Sir William Jones Monument
in the Chapel of University College, Oxford
By John Flaxman, 1798

Photo by Stephen Sheppard

INSTITUTES

OF

HINDU LAW:

OR, THE

ORDINANCES OF MENU,

ACCORDING TO THE

GLOSS OF CULLÚCA.

COMPRISING THE

INDIAN SYSTEM OF DUTIES,

RELIGIOUS AND CIVIL.

———

VERBALLY TRANSLATED FROM THE ORIGINAL
SANSCRIT.

WITH A PREFACE,

BY SIR WILLIAM JONES.

———

With a new introduction by
Steve Sheppard
University of Arkansas School of Law

THE LAWBOOK EXCHANGE, LTD.
Clark, New Jersey

ISBN 978-1-58477-731-1

Lawbook Exchange Edition 2007, 2018

THE LAWBOOK EXCHANGE, LTD.

33 Terminal Avenue

Clark, New Jersey 07066-1321

*Please see our website for a selection of our other publications
and fine facsimile reprints of classic works of legal history:*
www.lawbookexchange.com

Library of Congress Cataloging-in-Publication Data

Manu (Lawgiver)
[Manavadharmasastra. English]
Institutes of Hindu law, or, The ordinances of Manu, according
to the gloss of Cullúca, comprising the Indian system of duties,
religious, and civil / Manu, Jones, William.
p. cm.
Originally published: London: Reprinted for J. Sewell, Cornhill
and J. Debrett, Piccadilly, 1796.
ISBN-13: 978-1-58477-731-1 (alk. paper)
ISBN-10: 1-58477-731-1 (alk. paper)
1. Manu (Lawgiver). Manavadharmasastra. 2. Hindu law--Sources.
3. Law--India--Sources. 4. Law, Ancient--Sources. I. Jones,
William, Sir, 1746-1794. II. Title. III. Title: Institutes of Hindu
law. IV. Title: Ordinances of Manu, according to the gloss of
Cullúca, comprising the Indian system of duties, religious, and civil.
KNS127.3.A4E54 2007
294.5'94--dc22
2006019724

Printed in the United States of America on acid-free paper

Table of Contents

Law, God, Custom, and Duties in Sir William Jones's *Ordinances of Menu*
An Introduction for the American Reader

Stephen Sheppard

Sir William Jones's *Institutes of Hindu Law: or, The Ordinances of Menu,* is a unique rendition of what later Western audiences know as the *Laws of Manu* and has long been known to Hindu legal scholars as the *Mānava-Dharmasāstra* or the *Manu Smṛti.* It is one of the most significant texts in the history of the law. The first translation of a major Asian legal work into a European language, the text represents an important step in the identity and accessibility of written works of law. In this, the *Ordinances* implicitly challenge the dominant Western acceptance of law as a distinct creation of state action, while Jones's own efforts reflect a simultaneous desire to reduce the sources of law to writing while respecting religion, culture, and history as sources of law apart from government. More challengingly, the *Ordinances* mandate a caste system enshrined by religion, culture, and history – a system that, even when Jones wrote, contradicted the modern respect for freedom of the individual, a respect that Jones himself deeply held. Through it all threads the erudition of one of Britain's most scholarly lawyers of the eighteenth-century, a gifted linguist whose rare efforts to

VII

master Sanskrit combined with a poet's sensibility present a translation of beauty that is rare in the law.

The Ordinances of Menu

Though the text describes its own writing, and though Jones was convinced of its origin around 1280 B.C.E., its actual origin is unknown. The work has long been regarded by some scholars as the archive of an oral tradition, yet most eminent translators believe its core was written by one author. In either case, there is now wide agreement that it was likely composed in what is now northern India in or near the first century of the common era. Surviving manuscripts share a high degree of consistency, supporting this hypothesis.

The *Ordinances* is written in the voice of Menu, as Jones spelled his name from the Sanskrit according to the pronunciation of the Indian pandits he consulted. Although his name is now more often rendered in English as "Manu," Jones's spelling will be followed here.

Menu is the first man and so the father of all mankind as well as the first king, and he figures often in the revelatory works of the Hindu canon. Famously, Menu is warned by the fish avatar of Vishna of the approach of the great flood, which Menu alone survived. Book one of the *Māhābharatha* declares that Menu was endowed with "great wisdom and devoted to virtue." Indeed, not unlike the name of Adam, there is a dual meaning in the name Menu. Indeed here three meanings, for Menu means the individual and "man" and "knowledge." The American reader might recognize parallels in the Jewish and Christian traditions in Adam, Noah, and Solomon. By ascribing authorship of the *Ordinances* to Menu, the author added to him the law-giving role of Moses.

This ascription of authorship does not, however, render the *Ordinances* a revealed text or *śruti*, such as the four *Vedas* or the *Upanishads*. Rather, it is a *smṛti*, a text valued through tradition – what was remembered from the beginning – instead of revelation – what was learned from above. Considering a further parallel for the benefit of the American reader, the *Ordinances* is not unlike a prayer book, incorporating a host of traditional duties and obligations, derived from the edicts and stories of revered texts, which are frequently quoted, but developed through intervening custom.

Besides being a *smṛti*, the *Ordinances* is a *śāstra*, or treatise on a significant topic. This being the *śāstra* on *dharma* (see page X) that is attributed to Menu, it is also Menu's *smṛti*, hence the names in the opening paragraph, above. The *Ordinances* are by no means the exclusive source of Hindu literature on duties: *dharmaśāstras* are based on the *śruti*, that deal with *dharma*, including specific *dharmasūtras* that are much older than the *Ordinances*, and there are other *dharmaśāstras* as well as *smṛti* on other topics.

Owing to its apparent age and the successful ascription to Manu, the *Ordinances* have held a form of precedence over similar works. This precedence may also have resulted from the unusual comprehensiveness of the duties it collected, incorporating a variety of earlier traditions and reaching both higher and lower in the social order in the roles it considered than had earlier texts. Even so, the extent to which the *Ordinances* were known or followed on the Indian subcontinent before the arrival of the British East India Company in the eighteenth-century has been a matter of some dispute. The text was disseminated widely thanks to the edition of Sir William Jones reprinted here, and Jones had a variety of quite practical reasons for promoting a work of such breadth on *dharma*. Even so, scholars, notably Patrick Olivelle, have rather conclusively demonstrated the central place for Menu's work in the pre-colonial Hindu literature of *dharma*.

Dharma is famously hard to translate. It is rendered by Jones in the title as "duties, religious and civil." This rendering is quite helpful, so long as one does not try too hard to distinguish a particular obligation as either religious or civil. *Dharma* can be thought of as the sum of all true duties and their justifications, which are tied to a role every person has in existence. It makes no sense in such a concept to justify a given obligation by dividing religious authority from civil authority and basing an obligation on one alone.

The *Ordinances* were traditionally rendered in Sanskrit verse into twelve lessons, or chapters, in 2,694 stanzas. The divisions among chapters and transitions from topic to topic are integrated into the original text.

The first chapter begins with a prologue, of Menu in meditation when he is asked by the great sages to tell them the law. In answer, Menu gives summaries of Vedic stories of Brahmā's creation of the world, of plants and animals, the cosmos, law, time, and social class, a defense of the excellence of the Brahman class, followed by a description and overview of the treatise. This synopsis, the end of chapter one, runs from verses 111 to 119, on pp. 15 and 16.

The first third of the text details the life of the Brahman. The second chapter deals primarily with legal education, which is to say all education, because the purpose of learning is to understand the Law, which is based on the Vedas and on the traditions that follow them. The chronicle of the student's life of preparation, discipline, and instruction is presented in great detail, particularly in the decorum required between the student and the teacher and teacher's family. The third, fourth, and fifth chapters deal with domestic obligations of marriage and individual morals that govern a man during the time of his family life. Obligations of ceremony and decorum are interspersed with strict observances regarding food and voiding of the body, modesty and chastity, labor and wealth, courtesy and manners. A strong aspect of humility and modesty is constantly reinforced. The sixth chapter describes the retreat of the Brahman after family life to the life of a forest hermit, a wandering anchorite (or ascetic), or an ascetic retired in the house of his son.

Despite being a *dharmasāstra*, the text of Menu in the *Ordinances* goes beyond the usual construction of *dharma* to include *artha*, a separate tradition in prior literature that dealt specifically with the tasks of government and law. Chapters seven, eight, and nine derive from this tradition. Chapter seven depicts the law for the king, as well as the organization of government for the state and town, the supervision and payment of officials, the allocation and collection of taxes, the adjudication of lawsuits, protection of subjects and daily routine of the royal household. Chapters eight and nine are a manual for litigation, including the selection and role of judges and various grounds for liability arising from what an American would recognize as debt, tort, breach of contract, crimes, and property.

Chapters ten, eleven, and twelve consider the results of successes and failures of one's duties. Chapter ten considers variations in duties that arise from circumstance, such as when children are born from parents of two classes, changing expectations for members of each class that result from circumstances beyond their control. Chapter eleven lists blessings for the virtuous and penance for sinners, assessing some forms of inherent penance, such as a reduction in caste, and leaving others to be decreed by the king or wise legislators. The culmination of the book, though, is chapter twelve, in which actions are judged by the Law as good or evil, and the actors accordingly rise or fall in spirit. One result of the keeping of the Law is the ability of Brahmans to determine what the law is and to adjudicate claims under it. Yet the highest result is the transmigration of the soul into progressively higher states until one attains beatitude.

The text of the *Ordinances* as Jones presents it here is more than the manuscript he believed was written by Menu. With the confidence of a legal scholar used to reading a glossed text, Jones inserted hundreds of alterations derived from a later commentary by the Bengal scholar Kullūkabhaṭṭa, whom Jones spells Cullúca. As Jones describes on page xiii, the print in Roman print is the core text ascribed to Menu, and the print in italics is the later gloss.

The gloss illuminates only one of many choices Jones made in producing an authoritative text. He was aware of variations among manuscripts, as well as many of the limitations of his translation. Efforts at establishing a more perfect Sanskrit text and generating a more accurate translation have followed Jones's groundbreaking work. The translations of greatest significance are probably those of George Bühler in the nineteenth century and Patrick Olivelle in the twentieth, but there are others, the most accessible of which is probably that of Wendy Doniger O'Flaherty and Brian Smith.

Still, Jones's *Ordinances* remains more than just a starting point for later transmission and translation. It was a milestone in European understanding of Indian culture, with an influence all its own on the development of Hindu India. As the text in fact employed in Indian courts, it retains an independent significance that can only be obscured by reliance on later works.

Sir William Jones

William Jones was born in Westminster on September 28, 1746. His parents, William and Mary Jones, were clever but of modest means – his father being a well known mathematician and member of the Royal Society and his mother the educated daughter of a successful cabinet maker. His father died when William was only three, and young William was raised by his mother in a world of books, abetted by William's older sister Mary and by a Welsh relation and scholar, Lewis Morris. Young William memorized Shakespearean orations, Gay's fables, Biblical passages, Pope, Dryden, and other English works.

The study of languages and law would be the hallmark of Jones's life, and it is worth considering his early study in some detail. The classics awaited William at Harrow, which he entered when he was seven. Jones's first years at Harrow were marked more by beatings than by education, and in his third year, he began a program of self-instruction through private study and literary imitation, which persisted the rest of his life. A successful program it was, too. He began to act through the texts he read, leading his classmates in games organized around the histories and geographies, and holding debates after Plato. By the time he was twelve, Jones was designing a schedule of lectures and exercises for the school, while writing his own translations of Virgil and Horace, and imitations of other heroic poetry. Later in school, Jones taught himself Hebrew and began to study both Arabic writing as well as the common law, particularly the works of Sir Edward Coke. A popular if somewhat frail child, Jones acquired friendships in school that continued through his lifetime, including Joseph Banks, who would later lead the Royal Society and, perhaps not coincidentally, the British intelligence service.

In 1764, Jones entered University College, Oxford. He was not much impressed by the caliber of the Oxford lecture or of its students, and he spent most of his money on the support of Mirza, an Arabic teacher he hired himself, and most of his time immersed in Arabic and Persian languages. With Mirza's help, he performed a reverse translation of *Arabian Nights* back into Arabic. He still followed the university curriculum in Plato and Aristotle, as well as John Milton's plan, *Of Education*, in English, Italian, Spanish, and Portuguese, to which Jones added German. Two years after his matriculation, Jones received his B.A., was elected a Fellow of the College and, on the advice of the Dean of Westminster, was appointed the tutor to Baron Spencer's son, Althorpe. At the age of twenty, Jones had achieved position and income as well as a place in a noble house, prompting him to master a few social graces, such as dancing, riding, and fencing.

His private studies turned again to law. He read Fortescue's *De laudibus legum Angliae* as well as Roman and Greek law, and he acquired a life-long commitment to the English constitution, particularly from the viewpoint he had gained from Coke. That perspective was Whiggish not Radical, and Jones had no sympathy for the contemporary demagoguery of John Wilkes. His study grew more formal when he entered Middle Temple in 1770.

Earlier that year, Jones had published his first major translation, Mahdi Khan's biography of Nadir Shar, the recent monarch of Persia, a complicated and hagiographic work that Danish King Christian VII had sought to be translated into French. In his preface and appendix Jones argued for Europeans to be more receptive of the poetry and literature of other traditions, rather than being like savages, "who thought the sun rose and set for them alone and could not imagine that the waves, which surrounded their island, left coral and pearls upon any other shore."

This was the first of many works on Persian and Arabic poetry, which he made accessible both through translations and through the creation of grammars and criticism. These not only accelerated the current European fashion for "Eastern" literature and art, they refined the English ideal of poetry. His fame, as well as his scholarship and geniality, led both to his membership in the Royal Society and a variety of private circles, including the friendship of Samuel Johnson, Edmund Burke, Edward Gibbon, and their lights of Georgian London.

Meanwhile, his study of the law bore its own fruit, and Jones was called to the bar in 1774. He practiced mainly on the circuits of Wales, where he carried forward several defenses that corrected unjust accusations.

During these years, he published two works of translated law, the first English translation of a monument of Attic legal oratory, *Speeches of Isaeus Concerning the Law of Succession to Property in Athens* (1779) and *The Mahomedan Law of Succession to the Property of Intestates* (1782). He emphasized, both in the texts he chose and his editorial appendices, the right of the individual to the protection of property. This theme was central to his major work on the common law, his *Essay on the Law of Bailments* (1781), which built upon and promoted Sir William Blackstone's new *Commentaries* and which influenced a wide range of English and American law.

In 1778 Jones learned of an opening on the colonial Indian Supreme Court in Calcutta, and he sought the post. He was thwarted for five years in its appointment by, among other things, running for Parliament in the Whig opposition and advocating the American cause during the Revolution. In that advocacy he went so far as to visit Benjamin Franklin and John Adams in Paris and to publish a plan for a treaty of compromise to end the war favorably for the colonists. Indeed, his increasingly radical politics led to several pamphlets that were widely distributed in England and America, arguing for the right to a jury trial, the reform of Parliament, freedoms for the working man, and universal male suffrage. These pamphlets would have considerable influence in colonial and early Federal America.

Despite his radicalism and his attacks on patronage, it was exactly such patronage, through the new Whig prime minister, the Earl of Shelburne, that secured Jones's appointment to the Indian court in 1783, leading to his knighthood, and, given his new salary and impending departure from England, marriage to Mary Anna Shipley, the long-admired daughter of an old friend and ally.

The Joneses arrived in India, where they stayed for the rest of William's life. Jones quickly became central to the efforts of Warren Hastings, the Governor General, to establish a society for training administrators in the East India Company, resulting in the Asiatic Society, which remains a vibrant center of Asian studies two centuries later. Jones served as its first president, contributing a variety of papers on science, language, and culture, ranging along the lines of papers sent to the Royal Society, but based in Asia.

His interest in both Persian and Arabic poetry flourished as Jones found rich new materials for study and translation. Following the lead of his friend Charles Wilkins, Jones also began the study of the ancient language of Sanskrit, from which most Hindu texts had been translated into Persian. This study led to the publication in England of Jones's translations and imitations of Sanskrit poems, hymns, and drama, including his editions of *Sacontalá* and *Gítagóvinda*, profoundly influencing British, American, and continental writers, including Coleridge, the Shelleys, Thoreau, Herder, Goethe and Nietzsche. It also led, in his third address to the Asiatic Society, to the remarkable insight that ancient Asian culture is the common ancestor to European culture, an understanding now widely shared but then revolutionary.

Jones's work on the courts was dogged by the need to rely on local interpreters of native law, inviting both inconsistency and corruption. Further, the integration of English law into the hierarchical caste system of India presented irreconcilable choices. Despite his liberal preference for universal enfranchisement, in India, Jones accepted Hastings's view that the caste system of India was too entrenched to convert to a system of liberty without becoming a new form of tyranny; the English courts in Bengal should apply the traditional constitution and laws.

Although Hastings's initial effort to create a digest of local laws had proved unsatisfactory, Jones resolved to produce suitable digests of both Hindu and Islamic law, projects that he oversaw but that were largely staffed by local experts in their respective fields. With the exception of the printing in 1792 of the Islamic property text, *Al Sirájiyyah*, neither was completed until after Jones's death.

During the research for this project, Jones visited numerous scholars, libraries, and universities, and in 1784, a pandit told him of the *Mānava-Dharmásāstra*, which Ali Ibrahim Khan sent him from the school in Benares in March 1785. One of his initial interests in the text was its emphasis on oaths, which he hoped to use to formulate an oath that would be binding to Hindus in order to secure more reliable evidence in court. Yet the following year, he set about developing a translation of what he described to his friend Patrick Russell as "a law tract of great intrinsic merit, and extremely curious, which the Hindus believe to be almost as old as the creation. It is ascribed to "Menu, the Minos of India, and like him the son of Jove." He

XVII

appears to have translated the middle chapters early on, describing them in a letter to Earl Spencer as "a fine collection of Moral Precepts, wonderfully like those collected by the son of Sirach," or Ecclesiasticus. A full draft was complete by January 1791, and he continued to polish it for some months, only presenting a manuscript to the Governor in Council in July 1793.

Jones did not live to see the publication the following July. His health, never strong, had faltered with the departure of his wife for England in December 1793, and he died on April 27, 1794. He is buried in Kolkata, India.

Assessing the *Ordinances*

Sir William Jones has been both praised and reviled for his work in the *Ordinances*. Some charges are fair, such as his naiveté in accepting the Brahman myths as universal views of Hindu thought, or at least partially fair, such as blame for his part in the perpetuation of a brutal caste system. Others are either anachronistic or dubious, such as the charge of later Hindu legal scholars, particularly by J.D.M. Derrett, that Jones set in motion the destruction of customary Hindu law, preferring to pursue certainty to the more difficult task of encouraging evolution through legal science.

Though some complaints are fair, some are quite misplaced. It is fine to say centuries later that Jones was wrong to maintain the social order he found in India, but he feared that wholesale change ran greater risks for the lower castes than did the status quo, a fear that is rarely considered by his critics. Further, Jones's daily labor as well as his intellectual legacy was to make that order fairer and more transparent, in the hope of mitigating its worst corruptions.

XVIII

As to the dangers of the transmission of law texts, Jones was much more concerned with the protection of tradition and recognition of legal custom and science than he is credited by Derrett. The notes and preface to the *Ordinances* testify to a nuanced understanding of legal change. The law cannot survive without a tension between predictability on the one hand and changeability on the other.

Other tension between the recognition of custom and the promotion of certainty abound in Jones's *Ordinances* and the place he intended for them in the courts. The role, for instance, of religion in the justification of legal norms, once universally accepted in Europe, remained central to Jones's employment of Hindu law in British courts. This justification was one that Jones accepted comfortably as according to the customs of the people governed by the law, though it amounted to an implicit rejection of the rising tide of positivism in England.

Perhaps the most wonderful aspects of Jones's work, though, is its robust challenge to the anti-colonial arguments of Orientalism. As charged by Edward Said and others, Orientalists assert a power relationship over Asian, particularly Arab, culture that amounts to a code for the superiority of European culture and an implied justification for subjugating the inferior Eastern culture. Jones's career, as a colonial administrator enforcing imperial power over a subject people would appear to fit Said's mold, but it does not. Jones thoroughly immersed himself in Indian culture and letters, in Hinduism, Islam, and in Persian and Sanskrit. Rejecting the label "Oriental" for Asian, or Hindu, or Mohammedan, Jones genuinely valued these cultures and their literatures in their own light, and indeed he defended them throughout his life as often superior to European models. It is an irony indeed that the greatest exception to Jones's preference for the

XIX

Asiatic over the European was the British constitution, which he believed the best in the world.

That he abandoned the constitution as infeasible for governance and dangerous to the poor, in then-prevailing Asiatic culture has always been the basis for his greatest criticism. In his "anti-Orientalism," Jones might well have established his true legacy: the model of a comparative scholar who considers subjects for their inherent merit rather than through a parochial bias.

Further Reading

The Laws of Manu (Wendy Doniger O'Flaherty & Brian K. Smith, trans.) (London: Penguin Books, 1999).

Patrick Olivelle & Suman Olivelle, Manu's Code of Law: A Critical Edition and Translation of the Mānava-Dharmaśāstra (New York: Oxford University Press, 2004).

-o-

Sir William Jones, Works: With the life of the author by Lord Teignmouth (London: J. Stockdale, 1807) (13 vols.).

–, The Works of Sir William Jones (New York, Garland, 1984) (2 vols.).

–, The Letters of Sir William Jones (Garland H. Cannon, ed.) (Oxford: Clarendon Press, 1970).

Charles Wilkins, Esq. F. R. S., *A Catalogue of Sanscrita Manuscripts Presented to the Royal Society by Sir William and Lady Jones*, Philosophical Transactions of the Royal Society of London, Vol. 88 (1798), pp. 582-593.

- o -

Jeremy Bernstein, Dawning of the Raj: The Life and Trials of Warren Hastings (Chicago: Ivan R. Dee, 2000).

Garland H. Cannon, Sir William Jones: A Bibliography of Primary and Secondary Sources (Amsterdam:

Benjamins. 1979).

–, Oriental Jones: A Biography of Sir William Jones, 1746-1794 (Bombay: Asia Pub. House Indian Council for Cultural Relations, 1964).

–, The Life and Mind of Oriental Jones: Sir William Jones, the Father of Modern Linguistics (Cambridge: Cambridge University Press, 1990).

–, Sir William Jones, *Sir Joseph Banks, and the Royal Society, Notes and Records of the Royal Society of London*, Vol. 29, No. 2 (Mar., 1975), pp. 205-230.

–, Sir William Jones, Orientalist; An Annotated Bibliography of His Works (Honolulu: University of Hawaii Press, 1952).

–, *Sir William Jones's Indian Studies* Journal of the American Oriental Society, Vol. 91, No. 3. (Jul. - Sep., 1971), pp. 418-425.

Garland H. Cannon & Kevin Brine, Objects of Enquiry: Life, Contributions and Influence of Sir William Jones (New York: New York University Press. (1995).

H.D. Cornish, Handooks of Hindu Law, Part II, Partition and Maintenance (Cambridge University Press, 1915).

A. Mervyn Davies, Strange Destiny: A Biography of Warren Hastings (New York: G.P. Putnam's Sons, 1935).

J. Duncan M. Derrett, Religion, Law and the State in India (London: Sweet & Maxwell, 1968).

XXII

Franklin Edgerton, *Sir William Jones: 1746-1794*, Journal of the American Oriental Society, Vol. 66, No. 3. (Jul. - Sep., 1946), pp. 230-239.

Robert A. Ferguson, *The Emulation of Sir William Jones in the Early Republic*, The New England Quarterly, Vol. 52, No. 1 (Mar., 1979), pp. 3-26.

Michael J. Franklin, *Jones, Sir William (1746–1794)*, Oxford Dictionary of National Biography, (New York: Oxford University Press, 2004).

Ariel Glucklich, Religious Jurisprudence in the Dharmaśāstra (New York: Macmillan, 1988).

David Ibbetson, Sir William Jones as Comparative Lawyer, in Alexander Murray, ed., Sir William Jones, 1746-1794: A Commemoration (Clark, N.J.: The Lawbook Exchange, Ltd., 2006).

Werner F. Menski, Hindu Law: Beyond Tradition and Modernity (New Delhi: Oxford University Press, 2003).

S. N. Mukherjee, Sir William Jones: A Study in Eighteenth-Century British Attitudes to India (Cambridge: Cambridge University Press, 1968).

Alexander Murray, ed., Sir William Jones, 1746-1794: A Commemoration (Clark, N.J.: The Lawbook Exchange, Ltd., 2006).

Ellen M. Raghavan & Barry Wood, Thoreau's Hindu Quotations in "A Week," American Literature, Vol. 51, No. 1 (Mar., 1979), pp. 94-98 (Discussing Henry David Thoreau's *A Week on the Concord and Merrimack Rivers*).

Shashi S. Sharma., Imagined Manuvad: The Dharmaśāstras and Their Interpreters (New Delhi: Rupa, 2005).

Śrāddha-sāgara of Kullūkabha (S.G. Moghe, ed.) (New Delhi: D.K. Printworld, 1994).

J. M. Steadman, *The Asiatick Society of Bengal,* Eighteenth-Century Studies, Vol. 10, No. 4. (Summer, 1977), pp. 464-483.

INSTITUTES

OF

H I N D U   L A W:

OR, THE

ORDINANCES OF MENU,

ACCORDING TO THE

GLOSS OF CULLÚCA.

COMPRISING THE

INDIAN SYSTEM OF DUTIES,

RELIGIOUS AND CIVIL.

———

VERBALLY TRANSLATED FROM THE ORIGINAL
SANSCRIT.

WITH A PREFACE,

BY SIR WILLIAM JONES.

———

CALCUTTA:

PRINTED BY ORDER OF THE GOVERNMENT.

LONDON:

REPRINTED FOR J. SEWELL, CORNHILL; AND J. DEBRETT,
PICCADILLY. 1796.

———

[Drawback.]

THE PREFACE.

IT is a maxim in the fcience of legiflation and government, that *Laws are of no avail without manners*, or, to explain the fentence more fully, that the beft intended legiflative provifions would have no beneficial effect even at firft, and none at all in a fhort courfe of time, unlefs they were congenial to the difpofition and habits, to the religious prejudices, and approved immemorial ufages of the people for whom they were enacted; efpecially if that people univerfally and fincerely believed, that all their ancient ufages and eftablifhed rules of conduct had the fanction of an actual revelation from heaven: the legiflature of *Britain* having fhown, in compliance with this maxim, an intention to leave the natives of thefe *Indian* provinces in poffeffion of their own Laws, at leaft on the titles of *contracts* and *inheritances*, we may humbly prefume, that all future provifions, for the adminiftration of juftice and government in *India*, will be conformable, as far as the natives are affected by them, to the manners and opinions of the natives themfelves; an object which cannot poffibly be attained, until thofe manners and opinions can be fully and accurately known. Thefe confiderations, and a few others more immediately within my

pro-

province, were my principal motives for wifh-
ing to know, and have induced me at length
to publifh, that fyftem of duties, religious and
civil, and of law in all its branches, which the
Hindus firmly believe to have been promulged
in the beginning of time by MENU, fon or
grandfon of BRAHMA', or, in plain language,
the firft of created beings, and not the oldeft
only, but the holieft of legiflators; a fyftem
fo comprehenfive and fo minutely exact, that
it may be confidered as the *Inftitutes* of *Hindu*
Law, preparatory to the copious *Digeft*, which
has lately been compiled by *Pandits* of eminent
learning, and introductory perhaps to a *Code*
which may fupply the many natural defects
in the old jurifprudence of this country, and,
without any deviation from its principles, ac-
commodate it juftly to the improvements of a
commercial age.

WE are loft in an inextricable labyrinth of
imaginary aftronomical cycles, *Yugas, Ma-
háyúgas, Calpas,* and *Menwantaras,* in attempting to calculate the time, when the firft MENU,
according to the *Bráhmens,* governed this
world, and became the progenitor of mankind,
who from him are called *Mánaváh*; nor can
we, fo clouded are the old hiftory and chronology of *India* with fables and allegories, afcertain the precife age, when the work, now prefented to the Publick, was actually compofed;
but we are in poffeffion of fome evidence,
partly extrinfick and partly internal, that it is

really

really one of the oldest compofition's exifting.
From a text of PARA'SARA difcovered by Mr.
DAVIS, it appears, that the vernal equinox had
gone back from the *tenth* degree of *Bharani*
to the *firft* of *Afwini*, or *twenty-three degrees
and twenty minutes*, between the days of that
Indian philofopher, and the year of our Lord
499, when it coincided with the origin of the
Hindu ecliptick; fo that PARA'SARA probably
flourifhed near the clofe of the *twelfth* century
before CHRIST; now PARA'SARA was the
grandfon of another fage, named VA SISHT'HA,
who is often mentioned in the laws of MENU,
and once as contemporary with the divine
BHRĬGU himfelf; but the character of BHRĬGU,
and the whole dramatical arrangement of the
book before us, are clearly fictitious and ornamental, with a defign, too common among
ancient lawgivers, of ftamping authority on
the work by the introduction of fupernatural
perfonages, though VA'SISHT'HA may have
lived many generations before the actual writer
of it, who names him, indeed, in one or two
places as a philofopher in an earlier period.
The ftyle, however, and metre of this work
(which there is not the fmalleft reafon to think
affectedly obfolete) are widely different from
the language and metrical rules of CA'LIDA's,
who unqueftionably wrote before the beginning of our era; and the dialect of MENU is even
obferved, in many paffages, to refemble that of
the *Véda*, particularly in a departure from the

A 3   more

more modern grammatical forms ; whence it
muſt, at firſt view, ſeem very probable, that the
laws, now brought to light, were conſiderably
older than thoſe of SOLON or even of LYCUR-
GUS, although the promulgation of them, before they were reduced to writing, might have
been coeval with the firſt monarchies eſtabliſhed in *Egypt* or *Aſia:* but, having had the
ſingular good fortune to procure ancient copies
of eleven *Upaniſhads*, with a very perſpicuous
comment, I am enabled to fix, with more ex-
actneſs, the probable age of the work before us,
and even to limit its higheſt poſſible age by a
mode of reaſoning, which may be thought
new, but will be found, I perſuade myſelf,
ſatisfactory ; if the Publick ſhall, on this occaſion, give me credit for a few very curious
facts, which, though capable of ſtrict proof,
can at preſent be only aſſerted.   The *Sanſcrit*
of the three firſt *Védas*, (I need not here ſpeak
of the fourth) that of the *Mánava Dherma
Sáſtra*, and that of the *Puránas*, differ from each
other in pretty exact proportion to the *Latin* of
NUMA, from whoſe laws entire ſentences are
preſerved, that of APPIUS, which we ſee in the
fragments of the Twelve Tables, and that of
CICERO, or of LUCRETIUS, where he has not
affected an obſolete ſtyle : if the ſeveral changes,
therefore, of *Sanſcrit* and *Latin* took place, as
we may fairly aſſume, in times very nearly
proportional, the *Védas* muſt have been written
about 300 years before theſe Inſtitutes, and
about

about 600 before the *Purànas* and *Itihàfas*, which, I am fully convinced, were not the productions of VYA'SA ; fo that, if the fon of PARA'SARA committed the traditional *Védas* to writing in the *Sanfcrit* of his father's time, the original of this book muft have received its prefent form about 880 years before CHRIST'S birth. If the texts, indeed, which VYA'SA collected, had been actually *written* in a much older dialect, by the fages preceding him, we muft inquire into the greateft poffible age of the *Védas* themfelves : now one of the longeft and fineft *Upanifhads* in the fecond *Véda* contains three lifts, in a regular, feries upwards, of at moft *forty·two* pupils and preceptors, who fucceffively received and tranfmitted (probably by oral tradition) the doctrines contained in that *Upanifhad*; and as the old *Indian* priefts were ftudents at *fifteen*, and inftructors at *twenty-five*, we cannot allow more than *ten* years, on an average, for each interval between the refpective traditions; whence, as there are *forty* fuch intervals, in two of the lifts between VYA'SA, who arranged the whole work, and AYA'SYA, who is extolled at the beginning of it, and juft as many, in the third lift, between the compiler and YA'JNYAWALCYA, who makes the principal figure in it, we find the higheft age of the *Yajur Véda* to be 1580 years before the birth of our Saviour, (which would make it older than the five books of MOSES) and that of our *Indian* law tract about

1280

1280 years before the fame epoch.   The former date, however, feems the more probable
of the two, becaufe the *Hindu* fages are faid
to have delivered their knowledge orally, and
the very word *Sruta*, which we often fee ufed
for the *Véda* itfelf, means *what was heard*;
not to infift that Cullu'ca exprefsly declares
the fenfe of the *Véda* to be conveyed in the
language of Vya'sa.   Whether Menu or
Menus in the nominative and Meno's in an
oblique cafe, was the fame perfonage with Minos, let others determine; but he muft indubitably have been far older than the work,
which contains his laws, and though perhaps
he was never in *Crete*, yet fome of his infti-
tutions may well have been adopted in that
ifland, whence Lycurgus, a century or two
afterwards, may have imported them to *Sparta:*
   There is certainly a ftrong refemblance,
though obfcured and faded by time, between
our Menu with his divine Bull, whom he
names as Dherma himfelf, or the genius of
abftract juftice, and the Mneues of *Egypt* with
his companion or fymbol *Apis*; and, though
we fhould be conftantly on our guard againft
the delufion of etymological conjecture, yet we
cannot but admit that Minos and Mneues,
or *Mneuis*, have only *Greek* terminations, but
that the crude noun is compofed of the fame
radical letters both in *Greek* and in *Sanfcrit.*
‘ That Apis and Mneuis,’ fays the Analyft
of ancient Mythology, ‘ were both reprefen-
                                    ‘ tations

‘ tations of some personage, appears from the
‘ testimony of LYCOPHRON and his scholiast;
‘ and that personage was the same, who in
‘ Crete was styled MINOS, and who was also
‘ represented under the emblem of the Mino-
‘ taur: DIODORUS, who confines him to Egypt,
‘ speaks of him by the title of the bull Mneuis,
‘ as the first lawgiver, and says, “ That he lived
“ after the age of the gods and heroes, when
“ a change was made in the manner of life
“ among men; that he was a man of a most
“ exalted soul, and a great promoter of civil
“ society, which he benefited by his laws;
“ that those laws were unwritten, and receiv-
“ ed by him from the chief Egyptian deity
“ HERMES, who conferred them on the world
“ as a gift of the highest importance.” He
‘ was the same, adds my learned friend, with
‘ MENES, whom the Egyptians represented as
‘ their first king and principal benefactor, who
‘ first sacrificed to the gods, and brought about
‘ a great change in diet.’   If MINOS, the son
of JUPITER, whom the Cretans, from national
vanity, might have made a native of their own
island, was really the same person with MENU,
the son of BRAHMA', we have the good fortune
to restore, by means of Indian literature, the
most celebrated system of heathen jurisprudence, and this work might have been entitled
The Laws of MINOS ; but the paradox is too
singular to be confidently asserted, and the
geographical part of the book, with most of
the

the allufions to natural hiftory, muft indubitably have been written after the *Hindu* race
had fettled to the fouth of *Himálaya.* We cannot but remark that the word MENU has no
relation whatever to the *Moon* ; and that it
was the *feventh,* not the *firft* of that name,
whom the *Bráhmens* believe to have been preferved in an ark from the general deluge :
him they call the *Child of the Sun,* to diftinguifh him from our legiflator ; but they affign
to his brother YAMA *the office* (which the
Greeks were pleafed to confer on MINOS) *of
Judge in the fhades below.*

THE name of MENU is clearly derived (like
menes, mens, and *mind*) from the root *men* to
underftand; and it fignifies, as all the *Pandits*
agree, *intelligent,* particularly in the doctrines
of the *Véda,* which the compofer of our *Dherma Sáftra* muft have ftudied very diligently;
fince great numbers of its texts, changed only in
a few fyllables for the fake of the meafure, are
interfperfed through the work, and cited at
length in the commentaries: the Publick may,
therefore, affure themfelves, that they now poffefs a confiderable part of the *Hindu* fcripture,
without the dullnefs of its profane ritual or
much of its myftical jargon. DA'RA SHUCU'H
was perfuaded, and not without found reafon,
that the firft MENU of the *Bráhmens* could be
no other perfon than the progenitor of mankind, to whom *Jews, Chriftians,* and *Mufelmáns,* unite in giving the name of ADAM ; but,
who-

whoever he might have been he is highly honoured by name in the *Véda* itself, where it is
declared, that ' whatever MENU pronounced,
' was a medicine for the foul,' and the fage
VRIHASPATI, now fuppofed to prefide over
the planet *Jupiter,* fays in his own law tract,
that ' ME'NU held the firft rank among legifla-
' tors, becaufe he had expreffed in his code the
' whole fenfe of the *Véda* ; that no code was
' approved, which contradicted MENU ; that
' other *Sáftras,* and treatifes on grammar or lo-
' gick, retained fplendour fo long only, as
' MENU, who taught the way to juft wealth, to
' virtue and to final happinefs, was not feen in
' competition with them :' VYA'SA too, the
fon of PARA'SARA before mentioned, has decided, that ' the *Véda* with its *Angas,* or the
' fix compofitions deduced from it, the reveal-
' ed fyftem of medicine, the *Puránas,* or fa-
' cred hiftories, and the code of MENU were
' four works of fupreme authority, which
' ought never to be fhaken by arguments
' merely human.'

IT is the general opinion of *Pandits,* that
BRAHMA' taught his laws to MENU in a *hundred thoufand verfes,* which MENU explained
to the primitive world, in the very words of
the book now tranflated, where he names himfelf, after the manner of ancient fages, in the
third perfon, but in a fhort preface to the law
tract of NA'RED, it is afferted, that ' MENU,
' having written the laws of BRAHMA' in a
' hundred

' hundred thoufand *ſlócas* or couplets, arrang-
' ed under *twenty-four* heads in a thoufand
' chapters, delivered the work to NA'RED,
' the fage among gods, who abridged it, for
' the ufe of mankind, in *twelve thoufand* verfes,
' and gave them to a fon of BHRĬGU, named
' SUMATI, who, for greater eafe to the hu-
' man race, reduced them to *four thoufand* ;
' that mortals read only the fecond abridge-
' ment by SUMATI, while the gods of the
' lower heaven, and the band of celeftial mufi-
' cians, are engaged in ſtudying the primary
' code, beginning with the fifth verfe, a little
' varied, of the work now extant on earth ;
' but that nothing remains of NA'RED's abridge-
' ment, except an elegant epitome of the *ninth*
' original title *on the adminiſtration of juſtice.*'
Now, fince thefe inſtitutes confiſt only of
two thoufand ſix hundred and *eighty five* verfes,
they cannot be the whole work aſcribed to
SUMATI, which is probably diſtinguiſhed by
the name of the *Vriddha*, or ancient *Mánava*,
and cannot be found entire; though feveral
paſſages from it, which have been preferved by
tradition, are occafionally cited in the new
digeſt.

A NUMBER of gloſſes or comments on MENU
were compofed by the *Munis*, or old phi-
loſophers, whofe treatifes, together with that
before us, conſtitute the *Dhermaſáſtra*, in a col-
lective ſenſe, or *Body of Law* ; among the
more modern commentaries, that called *Méd-
hátit'hi,*

hátit'hi, that by Go'vindara'ja, and that by
Dharani'-Dhera, were once in the greateſt
repute; but the firſt was reckoned prolix and
unequal; the ſecond conciſe but obſcure; and
the third often erroneous. At length appeared
Cullu'ca Bhatta; who, after a painful courſe
of ſtudy and the collation of numerous manu-
ſcripts, produced a work, of which it may,
perhaps, be ſaid very truly, that it is the ſhort-
eſt, yet the moſt luminous, the leaſt oſtenta-
tious, yet the moſt learned, the deepeſt, yet
the moſt agreeable, commentary ever compoſed
on any author ancient or modern, *European* or
Aſiatick. The *Pandits* care ſo little for genu-
ine chronology, that none of them can tell me
the age of Cullu'ca, whom they always
name with applauſe; but he informs us himſelf, that he was a *Bráhmen* of the *Váréndra*
tribe, whoſe family had been long ſettled
in *Gaur* or *Bengal*, but that he had choſen his
reſidence among the learned, on the banks of
the holy river at *Cáſi*. His text and interpreta-
tion I have almoſt implicitly followed, though
I had myſelf collated many copies of Menu,
and among them a manuſcript of a very ancient
date: his gloſs is here printed in *Italicks*; and
any reader, who may chooſe to paſs it over as
if unprinted, will have in *Roman* letters an exact
verſion of the original, and may form ſome idea
of its character and ſtructure, as well as of the
Sanſcrit idiom which muſt neceſſarily be preſerved in a verbal tranſlation; and a tranſlation,

tion, not fcrupuloufly verbal, would have been
highly improper in a work on fo delicate and
momentous a fubject as private and criminal
jurifprudence.

SHOULD a feries of *Bráhmens* omit, for three
generations, the reading of MENU, their facerdotal clafs, as all the *Pandits* affure me, would
in ftrictnefs be forfeited; but they muft explain it only to their pupils of the three higheft
claffes; and the *Bráhmen*, who read it with
me, requefted moft earneftly, that his name
might be concealed; nor would he have read it
for any confideration on a forbidden day of the
moon, or without the ceremonies prefcribed in
the fecond and fourth chapters for a lecture on
the VE'DA: fo great, indeed, is the idea of
fanctity annexed to this book, that, when the
chief native magiftrate at *Banares* endeavoured,
at my requeft, to procure a *Perfian* tranflation
of it, before I had a hope of being at any time
able to underftand the original, the *Pandits* of
his court unanimoufly and pofitively refufed to
affift in the work; nor fhould I have procured
it at all, if a wealthy *Hináu* at *Gayà* had not
caufed the verfion to be made by fome of his de-
pendants, at the defire of my friend Mr. LAW.
The *Perfian* tranflation of MENU, like all
others from the *Sanfcrit* into that language,
is a rude intermixture of the text, loofely rendered, with fome old or new comment, and
often with the crude notions of the tranflator;
and though it expreffes the general fenfe of the
original, yet it fwarms with errours, imputable

partly

partly to hafte, and partly to ignorance : thus where MENU fays, *that emiffaries are the eyes of a prince*, the *Perfian* phrafe makes him afcribe *four eyes* to the perfon of a king ; for the word *chár*, which means *an emiffary* in *Sanfcrit*, fignifies *four* in the populat dialect.

THE work, now prefented to the *European* world, contains abundance of curious matter extremely interefting both to fpeculative lawyers and antiquaries, with many beauties which need not be pointed out, and with many blemifhes which cannot be juftified or palliated. It is a fyftem of defpotifm and prieftcraft, both indeed limited by law, but artfully confpiring to give mutual fupport, though with mutual checks; it is filled with ftrange conceits in metaphyficks and natural philofophy, with idle fuperftitions, and with a fcheme of theology moft obfcurely figurative, and confequently liable to dangerous mifconception ; it abounds with minute and childifh formalities, with ceremonies generally abfurd and often ridiculous; the punifhments are partial and fanciful; for fome crimes, dreadfully cruel, for others, reprehenfibly flight; and the very morals, though rigid enough on the whole, are in one or two inftances (as in the cafe of light oaths and of pious perjury) unaccountably relaxed : neverthelefs, a fpirit of fublime devotion, of benevolence to mankind, and of amiable tendernefs to all fentient creatures, pervades the whole work; the ftyle of it has a certain

3 auftere

auftere majefty, that founds like the language
of legiflation, and extorts a refpectful awe ; the
fentiments of independence on all beings but
GOD, and the harfh admonitions, even to kings,
are truly noble; and the many panegyricks on
the *Gáyatrì*, the *Mother* as it is called, of the
Véda, prove the author to have *adored* (not the
vifible material *fun*, but) *that divine and in-
comparably greater light*, to ufe the words of
the moft venerable text in the *Indian* fcripture,
*which illumines all, delights all, from which all
proceed, to which all muft return, and which
alone can irradiate* (not our vifual organs
merely, but our fouls and) *our intellects*. Whatever opinion in fhort may be formed of MENU
and his laws, in a country happily enlightened
by found philofophy and the only true revelation, it muft be remembered, that thofe
laws are actually revered, as the word of the
Moft High, by nations of great importance
to the political and commercial interefts of
Europe, and particularly by many millions of
Hindu fubjects, whofe well directed induftry
would add largely to the wealth of *Britain,*
and who afk no more in return than protection for their perfons and places of abode, juftice in their temporal concerns, indulgence to
the prejudices of their old religion, and the
benefit of thofe laws, which they have been
taught to believe facred, and which alone they
can poffibly comprehend.

W. JONES.

LAWS OF MENU,

SON OF BRAHMÁ.

CHAPTER THE FIRST.

On the Creation; with a Summary of the Contents.

1. MENU *fat* reclined, with his attention fixed on one object, *the Supreme* GOD ; *when* the divine Sages approached *him, and,* after mutual falutations in due form, delivered the following addrefs :

2. ' Deign, fovereign ruler, to apprize us of ' the facred laws in their order, as they muft be ' followed by all the *four* claffes, and by each of ' them, in their feveral degrees, together with ' the duties of every mixed clafs ;

3. ' For thou, Lord, *and thou* only *among mor-* ' *tals,* knoweft the true fenfe, the firft principle, ' *and* the prefcribed ceremonies, of this univerfal, ' fupernatural *Véda,* unlimited in extent and un- ' equalled in authority.'

4. HE, whofe powers were meafurelefs, being thus requefted by the great Sages, whofe thoughts were profound, faluted them all with reverence, and gave them a comprehenfive anfwer, *faying :* ' Be it heard !

5. ' This *univerfe* exifted only *in the firft divine* ' *idea yet unexpanded, as if involved* in darknefs, ' imperceptible, undefinable, undifcoverable *by*

B ' *reafon,*

' *reason, and* undiscovered *by revelation,* as if it
' were wholly immersed in sleep:

   6. ' Then the *sole* self-existing power, himself
' undiscerned, but making this world discernible,
' with five elements and other principles *of nature,*
' appeared with undiminished glory, *expanding*
' *his idea, or* dispelling the gloom.

   7. ' HE, whom the mind alone can perceive,
' whose essence eludes the external organs, who
' has no visible parts, who exists from eternity,
' even HE, the soul of all beings, whom no being
' can comprehend, shone forth in person.

   8. ' HE, having willed to produce various
' beings from his own divine substance, first with
' a thought created the waters, and placed in
' them a productive seed:

   9. ' The *seed* became an egg bright as gold,
' blazing like the luminary with a thousand
' beams; and in that egg he was born himself,
' *in the form of* BRAHMA', the great forefather of
' all spirits.

   10. ' The waters are called *nárá,* because they
' were the production of NARA, *or the spirit of*
' GOD; and, since they were his first *ayana,* or
' *place of motion,* he thence is named NA´RA´YANA,
' or *moving on the waters.*

   11. ' From THAT WHICH IS, the first cause,
' not the object of sense, existing *every where in*
' *substance,* not existing *to our perception,* without
' beginning or end, was produced the divine male,
' famed in all worlds under the appellation of
' BRAHMA'.

   12. ' In that egg the great power sat inactive a
' whole year *of the Creator,* at the close of which,
' by his thought alone, he caused the egg to divide
' itself;

                          13. ' And

13. ' And from its two divifions he framed the
' heaven *above* and the earth *beneath:* in the midft
' *he placed* the fubtil ether, the eight regions, and
' the permanent receptacle of waters.

14. ' From the fupreme foul he drew forth
' Mind, exifting fubftantially though unperceived
' by fenfe, immaterial; and *before mind, or the*
' *reafoning power, he produced* confcioufnefs, the
' internal monitor, the ruler;

15. ' And, *before them both,* he produced the
' great *principle of the foul, or firft expanfion of the*
' *divine idea;* and all vital forms endued with the
' three qualities of *goodnefs, paffion,* and *darknefs;*
' and the *five* perceptions of fenfe, and the five
' organs of fenfation.

16. ' *Thus,* having at once pervaded, with ema-
' nations from the Supreme Spirit, the minuteft
' portions of fix principles immenfely operative,
' *confcioufnefs and the five perceptions,* He framed all
' creatures;

17. ' And fince the minuteft particles of vifible
' nature have a dependence on thofe *fix* emanations
' from GOD, the wife have accordingly given the
' name of *s'aríra* or *depending on fix, that is, the ten*
' *organs on confcioufnefs, and the five elements on as*
' *many perceptions,* to His *image or* appearance in
' vifible nature:

18. ' Thence proceed the great elements, en-
' dued with peculiar powers, and Mind with
' operations infinitely fubtil, the unperifhable
' caufe of all apparent forms.

19. ' This *univerfe,* therefore, is compacted
' from the minute portions of thofe feven divine
' and active principles, *the great Soul, or firft ema-*
' *nation, confcioufnefs, and five perceptions;* a mutable
' *univerfe* from immutable *ideas.*

B 2

20. ' Among

20. ' Among them each fucceeding element
' acquires the quality of the preceding; and, in
' as many degrees as each of them is advanced,
' with fo many properties is it faid to be endued.

21. ' HE too firft affigned to all creatures dif-
' tinct names, diftinct acts, and diftinct occupa-
' tions ; as they had been revealed in the pre-
' exifting *Véda*.

22. ' HE, the fupreme Ruler, created an affem-
' blage of inferior Deities, with divine attributes
' and pure fouls ; and a number of Genii exqui-
' fitely delicate; and he *prefcribed* the facrifice
' ordained from the beginning.

23. ' From fire, from air, and from the fun
' he milked out, *as it were*, the three primordial
' *Védas*, named *Rïch*, *Yajufh*, and *Sáman*, for the
' due performance of the facrifice.

24. ' HE gave being to time and the divifions
' of time, to the ftars alfo, and to the planets, to
' rivers, oceans, and mountains, to level plains,
' and uneven valleys.

25. ' To devotion, fpeech, complacency, de-
' fire, and wrath, and to the creation, which fhall
' prefently be mentioned; for He willed the exif-
' tence of all thofe created things.

26. ' For the fake of diftinguifhing actions,
' He made a total difference between right and
' wrong, and enured thefe fentient creatures to
' pleafure and pain, *cold and heat*, and other oppo-
' fite pairs.

27. ' With very minute transformable portions,
' called *mïtrás*, of the five elements, all this
' perceptible world was compofed in fit order;

28. ' And in whatever occupation the fupreme
' Lord firft employed any vital foul, to that occu-
' pation

‘ pation the fame foul attaches itfelf fpontaneoufly,
‘ when it receives a new body again and again:

29. ‘ Whatever quality, noxious or innocent,
‘ harfh or mild, unjuft, or juft, falfe or true, He
‘ conferred on any being at its creation, the fame
‘ quality enters it of courfe *on its future births*;

30. ‘ As the *fix* feafons of the year attain
‘ refpectively their peculiar marks in due time
‘ and of their own accord, even fo the feveral
‘ acts of each embodied fpirit *atten / it natu-*
‘ *rally.*

31. ‘ That the human race might be multi-
‘ plied, He caufed the *Brahmen*, the *Cfhatriya*,
‘ the *Vaifya*, and the *Sudra* (fo named from the
‘ *fcripture, protection, wealth,* and *labour*) to pro-
‘ ceed from his mouth, his arm, his thigh and his
‘ foot.

32. ‘ Having divided his own fubftance, the
‘ mighty Power became half male, half female,
‘ or *nature active and paffive*; and from *that fe-
‘ male he produced VIRA'J:

33. ‘ Know Me, O moft excellent of *Brahmens*,
‘ to be that perfon, whom the male *power* VIRA'J,
‘ having performed auftere devotion, produced
‘ by himfelf; Me, the *fecondary* framer of all this
‘ *vifible world.*

34. ‘ It was I, who, defirous of giving birth
‘ to a race of men, performed very difficult reli-
‘ gious duties, and firft produced ten Lords of
‘ created beings, eminent in holinefs,

35. ‘ MARI'CHI, ATRI, ANGERAS, PULASTYA,
‘ PULAHA, CRATU, PRACHE'TAS, or DACSHA,
‘ VASISHT'HA, BHRIGU, and NARADA:

36. ‘ They, abundant in glory, produced
‘ feven other *Menus*, together with deities, and

B 3   ‘ the

' the manſions of deities, and *Maharſhis*, or great
' Sages, unlimited in power;

37. ' Benevolent genii, and fierce giants, blood-
' thirſty ſavages, heavenly quiriſters, nymphs and
' demons, huge ſerpents and ſnakes of ſmaller
' ſize, birds of mighty wing, and ſeparate com-
' panies of *Pitris*, or progenitors of mankind;

38. ' Lightnings and thunder-bolts, clouds and
' coloured bows of *Indra*, falling meteors, earth-
' rending vapours, comets, and luminaries of va-
' rious degrees;

39. ' Horſe-faced ſylvans, apes, fiſh, and a
' variety of birds, tame cattle, deer, men, and
' ravenous beaſts with two rows of teeth;

40. ' Small and large reptiles, moths, lice,
' fleas, and common flies, with every biting gnat,
' and immoveable ſubſtances of diſtinct ſorts.

41. ' Thus was this whole aſſemblage of ſta-
' tionary and moveable bodies framed by thoſe
' high-minded beings, through the force of their
' own devotion, and at my command, with ſepa-
' rate actions allotted to each.

42. ' Whatever act is ordained for each of
' thoſe creatures here below, *that* I will now de-
' clare to you, together with their order in reſpect
' to birth.

43. ' Cattle and deer, and wild beaſts with two
' rows of teeth, giants, and blood-thirſty ſavages,
' and the race of men, are born from a ſecundine:

44. ' Birds are hatched from eggs, *ſo are*
' ſnakes, crocodiles, fiſh *without ſhells*, and tor-
' toiſes, with other animal kinds, terreſtrial, *as*
' *chamelions*, and aquatick, *as ſhell-fiſh:*

45. ' From hot moiſture are born biting gnats,
' lice, fleas, and common flies; theſe, and what-
' ever is of the ſame claſs, are produced by heat.

46. ' All

46. ' All vegetables, propagated by feed or by
' flips grow from fhoots: fome herbs, abounding
' in flowers and fruits, perifh when the fruit is
' mature ;

47. ' Other plants, called lords of the foreft,
' have no flowers, but produce fruit; and, whe-
' ther they have flowers alfo, or fruit only, *large*
' *woody plants* of both forts are named trees.

48. ' There are fhrubs with many ftalks from
' the root upwards, and reeds with fingle roots
' but united ftems, all of different kinds, and
' graffes, and *vines or* climbers, and creepers,
' which fpring from a feed or from a flip.

49. ' Thefe *animals and vegetables*, encircled
' with multiform darknefs, by reafon of paft ac-
' tions, have internal confcience, and are fenfible
' of pleafure and pain.

50. ' All tranfmigrations, recorded *in facred*
' *books*, from the ftate of BRAHMA', to that of
' plants, happen continually in this tremendous
' world of beings; a world *always* tending to
' decay.

51. ' HE, whofe powers are incomprehenfible,
' having thus created both me and this univerfe,
' was again abforbed in the fupreme Spirit, chang-
' ing *the* time *of energy* for *the* time *of repofe.*'

52. ' When that Power awakes, *(for, though*
' *flumber be not predicable of the fole eternal Mind,*
' *infinitely wife and infinitely benevolent, yet it is pre-*
' *dicated of* BRAHMA', *figuratively, as a general pro-*
' *perty of life)* then has this world its full expanfion;
' but, when he flumbers with a tranquil fpirit,
' then the whole fyftem fades away;

53. ' For, while he repofes, *as it were*, in calm.
' fleep, embodied fpirits, endued with principles

B 4 · ' - ' of

‘ of action, depart from their several acts, and the
‘ mind itself becomes inert;

54. ‘ And when they once are abforbed in that
‘ fupreme effence, then the divine foul of all
‘ beings withdraws his energy, and placidly flum-
‘ bers;

55. ‘ Then too this vital foul *of created bodies*,
‘ with all the organs of fenfe and of action, re-
‘ mains long immerfed *in the first idea or in* dark-
‘ nefs, and performs not its natural functions, but
‘ migrates from its corporeal frame:

56. ‘ When, being *again* compofed of minute
‘ elementary principles, it enters at once into
‘ vegetable or animal feed, it then affumes a
‘ *new* form.

57. ‘ Thus that immutable Power, by waking
‘ and repofing alternately, revivifies and deftroys
‘ in eternal fucceffion, this whole affemblage of
‘ locomotive and immoveable creatures.

58. ‘ HE, having enacted this code of laws,
‘ himfelf taught it fully to me in the beginning:
‘ afterwards I taught it MARICHI and the *nine*
‘ other holy fages.

59. ‘ This *my fon* BHRĬGU will repeat the divine
‘ code to you without omiffion; for that fage
‘ learned from me to recite the whole of it.’

60. BHRĬGU, great and wife, having thus been
appointed by MENU to promulge his laws, addreffed all the *Rifhis* with an affectionate mind,
.faying: ‘ Hear!

61. ‘ FROM this MENU named SWA'YAMBHUVA,
‘ or *Sprung from the felf-exifting*, came fix def-
‘ cendants, other MENUS, *or perfectly underftanding*
‘ *the fcripture*, each giving birth to a race of his
‘ own, all exalted in dignity, eminent in power;

62. ‘ SWARO'CHISHA, AUTTAMI, TA'MASA,
                                      RAIVATA

' RAIVATA likewife and CHA'CSHUSHA, beaming
' with glory, and VAIVASWATA, child of the fun.

63. ' The feven MENUS, (or *thofe firft created,*
' *who are to be followed by feven more*) of whom
' SWA'YAMBHUVA is the chief, have produced and
' fupported this world of moving and ftationary
' beings, each in his own *antara,* or *the period of*
' *his reign.*

64. ' Eighteen *niméfhas,* or *twinklings of an eye,*
' are one *cáfht'há;* thirty *cáfht'hás,* one *calá ;*
' thirty *calás,* one *muhúrta :* and juft fo many
' *muhúrtas* let mankind confider as the duration
' of their day and night.

65. ' The fun caufes the diftribution of day and
' night, both divine and human ; night being
' *intended* for the repofe of *various* beings, and day
' for their exertion.

66. ' A month *of mortals* is a day and a night
' of the *Pitris* or *patriarchs inhabiting the moon ;*
' and the divifion *of a month* being into equal
' halves, the half beginning from the full moon is
' their day for actions ; and that beginning from
' the new moon is their night for flumber :

67. ' A year *of mortals* is a day and a night of
' the Gods, or *regents of the univerfe feated round*
' *the north pole ;* and again their divifion is this,
' their day is the northern, and their night the
' fouthern courfe of the fun.

68. ' Learn now the duration of a day and a
' night of BRAHMA', and of the feveral ages
' which fhall be mentioned in order fuccinctly.

69. ' Sages have given the name of *Crĭta* to an
' age containing four thoufand years of the Gods ;
' the twilight preceding it confifts of as many
' hundreds, and the twilight following it, of the
' fame number :

70. ' In

70. ' In the other three *ages*, with their twilights
' preceding and following, are thousands and
' hundreds diminished by·one.

71. ' The divine years, in the four *human* ages
' just enumerated, being added· together, their
' sum, *or* twelve thousand, is called the age of the
' Gods :

72. ' And, by reckoning a thousand such divine
' ages, a day of BRAHMA' may be known : his
' night also has an equal duration :

73. ' Those persons best know the divisions of
' the days and nights, who understand that the
' day of BRAHMA', which endures to the end of a
' thousand such ages, gives rise to virtuous ex-
' ertions; and that his night endures as long as
' his day.

74. ' At the close of his night, having long
' reposed, he awakes, and awaking, exerts in-
' tellect, *or reproduces the great principle of anima-*
' *tion,* whose property it is to exist unperceived by
' sense :

75. ' Intellect, called into action by his will
' to create worlds, performs *again* the work of
' creation; and thence *first* emerges the subtil
' ether, to which philosophers ascribe the quality
' of conveying sound ;

76. ' From ether, effecting a transmutation
' in form, springs the pure and potent air, a ve-
' hicle of all scents ; and air is held endued with
' the quality of touch :

77. ' Then from air, operating a change, rises
' light *or fire,* making objects visible, dispelling
' gloom, spreading bright rays ; and it is declared
' to have the quality of figure ;

78. ' But from light, a change being effected,
' comes water with the quality of taste ; and from
'   ' water

' water *is deposited* earth with the quality of smell :
' such were they created in the beginning.

79. ' The before-mentioned age of the Gods,
' or twelve thousand *of their* years, being mul-
' tiplied by seventy-one, *constitutes what* is here
' named a *Menwantara, or the reign of a* MENU.

80. ' There are numberless *Menwantaras ;*
' creations also and destructions of worlds, *in-*
' *numerable :* the Being supremely exalted per-
' forms all this, *with as much ease* as if in sport ;
' again and again, *for the sake of conferring hap-*
' *piness.*

81. ' In the *Crita* age *the Genius of* truth and
' right, *in the form of a Bull,* stands firm on his
' four feet ; nor does any advantage accrue to
' men from iniquity ;

82. ' But in the following ages, by reason of
' unjust gains, he is deprived successively of one
' foot ; and even just emoluments, through the
' prevalence of theft, falsehood, and fraud, are
' *gradually* diminished by a fourth part.

83. ' Men, free from disease, attain all sorts of
' prosperity, and live four hundred years in the
' *Crita* age ; but, in the *Trētà* and the succeeding
' ages, their life is lessened gradually by one
' quarter.

84. ' The life of mortals, which is mentioned
' in the *Véda*, the rewards of good works, and the
' powers of embodied spirits, are fruits propor-
' tioned among men to the order of the *four*
' ages.

85. ' Some duties are performed by *good* men
' in the *Crita* age ; others, in the *Trētà* ; some,
' in the *Dwápara* ; others, in the *Cali* ; in pro-
' portion as those ages decrease in length.

86. ' In the *Crita* the prevailing virtue is de-
                                        ' clared

' clared to be in devotion; in the *Trétà*, divine
' knowledge; in the *Dwápara*, holy sages call
' sacrifice the duty chiefly performed; in the
' *Cali*, liberality alone.

87. ' FOR the sake of preserving this universe,
' the Being, supremely glorious, allotted separate
' duties to those who sprang respectively from his
' mouth, his arm, his thigh, and his foot.

88. ' To *Bráhmens* he assigned the duties of
' reading the *Véda*, of teaching it, of sacrificing,
' of assisting others to sacrifice, of giving alms,
' *if they be rich*, and, *if indigent*, of receiving
' gifts:

89. ' To defend the people, to give alms, to
' sacrifice, to read the *Véda*, to shun the allure-
' ments of sensual gratification, are, in a few
' words, the duties of a *Chatriya*:

90. ' To keep herds of cattle, to bestow lar-
' gesses, to sacrifice, to read the scripture, to carry
' on trade, to lend at interest, and to cultivate
' land are prescribed *or permitted* to a *Vaisya*:

91. ' One principal duty the supreme Ruler
' assigns to a *Súdra*; namely, to serve the be-
' fore-mentioned classes, without depreciating
' their worth.

92. ' Man is declared purer above the navel;
' but the self-creating Power declared the purest
' part of him to be his mouth.

93. ' Since the *Bráhmen* sprang from the most
' excellent part, since he was the first born, and
' since he possesses the *Véda*, he is by right the
' chief of this whole creation.

94. ' Him, the Being, who exists of himself,
' produced in the beginning from his own mouth,
' that, having performed holy rites, he might
' present clarified butter to the Gods, and cakes
                                                    ' of

'of rice to the progenitors of mankind, for the
'prefervation of this world:

95. 'What created being then can furpafs
'Him, with whofe mouth the Gods of the fir-
'mament continually feaft on clarified butter, and
'the manes of anceftors, on hallowed cakes?

96. 'Of created things, the moft excellent are
'thofe which are animated; of the animated,
'thofe which fubfift by intelligence; of the in-
'telligent, mankind; and of men, the facerdotal
'clafs;

97. 'Of priefts, thofe eminent in learning;
'of the learned, thofe who know their duty; of
'thofe who know it, fuch as perform it virtuoufly;
'and of the virtuous, thofe who feek beatitude
'from a perfect acquaintance with fcriptural doc-
'trine.

98. 'The very birth of *Bráhmens* is a conftant
'incarnation of DHERMA, *God of Juftice*; for the
'*Bráhmen* is born to promote juftice, and to pro-
'cure ultimate happinefs.

99. 'When a *Bráhmen* fprings to light, he is
'born above the world, the chief of all creatures,
'affigned to guard the treafury of duties, religious
'and civil.

100. 'Whatever exifts in the univerfe, is all
'in effect, *though not in form*, the wealth of
'the *Bráhmen*; fince the *Bráhmen* is entitled
'to it all by his primogeniture and eminence
'of birth:

101. 'The *Bráhmen* eats but his own food;
'wears but his own apparel; and beftows but his
'own in alms: through the benevolence of the
'*Bráhmen*, indeed, other mortals enjoy life.

102. 'To declare the facerdotal duties, and
'thofe of the other claffes in due order, the fage

6   MENU,

' Menu, sprung from the self-exifting, promulged
' this code of laws:

103. ' A code which muft be ftudied with ex-
' treme eafe by every learned *Bráhmen*, and fully
' explained to his difciples, but *muſt be taught* by
' no other man *of an inferior claſs.*

104. ' The *Bráhmen* who ftudies this book,
' having performed facred rites, is perpetually
' free from offence in thought, in word, and in
' deed;

105. ' He confers purity on his living family,
' on his anceftors, and on his defcendants, as far
' as the feventh perfon; and He alone deferves
' to poffefs this whole earth.

106. ' This moft excellent code produces every
' thing aufpicious; this code increafes under-
' ftanding; this code procures fame and long life;
' this code leads to fupreme blifs.

107. ' In this book appears the fyftem of law
' in its full extent, with the good and bad pro-
' perties of human actions, and the immemorial
' cuftoms of the four claffes.

108. ' Immemorial cuftom is tranfcendent law,
' approved in the facred fcripture, and in the
' codes of divine legiflators: let every man, there-
' fore, of the three principal claffes, who has a due
' reverence for the *fupreme* fpirit *which dwells in*
' *him*, diligently and conftantly obferve imme-
' morial cuftom :

109. ' A man of the prieftly, military, or
' commercial clafs, who deviates from imme-
' morial ufage, taftes not the fruit of the *Véda*;
' but, by an' exact obfervance of it, he gathers
' that fruit in perfection.

110. ' Thus have holy fages, well knowing
' that law is grounded on immemorial cuftom,
                                        embraced,

' embraced, as the root of all piety, good ufages
' long eftablifhed.

111. ' THE creation of this univerfe, the forms
' of inftitution and education, with the obfervances
' and behaviour of a ftudent in theology; the beft
' rules for the ceremony on his return from the
' manfion of his preceptor;

112. ' The law of marriage in general, and
' of nuptials in different forms; the regulations
' for the great facraments, and the manner,
' primevally fettled, of performing obfequies;

113. ' The modes of gaining fubfiftence, and
' the rules to be obferved by the mafter of a
' family; the allowance and prohibition of diet,
' with the purification of men and utenfils;

114. ' Laws concerning women, the devotion
' of hermits, and of anchorets wholly intent on
' final beatitude, the whole duty of a king, and
' the judicial decifion of controverfies,

115. ' With the law of evidence and examina-
' tion; laws concerning hufband and wife, canons
' of inheritance; the prohibition of gaming, and
' the punifhments of criminals;

116. ' Rules ordained for the mercantile and
' fervile claffes, with the origin of thofe that are
' mixed; the duties and rights of all the claffes in
' time of diftrefs for fubfiftence; and the penances
' for expiating fins;

117. ' The feveral tranfmigrations in this uni-
' verfe, caufed by offences of three kinds, with
' the ultimate blifs attending good actions, on the
' full trial of vice and virtue;

118. ' All thefe titles of law, promulgated
' by MENU, and *occafionally* the cuftoms of dif-
' ferent countries, different tribes, and different
7   ' families,

' families, with rules concerning hereticks and
' companies of traders, are difcuffed in this
' code.

119. ' Even as MENU, at my requeft, formerly
' revealed this divine *Sáftra*, hear it now from
' me without any diminution or addition.

CHAPTER THE SECOND.

On Education; or on the Sacerdotal Clafs, and
The Firft Order.

———

1. ' Know that fyftem of duties, which is re-
' vered by fuch as are learned in the *Védas,* and
' impreffed, *as the means of attaining beatitude,* on
' the hearts of the juft, who are ever exempt
' from hatred and inordinate affection.

2. ' Self-love is no laudable motive, yet an
' exemption from felf-love is not *to be found* in
' this world : on felf-love is grounded the ftudy
' of fcripture, and the practice of actions re-
' commended in it.

3. ' Eager defire *to act* has its root in expecta-
' tion of fome advantage ; and with fuch expec-
' tation are facrifices performed ; the rules of
' religious aufterity and abftinence from fins are
' all known to arife from hope of remuneration.

4. ' Not a fingle act here below appears ever
' to be done by a man free from felf-love ; what-
' ever he performed, it is wrought from his defire
' of a reward.

5. ' He, indeed, who fhould perfift in *difcharg-*
' *ing* thefe duties without any view to their fruit,
' would attain hereafter the ftate of the immortals,
' and even in this life, would enjoy all the vir-
' tuous gratifications, that his fancy could fuggeft.

C   6. ' The

6. ' The roots of law are the whole *Véda*,
' the ordinances` and moral practices of such as
' perfectly understand it, the immemorial customs
' of good men, and, *in cases quite indifferent*, self-
' satisfaction.

7. ' Whatever law has been ordained for any
' person by MENU, that law is fully declared in
' the *Véda :* for He was perfect in divine know-
' ledge :

8. ' A man of true learning, who has viewed
' this complete system with the eye of sacred
' wisdom, cannot fail to perform all those duties,
' which are ordained on the authority of the *Véda.*

9. ' No doubt, that man who shall follow the
' rules prescribed in the *Sruti* and in the *Smṛti*,
' will acquire fame in this life, and, in the next,
' inexpressible happiness :

10. ' By *Sruti*, or *what was heard from above*,
' is meant the *Véda ;* and by *Smṛti*, or *what was
' remembered from the beginning*, the body of law :
' those two must not be oppugned by heterodox
' arguments; since from those two, proceeds the
' whole system of duties.

11. ' Whatever man of the three highest classes,
' having addicted himself to heretical books, shall
' treat with contempt those two roots of law, he
' must be driven, as an Atheist and a scorner of
' revelation, from the company of the virtuous.

12. ' The scripture, the codes of law, ap-
' proved usage, and, *in all indifferent cases*, self-
' satisfaction, the wise have openly declared to
' be the quadruple description of the juridical
' system.

13. ' A knowledge of right is a sufficient in-
' centive for men unattached to wealth or to sen-
' suality ; and to those who seek a knowledge of
                                        ' right,

' right, the supreme authority is divine revela-
' tion ;

14. ' But, when there are two sacred texts, *ap-*
' *parently inconsistent,* both are held to be law ; for
' both are pronounced by the wise to be valid
' and reconcileable ;

15. ' Thus in the *Véda* are these texts : " let
' the sacrifice be when the sun has arisen," and,
" before it has risen," and, " when neither sun
' nor stars can be seen :" the sacrifice, therefore,
' may be performed at any or all of those times.

16. ' He, whose life is regulated by holy texts,
' from his conception even to his funeral pile,
' has a decided right to study this code ; but no
' other man whatsoever.

17. ' BETWEEN the two divine rivers *Saraswatí*
' and *Drishadwatí,* lies the tract of land, which
' the sages have named *Brahmáverta,* because it
' was frequented by Gods :

18. ' The custom preserved by immemorial
' tradition in that country, among the four pure
' classes, and among those which are mixed, is
' called approved usage.

19. ' *Curucshétra, Matsya, Panchála,* or *Cánya-*
' *cubja,* and *Súraséna,* or *Mat'hurà,* form the re-
' gion called *Brahmarshi,* distinguished from *Brah-*
' *máverta :*

20. ' From a *Bráhmen* who was born in that
' country, let all men on earth learn their several
' usages.

21. ' That country which lies between *Hima-*
' *wat* and *Vindhya,* to the east of *Vinas'ana,* and to
' the west of *Prayága,* is celebrated by the title of
' *Medhya-d'Ja,* or *the central region.*

22. ' As far as the eastern, and as far as the
' western oceans, between the two mountains just

' men-

' mentioned, lies the tract which the wife have
' named *Ariáverta*, or *inhabited by respectable men.*

23. ' That land, on which the black antelope
' naturally grazes, is held fit for the performance
' of sacrifices; but the land of *Mléch'has,* or *those*
' *who speak barbarously,* differs widely from it.

24. ' Let the three first classes invariably dwell
' in those before-mentioned countries; but a *Sú-*
' *dra,* distressed for subsistence, may sojourn
' wherever he chuses.

25. ' Thus has the origin of law been succinct-
' ly declared to you, together with the formation
' of this universe: now learn the laws of the
' several classes.

26. ' WITH auspicious acts prescribed by the
' *Véda,* must ceremonies on conception, and so
' forth, be duly performed, which purify the
' bodies of the three classes in this life, and *qualify*
' *them* for the next.

27. ' By oblations to fire during the mother's
' pregnancy, by holy rites on the birth of the
' child, by the tonsure of his head with a lock of
' hair left on it, by the ligation of the sacrificial
' cord, are the seminal and uterine taints of the
' three classes wholly removed:

28. ' By studying the *Véda,* by religious ob-
' servances, by oblations to fire, by the ceremony
' of *Traividia,* by offering to the Gods and Manes,
' by the procreation of children, by the five great
' sacraments, and by solemn sacrifices, this human
' body is rendered fit for a divine state.

29. ' Before the section of the navel string a
' ceremony is ordained on the birth of a male:
' he must be made, while sacred texts are pro-
' nounced, to taste a little honey and clarified
' butter from a golden spoon.

30. ' Let

30. ' Let the father *perform or*, *if abfent*, caufe
' to be performed, on the tenth or twelfth day
' *after the birth*, the ceremony of giving a name ;
' or on fome fortunate day of the moon, at a
' lucky hour, and under the influence of a ftar
' with good qualities.

31. ' The firft part of a *Bráhmen*'s compound
' name fhould indicate holinefs ; of a *Cfhatriya's*,
' power ; of a *Vaifya's*, wealth ; and of a *Súdra's*
' contempt :

32. ' Let the fecond part of the prieft's name
' imply profperity ; of the foldier's, prefervation ;
' of the merchant's, nourifhment ; of the fervant's,
' humble attendance.

33. ' The names of women fhould be agreeable,
' foft, clear, captivating the fancy, aufpicious,
' ending in long vowels, refembling words of
' benediction.

34. ' In the fourth month the child fhould be
' carried out of the houfe *to fee the fun:* in the
' fixth month, he fhould be fed with rice ; or
' that *may be done*, which, by the cuftom of the
' family, is thought moft propitious.

35. ' By the command of the *Véda*, the cere-
' mony of tonfure fhould be legally performed
' by the three *firft* claffes in the firft or third
' year *after birth*.

36. ' In the eighth year from the conception
' of a *Bráhmen*, in the, eleventh from that of a
' *Cfhatriya*, and in the twelfth from that of a
' *Vaifya*, let the father inveft the child with the
' mark of his clafs :

37. ' Should a *Bráhmen*, or *his father for him*,
' be defirous of his advancement in facred know-
' ledge ; a *Cfhatriya*, of extending his power ; or a
' *Vaifya* of engaging in mercantile bufinefs ; the

' in-

' investiture may be made in the fifth, sixth, or
' eighth years respectively.

 38. ' The ceremony of investiture hallowed by
' the *gáyatrí* must not be delayed, in the case of a
' priest, beyond the sixteenth year; nor in that
' of a soldier, beyond the twenty-second; nor in
' that of a merchant, beyond the twenty-fourth.

 39. ' After that *all youths* of these three classes,
' who have not been invested at the proper time,
' become *vrátyas*, or outcasts, degraded from the
' *gáyatrí*, and contemned by the virtuous:

 40. ' With such impure men, let no *Bráhmen*,
' even in distress for subsistence, ever form a con-
' nexion in law, either by the study of the *Véda*,
' or by affinity.

 41. ' Let students in theology wear *for their*
' *mantles*, the hides of black antelopes, of common
' deer, or of goats, with *lower vests of* woven *s'ana*,
' of *cshumà*, and of wool, in the direct order of their
' classes.

 42. ' The girdle of a priest must be made of
' *munja*, in a triple cord, smooth and soft; that
' of a warrior must be a bow string of *múrvá*;
' that of a merchant, a triple thread of *s'ana*.

 43 ' If the *munja* be not procurable, their zones
' must be formed *respectively* of the grasses *cusa*
' *asmántaca, valvaja*, in triple strings with one, three,
' or five knots, *according to the family custom.*

 44. ' The sacrificial thread of a *Bráhmen* must
' be made of cotton, so as to be put on over his
' head, in three strings; that of a *Cshatriya*, of
' *s'ana* thread only; that of a *Vais'ya* of woollen
' thread.

 45. ' A priest ought by law to carry a staff of
' *Bilva* or *Palása*; a soldier, of *Bata* or *C'hadira*;
' a merchant of *Vénu* or *Udumbara*;

       46. ' The

46. ' The ſtaff of a prieſt muſt be of ſuch length
' as to reach his hair ; that of a ſoldier, to reach
' his forehead ; and that of a merchant, to reach
' his noſe.

47. ' Let all the ſtaves be ſtraight, without
' fracture, of a handſome appearance, not likely
' to terrify men, with their bark perfect, unhurt
' by fire.

48. ' Having taken a legal ſtaff to his liking,
' and ſtanding oppoſite to the ſun, let the ſtudent
' thrice walk round the fire from left to right, and
' perform, according to law, the ceremony of aſk-
' ing food :

49. ' The moſt excellent of the three claſſes,
' being girt with the ſacrificial thread, muſt aſk
' food with the reſpectful word *bhavati*, at the
' beginning of the phraſe ; thoſe of the ſecond
' claſs, with that word in the middle ; and thoſe
' of the third, with that word at the end.

50. ' Let him firſt beg food of his mother, or
' of his ſiſter, or of his mother's whole ſiſter ; then
' of ſome other female who will not diſgrace him.

51. ' Having collected as much of the deſired
' food as he has occaſion for, and having preſented
' it without guile to his preceptor, let him eat
' ſome of it, being duly purified, with his face to
' the eaſt :

52. ' If he ſeek long life, he ſhould eat with his
' face to the eaſt, if exalted fame to the ſouth ; if
' proſperity to the weſt ; if truth *and its reward* to
' the north.

53. ' Let the ſtudent, having performed his
' ablution, always eat his food without diſtraction
' of mind ; and, having eaten, let him *thrice* waſh
' his mouth completely, ſprinkling with water the

' ſix

' *fix* hollow parts of his head, *or his eyes, ears, and*
' *noſtrils.*

54. ' Let him honour all his food, and eat it
' without contempt; when he ſees it, let him
' rejoice and be calm, and pray, that he may
' always obtain it.

55. ' Food, eaten conſtantly with reſpect, gives
'muſcular force and generative power; but, eaten
' irreverently, deſtroys them both.

56. ' He muſt beware of giving any man what
' he leaves; and of eating any thing between
' *morning and evening:* he muſt alſo beware of
' eating too much, and of going any whither with
' a remnant of his food unſwallowed.

57. ' Exceſſive eating is prejudicial to health,
' to fame, and to 'future bliſs in Heaven; it is
' injurious to virtue, and odious among men:
' he muſt, for theſe reaſons, by all means avoid it.

58. ' Let a *Bráhmen* at all times perform the
' ablution with the pure part of his hand denomi-
' nated from the *Véda,* or with the part ſacred to
' the Lord of creatures, or with that dedicated to
' the Gods; but never with the part named from
' the *Pitris:*

59. ' The pure part under the root of the
' thumb is called *Bráhma,* that at the root of the
' little finger, *Cáya;* that at the tips of the fingers,
' *Daiva;* and the part between the thumb and
' index *Pitrya.*

60. ' Let him firſt ſip water thrice; then twice
' wipe his mouth; and laſtly touch with water
' the *fix before mentioned* cavities, his breaſt,
' and his head.

61. ' He who knows the law and ſeeks purity
' will ever perform his ablution with the pure part
' of his hand, and with water neither hot nor
                              ' frothy

' frothy, ſtanding in a lonely place, and turning
' to the eaſt or the north.

62. ' A *Bráhmen* is purified by water that
' reaches his boſom; a *Chatriya*, by water deſcend-
' ing to his throat; a *Vaiſya*, by water barely
' taken into his mouth; a *Súdra* by water touched
' with the extremity of his lips.

63. ' A youth of the three higheſt claſſes is
' named *upaviti*, when his right hand is extended
' *for the cord to paſs over his head and be fixed on his*
' *left ſhoulder*; when his left hand is extended,
' *that the thread may be placed on his right ſhoulder*,
' he is called *práchinávíti*; and *niviti*, when it is
' faſtened on his neck.

64. ' His girdle, his leathern mantle, his ſtaff,
' his ſacrificial cord, and his ewer, he muſt throw
' into the water, when they are worn out or
' broken, and receive others hallowed by myſtical
' texts.

65. ' The ceremony of *céſánta*, or *cutting off the*
' *hair*, is ordained for a prieſt in the ſixteenth year
' from conception; for a ſoldier, in the twenty-
' ſecond; for a merchant, two years later than
' that.

66. ' The ſame ceremonies, *except that of the*
' *ſacrificial thread*, muſt be duly performed for
' women at the ſame age and in the ſame order,
' that the body may be made perfect; but with-
' out any text from the *Véda*:

67. ' The nuptial ceremony is confidered as
' the complete inſtitution of women, ordained for
' them in the *Véda*, together with reverence to
' their huſbands, dwelling firſt in their father's
' family, the buſineſs of the houſe, and attention
' to ſacred fire.

7

68. ' Such

68. ' Such is the real law of inftitution for the
' twice born ; an inftitution in which their fecond
' birth clearly confifts, and which caufes their ad-
' vancement in holinefs : now learn to what du-
' ties they muft afterwards apply themfelves.

69. ' THE venerable preceptor, having girt his
' pupil with the thread, muft firft inftruct him
' in purification, in good cuftoms, in the manage-
' ment of the confecrated fire, and in the holy
' rites of morning, noon, and evening.

70. ' When the ftudent is going to read the
' *Véda*, he muft perform an ablution, as the law
' ordains, with his face to the north, and, having
' paid fcriptural homage, he muft receive inftruc-
' tion, wearing a clean veft, his members being
' duly compofed :

71. ' At the beginning and end of the lecture,
' he muft always clafp both the feet of his precep-
' tor ; and he muft read with both his hands
' clofed : (this is called fcripture homage.)

72. ' With croffed hands let him clafp the feet
' of his tutor, touching the left foot with his left,
' and the right, with his right hand.

73. ' When he is prepared for the lecture, the
' preceptor, conftantly attentive, muft fay : "hoa !
' read ;" and at the clofe of the leffon he muft
' fay : " take reft."

74. ' A *Bráhmen*, beginning and ending a
' lecture on the *Véda*, muft always pronounce to
' himfelf the fyllable *óm*; for, unlefs the fyllable
' *óm* precede, his learning will flip away from him ;
' and, unlefs it follow, nothing will be long
' retained.

75. ' If he have fitten on culms of *cus'a* with
' their points toward the eaft, and be purified
' by *rubbing* that holy grafs on both his hands,
              and

' and be 'further prepared by three fuppreffions of
' breath *each equal in time to five short vowels*, he
' then may fitly pronounce *óm*.

76. ' BRAHMA' milked out, *as it were*, from the
' three *Védas*, the letter A, the letter U, and
' the letter M, *which form by their coalition the trilite-*
' *ral monofyllable*, together with three myfterious
' words, *bhur, bhuvah, fwer*, or *earth, fky, heaven*:

77. ' From the three *Védas*, alfo, the Lord of
' creatures, incomprehenfibly exalted, fucceffively
' milked out the three meafures of that ineffable
' text, beginning with the word *tad*, and entitled
' *fávitri* or *gáyatrí*.

78. ' A prieft who fhall know the *Véda*, and fhall
' pronounce to himfelf, both morning and even-
' ing, that fyllable, and that holy text preceded
' by the three words, fhall attain the fanctity
' which the *Véda* confers ;

79. ' And a twice born man, who fhall a thou-
' fand times repeat thofe three (or *óm*, the *vyáhrĭtis*,
' and the *gayatrí*,) apart *from the multitude*, fhall be
' releafed in a month even from a great offence,
' as a fnake from his flough.

80. ' The prieft, the foldier, and the merchant,
' who fhall neglect this myfterious text, and fail
' to perform in due feafon his peculiar acts of
' piety, fhall meet with contempt among the
' virtuous.

81. ' The three great immutable words, pre-
' ceded by the triliteral fyllable, and *followed by*
' the *gáyatrí* which confifts of three meafures, muft
' be confidered as the mouth, or *principal part*
' of the *Véda* :

82. ' Whoever fhall repeat, day by day, for
' three years, without negligence, that facred
' text, fhall *hereafter* approach the divine effence,
' move

5

' move as freely as air, and affume an ethereal
' form.

83. ' The triliteral monofyllable is *an emblem of*
' the fupreme, the fuppreffions of breath *with a*
' *mind fixed on* GOD are the higheft devotion ; but
' nothing is more exalted than the *gáyatrí : a de-*
' *claration of* truth is more excellent than filence.

84. ' All rites ordained in the *Véda,* oblations to
' fire, and folemn facrifices pafs away ; but that
' which paffes not away, is declared to be the
' fyllable *óm,* thence called *acfhara;* fince it is a
' *fymbol of* GOD, the Lord of created beings.

85. ' The act of repeating his Holy Name is
' ten times better than the appointed facrifice ;
' an hundred times better when it is heard by no
' man ; and a thoufand times better when it is
' purely mental :

86. ' The four domeftic factaments which are
' accompanied with the appointed facrifice, are not
' equal, though all be united, to a fixteenth part
' of the facrifice performed by a repetition of the
' *gáyatrí :*

87. ' By the fole repetition of the *gáyatrí,* a
' prieft may indubitably attain beatitude, let him
' perform, or not perform, any other religious
' act ; if he be *Maitra,* or a *friend to all creatures,*
' he is *juftly* named *Bráhmena,* or *united to the Great*
' *One.*

88. ' In reftraining the organs which run wild
' among ravifhing fenfualities, a wife man will
' apply diligent care, like a charioteer in ma-
' naging reftive horfes.

89. ' Thofe eleven organs, to which the firft
' fages gave names, I will comprehenfively enu-
' merate as the law confiders them in due order.

90. ' The

90. ' The nofe is the fifth after the ears, the
' fkin, the eyes, and the tongue; and the organs
' of fpeech are reckoned the tenth, after thofe
' of excretion and generation, and the hands and
' feet :

91. ' Five of them, the ear and the reft in fuc-
' ceffion, learned men have called organs of fenfe;
' and the others, organs of action :

92. ' The heart muft be confidered as the
' eleventh; which, by its natural property, com-
' prifes both fenfe and action; and which being
' fubdued, the two other fets, with five in each,
' are alfo controled.

93. ' A man, by the attachment of his organs
' to fenfual pleafure incurs certain guilt; but,
' having wholly fubdued them, he thence attains
' heavenly blifs.

94. ' Defire is never fatisfied with the enjoyment
' of defired objects; as the fire is not appeafed
' with clarified butter; it only blazes more ve-
' hemently.

95. ' Whatever man may obtain all thofe gra-
' tifications, or whatever man may refign them
' completely, the refignation of all pleafures is far
' better than the attainment of them.

96. ' The organs being ftrongly attached to
' fenfual delights cannot fo effectually be reftrained
' by avoiding incentives to pleafure, as by a con-
' ftant purfuit of divine knowledge.

97. ' To a man contaminated by fenfuality
' neither the *Védas*, nor liberality, nor facrifices,
' nor ftrict obfervances, nor pious aufterities, ever
' procure felicity.

98. ' He muft be confidered as really triumph-
' ant over his organs, who, on hearing and touch-
' ing, on feeing and tafting and fmelling, *what*
' *may*

‘ *may pleafe or offend the fenfes*, neither greatly re-
‘ joices nor greatly repines :

99. ‘ But, when one among all his organs fails,
‘ by that fingle failure his knowledge of GOD
‘ paffes away, as water flows through one hole in
‘ a leathern bottle.

100. ‘ Having kept all his members *of fenfe*
‘ *and action* under control, and obtained alfo com-
‘ mand over his heart, he will enjoy every ad-
‘ vantage, even though he reduce not his body
‘ by religious aufterities.

101. ‘ AT the morning twilight let him ftand
‘ repeating the *gáyatrí* until he fee the fun ; and
‘ at evening twilight, let him repeat it fitting,
‘ until the ftars diftinctly appear :

102. ‘ He who ftands repeating it at the morn-
‘ ing twilight, removes *all unknown* nocturnal fin ;
‘ and he who repeats it fitting at evening twilight,
‘ difperfes the taint, that has *unknowingly* been
‘ contracted in the day ;

103. ‘ But he who ftands not repeating it in
‘ the morning, and fits not repeating it in the
‘ evening, muft be precluded, like a *Súdra*, from
‘ every facred obfervance of the twice born
‘ claffes.

104. ‘ Near pure water, with his organs holden
‘ under control, *and* retiring from circumfpection
‘ to fome unfrequented place, let him pronounce
‘ the *gáyatrí*, performing daily ceremonies.

105. ‘ IN reading the *Védángas*, or *grammar*,
• *profody, mathematicks, and fo forth*, or even fuch
‘ parts of the *Véda* as ought conftantly to be read,
‘ there is no prohibition on particular days ; nor
‘ in pronouncing the texts appointed for oblations
‘ to fire :

106. ‘ Of

106. ' Of that, which muſt conſtantly be read,
' and is therefore called *Bráhmaſatra*, there can
' be no ſuch prohibition; and the oblation to
' fire, according to the *Véda*, produces good fruit,
' though accompanied with the text *vaſhat*, which
' *on other occaſions* muſt be intermitted on cer-
' tain days.

107. ' For him, who ſhall perſiſt a whole year
' in reading the *Véda*, his organs being kept in
' ſubjection, and his body pure, there will always
' riſe good fruit from his *offerings of* milk and
' curds, *of* clarified butter and honey.

108. ' Let the twice born youth, who has
' been girt with the ſacrificial cord, collect wood
' for the holy fire, beg food of his relations, ſleep
' on a low bed, and perform ſuch offices as may
' pleaſe his preceptor, until his return to the
' houſe of his natural father.

109. ' Ten perſons may legally be inſtructed
' in the *Véda*; the ſon of a ſpiritual teacher;
' a boy who is aſſiduous; one who can impart
' other knowledge; one who is juſt; one who
' is pure; one who is friendly; one who is
' powerful; one who can beſtow wealth; one
' who is honeſt; and one who is related by
' blood.

110. ' Let not a ſenſible teacher tell any *other*
' what he is not aſked, nor what he is aſked im-
' properly; but let him however intelligent, act
' in the multitude as if he were dumb:

111. ' Of the two perſons, him, who illegally
' aſks, and him, who illegally anſwers, one will
' die, or incur odium.

112. ' Where virtue, and wealth *ſufficient to ſe-*
' *cure it*, are not found, or diligent attention, *at*
' *leaſt* proportioned *to the holineſs of the ſubject*, in
' that

‘ that foil divine inſtruction muſt not be fown : it
‘ would periſh like fine feed in barren land.

113. ‘ A teacher of the *Véda* ſhould rather die
‘ with his learning, than fow it in ſterile foil, even
‘ though he be in grevious diſtreſs for ſubſiſtence.

114. ‘ Sacred Learning, having approached a
‘ *Bráhmen*, faid to him : “ I am thy precious
‘ gem ; preferve me with care ; deliver me not to
‘ a fcorner ; (fo *preferved* I ſhall become ſupremely
‘ ſtrong.)

115. ‘ But communicate me, as to a vigilent de-
‘ poſitory of thy gem, to that ſtudent, whom thou
‘ ſhalt know to be pure, to have ſubdued his
‘ paſſions, to perform the duties of his order.”

116. ‘ He who ſhall acquire *knowledge of* the
‘ *Véda* without the aſſent of his preceptor, incurs
‘ the guilt of ſtealing the ſcripture, and ſhall fink
‘ to the region of torment.

117. ‘ From whatever teacher a ſtudent has
‘ received inſtruction, either popular, ceremonial,
‘ or facred, let him firſt falute his inſtructor, when
‘ they meet.

118. ‘ A *Bráhmen*, who completely governs his
‘ paſſions, though he know the *gáyatrí* only, is
‘ more honourable than he, who governs not his
‘ paſſions, who eats all *ſorts of food,* and fells all
‘ *ſorts of commodities,* even though he know the
‘ three *Védas*.

119. ‘ When a ſuperior fits on a couch or
‘ bench, let not an inferior fit on it with him ;
‘ and, if an inferior be fitting on a couch, let him
‘ rife to falute a ſuperior.

120. ‘ The vital ſpirits of a young man mount
‘ upwards *to depart from him,* when an elder ap-
‘ proaches ; but by rifing and falutation he reco-
‘ vers them.

121. ‘ A

121. ' A youth who habitually greets and con-
' ftantly reveres the aged, obtains an increafe of
' four things ; life, knowledge, fame, ftrength.

122. ' After the word of falutation, a *Bráhmen*
' muft addrefs an elder ; faying, " I am fuch an
' one," pronouncing his own name.

123. ' If any perfons, *through ignorance of the*
' Sanfcrit *language*, underftand not the import of
' his name, to them fhould a learned man fay,
" It is I ;" and in that manner he fhould addrefs
' all *claffes of* women.

124. ' In the falutation he fhould pronounce,
' after his own name, the vocative particle *bhós* ;
' for the particle *bhós* is held by the wife to have
' the fame property with names *fully expreffed*.

125. ' A *Bráhmen* fhould thus be faluted in re-
' turn : " May'ft thou live long, excellent man !"
' and at the end of his name, the vowel and pre-
' ceding confonant fhould be lengthened, *with an*
' *acute accent*, to three fyllabick moments *or fhort*
' *vowels*.

126. ' That *Bráhmen*, who knows not the form
' of returning a falutation, muft not be faluted by
' a man of learning: as a *Súdra*, even fo is he.

127. ' Let a learned man afk a prieft, when he
' meets him, if his devotion profpers ; a warriour,
' if he is unhurt ; a merchant, if his wealth is
' fecure ; and one of the fervile clafs, if he enjoys
' good health ; *ufing refpectively the words*, cus'alam,
' anámayam, cfhémam, *and* árógyam.

128. ' He, who has juft performed a folemn
' facrifice and ablution, muft not be addreffed by
' his name, even though he be a younger man ;
' but he, who knows the law, fhould accoft him
' with the vocative particle, or with *bhavat*, the
' the pronoun of refpect.

D   129. ' To

129. ' To the wife of another, and to any wo-
' man not related by blood, he muft fay, " *bhavati*,
' and amiable fifter.''

130. ' To his uncles paternal and maternal, to
' his wife's father, to performers of the facrifice,
' and to fpiritual teachers; he muft fay, " I am
' fuch an one"—rifing up to falute them, even
' though younger than himfelf.

131. ' The fifter of his mother, the wife of his
' maternal uncle, his own wife's mother, and the
' fifter of his father, muft be faluted like the wife
' of his father or preceptor: they are equal to his
' father's or his preceptor's wife.

132. ' The wife of his brother, if fhe be of the
' fame clafs, muft be faluted every day; but his
' paternal and maternal kinfwomen need only be
' greeted on his return from a journey.

133. ' With the fifter of his father and of his
' mother, and with his own elder fifter, let him
' demean himfelf as with his mother; though his
' mother be more venerable than they.

134. ' Fellow citizens are equal for ten years;
' dancers and fingers, for five; learned theolo-
' gians, for lefs than three; but perfons related by
' blood, for a fhort time: *that is, a greater difference*
' *of age deftroys their equality.*

135. ' The ftudent muft confider a *Bráhmen*,
' though but ten years old, and a *Cfhatriya*, though
' aged a hundred years, as father and fon; as
' between thofe two, the young *Bráhmen* is *to be*
' *refpected as* the father.

136. ' Wealth, kindred, age, moral conduct,
' and, fifthly, divine knowledge, entitle men to
' refpect; but that which is laft mentioned in
' order, is the moft refpectable.

I   137. ' Whatever

137. ' Whatever man of the three *higheſt* claſſes
' poſſeſſes the moſt of thoſe five, both in number
' and degree, that man is entitled to moſt reſpeƈt;
' even a *Súdra*, if he have entered the tenth decad
' of his age.

138. ' Way muſt be made for a man in a
' wheeled carriage, or above ninety years old, or
' afflicted with diſeaſe, or carrying a burthen; for
' a woman; for a prieſt juſt returned from the
' manſion of his preceptor; for a prince, and for
' a bridegroom:

139. ' Among all thoſe, if they be met at one
' time, the prieſt juſt returned home and the
' prince are moſt to be honoured; and of thoſe
' two, the prieſt juſt returned, ſhould be treated
' with more reſpeƈt than the prince.

140 ' That prieſt who girds his pupil with the
' ſacrificial cord, and afterwards inſtruƈts him in
' the whole *Véda*, with the law of ſacrifice and
' the ſacred *Upaniſhads*, holy ſages call an *áchárya :*

141. ' But, he, who for his livelihood, gives
' inſtruƈtion in a part only of the *Véda*, or in gram-
' mar, and in other *Védángas*, is called an *upádhyáya*,
' or ſubleƈturer.

142. ' The father, who performs the ceremo-
' nies on conception and the like, according to
' law, and who nouriſhes the child with his firſt
' rice, has the epithet of *guru*, or venerable.

143. ' He, who receives a ſtipend for preparing
' the holy fire, for conduƈting the *páca* and
' *agniſhtóma*, and for performing other ſacrifices,
' is called in this code the *ritwij* of his employer.

144. ' He, who truly and faithfully fills both
' ears with the *Véda*, muſt be conſidered as equal
' to a mother; he muſt be revered as a father;
' him the pupil muſt never grieve.

145. ' A

145. ' A mere *áchárya*, or *a teacher of the* gá-
' yatrí *only*, furpaffes ten *upádhyáyas* ; a father, a
' hundred fuch *áchárya*s; and a mother, a thoufand
' natural fathers.

146. ' Of him, who gives natural birth, and
' him, who gives knowledge of the whole *Véda*,
' the giver of facred knowledge is the more ve-
' nerable father ; fince the *fecond or* divine birth
' enfures life to the twice born both in this world
' and hereafter eternally.

147. ' Let a man confider that as a mere
' human birth, which his parents gave him for
' their mutual gratification, and which he receives
' after lying in the womb ;

148. ' But that birth, which his principal
' *áchárya*, who knows the whole *Véda*, procures for
' him by *his divine mother* the *gáyatrí*, is a true
' birth : that birth is exempt from age and from
' death.

140. ' Him, who confers on a man the benefit
' of facred learning, whether it be little or much,
' let him know to be here named *guru*, or *ve-*
' *nerable father*, in confequence of that heavenly
' benefit.

150. ' A *Bráhmen*, who is the giver of fpiritual
' birth, the teacher of prefcribed duty, is by right
' *called* the father of an old man, though himfelf
' be a child.

151. ' CAVI, or *the learned*, child of ANGIRAS,
' taught his paternal uncles and coufins to read the
' *Véda*, and, excelling them in divine knowledge,
' faid to them, '' little fons :"

152. ' They, moved with refentment, afked the
' Gods the meaning of that *expreffion* ; and the
' Gods, being affembled, anfwered them : '' The
' child has addreffed you properly ;

153. ' For

152. ' For an unlearned man is in truth a
' child ; and he who teaches him the *Véda*, is his
' father : holy sages have always said child to an
' ignorant man, and father to a teacher of scrip-
' ture."

154. ' Greatnefs is not conferred by years, not
' by gray hairs, not by wealth, not by powerful
' kindred : the divine sages have eftablifhed this
' rule ; " Whoever has read the *Védas* and their
' *Angas*, he among us is great."

155. ' The feniority of priefts is from facred
' learning ; of warriours from valour ; of mer-
' chants from abundance of grain ; of the fervile
' clafs only from priority of birth.

156. ' A man is not therefore aged, becaufe his
' head is gray : him, furely, the Gods confidered
' as aged, who, though young in years, has read
' *and underftands* the *Véda*.

157. ' As an elephant made of wood, as an
' antelope made of leather, fuch is an unlearned
' *Bráhmen :* thofe three have nothing but names.

158. ' As an eunuch is unproductive with wo-
' men, as cow with a cow is unprolifick, as libe-
' rality to a fool is fruitlefs, fo is a *Bráhmen* ufelefs,
' if he read not the holy texts.

159. ' Good inftruction muft be given without
' pain to the inftructed ; and fweet gentle fpeech
' muft be ufed by a preceptor, who cherifhes virtue.

160. ' He, whofe difcourfe and heart are pure,
' and ever perfectly guarded, attains all the fruit
' arifing from his complete courfe of ftudying the
' *Véda*.

161. ' Let not a man be querulous even
' though in pain ; let him not injure another in
' deed or in thought ; let him not even utter a word,
' by which his fellow creature may fuffer uneafi-
' nefs ;

D 3

' nefs; fince that will obftruct his own progrefs to
' future beatitude.

162. ' A *Bráhmen* fhould conftantly fhun wordly
' honour, as he fhould fhun poifon ; and rather
' conftantly feek difrefpect, as he would feek nectar;

163. ' For though fcorned, he may fleep with
' pleafure; with pleafure may he awake; with
' pleafure may he pafs through this life : but the
' fcorner utterly perifhes.

164. ' Let the twice born youth, whofe foul
' has been formed by this regular fucceffion of
' prefcribed acts, collect by degrees, while he
' dwells with his preceptor, the devout habits
' proceeding from the ftudy of fcripture.

165. ' With various modes of devotion, and
' with aufterities ordained by the law, muft the
' whole *Véda* be read, and above all the facred
' *Upanifhads*, by him, who has received a new birth.

166. ' Let the beft of the twice born claffes,
' intending to practife devotion, continually repeat
' the reading of fcripture; fince a repetition of
' reading the fcripture is here ftyled the higheft
' devotion of a *Bráhmen*.

167. Yes verily; that ftudent in theology per-
' forms the higheft act of devotion *with his whole*
' *body*, to the extremities of his nails, even though
' he *be fo far fenfual as to* wear a chaplet of fweet
' flowers, who to the utmoft of his ability daily
' reads the *Véda*.

168. ' A twice born man, who not having ftu-
' died the *Véda*, applies diligent attention to a dif-
' ferent *and worldly* ftudy, foon falls, even when
' living, to the condition of a *Súdra*; and his def-
' cendants after him.

169. ' The firft birth is from a natural mother;
' the fecond, from the ligation of the zone; the
                                                  ' third

' thitd from the due performance of the facrifice ;
' fuch are the births of him who is ufually called
' twice born, according to a text of the *Véda* :

170. ' Among them his divine birth is that,
' which is diftinguifhed by the ligat ion of the
' zone, *and facrificial eord*; and in that *birth* the
' *Gáyatrí* is his mother, and the *Achárya*, his father.

171. ' Sages call the *Achárya* father, from his
' giving inftruction in the *Véda* : nor can any holy
' rite be performed by a young man, before his
' inveftiture.

172. ' *Till he be invefted with the figns of his clafs,*
' he muft not pronounce any facred text, except
' what ought to be ufed in obfequies to an anceftor;
' fince he is on a level with a *Súdra* before his new
' birth from the revealed fcripture :

173. ' From him, who has been duly invefted,
' are required both the performance of devout acts
' and the ftudy of the *Véda* in order, preceded by
' ftated ceremónies.

174. ' Whatever fort of leathern mantle, facri-
' ficial thread, and zone, whatever ftaff, and what-
' ever under-apparel are ordained, *as before men-*
' *tioned*, for a youth of each clafs, the like muft
' alfo be ufed in his religious acts.

175. ' Thefe *following* rules muft a *Brahmachárí*
' or *ftudent in theology*, obferve, while he dwells
' with his preceptor; keeping all his members
' under control, for the fake of increafing his ha-
' bitual devotion.

176. ' Day by day, having bathed and being
' purified, let him offer frefh water to the Gods;
' the Sages, and the Manes; let him fhow refpect
' to the images of the deities, and bring wood for
' the oblation to fire.

177. ' Let

:177. ' Let him abstain from honey, from flesh
' meat, from perfumes, from chaplets of flowers,
' from sweet vegetable juices, from women, from
' all sweet substances turned acid, and from in-
' jury to animated beings;

178. ' From unguents for his limbs, and from
' black powder for his eyes, from wearing san-
' dals, and carrying an umbrella, from sensual
' desires, from wrath, from covetousness, from
' dancing, and from vocal and instrumental musick;

179 ' From gaming, from disputes, from de-
' traction, and from falsehood, from embracing
' or wantonly looking at women, and from dis-
' service to other men.

180. ' Let him constantly sleep alone: let him
' never waste his own manhood; for he, who vo-
' luntarily wastes his manhood, violates the rule of
' his order, *and becomes an* avacírní:

181. ' A twice born youth, who has involun-
' tarily wasted his manly strength during sleep,
' must repeat with reverence, having bathed and
' paid homage to the sun, this text of scripture:
" *Again let my strength return to me.*"

182. ' Let him carry water pots, flowers, cow-
' dung, fresh earth, and *cus'a*-grass, as much as
' may be useful to his preceptor; and let him per-
' form every day the duty of a religious mendicant.

183. ' Each day must a *Bráhmen* student receive
' his food by begging, with due care, from the
' houses of persons renowned for discharging their
' duties, and not deficient in performing the sacri-
' fices which the *Véda* ordains.

184. ' Let him not beg from the cousins of his
' preceptor; nor from his own cousins; nor from
' other kinsmen by the father's side, or by the
' mother's; but, if other houses be not accessible,
                                        ' let

' let him begin with the laſt of thoſe in order,
' avoiding the firſt ;

185. ' Or, if none of thoſe *houſes* juſt mentioned
' can be found, let him go begging through the
' whole diſtrict, round the village, keeping his
' organs in ſubjection, and remaining ſilent; but
' let him turn away from ſuch as have committed
' any deadly ſin.

186. ' Having brought logs of wood from a
' diſtance, let him place them in the open air ; and
' with them let him make an oblation to fire with-
' out remiſſneſs, both evening and morning.

187. ' He, who for ſeven ſucceſſive days omits
' the ceremony of begging food, and offers not wood
' to the ſacred fire, muſt perform the penance of
' an *avacírní*, unleſs he be afflicted with illneſs.

188. ' Let the ſtudent perſiſt conſtantly in ſuch
' begging, but let him not eat the food of one
' perſon only : the ſubſiſtence of a ſtudent by beg-
' ging is held equal to faſting *in religious merit*.

189. ' Yet, when he is aſked in a ſolemn act in
' honour of the Gods or the Manes, he may eat
' at his pleaſure the food of a ſingle perſon ; ob-
' ſerving, however, the laws of abſtinence and the
' auſterity of an anchoret : thus the rule of his
' order is kept inviolate.

190. ' This duty of a mendicant is ordained by
' the wiſe for a *Bráhmen* only ; but no ſuch act is
' appointed for a warriour, or for a merchant.

191. ' Let the ſcholar, when commanded by his
' preceptor, and even when he has received no
' command, always exert himſelf in reading,
' and in all acts uſeful to his teacher.

192. ' Keeping in due ſubjection his body, his
' ſpeech, his organs of ſenſe, and his heart, let him
                                                    ' ſtand

' ftand, with the palms of his hands joined, looking
' at the face of his preceptor.

193. ' Let him always keep his right arm un-
' covered, be always decently apparelled, and pro-
' perly compofed; and when his inftructor fays,
" be feated," let him fit oppofite to his venerable
' guide.

194. ' In the prefence of his preceptor let him
' always eat lefs, and wear a coarfer mantle with
' worfe appendages; let him rife before, and go
' to reft after his tutor.

195. ' Let him not anfwer his teacher's orders,
' or converfe with him, reclining on a bed; nor
' fitting, nor eating, nor ftanding, nor with an
' averted face:

196. ' But let him both *anfwer and converfe*, if
' his preceptor fit, ftanding up; if he ftand, ad-
' vancing toward him; if he advance, meeting
' him; if he run, haftening after him;

197. ' If his face be averted, going round to
' front him, *from left to right*; if he be at a little
' diftance, approaching him; if reclined, bending
' to him; and, if he ftand ever fo far off, running
' toward him.

198. ' When his teacher is nigh, let his couch
' or his bench be always placed low: when his
' preceptor's eye can obferve him, let him not fit
' carelefsly at eafe.

199. ' Let him never pronounce the mere name
' of his tutor, even in his abfence; nor ever mimick
' his gait, his fpeech, or his manner.

200. ' In whatever place, either true but cenfo-
' rious, or falfe and defamatory, difcourfe is held
' concerning his teacher, let him there cover his
' ears or remove to another place:

201. ' By cenfuring his preceptor, though juftly,
' he will be born an afs; by falfely defaming him,
a dog;

' a dog; by using his goods without leave, a small
' worm; by envying his merit, a larger insect
' or reptile.

202 ' He must not serve his tutor by the in-
' tervention of another, while himself stands aloof;
' nor must he attend him in a passion, nor when a
' woman is near; from a carriage or raised seat
' he must descend to salute his heavenly director.

203. ' Let him not sit with his preceptor to the
' leeward, or to the windward of him; nor let
' him say any thing which the venerable man can-
' not hear.

204. ' He may sit with his teacher in a carriage
' drawn by bulls, horses, or camels; on a terrace,
' on a pavement of stones, or on a mat of woven
' grass; on a rock, on a wooden bench, or in
' a boat.

205. ' When his tutor's tutor is near, let him
' demean himself as if his own were present; nor
' let him, unless ordered by his spiritual father,
' prostrate himself *in his presence* before his natural
' father, or paternal uncle.

206. ' This is likewise ordained as his constant
' behaviour toward his other instructors in science;
' toward his elder paternal kinsmen; toward all
' who may restrain him from sin, and all who
' give him salutary advice.

207. ' Toward men also, who are truly vir-
' tuous, let him always behave as toward his pre-
' ceptor; and, in like manner, toward the sons of
' his teacher, who are entitled to respect *as older*
' *men, and are not students*; and toward the paternal
' kinsmen of his venerable tutor.

208. ' The son of his preceptor, whether
' younger or of equal age, or a student, if he be
' capable of teaching the *Véda*, deserves the same
                                        honour

' honour with the preceptor himſelf, *when he is*
' *preſent* at any ſacrificial act :

' 209. ' But he muſt not perform for the ſon of
' his teacher, the duty of rubbing his limbs, or of
' bathing him, or of eating what he leaves, or of
' waſhing his feet.

  210. ' The wives of his preceptor, if they be
' of the ſame claſs, muſt receive equal honour
' with their venerable huſband ; but if they be of a
' different claſs, they muſt be honoured only by
' riſing and ſalutation.

  211. ' For no wife of his teacher muſt he per-
' form the offices of pouring ſcented oil on them,
' of attending them while they bathe, of rubbing
' their legs and arms, or of decking their hair ;

  212. Nor muſt a young wife of his preceptor
' be greeted even by the ceremony of touching her
' feet, if he have completed his twentieth year, or
' can diſtinguiſh virtue from vice.

  213. ' It is the nature of women in this world
' to cauſe the ſeduction of men ; for which reaſon
' the wiſe are never unguarded in the company of
' females :

  214. ' A female indeed, is able to draw from
' the right path in this life not a fool only, but
' even a ſage, and can lead him in ſubjection to
' deſire or to wrath.

  215. ' Let not a man, therefore, ſit in a ſequeſ-
' tered place with his neareſt female relations :
' the aſſemblage of corporeal organs is powerful
' enough to ſnatch wiſdom from the wiſe.

  216. ' A young ſtudent may, as the law directs,
' make proſtration at his pleaſure on the ground
' before a young wife of his tutor, ſaying, " I am
' ſuch an one ;"

                                217. ' And

217. ' And on his return from a journey, he
' muft once touch the feet of his preceptor's *aged*
' wife, and falute her each day by proftration,
' calling to mind the practice of virtuous men.

218. ' As he who digs deep with a fpade
' comes to a fpring of water, fo the ftudent, who
' humbly ferves his teacher, attains the knowledge
' which lies deep in his teacher's mind.

219. ' Whether his head be fhorn, or his hair
' long, or one lock be bound above in a knot, let
' not the fun ever fet or rife while he lies afleep
' in the village.

220. ' If the fun fhould rife or fet, while he
' fleeps through fenfual indulgence, and knows it
' not, he muft faft a whole day, repeating the
' *gáyatrí:*

221. ' He, who has been furprifed afleep by the
' fetting or by the rifing fun, and performs not
' that penance, incurs great guilt.

222. ' Let him adore God both at funrife
' and at funfet, as the law ordains, having made
' his ablution and keeping his organs controled;
' and, with fixed attention, let him repeat the
' text, which he ought to repeat, in a place free
' from impurity.

223. ' If a woman or a *Súdra* perform any act
' leading to the chief temporal good, let the ftu-
' dent be careful to emulate it; and he may do
' whatever gratifies his heart, unlefs it be for-
' bidden by law:

224. ' The chief temporal good is by fome
' declared to confift in virtue and wealth; by
' fome, in wealth and lawful pleafure; by fome,
' in virtue alone; by others, in wealth alone;
' but the chief good here below is an affemblage
' of all three: this is a fure decifion.

225. ' A

225. ' A TEACHER of the *Véda* is the image of
' GOD; a natural father, the image of BRAHMA';
' a mother, the image of the earth; an elder
' whole brother, the image of the foul:

226. ' Therefore a fpiritual and a natural fa-
' ther, a mother, and an elder brother, are not to
' be treated with difrefpect, efpecially by a *Bráh-
' men*, though the ftudent be grievoufly pro-
' voked.

227. ' That pain and care which a mother and
' father undergo in producing and rearing chil-
' dren, cannot be compenfated in an hundred
' years.

228. ' Let every man conftantly do what may
' pleafe his parents; and, on all occafions, what
' may pleafe his preceptor: when thofe three are
' fatisfied, his whole courfe of devotion is accom-
' plifhed.

229. ' Due reverence to thofe three is con-
' fidered as the higheft devotion; and without their
' approbation he muft perform no other duty.

230. ' Since they alone are held equal to' the
' three worlds; they alone, to the three principal
' orders; they alone, to the three *Védas*; they
' alone, to the three fires:

231. ' The natural father is confidered as the
' *gárbapatya*, or nuptial fire; the mother as the
' *dacfhina*, or ceremonial; the fpiritual guide, as
' the *áhavaniya* or facrificial: this triad of fires is
' moft venerable.

232. ' He, who neglects not thofe three, when
' he becomes a houfe-keeper, will ultimately ob-
' tain dom.nion over the three worlds; and his
' body being irradiated like a God, he will enjoy
' fupreme blifs in heaven.

233. ' By

233. ' By honouring his mother he gains this
' *terreſtrial* world ; by honouring his father, the
' intermediate, or *etherial* ; and, by aſſiduous at-
' tention to his preceptor, even the *celeſtial* world
' of BRAHMA':

234. ' All duties are completely performed by
' that man, by whom thoſe three are completely
' honoured ; but to him by whom they are diſ-
' honoured, all other acts of duty are fruitleſs.

235. ' As long as thoſe three live, ſo long he
' muſt perform no other duty *for his own ſake* ;
' but delighting in what may conciliate their af-
' fections and gratify their wiſhes, he muſt from
' day to day aſſiduouſly wait on them :

236. ' Whatever duty he may perform in
' thought, word, or deed, with a view to the
' next world, without derogation from his reſpect
' to them ; he muſt declare to them his entire
• performance of it.

237. ' By honouring thoſe three, without more,
' a man effectually does whatever ought to be
' done : this is the higheſt duty, appearing before
. ' us like DHERMA himſelf, and every other act is
' an *upadherma*, or ſubordinate duty.

238. ' A believer in ſcripture may receive pure
' knowledge even from a *Súdra* ; a leſſon of the
' higheſt virtue, even from a *Chandála* ; and a
' woman, bright as a gem, even from the baſeſt
' family :

239. ' Even from poiſon may nectar be taken ;
' even from a child, gentleneſs of ſpeech ; even
' from a foe, prudent conduct ; and even from
• an impure ſubſtance, gold.

240. ' From every quarter, therefore, muſt be
' ſelected women bright as gems, knowledge,
          ' virtue,

' virtue, purity, gentle fpeech, and various liberal
' arts.

241. ' In cafe of neceffity, a ftudent is required
' to learn the *Véda* from one who is not a *Bráh-*
' *men*, and, as long as that inftruction continues, to
' honour his inftructor with obfequious affiduity ;

2 2. ' But a pupil who feeks the incomparable
' path to heaven, fhou'd not live to the end of
' his days in the dwelling of a preceptor who is
' no *Bráhmen*, or who has not read all the *Védas*
' with their *Angas*.

243. ' If he anxioufly defire to pafs his whole
' life in the houfe of a facerdotal teacher, he muft
' ferve him with affiduous care, till he be releafed
' from his mortal frame :

244. ' That *Bráhmen*, who has dutifully at-
' tended his preceptor, till the diffolution of his
' body, paffes directly to the eternal manfion of
' GOD.

245. ' LET not a ftudent, who knows his duty,
' prefent any gift to his preceptor *before his return*
' *home* ; but when, by his tutor's permiffion, he
' is going to perform the ceremony on his return,
' let him give the venerable man fome valuable
' thing to the beft of his power ;

246 ' A field, or gold, a jewel, a cow, or an
' horfe, an umbrella, a pair of fandals, a ftool,
' corn, cloths, or even any very excellent vege-
' table : thus will he gain the affectionate re-
' membrance of his inftructor.

247. ' The ftudent for life muft, if his teacher
' die, attend on his virtuous fon, or his widow,
' or on one of his paternal kinfmen, with the fame
' refpect which he fhowed to the living :

248. ' Should none of thofe be alive, he muft
occupy

' occupy the station of his preceptor, the seat,
' and the place of religious exercises ; must con-
' tinually pay due attention to the fires, which he
' had confecrated ; and must prepare his own
' soul for heaven.

249. ' The twice born man, who shall thus
' without intermission have passed the time of his
' studentship, shall ascend, after death, to the most
' exalted of regions, and no more again spring to
' birth in this lower world.

CHAPTER THE THIRD.

On Marriage ; or on the Second Order.

1. ' The difcipline of a ftudent in the three
' *Védas* may be continued for thirty-fix years, in
' the houfe of his preceptor ; or for half that time,
' or for a quarter of it, or until he perfectly com-
' prehend them :

2. ' A ftudent, whofe rules have not been vio-
' lated, may affume the order of a married man,
' after he has read in fucceffion a *s'áé'há*, or branch
' from each of the three, or from two, or from
' any one of them.

3. ' Being juftly applauded for the ftrict per-
' formance of his duty, and having received from
' his *natural or fpiritual* father the facred gift of the
' *Véda*, let him fit on an elegant bed, decked with
' a garland of flowers, and let his father honour
' him before his nuptials, with a prefent of a cow.

4. ' Let the twice born man, having obtained
' the confent of his venerable guide, and having
' performed his ablution with ftated ceremonies,
' on his return home, as the law directs, efpoufe a
' wife of the fame clafs ·with himfelf and endued
' with the marks of excellence.

5. ' She, who is not defcended from his *pater-*
' *nal or maternal* anceftors, within the fixth degree,
' and who is not *known by her family name to be* of
' the fame primitive ftock with his father *or mother,*

' is

‘ is eligible by a twice born man for nuptials and
‘ holy union :

6. ‘ In connecting himself with a wife, let him
‘ studiously avoid the ten following families, be
‘ they ever so great, or ever so rich in kine, goats,
‘ sheep, gold and grain :

7. ‘ The family which has omitted pre-
‘ scribed acts of religion ; that, which has pro-
‘ duced no male children; that, in which the *Véda*
‘ has not been read ; that, which has thick hair
‘ on the body ; and those, which have been sub-
‘ ject to hemorrhoids, to phthisis, to dispepsia, to
‘ epilepsy, to leprosy, and to elephantiasis.

8. ‘ Let him not marry a girl with reddish hair,
‘ nor with any deformed limb ; nor one troubled
‘ with habitual sickness ; nor one either with no
‘ hair or with too much ; nor one immoderately
‘ talkative ; nor one with inflamed eyes ;

9. ‘ Nor one with the name of a constellation,
‘ of a tree or of a river, of a barbarous nation, or
‘ of a mountain, of a winged creature, a snake, or
‘ a slave ; nor with any name raising an image of
‘ terrour.

10. ‘ Let him chuse for his wife a girl, whose
‘ form has no defect ; who has an agreeable name ;
‘ who walks *gracefully* like a phenicopteros, or like
‘ a young elephant ; whose hair and teeth are
‘ moderate respectively in quantity and in size ;
‘ whose body has exquisite softness.

11. ‘ Her, who has no brother, or whose father
‘ is not well known, let no sensible man espouse,
‘ through fear left, *in the former case*, her father
‘ should take her first son as his own *to perform his*
‘ *obsequies* ; or, *in the second case*, left an illicit mar-
‘ riage should be contracted.

12. ‘ For

12. ' For the firſt marriage of the twice born
' claſſes, a woman of the ſame claſs is recom-
' mended ; but for ſuch as are impelled by in-
' clination to marry again, women in the direct
' order of the claſſes are to be preferred :

13. ' A Súdra woman only muſt be the wife of
' a Súdra ; ſhe and a Vaiſyà, of a Vaiſya ; they two
' and a Cſhatriyá, of a Cſhatriya ; thoſe two and a
' Bráhmanì of a Bráhmen.

14. ' A woman of the ſervile claſs is not menti-
' oned, even in the recital of any ancient ſtory, as
' the firſt wife of a Bráhmen or of a Cſhatriya, though
' in the greateſt difficulty to find a ſuitable match.

15. ' Men of the twice born claſſes, who through
' weakneſs of intellect, irregularly marry women
' of the loweſt claſs, very ſoon degrade their fa-
' milies and progeny to the ſtate of Súdras :

16. ' According to ATRI and to (GO'TAMA)
' the ſon of UTAT'HYA, he who thus marries a wo-
' man of the ſervile claſs, if he be a prieſt, is de-
' graded inſtantly ; according to SAUNACA, on
' the birth of a ſon, if he be a warriour ; and, if he
' be a merchant, on the bith of a ſon's ſon, accord-
' ing to (me) BHRĭGU.

17. ' A Bráhmen, if he take a Súdra to his bed,
' as his firſt wife, ſinks to the regions of torment ;
' if he beget a child by her, he loſes even his
' prieſtly rank :

18. ' His ſacrifices to the Gods, his oblations
' to the Manes, and his hoſpitable attentions to
' ſtrangers, muſt be ſupplied principally by her ;
' but the Gods and Manes will not eat ſuch offer-
' ings ; nor can heaven be attained by ſuch hoſ-
' pitality.

19. ' For the crime of him, who thus illegally
' drinks the moiſture of a Súdra's lips, who is

E 3   ' tainted

' tainted by her breath, and who even begets a
' child on her body, the law declares no ex-
' piation.

20. ' Now learn compendiously the eight forms
' of the nuptial ceremony, used by the four classes,
' some good and some bad in this world, and in
' the next :

21. ' The ceremony of BRAHMA', of the *Dévas*
' of the *Rĭ́shis*, of the *Prajápatis*, of the *Asuras*,
' of the *Gandharvas*, and of the *Racshasas* ; the
' eighth and basest is that of the *Pisáchas*.

22. ' Which of them is permitted by law to
' each class and what are the good and bad pro-
' perties of each ceremony, all this I will fully
' declare to you, together with the qualities, good
' and bad, of the offspring.

23. ' Let mankind know, that *the* six *first* in
' direct order are *by some held* valid in the case of
' a priest ; the four last, in that of a warriour ; and
' the same four, except the *Racshasa* marriage, in
' the cases of a merchant and a man of the servile
' class :

24. Some consider the four first only as ap-
' proved in the case of a priest ; one, that of *Racshasas*,
' as peculiar to a soldier ; and that of *Asuras*, to
' a mercantile and a servile man :

25. ' But in this code, three of *the* five *last* are
' held legal, and two illegal : the ceremonies of
' *Pisáchas* and *Asuras* must never be performed.

26. ' For a military man the before mentioned
' marriages of *Gandharvas* and *Racshasas*, whether
' separate or mixed, *as when a girl is made captive*
' *by her lover, after a victory over her kinsmen,* are
' permitted by law.

27. ' The gift of a daughter, clothed only with
' a single robe, to a man learned in the *Véda,*
' whom

' whom her father voluntarily invites, and re-
' spectfully receives, is the nuptial right called
' *Bráhma.*

28. ' The rite which sages call *Daiva*, is the
' gift of a daughter, whom her father has decked
' in gay attire, when the sacrifice is already begun,
' to the officiating priest, who performs that act
' of religion.

29. ' When the father gives his daughter away,
' after having received from the bridegroom one
' pair of kine, or two pairs, for uses prescribed
' by law, that marriage is termed *Arsha.*

30. The nuptial rite called *Prájápatya*, is when
' the father gives away his daughter with due ho-
' nour, saying distinctly, " May both of you
' perform together your civil and religious
' duties !"

31. ' When the bridegroom, having given as
' much wealth as he can afford to the father and
' paternal kinsmen, and to the damsel herself,
' takes her voluntarily as his bride, that marriage
' is named *Asura.*

32. ' The reciprocal connection of a youth and
' a damsel, with mutual desire, is the marriage
' denominated *Gandharva*, contracted for the
' purpose of amorous embraces, and proceeding
' from sensual inclination.

33. ' The seizure of a maiden by force from
' her house, while she weeps and calls for assist-
' ance, after her kinsmen and friends have been
' slain in battle, or wounded, and their houses
' broken open, is the marriage styled *Racshasa.*

34. ' When the lover secretly embraces the
' damsel, either sleeping or flushed with strong
' liquor, or disordered in her intellect, that sinful

E 4 ' marriage,

' marriage, called *Piſácha*, is the eighth and the
' baſeſt.

35. ' The gift of daughters in marriage by the
' ſacerdotal claſs, is moſt approved, when they
' previouſly have poured water into the hands of
' the bridegroom; but the ceremonies of the other
' claſſes may be performed according to their ſe-
' veral fancies.

36. ' Among theſe nuptial rites, what quality is
' aſcribed by MENU to each, hear now ye
' *Bráhmens*, hear it all from me, who fully de-
' clare it!

37. ' The ſon of a *Bráhmì*, or wife by the firſt
' ceremony, redeems from ſin, if he perform vir-
' tuous acts, ten anceſtors, ten deſcendants, and
' himſelf the twenty-firſt perſon.

38. ' A ſon, born of a wife by the *Daiva* nuptials,
' redeems ſeven and ſeven in higher and lower de-
' grees; of a wife by the *A'rſha* three and three;
' of a wife by the *Prájápatya* ſix and ſix.

39. ' By four marriages, the *Bráhma* and ſo
' forth, in direct order, are born ſons illumi-
' ned by the *Véda*, learned men, beloved by the
' learned,

40. ' Adorned with beauty, and with the qua-
' lity of goodneſs, wealthy, famed, amply gra-
' tified with lawful enjoyments, performing all
' duties, and living an hundred years:

41. ' But in the other *four* baſe marriages, which
' remain, are produced ſons acting cruelly, ſpeak-
' ing falſely, abhorring the *Véda*, and the duties
' preſcribed in it.

42. ' From the blameleſs nuptial rites of men
' ſprings a blameleſs progeny; from the reprehen-
' ſible, a reprehenſible offspring: let mankind,
'   ' therefore,

' therefore, ftudioufly avoid the culpable forms
' of marriage.

43. ' The ceremony of joining hands is ap-
' pointed for thofe, who marry women of their
' own clafs ; but, with women of a different clafs,
' the following nuptial ceremonies are to be ob-
' ferved :

44. ' By a *Cfhatriyà* on her. marriage with a
' *Bráhmen,* an arrow muft be held in her hand ;
' by a *Vaifyà* woman, with a bridegroom *of the*
' *facerdotal or military clafs,* a whip ; *and by a Súdrà*
' bride, *marrying a prieft, a foldier, or a merchant,*
' muft be held the fkirt of a mantle.

45. ' LET the hufband approach his wife in
' due feafon, *that is, at the time fit for pregnancy ;*
' let him be conftantly fatisfied with her alone ;
' but, except on the forbidden days of the moon;
' he may approach her, being affectionately dif-
' pofed, *even out of due feafon,* with a defire of con-
' jugal intercourfe.

46. ' Sixteen days and nights in each month,
' with four diftinct days neglected by the vir-
' tuous, are called the natural feafon of women : '

47. ' Of thofe fixteen, the four firft, the ele-
' venth, and the thirteenth, are reprehended; the
' ten remaining nights are approved.

48. ' Some fay, that on the even nights are
' conceived fons ; on the odd nights daughters ;
' therefore let the man, who wifhes for a fon,
' approach his wife in due feafon on the even
' nights;

49. ' But a boy is in truth produced by the
' greater quantity of the male ftrength ; and a
' girl by a greater quantity of the female ; by
' equality, an hermaphrodite, or a boy and a girl;
' by

' by weaknefs or deficiency, is occafioned a
' failure of conception.

50. ' He, who avoids conjugal embraces on
' the fix reprehended nights and on eight others,
' is equal in chaftity to a *Brahmachári*, in which-
' ever of the *two next* orders he may live.

51. ' LET no father, who knows the law, re-
' ceive a gratuity, however fmall, for giving his
' daughter in marriage; fince the man, who,
' through avarice, takes a gratuity *for that purpofe*,
' is a feller of his offspring.

52. ' Whatever male relations, through delu-
' fion of mind, take poffeffion of a woman's
' property, be it only her carriages or her clothes,
' fuch offenders will fink to a region of torment.

53. ' Some fay that the bull and cow *given* in
' the nuptial ceremony of the *Rìſhis*, are a bribe
' to the father; but this is untrue : a bribe *in-*
' *deed*, whether large or fmall, is an actual fale of
' *the daughter.*

54. ' When money or goods are given to
' damfels, whofe kinfmen receive them not for
' their own ufe, it is no fale : it is merely a token
' of courtefy and affection to the brides.

55. ' Married women muft be honoured and
' adorned by their fathers and brethren, by their
' hufbands, and by the brethren of their hufbands,
' if they feek abundant profperity :

56. ' Where females are honoured, there the
' deities are pleafed ; but where they are difho-
' noured, there all religious acts become fruitlefs.

57. ' Where female relations are made mifera-
' ble, the family of him who makes them fo,
' very foon wholly perifhes ; but, where they are
' not unhappy, the family always increafes.

58. ' On

58. ' On whatever houses the women of a
' family, not being duly honoured, pronounce an
' imprecation, those houses, with all that belong
' to them, utterly perish, as if destroyed by a
' sacrifice for the death of an enemy.

59. ' Let those women, therefore, be con-
' tinually supplied with ornaments, apparel and
' food, at festivals and at jubilees, by men de-
' sirous of wealth.

60. ' In whatever family the husband is con-
' tented with his wife, and the wife with her
' husband, in that house will fortune be assuredly
' permanent.

61. ' Certainly, if the wife be not elegantly
' attired, she will not exhilirate her husband; and
' if her lord want hilarity, offspring will not be
' produced.

62. ' A wife being gaily adorned, her whole
' house is embellished; but, if she be destitute of
' ornament, all will be deprived of decoration.

63. ' By culpable marriages, by omission of
' prescribed ceremonies, by neglect of reading the
' *Véda*, and by irreverence toward a *Bráhmen*,
' great families are sunk to a low state.

64. ' So they are by practising manual arts, by
_' *lending at interest and other* pecuniary transactions,
' by begetting children on *Súdrás* only, by traffick
' in kine, horses, and carriages, by agriculture
' and by attendance on a king.

65. ' By sacrificing for such as have no right
' to sacrifice, and by denying a future compensa-
' tion for good works, great families, being de-
' prived of sacred knowledge, are quickly de-
' stroyed;

66. ' But families, enriched by a knowledge of
' the

' the *Véda*, though poffeffing little temporal
' wealth, are numbered among the great, and ac-
' quire exalted fame.

67. ' Let the houfe-keeper perform domeftic
' religious rites, with the nuptial fire, according
' to law, and the ceremonies of the five great
' facraments, and the feveral acts which muft day
' by day be performed.

68 ' A houfe-keeper has five places of flaughter,
' *or where fmall living creatures may be flain*; his
' kitchen hearth, his grindftone, his broom, his
' peftle and mortar, his water pot; by ufing
' which, he becomes in bondage to fin:

69. ' For the fake of expiating *offences committed*
' *ignorantly* in thofe places *mentioned* in order, the
' five great facraments were appointed by eminent
' fages to be performed each day by fuch as keep
' houfe.

70. ' Teaching and ftudying the fcripture is
' the facrament of the *Véda*; offering cakes and
' water, the facrament of the Manes; an oblation
' to fire, the facrament of the Deities; giving
' rice or other food to living creatures, the facra-
' ment of fpirits; receiving guefts with honour,
' the facrament of men;

71. ' Whoever omits not thofe five great ce-
' remonies, if he have ability *to perform them*, is
' untainted by the fins of the *five* flaughtering
' places, even though he conftantly refide at
' home;

72. ' But whoever cherifhes not five orders of
' beings, *namely*, the deities; thofe, who demand
' hofpitality; thofe, whom he ought by law to
' maintain; his departed forefathers; and him-
' felf; that man lives not even though he
' breathe.

73. ' Some

73. ' Some call the five facraments *abuta* and
' *huta, prahuta, bráhmya-huta* and *práfita* :

74. ' *Abuta*, or unoffered, is divine ftudy ; *huta,*
' or offered, is the oblation to fire ; *prahuta*, or
' well offered, is the food given to fpirits ; *bráh-*
' *mya-huta*, is refpect fhewn to twice born guefts ;
' and *práfita*, or well eaten, is the offering of rice
' or water to the manes of anceftors.

75. ' Let every man in this fecond order em-
' ploy himfelf daily in reading the fcripture, and
' in performing the facrament of the Gods ; for,
' being employed in the facrament of deities, he
' fupports this whole animal and vegetable world ;

76. ' Since his oblation of clarified butter, duly
' caft into the flame, afcends in fmoke to the fun ;
' from the fun it falls in rain ; from rain comes
' vegetable food ; and from fuch food animals
' derive their fubfiftence.

77. ' As all creatures fubfift by receiving fup-
' port from air, thus all orders of men exift by
' receiving fupport from houfe-keepers ;

78. ' And fince men of the three other orders
' are each day nourifhed by them with divine
' learning and with food, a houfe-keeper is for
' this reafon of the moft eminent order :

79. ' That order, therefore, muft be conftantly
' fuftained with great care by the man who feeks
' unperifhable blifs in heaven, and in this world
' pleafurable fenfations ; an order which cannot
' be fuftained by men with uncontroled organs.

80. ' The divine fages, the manes, the gods,
' the fpirits, and guefts, pray for benefits to
' mafters of families ; let thefe honours, there-
' fore, be done to them by the houfe-keeper who
' knows his duty :

81. ' Let

81. ' Let him honour the Sages by studying
' the *Véda* : the Gods, by oblations to fire or-
' dained by law ; the Manes, by pious obsequies ;
' men by supplying them with food ; and spirits,
' by gifts to all animated creatures.

82. ' Each day let him perform a *sráddha*
' with boiled rice and the like, or with water, or
' with milk, roots, and fruit ; for thus he obtains
' favour from departed progenitors.

83. ' He may entertain one *Bráhmen* in that sa-
' crement among the five, which is performed for
' the *Pitr̃s* ; but, at the oblation to all the Gods,
' let him not invite even a single priest.

84. ' In his domestic fire for dressing the food
' of all the Gods, after the prescribed ceremony,
' let a *Bráhmen* make an oblation each day to these
' *following* divinities ;

85. ' First to AGNI, god of fire, and to the
' Lunar God, severally ; then, to both of them
' at once ; next to the assembled gods ; and after-
' wards, to DHANWANTARI, god of medicine ;

86. ' To CUHU', goddess of the day, when the
' new moon is discernible ; to ANUMATI, goddess
' of the day, after the opposition ; to PRAJA'PATI,
' or the Lord of Creatures ; to DYA'VA' and PRIT-
' HIVI', goddesses of sky and earth ; and lastly,
' to the fire of the good sacrifice.

87. ' Having thus, with fixed attention, offered
' clarified butter in all quarters, proceeding *from*
' *the east* in a southern direction to INDRA, YAMA,
' VARUNA, and the god SOMA, let him offer his
' gift to animated creatures :

88: ' *Saying*, " I salute the *Maruts*," or *Winds*,
' let him throw dressed rice near the door ; *saying*,
" I salute the water gods," in water ; and on his
' pestle

' peftle and mortar, *faying*, " I falute the gods of
' large trees."

89. ' Let him do the like *in the north eaft, or*
' near his pillow, to SRI', the goddefs of abun-
' dance; *in the fouth weft, or* at the foot of his bed,
' to the propitious goddefs BHADRACA'LI'; in
' the centre of his manfion, to BRAHMA' and his
' houfehold God;

90. ' To all the Gods affembled, let him throw
' up his oblation in the open air; by day, to the
' fpirits who walk in light; and by night, to thofe
' who walk in darknefs :

91. In the building on his houfe top, *or behind*
' *his back*, let him caft his oblation for the welfare
' of all creatures; and what remains let him give
' to the *Pitris* with his face toward the fouth :

92. ' The fhare of dogs, of outcafts, of dog-
' feeders, of finful men, punifhed with elephan-
' tiafis or confumption, of crows, and of reptiles,
' let him drop on the ground by little and little.

93. ' A *Bráhmen*, who thus each day fhall ho-
' nour all beings, will go to the higheft region in
' a ftraight path, in an irradiated form.

94. ' When he has performed his duty of mak-
' ing oblations, let him caufe his gueft to take
' food before himfelf; and let him give a portion
' of rice, as the law ordains, to the mendicant
' who ftudies the *Véda :*

' 95. ' Whatever fruit fhall be obtained by that
' ftudent, as the reward of his virtue, when he fhall
' have given a cow to his preceptor, according to
' law, the like reward to virtue fhall be obtained
' by the twice born houfe-keeper, when he has
' given a mouthful of rice to the religious men-
' dicant.

96. ' To

I

96. ' To a *Bráhmen* who knows the true prin-
' ciple of the *Véda*, let him present a portion of
' rice, or a pot of water, garnished with fruit and
' flowers, due ceremonies having preceded :

97. ' Shares of oblations to the Gods, or to the
' Manes, utterly perish, when presented, through
' delusion of mind, by men regardless of duty, to
' such ignorant *Bráhmens* as are mere ashes ;

98. ' But an offering in the fire of a sacerdotal
' mouth, which richly blazes with true know-
' ledge and piety, will release the giver from dis-
' tress, and even from deadly sin.

99. ' To the guest who comes of his own
' accord, let him offer a seat and water, with such
' food as he is able to prepare, after the due rites
' of courtesy.

100. ' A *Bráhmen* coming as a guest, and not
' received with just honour, takes to himself all the
' reward of the house-keeper's former virtue,
' even though he had been so temperate as to live
' on the gleanings of harvests, and so pious as to
' make oblations in five distinct fires.

101. ' Grass and earth to sit on, water to wash
' the feet, and, fourthly affectionate speech are at
' no time deficient in the mansions of the good,
' *although they may be indigent.*

102. ' A *Bráhmen*, staying but one night as a
' guest, is called an *atit'hi* ; since continuing so
' short a time, he is not even a sojourner for a
' whole *tit'hi*, or *day of the moon.*

103. ' The house-keeper must not consider as
' an *atit'hi* a mere visitor of the same town, or a
' *Bráhmen*, who attends him on business, even
' though he come to the house where his wife
' dwells, and where his fires are kindled.

104. ' Should

104. ' Should any houſe-keepers be ſo ſenſeleſs,
' as to ſeek, on pretence of being gueſts, the food
' of others, they would fall after death, by reaſon
' of that baſeneſs, to the condition of cattle be-
' longing to the giver of ſuch food.

105. ' No gueſt muſt be diſmiſſed in the even-
' ing by a houſe-keeper ; he is ſent by the retir-
' ing ſun ; and, whether he come in fit ſeaſon or
' unſeaſonably, he muſt not ſojourn in the houſe
' without entertainment.

106. ' Let not himſelf eat any delicate food,
' without aſking his gueſt to partake of it : the
' ſatisfaction of a gueſt will aſſuredly bring the
' houſe-keeper wealth, reputation, long life, and a
' place in heaven.

107. ' To the higheſt gueſts in the beſt form,
' to the loweſt in the worſt, to the equal, equally,
' let him offer ſeats, reſting places, couches; giv-
' ing them proportionable attendance, when they
' depart ; and honour as long as they ſtay.

108. ' Should another gueſt arrive, when the
' oblation to all the Gods is concluded, for him
' alſo let the houſe-keeper prepare food, accord-
' ing to his ability ; but let him not repeat his
' offerings to animated beings.

109. ' Let no *Bráhmen* gueſt proclaim his fa-
' mily and anceſtry for the ſake of an entertain-
' ment ; ſince he, who thus proclaims them, is
' called by the wiſe a *vántáſi*, or foul-feeding
' demon.

110. ' A military man is not denominated a
' gueſt in the houſe of a *Bráhmen*; nor a man of
' the commercial or ſervile claſs ; nor his fa-
' miliar friend ; nor his paternal kinſman ; nor
' his preceptor :

F   111. ' But

111. ' But if a warriour come to his houfe in
' the form of a gueft, let food be prepared for
' him, according to his defire, after the before-
' mentioned *Bráhmens* have eaten.

112. ' Even to a merchant or a labourer, ap-
' proaching his houfe in the manner of guefts,
' let him give food, fhowing marks of benevo-
' lence at the fame time with his domefticks :

113. ' To others, as familiar friends, and' the
' reft before-named, who come with affection
' to his place of abode, let him ferve a repaft at
' the fame time with his wife *and himfelf*, having
' amply provided it according to his beft means.

114. ' To a bride, and to a damfel, to the fick,
' and to pregnant women, let him give food, even
' before his guefts, without hefitation.

115. ' The idiot, who firft eats his own mefs,
' without having prefented food to the perfons
' juft enumerated, knows not, while he crams, that
' he will himfelf be food after death for bandogs
' and vultures.

116. ' After the repaft of the *Bráhmen* gueft,
' of his kinfmen, and his domefticks, the married
' couple may eat what remains untouched.

117. ' The houfe-keeper, having honoured
' fpirits, holy fages, men, progenitors, and houfe-
' hold gods, may feed on what remains after thofe
' oblations.

118. ' He, who eats what has been dreffed for
' himfelf only, eats nothing but fin : a repaft on
' what remains after the facrament is called the
' banquet of the good.

119. ' After a year from the reception of a
' vifitor, let the houfe-keeper again honour a
' king, a facrificer, a ftudent returned from his
preceptor,

' preceptor, a fon-in-law, a father-in-law, and
' a maternal uncle, with a *madhuperca*, or prefent
' of honey, curds, and fruit.

120. ' A king or a *Bráhmen* arriving at the
' celebration of the facrament, are to be honoured
' with a *madhuperca*; but not, if the facrament
' be over: this is a fettled rule.

121. ' In the evening let the wife make an
' offering of the dreffed food, but without pro-
' nouncing any text of the *Véda*: one oblation to
' the affembled gods, thence named *Vaifwadéva*,
' is ordained both for evening and morning.

122. ' FROM month to month, on the dark day
' of the moon, let a twice born man, having
' finifhed the daily facrament of the *Pitris*, and
' his fire being ftill blazing, perform the folemn
' *fráddha*, called *pindánwáhárya*:

123. ' Sages have diftinguifhed the monthly
' *fráddha* by the title of *anwáhárya*, or *after eaten*,
' that is, eaten after the *pinda* or ball of rice; and
' it muft be performed with extreme care, and
' with flefh meat in the beft condition.

124. ' What *Bráhmens* muft be entertained at
' that ceremony, and who muft be accepted, how
' many are to be fed, and with what forts of food,
' on all thofe articles, without omiffion, I will fully
' difcourfe.

125. ' At the *fráddha* of the gods he may en-
' tertain two *Bráhmens*; at that of his father,
' paternal grandfather, and paternal great-grand-
' father, three; or one only at that of the gods,
' and one at that for his three paternal ancestors:
' though he abound in wealth, let him not be fo-
' licitous to entertain a large company.

126. ' A large company deftroys thefe five ad-
' vantages; reverence to priefts, propriety of time

and

' and place, purity, and the acquifition of virtuous
' Bráhmens : let him not therefore, endeavour to
' feed a fuperfluous number.

127. ' This act of due honour to departed fouls,
' on the dark day of the moon, is famed by the
' appellation of *pitrya*, or anceftral : the legal ce-
' remony, in honour of departed fpirits, rewards
' with continual fruit, a man engaged in fuch ob-
' fequies.

128. ' Oblations to the gods and to anceftors
' fhould be given to a moft reverend Bráhmen,
' perfectly converfant with the *Véda* ; fince what is
' given to him produces the greateft reward.

129. ' By entertaining one learned man at the
' oblation to the gods and at that to anceftors, he
' gains more exalted fruit than by feeding a mul-
' titude, who know not the holy texts.

130. ' Let him inquire into the anceftry, even
' in a remote degree, of a Bráhmen, who has ad-
' vanced to the end of the *Véda :* fuch a man, if
' fprung from good men, is a fit partaker of ob-
' lations to gods and to anceftors ; fuch a man
' may juftly be called an *atit'hi*, or gueft. '

131. ' Surely, though a million of men, un-
' learned in holy texts, were to receive food, yet
' a fingle man, learned in fcripture, and fully fa-
' tisfied with his entertainment, would be of more
' value than all of them together.

132. ' Food, confecrated to the gods and the
' manes, muft be prefented to a theologian of
' eminent learning ; for certainly, when hands
' are fmeared with blood, they cannot be cleaned
' with blood only, *nor can fin be removed by the*
' *company of finners.*

133. ' As many mouthfuls as an unlearned man
                                          fhall

' shall swallow at an oblation to the gods and to
' anceftors, so many red hot iron balls muft the
' giver of the *sráddha* swallow in the next world.

134. ' Some *Bráhmens* are intent on scriptural
' knowledge; others, on auftere devotion; some
' are intent both on religious aufterity and on the
' ftudy of the *Véda*; others on the performance
' of sacred rites:

135. ' Oblations to the manes of anceftors
' ought to be placed with care before such as are
' intent on sacred learning: but offerings to the
' gods may be presented, with due ceremonies, to
' *Bráhmens* of all the four descriptions.

136. ' There may be a *Bráhmen*, whose father
' had not ftudied the scripture, though the son
' has advanced to the end of the *Véda*; or there
' may be one, whose son has not read the *Véda*,
' though the father had travelled to the end of it:

137. ' Of those two let mankind confider him
' as the superiour, whose father had ftudied the
' scripture, yet for the sake of performing rites
' with holy texts, the other is worthy of honour.

138. ' Let no man, at the prescribed obsequies,
' give food to an intimate friend; since advantage
' to a friend muft be procured by gifts of different
' property: to that *Bráhmen* let the performer of
' a *sráddha* give food, whom he confiders neither
' as a friend nor as a foe.

139. ' For him, whose obsequies and offerings
' of clarified butter are provided chiefly through
' friendship, no fruit is reserved in the next life,
' on account either of his obsequies or of his
' offerings.

140. ' The man, who, through delufion of in-
' tellect, forms temporal connexions by obsequies,

' is

' is excluded from heavenly manfions, as a giver
' of the *fráddha* for the fake of friendfhip, and the
' meaneft of twice born men :

141. ' Such a convivial prefent, by men of the
' three higheft claffes, is called the gift of *Pisáchas*,
' and remains fixed here below, like a blind cow
' in one ftall.

142. ' As a hufbandman, having fown feed in
' a barren foil, reaps no grain, thus a performer
' of holy rites, having given clarified butter to
' an unlearned *Bráhmen*, attains no reward in
' heaven ;

143. ' But a prefent made, as the law ordains,
' to a learned theologian, renders both the giver
' and the receiver partakers of good fruits in this
' world and in the next.

144. ' If no learned *Bráhmen* be at hand, he
' may at his pleafure invite a friend to the *fráddha*,
' but not a foe, be he ever fo learned ; fince the
' oblation, being eaten by a foe, lofes all fruit in
' the life to come.

145. ' With great care let him give food at
' the *fráddha* to a prieft, who has gone through
' the fcripture, but has chiefly ftudied the *Rĭgvéda*;
' to one, who has read all the branches, but prin-
' cipally thofe of the *Yajufh*; or to one who has
' finifhed the whole, with particular attention to
' the *Sáman :*

146. ' Of that man whofe oblation has been
' eaten, after due honours, by any one of thofe
' three *Bráhmens*, the anceftors are conftantly
' fatisfied as high as the feventh perfon, *or to the*
' *fixth degree.*

147. ' This is the chief rule in offering the
' *fráddha* to the gods and to anceftors; but the fol-
                                        ' lowing

' lowing may be confidered as a fubfidiary rule,
' *where no fuch learned priefts can be found*, and is
' ever obferved by good men :

148. ' Let him entertain his maternal grand-
' father, his maternal uncle, the fon of his fifter,
' the father of his wife, his fpiritual guide, the
' fon of his daughter, or her hufband, his mater-
' nal coufin, his officiating prieft, or the performer
' of his facrifice.

149. ' For an oblation to the gods, let not the
' man, who knows what is law, fcrupuloufly in-
' quire into the parentage of a *Bráhmen*; but for
' a prepared oblation to anceftors let him examine
' it with ftrict care.

150. ' Thofe *Bráhmens*, who have committed
' any inferiour theft or any of the higher crimes,
' who are deprived of virility, or who profefs a
' difbelief in a future ftate, MENU has pronounced
' unworthy of honour at a *fráddha* to the gods or
' to anceftors.

151. ' To a ftudent in theology, who has not
' read the *Véda*, to a man *punifhed for paft crimes*
' *by being* born without a prepuce, to a gamefter,
' and to fuch' as perform many facrifices for other
' men, let him never give food at the facred
' obfequies.

152. ' Phyficians, image worfhippers for gain,
' fellers of meat, and fuch as live by low traffick,
' muft be fhunned in oblations both to the deities
' and to progenitors.

153. ' A public fervant of the whole town, or
' of the prince, a man with whitlows on his nails,
' or with black yellow teeth, an oppofer of his
' preceptor, a deferter of the facred fire, and an
' ufurer,

154. ' A

154. ' A phthifical man, a feeder of cattle, one
' omitting the five great facraments, a contemner
' of *Bráhmens*, a younger brother married before
' the elder, an elder brother not married before
' the younger, an a man who fubfifts by the
' wealth of many relations,

155. ' A dancer, one who has violated the
' rule of chaftity in the firft or fourth order, the
' hufband of a *Súdra*, the fon of a twice married
' woman, a man who has loft one eye, and a huf-
' band in whofe houfe an adulterer dwells,

156. ' One who teaches the *Véda* for wages, and
' one who gives wages to fuch a teacher, the
' pupil of a *Súdra*, and the *Súdra* preceptor, a rude
' fpeaker, and the fon of an adulterefs, born either
' before or after the death of the hufband,

157. ' A forfaker, without juft caufe, of his
' mother, father or preceptor, and a man who
' forms a connexion, either by fcriptural or
' connubial affinity, with great finners, ·

158. ' A houfe-burner, a giver of poifon, an
' eater of food offered by the fon of an adulterefs,
' a feller of the moon plant, *a fpecies of mountain*
' *rue*, a navigator of the ocean, a poetical enco-
' miaft, an oilman, and a fuborner of perjury,

159. ' A wrangler with his father, an employer
' of gamefters for his own benefit, a drinker of
' intoxicating fpirits, a man punifhed for fin with
' elephantiafis, one of evil repute, a cheat, and a
' feller of liquids,

160. ' A maker of bows and arrows, the huf-
' band of a younger fifter married before the elder
' *of the whole blood*, an injurer of his friend, the
' keeper of a gaming-houfe, and a father inftructed
' in the *Véda* by his own fon,

5   161. ' An

161. ' An epileptick perſon, one who has the
' eryſipelas or the leproſy, a common informer,
' a lunatick, a blind man, and a deſpiſer of ſcrip-
' ture, muſt all be ſhunned.   ,

162. ' A tamer of elephants, bulls, horſes, or
' camels, a man who ſubſiſts by aſtrology, a
' keeper of birds, and one who teaches the uſe
' of arms,

163. ' He, who diverts watercourſes, and he,
' who is gratified by obſtructing them, he, who
' builds houſes for gain, a meſſenger, and a plan-
' ter of trees for pay,

164. ' A breeder of ſporting dogs, a falconer,
' a ſeducer of damſels, a man delighting in miſ-
' chief, a Bráhmen living as a Súdra, a ſacrificer
' to the inferiour gods only,

165. ' He, who obſerves not approved cuſtoms,
' and he, who regards not preſcribed duties, a con-
' ſtant importunate aſker of favours, he, who ſup-
' ports himſelf by tillage, a clubfooted man, and
' one deſpiſed by the virtuous,

166. ' A ſhepherd, a keeper of buffalos, the
' huſband of a twice married woman, and the re-
' mover of dead bodies for pay, are to be avoided
' with great care.

167. ' Thoſe loweſt of Bráhmens, whoſe man-
' ners are contemptible, who are not admiſſible
' into company at a repaſt, an exalted and learned
' prieſt muſt avoid at both ſráddhas.

168. ' A Bráhmen unlearned in holy writ, is
' extinguiſhed in an inſtant like a fire of dry graſs:
' to him the oblation muſt not be given ; for the
' clarified butter muſt not be poured on aſhes.

169. ' What retribution is prepared in the next
' life for the giver of food to men inadmiſſible into
company,

' company, at the *fráddha* to the gods and to an-
' ceftors, 1 will now declare without omiffion.

170. ' On that food, which has been given to
' *Brahmens* who have violated the rules of their
' order, to the younger brother married before the
' elder, and to the reft who are not admiffible
' into company, the *Racfhafes* eagerly feaft.

171. ' He, who makes a marriage contract
' with the connubial fire, while his elder brother
' cot inues unmarried, is called a *perivéttri* ; and
' the elder brother a *perivitti* :

172. ' The *perivéttri*, the *perivitti*, the dam-
' fel thus wedded, the giver of her in wedlock,
' and, fifthly, the performer of the nuptial facri-
' fice, all fink to a region of torment.

173. ' He, who lafcivioufly dallies with the
' widow of his deceafed brother, though fhe be le-
' gally married to him, is denominated the huf-
' band of a *didhifhú*.

174. ' Two fons, named a *cunda* and a *gólaca*,
' are born in adultery ; the *cunda*, while the hufband
' is alive, and the *gólaca*, when the hufband is dead :

175. ' Thofe animals begotten by adulterers,
' deftroy, both in this world and in the next, the
' food prefented to them by fuch as make obla-
' tions to the gods or to the manes.

176. ' The foolifh giver of a *fráddha* lofes, in
' a future life, the fruit of as many admiffible
' guefts, as a *thief or the like* perfon, inadmiffible
' into company, might be able to fee.

177. ' A blind man placed where one with eyes
' might have feen, deftroys the reward of ninety ;
' he, who has loft one eye, of fixty ; a leper, of
' an hundred ; one punifhed with elephantiafis, of
' a thoufand.

178. ' Of

178. ' Of the gift at a *sráddha*, to as many
' *Bráhmens*, as a sacrificer for a *Súdra* might be
' able to touch on the body, the fruit is lost to the
' giver, *if he invite such a wretch* ;

179. ' And if a *Bráhmen* who knows the *Véda*,
' receive through covetousness a present from such
' a sacrificer, he speedily sinks to perdition, like a
' figure of unburnt clay in water.

180. ' Food given to a seller of the moon plant,
' becomes ordure in another world ; to a physician
' purulent blood ; *and the giver will be a reptile*
' *bred in them* : if offered to an image worshipper,
' it is thrown away ; if to an usurer, infamous.

181. ' That which is given to a trader, endures
' neither in this life nor in the next, and that be-
' stowed on a *Bráhmen*, who has married a widow,
' resembles clarified butter poured on ashes as an
' oblation to fire.

182. ' That food, which is given to other base
' and inadmissible men, before mentioned, the
' wise have pronounced to be no more than
' animal oil, blood, flesh, skin, and bones.

183. ' Now learn comprehensively, by what
' *Bráhmens* a company may be purified, when it has
' been defiled by inadmissable persons ; *Bráhmens*,
' the chief of their class, the purifiers of every as-
' sembly.

184. ' Those priests must be considered as the
' purifiers of a company who are most learned in
' all the *Védas* and all their *Angas*, together with
' their descendants who have read the whole
' scripture ;

185. ' A priest learned in a principal part of
' the *Yajurvéda* ; one who keeps the five fires
' constantly burning ; one skilled in a principal
' part of the *Rigvéda* ; one who explains the six
' *Védángas* ;

' *Védángas* ; the fon of a *Bráhmì*, or woman mar-
' ried by the *Bráhma* ceremony ; and one who
' chants the principal *Sáman* ;

186. ' One who propounds the fenfe of the
' *Védas*, which he learnt from his preceptor, a ftu-
' dent who has given a thoufand *cows for pious*
' *ufes*, and a *Bráhmen* a hundred years old, muft
' all be confidered as the purifiers of a party at a
' *fráddha.*

187. ' On the day before the facred obfequies,
' or on the very day when they are prepared, let
' the performer of them invite, with due honour,
' fuch *Bráhmens* as have been mentioned ; *ufually*
' one fuperiour, who has three inferiour to him.

188. ' The *Bráhmen*, who has been invited to a
' *fráddha* for departed anceftors, muft be continu-
' ally abftemious ; he muft not even read the
' *Védas* ; and he who performs the ceremony,
' muft act in the fame manner.

189. ' Departed anceftors, no doubt, are at-
' tendant on fuch invited *Bráhmens* ; hovering
' around them like pure fpirits, and fitting by them,
' when they are feated.

190. ' The prieft who having been duly invited
' to a *fráddha*, breaks the appointment, commits
' a grievous offence, and in his next birth becomes
' a hog.

191. ' He, who careffes a *Súdra* woman, after
' he has been invited to facred obfequies, takes on
' himfelf all the fin that has been committed by
' the giver of the repaft.

192. ' The *Pitrïs* or *great progenitors*, are free
' from wrath, intent on purity, ever exempt from
' fenfual paffions, endued with exalted qualities :
' they are primeval divinities, who have laid
' arms afide.

193. ' HEAR

193. ' Hear now completely, from whom they
' fprang; who they are; by whom and by what
' ceremonies they are to be honoured.

194. ' The fons of Mari'chi and of all the other
' Rifhis, who were the offspring of Menu, fon of
' Brahma', are called the companies of Pitrĭs,
' or forefathers.

195. ' The Sŏmafads, who fprang from Vira'j,
' are declared to be the anceftors of the Sádhyhas;
' and the Agnifhwáttas, who are famed among
' created beings as the children of Mari'chi, to
' be the progenitors of the Dévas.

196. ' Of the Daityas, the Dánavas, the Yac-
' fhas, the Gandharvas, the Uragas, or Serpents,
' the Racfhafhes, the Garudas, and the Cinnaras,
' the anceftors are Barhifhads defcended from
' Atri;

197. ' Of Bráhmens, thofe named Sŏmapas; of
' Cfhatriyas, the Havifhmats; of Vaifyas, thofe
' called Abjyapas; of Súdras, the Sucálins:

198. ' The Sŏmapas defcended from Me, Bhrĭ-
' gu; the Havifhmats, from Angiras; the Ajya-
' pas, from Pulastya; the Sucálins, from Va-
' sisht'ha.

199. ' Thofe who are, and thofe who are not,
' confumable by fire, called Agnidagdhas, and
' Anagnidagdhas, the Cávyas, the Barhifhads, the
' Agnifhwáttas, and the Saumyas, let mankind
' confider as the chief progenitors of Bráhmens.

200. ' Of thofe juft enumerated, who are ge-
' nerally reputed the principal tribes of Pitrĭs,
' the fons and grandfons indefinitely, are alfo in
' this world confidered as great progenitors.

201. ' From the Rĭfhis come the Pitrĭs, or
' patriarchs; from the Pitrĭs, both Dévas and Dánavas;

' *navas*; from the *Dévas*, this whole world of
' animals and vegetables, in due order.

202. ' Mere water, offered with faith to the
' progenitors of men, in veffels of filver, or
' adorned with filver, proves the fource of in-
' corruption.

203. ' An oblation by *Bráhmens* to their an-
' ceftors tranfcends an oblation to the deities;
' becaufe that to the deities is confidered as the
' opening and completion of that to anceftors :

204. ' As a prefervative of the oblation to the
' patriarchs, let the houfe-keeper begin with an
' offering to the gods; for the *Racfhafes* rend
' in pieces an oblation which has no fuch pre-
' fervative.

205. Let an offering to the gods be made at the
' beginning and end of the *fráddha* : it muft not
' begin and end with an offering to anceftors ; for
' he who begins and ends it with an oblation to the
' *Pitrĭs*, quickly perifhes with his progeny.

206. ' LET the *Bráhmen* fmear with cow dung
' a purified and fequeftered piece of ground ; and
' let him, with great care, felect a place with a
' declivity toward the fouth :

207. ' The divine manes are always pleafed
' with an oblation in empty glades, naturally
' clean, on the banks of rivers, and in folitary
' fpots.

208. ' Having duly made an ablution with
' water, let him place the invited *Bráhmens*, who
' have alfo performed their ablutions, one by
' one, on allotted feats purified with *cus'a*-grafs.

209. ' When he has placed them with re-
' verence on their feats, let him honour them,
' (having firft honoured the Gods) with fragrant
' garlands and fweet odours.

210. ' Having

210. ' Having brought water for them with
' cus'a-grafs and tila, let the Bráhmen, with the
' Bráhmens; pour the oblation, as the law directs,
' on the holy fire.

211. ' Firft, as it is ordained, having fatisfied
' Agni, Soma and Yama, with clairfied butter,
' let him proceed to fatisfy the manes of his pro-
' genitors.

212. ' If he have no confecrated fire, as if he be
' yet unmarried, or his wife be juft deceafed, let him
' drop the oblation into the hand of a Bráhmen ;
' fince, what fire is, even fuch is a Bráhmen ; as
' priefts who know the Véda declare :

213. ' Holy fages call the chief of the twice
' born the gods of obfequies, free from wrath, with
' placid afpects, of a primeval race, employed in
' the advancement of human creatures.

214. ' Having walked in order from eaft to
' fouth, and thrown into the fire all the ingredients
' of his oblation, let him fprinkle water on the
' ground with his right hand.

215. ' From the remainder of the clarified
' butter having formed three balls of rice, let him
' offer them, with fixed attention, in the fame
' manner as the water, his face being turned to
' the fouth :

216. ' Then, having offered thofe balls, after
' due ceremonies and with an attentive mind, to the
' manes of his father, his paternal grandfather, and
' great grandfather, let him wipe the fame hand
' with the roots of cus'a, which he had before ufed,
' for the fake of his paternal anceftors in the fourth,
' fifth, and fixth degrees, who are the partakers of
' the rice and clarified butter thus wiped off.

217. ' Having made an ablution, returning to-
' ward the north, and thrice fuppreffing his breath
slowly,

' flowly, let him falute the Gods of the fix feafons;
' and the *Pitris* alfo, being well acquainted with
' proper texts of the *Véda.*

218. ' Whatever water remains in his ewer, let
' him carry back deliberately near the cakes of
' rice; and with fixed attention, let him fmell
' thofe cakes, in order as they were offered :

219. ' Then, taking a fmall portion of the cakes
' in order, let him firft, as the law directs, caufe
' the *Bráhmens* to eat of them, while they are
' feated.

220. ' If his father be alive, let him offer the
' *fráddha* to his anceftors in *three* higher degrees;
' or let him caufe his own father to eat, as a
' *Bráhmen* at the obfequies :

221. ' Should his father be dead, and his grand-
' father living, let him, in celebrating the name
' of his father, *that is, in performing obfequies to*
' *him,* celebrate alfo his paternal great grand-
' father;

222. ' Either the paternal grandfather may par-
' take of the *fráddha* (fo has MENU declared) or
' the grandfon, authorized by him, may perform
' the ceremony at his difcretion.

223. ' Having poured water, with *cus'a*-grafs
' and *tila,* into the hands of the *Bráhmens,* let him
' give them the upper part of the cakes, faying,
" *Swadhá* to the manes !"

224. ' Next, having himfelf brought with both
' hands, a veffel full of rice, let him, ftill medi-
' tating on the *Pitris,* place it before the *Bráhmens*
' without precipitation.

225. ' Rice taken up, but not fupported with
' both hands, the malevolent *Afuras* quickly rend
' in pieces.

226. ' Broths,

226. ' Broths, potherbs, and other eatables ac-
' companying the rice, together with milk and
' curds, clarified butter and honey, let him firſt
' place on the ground, after he has made an ablu-
' tion ; and let his mind be intent on no other
' objeЄt :

227. ' Let him add ſpiced puddings, and milky
' meſſes of various ſorts, roots of herbs and ripe
' fruits, ſavoury meats and ſweet ſmelling drinks.

228. ' Then being duly purified, and with per-
' fect preſence of mind, let him take up all the
' diſhes, one by one, and preſent them in order to
' the Bráhmens, proclaiming their qualities.

229. ' Let him at no time drop a tear ; let him
' on no account be angry ; let him ſay nothing
' falſe ; let him not touch the eatables with his
' foot ; let him not even ſhake the diſhes :

230. ' A tear ſends the meſſes to reſtleſs ghoſts ;
' anger, to foes ; falſehood, to dogs ; contact with
' his foot, to demons ; agitation, to ſinners.

231. ' Whatever is agreeable to the Bráhmens,
' let him give without envy ; and let him diſcourſe
' on the attributes of GOD : ſuch diſcourſe is ex-
' pected by the manes.

232. ' At the obſequies to anceſtors, he muſt
' let the Bráhmens hear paſſages from the Véda,
' from the codes of law, from moral tales, from
' heroick poems, from the Puránas, and from
' theological texts.

233. ' Himſelf being delighted, let him give
' delight to the Bráhmens, and invite them to eat
' of the proviſions by little and little ; attracting
' them often with the dreſſed rice and other eata-
' bles, and mentioning their good properties.

234. ' To the ſon of his daughter, though a
' ſtudent in theology, let him carefully give food

G　　　　　　　' at

' at the *fráddha*; offering him a blanket from
' *Népàl* as his feat, and fprinkling the ground with
' *tila*.

235. ' Three things are held pure at fuch obfe-
' quies, the daughter, fon, the *Népàl* blanket,
' and the *tila*; and three things are praifed in it
' by the wife, cleanlinefs, freedom from wrath,
' and want of precipitate hafte.

236. ' Let all the dreffed food be very hot;
' and let the *Bráhmens* eat it in filence; nor let
' them declare the qualities of the food, even
' though afked by the giver.

237. ' As long as the meffes continue warm,
' as long as they eat in filence, as long as the qua-
' lities of the food are not declared by them, fo
' long the manes feaft on it.

' 238. ' What a *Bráhmen* eats with his head
' covered, what he eats with his face to the fouth,
' what he eats with fandals on his feet, the demons
' affuredly devour.

239. ' Let not a *Chandála*, a town boar, a cock,
' a dog, a woman in her courfes, or an eunuch,
' fee the *Bráhmens* eating:

240. ' That which any one of them fees at the
' oblation to fire, at a folemn donation of cows
' and gold, at a repaft given to *Bráhmens*, at holy
' rites to the gods, and at the obfequies to ancef-
' tors, produces not the intended fruit:

241. ' The boar deftroys it by his fmell; the
' cock, by the air of his wings; the dog, by the
' caft of a look; the man of the loweft clafs, by
' the touch.

242. ' If a lame man, or a man with one eye,
' or a man with a limb defective or redundant,
' be even a fervant of the giver, him alfo let his
' mafter remove from the place.

243. ' Should

243. ' Should another *Bráhmen*, or a mendicant,
' come to his houfe for food, let him, having ob-
' tained permiffion from the invited *Bráhmens*, en-
' tertain the ftranger to the beft of his power.

244. ' Having brought together all the forts of
' food, as dreffed rice and the like, and fprinkling
' them with water, let him place them before the
' *Bráhmens*, who have eaten ; dropping fome *on*
' *the blades of* cus'a-grafs, *which have been fpread*
' on the ground.

245. ' What remains in the difhes, and what
' has been dropped on the blades of *cus'a*, muft
' be confidered as the portion of deceafed *Bráh-*
' *mens*, not girt with the facrificial thread, and of
' fuch as have deferted unreafonably the women of
' their own tribe.

246. ' The refidue, that has fallen on the ground
' at the *fráddha* to the manes, the wife have de-
' cided to be the fhare of all the fervants, who are
' not crooked in their ways, nor lazy and ill
' difpofed.

247. ' Before the obfequies to anceftors as far
' as the fixth degree, they muft be performed to a
' *Bráhmen* recently deceafed ; but the performer of
' them muft, *in that cafe*, give the *fráddha* without
' the ceremony to the gods, and offer only one
' round cake ; *and thefe obfequies for a fingle anceftor*
' *fhould be annually performed on the day of his death:*

248. ' When, *afterwards*, the obfequies to an-
' ceftors as far as the fixth degree, inclufively of
' him, are performed according to law, then muft
' the offering of cakes be made by the defcen-
' dants in the manner before ordained *for the*
' *monthly ceremonies*.

249. ' THAT fool, who, having eaten of the
' *fráddha*, gives the refidue of it to a man of the

' fervile

' servile clafs, falls headlong down to the hell
' named *Cálafútra.*

250. ' Should the eater of a *fráddha* enter, on
' the fame day, the bed of a feducing woman, his
' anceftors would fleep for that month on her ex-
' crement.

251. ' HAVING, by the word *fwaditam,* afked
' the *Bráhmens* if they have eaten well, let him
' give them, being fatisfied, water for an ablution,
' and courteoufly fay to them, "Reft either at
' home or here."

252. ' Then let the *Bráhmens* addrefs him, faying
' *fwadhá;* for in all ceremonies relating to deceafed
' anceftors, the word *fwadhá* is the higheft benifon.

253. ' After that, let him inform thofe, who
' have eaten of the food that remains ; and being
' inftructed by the *Bráhmens,* let him difpofe of it
' as they may direct.

254. ' At the clofe of the *fráddha* to his ancef-
' tors, he muft afk if the *Bráhmens* are fatisfied,
' by the word *fwadita* ; after that for his family,
' by the word *fufruta* ; after that for his own ad-
' vancement, by the word *fampanna,* after that
' which has been offered to the gods, by the word
' *ruchita.*

255. ' The afternoon, the *cufa*-grafs, the clean-
' fing of the ground, the *tilas,* the liberal gifts of
' food, the due preparation for the repaft, and the
' company of moft exalted *Bráhmens,* are true riches
' in the obfequies to anceftors.

256. ' The blades of *cufa,* the holy texts, the
' forenoon, all the oblations, *which will prefently*
' *be enumerated,* and the purification before men-
' tioned, are to be confidered as wealth in the
' *fráddha* to the gods :

257. ' Such wild grains as are eaten by hermits,
' milk, the juice of the moonplant, meat untainted,
' and

' and falt unprepared by art, are held things fit, in
' their own nature, for the laft mentioned offering.

258. ' Having difmiffed the invited *Bráhmens*,
' keeping his mind attentive, and his fpeech fup-
' preffed, let him, after an ablution, look toward
' the fouth, and afk thefe bleffings of the *Pitrís* :

259. " May generous give s abo nd in our
' houfe ! may the fcriptures be ftudied, and pro-
' geny increafe in it ! may faith never depart from
' us ! and may we have much to beftow on the
' needy !"

260. ' Thus having ended the *fráddhá*, let him
' caufe a cow, a prieft, a kid, or the fire to de-
' vour what remains of the cakes ; or let him caft
' them into the waters.

261. ' Some make the offering of the round
' cakes after the repaft of the *Bráhmens*; fome
' caufe the birds to eat what remains, or caft it
' into water or fire.

262. ' Let a lawful wife, ever dutiful to her
' lord, and conftantly honouring his anceftors, eat
' the middlemoft of the three cakes, *or that offered*
' *to his paternal grandfather*, with due ceremonies,
' praying for offspring :

263. ' So may fhe bring forth a fon, who will
' be long lived, famed, and ftrong minded,
' wealthy, having numerous defcendants, endued
' with the beft of qualities, and performing all
' duties religious and civil.

264. ' Then, having wafhed both his hands and
' fipped water, let him prepare fome rice for his
' paternal kinfmen ; and, having given it them
' with due reverence, let him prepare food aifo
' for his maternal relations.

265. ' Let the refidue continue in its place,
' until the *Bráhmens* have been difmiffed ; and

G 3   ' then

‘ then let him perform the *remaining* domeftick
‘ facraments.

266. ‘ W HAT fort of oblations, given duly to
‘ the manes   are apable of fati-fying them, for a
‘ long time or for eterni:y, I will now declare
‘ without omiffion.

267. ‘ The anceftors of men are fatisfied a
‘ whole month with   *tila,* rice, barley,   black
‘ lentils or vetches, water, roots, and fruit, given
‘ with prefcribed ceremonies ;

268. ‘ Two months, with fifh ; three months,
‘ with venifon ; four, with mutton; five; with the
‘ flefh of *fuch* birds, *as* the twice born may eat :

269. ‘ Six months, with the flefh of kids ; fe-
‘ ven, with that of fpotted deer ; eight, with that
‘ of the deer, or antelope, called *éna* ; nine, with
‘ that of the *ruru :*

270. ‘ Ten months are they fatisfied with the
‘ flefh of wild boars and wild buffalos ; eleven,
‘ with that of rabbits or hares, and of tortoifes ;

271. ‘ A whole year with the milk of cows,
‘ and food made of that milk ; from the flefh of
‘ the long eared white goat, their fatisfaction en-
‘ dures twelve years.

272. ‘ The potherb *câlafáca*, the fifh *maháfalca*,
‘ or the *diodon*, the flefh of a rhinoceros, or of an
‘ iron-coloured kid, honey, and all fuch foreft
‘ grains as are eaten by hermits, are formed for
‘ their fatisfaction without end.

273. ‘ Whatever pure food, mixed with honey,
‘ a man offers on the thirteenth day of the moon,
‘ in the feafon of rain, and under the lunar afte-
‘ rifm *Maghà*, has likewife a ceafelefs duration.

274. “ Oh ! may that man, *fay the manes*, be
‘ born in our line, who may give us milky food,
‘ with honey and pure butter, both on the thir-
                                        ‘ teenth

' teenth of the moon, and when the fhadow of an
' elephant falls to the eaft !"

275. ' Wha ever a man, endued with ftrong
' faith, pioufly offers, as the law has directed,
' becomes a perpetual unperifhable gratification
' to his anceftors in the other world :

276. ' The tenth and fo forth, except the
' fourteenth, in the dark half of the month, are
' the lunar days moft approved for facred obfe-
' quies: as they *are*, fo *are* not the others.

277. ' He, who does honour to the manes, on
' even lunar days, and under even lunar ftations,
' enjoys all his defires ; on odd lunar days, and
' under odd lunar afterifms, he procures an illuf-
' trious race.

278. ' As the latter *or dark* half of the month
' furpaffes, for the celebration of obfequies, the
' former, *or bright* half, fo the latter half of the
' day furpaffes, *for the fame purpofe*, the former
' half of it.

279. ' The oblation to anceftors muft be duly
' made, even to *the conclufion of it with the diftri-*
' *bution to* the fervants, (or even to the clofe of
' life,) in the form prefcribed, by a *Bráhmen* wear-
• ing his thread on his right fhoulder, proceeding
' from left to right, without remiffnefs, and with
' *cus'a*-grafs in his hand.

280. ' Obfequies muft not be performed by
' night ; fince the night is called *rácfhasì* or *infefted*
' *by demons* ; nor while the fun is rifing or fetting,
' nor when it has juft rifen.

281. ' A houfe-keeper, *unable to give a monthly*
' *repaft*, may perform obfequies here below, ac-
' cording to the facred ordinance, only thrice a
' year, in the feafons of *hémanta, grifhma,* and

' *verfhà;*

‘ *verſhà* ; but the five ſacraments he muſt perform
‘ daily.

282. ‘ The ſacrificial oblation at obſequies to
‘ anceſtors, is ordained to be made in no vulgar
‘ fire ; nor ſhou'd the monthly *ſráddha* of that
‘ *Bráhmen,* who keeps a perpetual fire, be made on
‘ any day, except on that of the conjunction.

283. ‘ When a twice born man, having per-
‘ formed his ablution, offers a ſatisfaction to the
‘ manes with water only, *being unable to give a*
‘ *repaſt,* he gains by that offering all the fruit of a
‘ *ſráddha.*

284. ‘ The wife call our fathers, *Vaſus* ; our
‘ paternal grandfathers, *Rudras* ; our paternal great
‘ grandfathers, *Adityas* ; (that is *all are to be re-*
‘ *vered as deities,*) and to this effect there is a pri-
‘ meval text in the *Véda.*

285. ‘ Let a man, who is able, continually feed
‘ on *vighaſa,* and continually feed on *amrĭta* ; by
‘ *vighaſa* is meant the reſidue of a repaſt at obſe-
‘ quies ; and by *amrĭta,* the reſidue of a ſacrifice
‘ to the gods.

286. ‘ THIS complete ſyſtem of rules, for the
‘ five ſacraments and the like, has been declared to
‘ you : now hear the law for thoſe means of ſub-
‘ ſiſtence, which the chief of the twice born may
‘ ſeek.

CHAPTER THE FOURTH.

On Economicks; and Private Morals.

———

1. ' Let a *Bráhmen*, having dwelt with a pre-
' ceptor during the firſt quarter of a man's life,
' paſs the ſecond quarter of human life in his own
' houſe, when he has contracted a legal marriage.

2. ' He muſt live, with no injury, or with the
' leaſt poſſible injury, to animated beings, by
' purſuing thoſe means of gaining ſubſiſtence,
' which are ſtrictly preſcribed by law, except in
' times of diſtreſs :

3. ' For the ſole purpoſe of ſupporting life,
' let him acquire property by thoſe irreproach-
' able occupations, which are peculiar to his claſs,
' and unattended with bodily pain.

4. ' He may live by *rĭta* and *amrĭta*, or, *if ne-*
' *ceſſary*, by *mrĭta* or *pramrĭta*, or even by *ſat-*
' *yanrĭta* ; but never let him ſubſiſt by *ſwavrĭtti* :

5. ' By *rĭta*, muſt be underſtood lawful glean-
' ing and gathering ; by *amrĭta*, what is given
' unaſked ; by *mrĭta*, what is aſked as alms ; til-
' lage is called *pramrĭta* ;

6. ' Traffick and money lending are *ſatyanrĭta* ;
' even by them, *when he is deeply diſtreſſed*, may
' he ſupport life ; but ſervice for hire is named
' *ſwavrĭtti*, or *dog living*, and of courſe he muſt by
' all means avoid it.

7. ' He

7. ' He may either store up grain for three
' years; or garner up enough for one year; or
' collect what may last three days, or make no
' provision for the morrow.

8. ' Of the four *Bráhmens* keeping house, *who*
' *follow those four different modes*, a preference is
' given to the last in order succeffively; as to
' him, who most completely by virtue has van-
' quished the world :

9. ' One of them subfifts by all the six means
' of livelihood; another by three of them; a
' third by two only; and a fourth lives barely on
' continually teaching the *Véda*.

10. ' He, who suftains himself by picking up
' grains and ears, muft attach himself to some
' altar of confecrated fire, but conftantly perform
' those rites only, which end with the dark and
' bright fortnights and with the folftices.

11. ' Let him never, for the fake of a fub-
' fiftence, have recourfe to popular converfation ;
' let him live by the conduct of a prieft, neither
' crooked, nor artful, nor blended *with the manners*
' *of the mercantile clafs.*

12. ' Let him, if he feek happinefs, be firm in
' perfect content, and check all defire of acquiring
' more *than he poffeffes*; for happinefs has its root
' in content, and difcontent is the root of mifery.

13. ' A *Bráhmen* keeping houfe, *and* fupport-
' ing himfelf, by any of the *legal* means before-
' mentioned, muft difcharge thefe *following* duties,
' which conduce to fame, length of life, and bea-
' titude.

14. ' Let him daily, without floth, perform his
' peculiar duty, which the *Véda* prefcribes ; for
' he who performs that *duty*, as well as he is able,
' attains the higheft path to fupreme blifs.

15. ' He

15. ' He muſt not gain wealth *by muſick or*
' *dancing, or* by any art that pleaſes the ſenſe ; nor
' by any prohibited art ; nor, whether he be rich
' or poor, *muſt he receive gifts* indiſcriminately.

16. ' Let him not, from a ſelfiſh appetite, be
' ſtrongly addicted to any ſenſual gratification ;
' let him, by improving his intellect, ſtudiouſly
' preclude an exceſſive attachment to ſuch plea-
' ſures, *even though lawful.*

17. ' All kinds of wealth, that may impede
' his reading the *Véda*, let him wholly abandon,
' perſiſting by all means in the ſtudy of ſcripture ;
' for that will be found his moſt beneficial at-
' tainment.

18. ' Let him paſs through this life, bringing
' his apparel, his diſcourſe, and his frame of mind,
' to conformity with his age, his occupations, his
' property, his divine knowledge, and his family.

19. ' Each day let him examine thoſe holy
' books, which ſoon give increaſe of wiſdom ; and
' thoſe, which teach the means of acquiring wealth ;
' thoſe, which are ſalutary to life ; and thoſe
' *nigamas,* which are explanatory of the *Véda* ;

20. ' Since, as far as a man ſtudies completely
' the ſyſtem of ſacred literature, ſo far only can he
' become eminently learned, and ſo far may his
' learning ſhine brightly.

21. ' The ſacramental oblations to ſages, to
' the gods, to ſpirits, to men, and to his anceſtois,
' let him conſtantly perform to the beſt of his
' power.

22. ' Some, who well know the ordinances
' for thoſe oblations, perform not always exter-
' nally the five great ſacraments, but continually
' make offerings in their own organs *of ſenſation*
' *and intellect :*

23. ' Some

23. ' Some conftantly facrifice their breath in
' their fpeech, *when they inftruct others, or praife*
' GOD *aloud*, and their fpeech in their breath, *when*
' *they medidate in filence*; perceiving in their fpeech
' and breath, *thus employed*, the unperifhable fruit
' of a facrificial offering:

24. ' Other *Bráhmens* inceffantly perform thofe
' facrifices with fcriptural knowledge only; feeing
' with the eye of divine learning, that fcriptural
' knowledge is the root of every ceremonial ob-
' fervance.

25. ' Let a *Bráhmen* perpetually make obla-
' tions to confecrated fire at the beginning and
' end of day and night, and at the clofe of each
' fortnight, *or at the conjunction and oppofition:*

26. ' At the feafon, when old grain is ufually
' confumed, let him offer new grain for a plenti-
' ful harveft; and at the clofe of the feafon, let
' him perform the rites called *adhvara*; at the
' folftices, let him facrifice cattle; at the end of
' the year, let his oblations be made with the
' juice of the moon plant:

27. ' Not having offered grain for the harveft,
' nor cattle *at the time of the folftice*, let no *Bráh-*
' *men*, who keeps hallowed fire, and wifhes for
' long life, tafte rice or flefh;

28. ' Since the holy fires, not being honoured
' with new grain and with a facrifice of cattle,
' are greedy for rice and flefh, and feek to devour
' his vital fpirits.

29. ' Let him take care, to the utmoft of his
' power, that no gueft fojourn in his houfe un-
' honoured with a feat, with food, with a bed, with
' water, with efculent roots, and with fruit:

30. ' But let him not honour with his conver-
' fation fuch as do forbidden acts; fuch as fubfift,
                                        ' like

' like cats, *by interefted craft*; fuch as believe
' not the fcripture; fuch as oppugn it by fo-
' phifms; or fuch as live like rapacious water
' birds.

31. ' With oblations to the gods and to an-
' ceftors, let him do reverence to *Bráhmens* of the
' fecond order, who are learned in theology, who
' have returned home from their preceptors, after
' having performed their religious duties and fully
' ftudied the *Véda*; but men of an oppofite de-
' fcription let him avoid.

32. ' Gifts muft be made by each houfekeeper,
' as far as he has ability, to religious mendicants,
' though heterodox; and a juft portion muft be
' referved, without inconvenience to his family,
' for all fentient beings, *animal and vegetable*.

33. ' A prieft, who is mafter of a family, and
' pines with hunger, may feek wealth from a
' king *of the military clafs*, from a facrificer, or
' his own pupil, but from no perfon elfe, *unlefs*
' *all other helps fail:* thus *will he fhew his* refpect
' for the law.

34. ' Let no prieft, who keeps houfe, *and is*
' able *to procure food*, ever wafte himfelf with
' hunger; nor, when he has any fubftance, let
' him wear old or fordid clothes.

35. ' His hair, nails, and beard being clipped;
' *his paffions*, fubdued; his mantle, white; his
' body, pure; let him diligently occupy himfelf
' in reading the *Véda*, and be conftantly intent on
' fuch acts, as may be falutary to him.

36. ' Let him carry a ftaff of *Vénu*, an ewer
' with water in it, a handful of *cus'a*-grafs, or *a*
' *copy of* the *Véda*; with a pair of bright golden
' rings in his ears.

37. ' He muft not gaze on the fun whether
rifing

' rifing or fetting, or eclipfed, or reflected in
' water, or advanced to the middle of the fky.

38. ' Over a ftring, to which a calf is tied, let
' him not ftep; nor let him run while it rains;
' nor let him look on his own image in water:
' this is a fettled rule.

39. ' By a mound of earth, by a cow, by an
' idol, by a *Bráhmen*, by a pot of clarified butter,
' or of honey, by a place where four ways meet,
' and by large trees well known in the diftrict,
' let him pafs with his right hand toward them.

40. ' Let him not, though mad with defire,
' approach his wife, when her courfes appear;
' nor let him then fleep with her in the fame bed ;

41. ' Since the knowledge, the manhood, the
' ftrength, the eye fight, even the vital fpirit of
' him, who approaches his wife thus defiled, ut-
' terly perifh ;

42. ' But the knowledge, the manhood, the
' ftrength, the fight, and the life of him, who
' avoids her in that ftate of defilement, are greatly
' increafed.

43. ' Let him neither eat with his wife, nor
' look at her eating, or fneezing, or yawning, or
' fitting carelefsly at her eafe ;

44. ' Nor let a *Bráhmen*, who defires manly
' ftrength, behold her fetting off her eyes with
' black powder, or fcenting herfelf with effences,
' or baring her bofom, or bringing forth a child.

45. ' Let him not eat his food, wearing only
' a fingle cloth ; nor let him bathe quite naked ;
' nor let him eject urine or feces in the highway,
' nor on afhes, nor where kine are grazing.

46. ' Nor on tilled ground, nor in water, nor
' on wood raifed for burning, nor, *unlefs be be in*
great

' *great need*, on a mountain, nor on the ruins of a
' temple, nor at any time on a neſt of white ants,

47. ' Nor in ditches with living creatures in
' them, nor walking, nor ſtanding, nor on the
' bank of a river, nor on the ſummit of a moun-
' tain :

48. ' Nor let him ever ejeᶜt them, looking at
' *things moved by* the wind, or at fire, or at a prieſt,
' or at the ſun, or at water, or at cattle ;

49. ' But let him void his excrements, having
' covered the earth with wood, potherbs, *dry* leaves
' and graſs, or the like, carefully ſuppreſſing his
' utterance, wrapping up his breaſt and his head :

50. ' By day let him void them with his face to
' the north ; by night, with his face to the ſouth ;
' at ſun riſe and at ſun ſet, in the ſame manner as
' by day ;

51. ' In the ſhade or in darkneſs, whether by
' day or by night, let a *Bráhmen* eaſe nature with
' his face turned as he pleaſes ; and in places where
' he fears injury to life, *from wild beaſts or from*
' *reptiles*.

52. ' Of him, who ſhould urine againſt fire,
' againſt the ſun, or the moon, againſt a twice
' born man, a cow, or the wind, all the ſacred
' knowledge would periſh.

53. ' Let him not blow the fire with his mouth ;
' let him not ſee his wife naked ; let him not
' throw any foul thing into fire ; nor let him
' warm his feet in it ;

54. ' Nor let him place it *in a chafing diſh* un-
' der *his bed* ; nor let him ſtride over it ; nor let
' him keep it, *while he ſleeps*, at his feet : let him
' do nothing that may be injurious to life.

55. ' At the time of ſunriſe or ſunſet, let
' him not eat, nor travel, nor lie down to reſt ; let

6   ' him

‘ him not idly draw lines on the ground ; nor let
‘ him take off his own chaplet of flowers.

56. ‘ Let him not caſt into the water either
‘ urine or ordure, nor ſaliva, nor cloth, or any
‘ other thing ſoiled with impurity, nor blood, nor
‘ any kinds of poiſon.

57. ‘ Let him not ſleep alone in an empty
‘ houſe; nor let him wake a ſleeping man *ſuperiour*
‘ *to himſelf in wealth and in learning* ; nor let him
‘ ſpeak to a woman at the time of her courſes ;
‘ nor let him go to *perform* a ſacrifice, unattended
‘ *by an officiating prieſt.*

58. ‘ In a temple *of conſecrated fire,* in the paſ-
‘ ture of kine, in the preſence of *Bráhmens,* in
‘ reading the *Véda,* and in eating his food, let him
‘ hold out his right arm uncovered.

59. ‘ Let him not interrupt a cow *while ſhe is*
‘ drinking, nor give notice to any, *whoſe milk or*
‘ *water ſhe drinks* ; nor let him who knows *right*
‘ *from wrong,* and ſees in the ſky the bow of INDRA,
‘ ſhow it to any man.

60. ‘ Let him not inhabit a town, in which
‘ civil and religious duties are neglected ; nor for
‘ a long time, one in which diſeaſes are frequent ;
‘ let him not begin a journey alone ; let him not
‘ reſide long on a mountain.

61. ‘ Let him not dwell in a city governed by
‘ a *Súdra* king, nor in one ſurrounded with men
‘ unobſervant of their duties, nor in one abounding
‘ with profeſſed hereticks, nor in one ſwarming
‘ with low born outcaſts.

62. ‘ Let him eat no vegetable, from which the
‘ oil has been extracted ; nor indulge his appetite
‘ to ſatiety ; nor eat either too early or too late ;
‘ nor *take any food* in the evening, if he have eaten
‘ to fullneſs in the morning.

63. Let

63. ' Let him make no vain corporeal exer-
' tion : let him not fip water *taken up* with his
' *clofed* fingers : let him eat nothing *placed* in his
' lap : let him never take pleafure in afking idle
' queftions.

64. ' Let him neither dance, nor fing, nor
' play on mufical inftruments, *except in religious*
' *rites;* nor let him ftrike his arm, or gnafh his
' teeth, or make a braying noife, though agitated
' by paffion.

65. ' Let him not wafh his feet in a pan of
' mixed yellow metal ; nor let him eat from a
' broken difh, nor where his mind is difturbed
' with anxious apprehenfions.

66. ' Let him not ufe either flippers or clothes,
' or a facerdotal ftring, or an ornament, or a gar-
' land, or a water pot, which before have been
' ufed by another.

67. ' With untrained beafts of burden let him
' not travel ; nor with fuch as are oppreffed by
' hunger or by difeafe ; nor with fuch as have im-
' perfeCt horns, eyes, or hoofs; nor with fuch as
' have ragged tails :

68. ' But let him conftantly travel with beafts
' well trained, whofe pace is quick, who bear all
' the marks of a good breed, who have an agree-
' able colour, and a beautiful form ; giving them
' very little pain with his whip.

69. ' The fun in the fign of *Canyà,* the fmoke
' of a burning corfe, and a broken feat, muft be
' fhunned : he muft never cut his own hair and
' nails, nor ever tear his nails with his teeth.

70. ' Let him not break mould or clay *without*
' *caufe :* let him not cut grafs with his nails : let
' him neither indulge any vain fancy, nor do any
' aCt that can bring no future advantage :

H   71. ' He

71. ' He, who *thus idly* breaks clay, or cuts
' grafs, or bites his nails, will fpeedily fink to
' ruin; and *fo fhall* a detractor, and an unclean
' perfon.

72. ' Let him ufe no contumelious phrafe;
' let him wear no garland except on his hair : to
' ride on the back of a bull or cow, is in all
' modes culpable.

73. ' Let him not pafs, otherwife than by the
' gate, into a walled town or an enclofed houfe;
' and by night let him keep aloof from the roots
' of trees.

74. ' Never let him play with dice : let him
' not put off his fandals with his hand : let him
' not eat, while he reclines on a bed, nor what is
' placed in his hand, or on a bench;

75. ' Nor, when the fun is fet, let him eat any
' thing mixed with *tila*; nor let him ever, in this
' world, fleep quite naked; nor let him go any
' whither with a remnant of food in his mouth.

76. ' Let him take his food, having fprinkled
' his feet with water; but never let him fleep
' with his feet wet : he, who takes his food with
' his feet fo fprinkled, will attain long life.

77. ' Let him never advance into a place un-
' diftinguifhable by his eye, or not eafily paffable :
' never let him look at urine or ordure; nor let
' him pafs a river *fwimming* with his arms.

78. ' Let not a man, who defires to enjoy long
' life, ftand upon hair, nor upon afhes, bones, or
' potfherds, nor upon feeds of cotton, nor upon
' hufks of grain.

79. ' Nor let him tarry *even under the fhade of*
' *the fame tree* with outcafts for great crimes, nor
' with *Chandálas*, nor with *Puccafas*, nor with
' idiots, nor with men proud of wealth, nor with

' wafher-

' *wafhermen and other* vile perfons, nor with *An-*
' *tyavafiyins.*

80. ' Let him not give *even temporal* advice to
' a *Shdra*; nor, *except to his own fervant*, what re-
' mains from his table; nor clarified butter, of
' which part has been offered *to the gods*; nor let
' him *in perfon* give fpiritual counfel to fuch a
' man, nor *perfonally* inform him of the legal ex-
' piation for his fin:

81. ' Surely he, who declares the law to a
' fervile man, and he, who inftructs him in the
' mode of expiating fin, *except by the intervention*
' *of a prieft*, finks with that very man into the
' hell named *Afamvr̃ita,*

82. ' Let him not ftroke his head with both
' hands; nor let him even touch it, while food
' remains in his mouth; not without *bathing it*,
' let him bathe his body.

83. ' Let him not *in anger* lay hold of hair, or
' fmite any one on the head; nor let him, after
' his head has been rubbed with oil, touch with
' oil any of his limbs.

84. ' From a king, not born in the military
' clafs, let him accept no gift, nor from fuch as
' keep a flaughter-houfe or an oil prefs, or put out
' a vintner's flag, or fubfift by the gain of pro-
' ftitutes:

85. ' One oil prefs is as bad as ten flaughter-
' houfes; one vintner's flag, as ten oil preffes;
' one proftitute, as ten vintner's flags; one *fuch*
' king, as ten proftitutes;

86. ' With a flaughterer, *therefore*, who em-
' ploys ten thoufand flaughter-houfes, a king, *not*
' *a foldier by birth*, is declared to be on a level;
' *and*, a gift from him is tremendous.

87. ' He, who receives a prefent from an ava-

H 2   ' ricious

' ricious king and a tranfgreffor of the facred
' ordinances, goes in fucceffion to the following
' twenty-one hells:

88. ' *Támifra, Andhatámifra, Mahiraurava, Rau-*
' *rava, Naraca, Cálasútra,* and *Mahinaraca;*

89. ' *Sanjívana, Mahavichi, Tapana, Samp-*
' *ratápana, Sanháta, Sacácóla, Cudmala, Pútim-*
' *rútt.ca;*

90. ' *Lóhafancu,* or *iron fpiked,* and *Rijífha,*
'· *Pant'hána,* the river *Sálmalí, Afipatravana,* or *the*
' *fword-leaved foreft,* and *Lóh'ángáraca,* or *the ·pit*
' *of red hot charcoal.*

91. ' *Bráhmens,* who know this *law,* who fpeak
' the words of the *Véda,* and who feek blifs after
' death, accept no gifts from a king.

92. ' LET the houfe-keeper wake in the time
' facred to BRA'HMI', *the goddefs of fpeech, that is*
' *in the laft watch of the night:* let him then reflect
' on virtue and virtuous emoluments, on the bo-
' dily labour which they require, and on the
' whole meaning and very effence of the *Véda.*

93. ' Having rifen, having done what nature
' makes neceffary, having then purified himfelf
' and fixed his attention, let him ftand a long
' time repeating the *gáyatrì* for the firft *or morning*
' twilight; as he muft for the laft *or evening*
' twilight in its proper time.

94. ' By continued repetition of the *gáyatrì,* at
' the twilights, the holy fages acquire length of
' days, perfect knowledge, reputation during life,
' fame after death, and celeftial glory.

95. ' Having duly performed the *upácarma,* or
' *domeftick ceremony with facred fire,* at the full moon
' of *Srávana,* or of *Bhádra,* let the *Bráhmen,* fully
' exerting his intellectual powers, read the *Védas*
' during four months and one fortnight:

96. ' Under

96. ' Under the lunar afterifm *Pufhya*, or on
' the firft day of the bright half of *Mágha*, and in
' the firft part of the day, let him perform out of
' the town, *the ceremony called* the *utferga* of the
' *Védas.*

97. ' Having performed that ceremony out of
' town, as the law directs, let him defift from
' reading for one *intermediate* night winged *with*
' *two days*, or for that day and *that following* night
' only ;

98. ' But after that *intermiffion*, let him atten-
' tively read the *Védas* in the bright fortnights
' and in the dark fortnights let him conftantly
' read all the *Védángas.*

99. ' He muft never read the *Véda* without
' accents and letters well pronounced ; nor ever in
' the prefence of *Súdras* ; nor *having begun to read*
' *it* in the laft watch of the night, muft he, though
' fatigued, fleep again.

100. ' By the rule juft mentioned let him con-
' tinually, with his faculties exerted, read the
' *Mantras*, or holy texts, compofed in regular
' meafures ; and, when he is under no reftraint,
' let him read both the *Mantras* and the *Bráhmanas*,
' or chapters on the attributes of God.

101. ' Let a reader of the *Véda*, and a teacher
' of it to his pupils, in the form prefcribed, al-
' ways avoid reading on the following prohibited
' days.

102. ' By night, when the wind meets his ear,
' and by day when the duft is collected, *he muft*
' *not read* in the feafon of rain ; fince both thofe
' times are declared unfit for reading, by fuch as
' know when the *Véda* ought to be read.

103. ' In lightning, thunder, *and* rain, or dur-
' ing the fall of lage fireballs on all fides, at fuch

' times

' times MENU has ordained the reading of fcrip-
' ture to be deferred till the fame time next day.

104. ' When the prieft perceives thofe accidents
' occurring at once, while his fires are kindled for
' *morning and evening* facrifices; then let him
' know, that the *Véda* muft not be read ; and
' when clouds are feen gathered out of feafon.

105. ' On the occafion of a preternatural found
' from the fky, of an earthquake, or an obfcura-
' tion of the heavenly bodies, even in due feafon,
' let him know, that his reading muft be poftponed
' till the proper time :

106. ' But if, while his fires are blazing, the
' found of lightning and thunder is heard *without*
' *rain*, his reading muft be difcontinued, only
' while the phenomenon lafts ; the remaining
' event, *or rain alfo*, happening, it muft ceafe for a
' night and a day.

107. ' The reading of fuch, as wifh to attain
' the excellent reward of virtue, muft continually
' be fufpended in towns and in cities, and always
' where an offenfive fmell prevails.

108. ' In a diftrict, through which a corpfe is
' carried, and in the prefence of an unjuft perfon,
' the reading of fcripture muft ceafe ; *and* while
' the found of weeping is heard ; and in a pro-
' mifcuous affembly of men.

109. ' In water, near midnight, and while the
' two natural excretions are made, or with a rem-
' nant of food in the mouth, or when the *fráddha*
' has recently been eaten, let no man even medi-
' tate in his heart *on the holy texts.*

110. ' A learned *Bráhmen*, having received an
' invitation to the obfequies of a fingle anceftor,
' muft not read the *Véda* for three days ; nor
                                        ' when

' when the king has a fon born; nor when the
' dragon's head caufes an eclipfe.

111. ' As long as the fcent and unctuofity of
' perfumes remain on the body of a learned prieft,
' who has partaken of an entertainment, fo long
' he muft abftain from pronouncing the texts of
' the *Véda*.

112. ' Let him not read lolling on a couch,
' nor with his feet raifed on a bench, nor with his
' thighs croffed, nor having lately fwallowed
' meat, or the rice and other food *given* on the
' birth or death of a relation;

113. ' Nor in a cloud of duft, nor while arrows
' whiz, *or a lute founds*, nor in either of the twi-
' lights, nor at conjunction, nor on the fourteenth
' day, nor at the oppofition, nor on the eighth
' day of the moon:

114. ' The dark lunar day deftroys the fpiritual
' teacher; the fourteenth deftroys the learner; the
' eighth and the day of the full moon deftroy *all*
' *remembrance of* fcripture; for which reafons he
' muft avoid reading on thofe lunar days.

115. ' Let no *Bráhmen* read, while duft falls
' like a fhower, nor while the quarters of the fir-
' mament are inflamed, nor while fhakals yell,
' nor while dogs bark or yelp, nor while affes or
' camels bray, nor while men in company chatter.

116. ' He muft not read near a cemetery, near
' a town, or in a pafture for kine; nor in a man-
' tle worn before a time of dalliance; nor having
' juft received the prefent ufual at obfequies:

117. ' Be it an animal, or a thing inanimate, or
' whatever be the gift at a *fráddha*, let him not,
' having lately accepted it, read the *Véda*; for
' fuch a *Bráhmen* is faid to have his mouth in his
' hand.

H 4 118. ' When

118. ' When the town is befet by robbers, or
' an alarm has been raifed by fire, and in all ter-
' rors from ftrange phenomena, let him know,
' that his lecture muft be fufpended till the due
' time *after the caufe of terror has ceafed*.

119. ' The fufpenfion of reading fcripture, af-
' ter a performance of the *upácarma* and *utferga*,
' muft be for three whole nights, *by the man who*
' *feeks virtue more than knowledge* ; alfo for one day
' and night, on the eighth lunar days which follow
' thofe ceremonies, and on the nights at the clofe
' of the feafons.

120. ' Never let him read on horfeback, nor
' on a tree, nor on an elephant, nor in a boat, nor
' on an afs, nor on a camel, nor ftanding on bar-
' ren ground, nor borne in a carriage ;

121. ' Nor during a verbal altercation, nor
' during a mutual affault, nor with an army, nor
' in battle, nor after food, *while his hand is moift*
' *from wafhing*, nor with an indigeftion, nor after
' vomiting, nor with four eructations ;

122. ' Nor without notice to a gueft juft arrived,
' nor while the wind vehemently blows, nor when
' blood gufhes from his body, nor when it is
' wounded by a weapon.

123. ' While the ftrain of the *Sáman* meets his
' ear, he fhall not read the *Rǐch*, or the *Yajufh* ;
' nor any part of the *Véda*, when he has juft con-
' cluded the whole ; nor *any other part*, when he
' has juft finifhed the book entitled *Aranyaca* :

124. ' The *Rigvéda* is held facred to the gods ;
' the *Yajurvéda* relates to mankind ; the *Sámavéda*
' concerns the manes of anceftors, and the found
' of it, *when chanted*, raifes therefore a notion of
' fomething impure.

125. ' Know-

125. ' Knowing this *collection of rules*, let the
' learned read the *Véda* on every *lawful* day, having
' firſt repeated, in order, the pure eſſence of the
' three *Védas*, namely, the *pranava*, the *vyáhritis*,
' and the *gáyatrì*.

126. ' If a beaſt uſed in agriculture, a frog, a
' cat, a dog, a ſnake, an ichneumon, or a rat,
' paſs between *the lecturer and his pupil*, let him
' know, that the lecture muſt be intermitted for a
' day and a night.

127. ' Two occaſions, when the *Véda* muſt not
' be read, let a *Bráhmen* conſtantly obſerve with
' great care ; *namely*, when the place for reading
' it is impure, and when he is himſelf unpurified.

128. ' On the dark night of the moon, and on
' the eighth, on the night of the full moon, and
' on the fourteenth, let a *Bráhmen*, who keeps
' houſe, be continually chaſte as a ſtudent in theo-
' logy, even in the ſeaſon of nuptial embraces.

129. ' Let him not bathe, having juſt eaten ;
' nor while he is afflicted with diſeaſe ; nor in the
' middle of the night; nor with many clothes;
' nor in a pool of water imperfectly known.

130. ' Let him not intentionally paſs over the
' ſhadow of ſacred images, of a natural or ſpiritual
' father, of a king, of a *Bráhmen*, who keeps houſe,
' or of any reverend perſonage ; nor of a red-haired
' *or copper-coloured* man, nor of one who has juſt
' performed a ſacrifice.

131. ' At noon or at midnight, or having eaten
' fleſh at a *ſráddha*, or in either of the twilights,
' let him not long tarry where four ways meet.

132. ' He muſt not ſtand knowingly near oil
' and other things, with which a man has rubbed
' his body, or water in which he has waſhed
'   ' himſelf,

' himfelf. or feces and urine, or blood, or mucus,
' or any thing chewed and fpitten out, or any
' thing vomited

133. ' Let him fhew no particular attention to
' his enemy or his enemy's friend, to an unjuft
' perfon, to a thief, or to the wife of another
' man ;

134. ' Since nothing is known in this world fo
' obftructive to length of days, as the culpable
' attention of a man to the wife of another.

135. ' Never let him, who defires an increafe of
' wealth, defpife a warriour, a ferpent, or a prieft
' verfed in fcripture, how mean foever *they may*
' *appear* ;

136. ' Since thofe three, when contemned, may
' deftroy a man ; let a wife man therefore, always
' beware of treating thofe three with contempt :

137. ' Nor fhould he defpife *even* himfelf on
' account of previous mifcarriages ; let him pur-
' fue fortune till death, nor ever think her hard
' to be attained.

138. ' Let him fay what is true, but let him
' fay what is pleafing ; let him fpeak no difagree-
' able truth, nor let him fpeak agreeable falfehood :
' this is a primeval rule.

139. ' Let him fay " well and good," or let
' him fay " well" only ; but let him not maintain
' fruitlefs enmity and altercation with any man.

140. ' Let him not journey too early in the
' morning or too late in the evening, nor too near
' the mid-day, nor with an unknown companion,
' nor alone, nor with men of the fervile clafs.

141. Let him not infult thofe who want a limb,
' or have a limb redundant, who are unlearned,
' who are advanced in age, who have no beauty,
                                        ' who

' who have no wealth, or who are of an ignoble
' race.

142. ' Let no prieft, unwafhed after food, touch
' with his hand a cow, a *Bráhmen,* or fire; nor
' being in good health *and* unpurified, let him even
' look at the luminaries in the firmament:

143. ' But, having accidentally touched them
' before his purification, let him ever fprinkle,
' with water in the palm of his hand, his organs of
' fenfation, all his limbs, and his navel.

144. ' Not being in pain from difeafe, let him
' never without caufe touch the cavities of his
' body; and carefully let him avoid his concealed
' hair.

145. ' Let him be intent on *thofe propitious ob-*
' *fervances which lead to* good fortune, and on the
' difcharge of his cuftomary duties, his body
' and mind being pure, and his members kept
' in fubjection; let him conftantly without re-
' miffnefs repeat the *gáyatrì,* and prefent his obla-
' tion to fire:

146. ' To thofe who are intent on good fortune
' and on the difcharge of their duties, who are
' always pure, who repeat the holy text, and
' make oblations to fire, no calamity happens.

147. ' In due feafon, let him ever ftudy the
' fcripture without negligence; for the fages call
' that his principal duty: every other duty is de-
' clared to be fubordinate.

148. ' By reading the *Véda* continually, by
' purity of body and mind, by rigorous devotion,
' and by doing no injury to animated creatures,
' he brings to remembrance his former birth:

149. ' A *Bráhmen,* remembering his former
' birth, again reads the *Véda,* and by reading it
' conftantly, attains blifs without end.

150. ' On

150. ' On the days of the conjunction and op-
' position, let him conftantly make thofe oblations,
' which are hallowed by the *gáyatrì*, and thofe
' which avert misfortune ; but on the eighth and
' ninth lunar days *of the three dark fortnights, after*
' *the end of Ágraháyan*, let him always do reverence
' to the manes of anceftors.

151. ' Far from the manfion of holy fire, let him
' remove all ordure ; far *let him remove* water, in
' which feet have been wafhed ; far *let him re-*
' *move* all remnants of food, and all feminal im-
' purity.

152. ' AT the beginning of each day let him
' difcharge his feces, bathe, rub his teeth, apply
' a collirium to his eyes, adjuft his drefs, and
' adore the gods.

153. ' On the dark lunar day, and on the
' other monthly *parvans*, let him vifit the images
' of deities and *Bráhmens* eminent in virtue, and
' the ruler of the land, for the fake of protection,
' and thofe whom he is bound to revere.

154. ' Let him humbly greet venerable men,
' *who vifit him*, and give them his own feat ; let
' him fit near them, clofing the palms of his
' hands ; and when they depart, let him walk
' fome way behind them.

155. ' Let him practife, without intermiffion,
' that fyftem of approved ufages, which is the root
' of all duty religious and civil, declared at large
' in the fcriptural and facred law tracts, together
' with the ceremonies peculiar to each act :

156. ' Since by fuch practice long life is at-
' tained ; by fuch practice *is gained* wealth un-
' perifhable ; fuch practice baffles every mark of
' ill fortune :

157. ' But

157. ' But by an opposite practice, a man surely
' sinks to contempt in this world, has always a
' large portion of misery, is afflicted with disease
' and short-lived;

158. ' While the man who is observant of ap-
' proved usages, endued with faith in scripture,
' and free from a spirit of detraction, lives a
' hundred years, even though he bear no bodily
' mark of a prosperous life.

159. ' Whatever act depends on another man,
' that act let him carefully shun; but whatever
' depends on himself, to that let him studiously
' attend :

160. ' ALL THAT DEPENDS ON ANOTHER,
' GIVES PAIN; AND ALL THAT DEPENDS ON
' HIMSELF, GIVES PLEASURE; let him know this
' to be in few words the definition of pleasure
' and pain.

161. ' When an act, *neither prescribed nor pro-*
' *hibited*, gratifies the mind of him who performs
' it, let him perform it with diligence, but let
' him avoid its opposite.

162. ' Him, by whom he was invested with
' the sacrificial thread, him, who explained the
' *Véda*, or even a part of it, his mother, and his
' father, natural or spiritual, let him never op-
' pose, nor priests, nor cows, nor persons truly
' devout.

163. ' Denial of a future state, neglect of the
' scripture, and contempt of the deities, envy and
' hatred, vanity and pride, wrath and severity,
' let him at all times avoid.

164. ' Let him not, when angry, throw a
' stick at another man, nor smite him with any
' thing; unless he be a son or a pupil; those
' two

' two he may chaftife for their *improvement* in
' learning.

165. ' A twice born man, who barely affaults
' a *Br hmen* with intention to hurt him, fhall be
' whirled about for a century in the hell named
' *Támifra* ;

166. ' *But,* having fmitten him in anger and
' by defign, even with a blade of grafs, he fhall
' be born, in one and twenty tranfmigrations,
' from the wombs of impure quadrupeds.

167. ' He, who, through ignorance of the law,
' fheds blood from the body of a *Bráhmen*, not
' engaged in battle, fhall feel exceffive pain in
' his future life :

168. ' As many particles of duft as the blood
' fhall roll up from the ground, for fo many years
' fhall the fhedder of that blood be mangled by
' other animals in his next birth.

169. ' Let not him then, who knows *this law,*
' even affault a *Br hmen* at any time, nor ftrike
' him even with grafs, nor caufe blood to gufh
' from his body.

170. ' Even here below an unjuft man attains
' no felicity ; nor he, whofe wealth proceeds from
' giving falfe evidence ; nor he, who conftantly
' takes delight in mifchief.

171. ' Though oppreffed by penury, in con-
' fequence of his righteous dealings, let him
' never give his mind to unrighteoufnefs ; for he
' may obferve the fpeedy overthrow of iniquitous
' and finful men.

172. ' Iniquity, committed in this world, pro-
' duces not fruit immediately, *but,* like the
' earth, *in due feafon* ; and, advancing by little
' and little, it eradicates the man . who commit-
' ted it

173. ' Yes ;

173. ' Yes; iniquity, once committed, fails
' not of producing fruit to him, who wrought it;
' if not in his own perfon, yet in his fons; or, if
' not in his fons, yet in his grandfons:

174. ' He grows rich for awhile through un-
' righteoufnefs; then he beholds good things;
' then it is, that he vanquifhes his foes; but he
' perifhes at length from his whole root up-
' wards.

175. ' LET a man continually take pleafure in
' truth, in juftice, in laudable practices, and in
' purity; let him chaftife thofe whom he may
' chaftife in a legal mode; let him keep in
' fubjection his fpeech, his arm, and his ap-
' petite:

176. ' Wealth and pleafures, repugnant to law,
' let him fhun; and even lawful acts, which may
' caufe future pain, or be offenfive to mankind.

177. ' Let him not have nimble hands, reftlefs
' feet, or voluble eyes; let him not be crooked in
' his ways; let him not be flippant in his fpeech,
' nor intelligent in doing mifchief.

178. ' Let him walk in the path of good men;
' the path in which his parents and forefathers
' walked: while he moves in that path he can
' give no offence.

179. ' WITH an attendant on confecrated fire,
' a performer of holy rites, and a teacher of the
' *Véda,* with his maternal uncle, with his gueft
' or a dependent, with a child, with a man either
' aged or fick, with a phyfician, with his pa-
' ternal kindred, with his relations by marriage,
' and with coufins on the fide of his mother,

180. ' With his mother herfelf, or with his
' father, with his kinfwomen, with his brother,
' with

' with his fon, his wife, or his daughter, and
' with his whole fet of fervants let him have no
' ftrife.

181. ' A houfe-keeper, who fhuns altercation
' with thofe *juft mentioned*, is releafed from all
' fecret faults; and, by fuppreffing all fuch dif-
' putes, he obtains a victory over the following
' worlds:

182. ' The teacher of the *Véda* fecures him
' the world of BRAHMA'; his father, the world *of*
' *the Sun, or* of the *Prajápetis*; his gueft, the
' world of INDRA; his attendants on holy fire,
' the world of *Dévas*;

183. '. His female relations, the world of ce-
' leftial nymphs; his maternal coufins, the world
' of the *Vifvadévas*; his relations by affinity, the
' world of waters; his mother and maternal uncle
' give him power on earth;

184. ' Children, old men, poor dependents,
' and fick perfons, muft be confidered as rulers
' of the pure ether; his elder brother, as equal
' to his father; his wife and fon, as his own
' body;

185. ' His affemblage of fervants, as his own
' fhadow; his daughter, as the higheft object
' of tendernefs: let him therefore, when of-
' fended by any of thofe, bear the offence without
' indignation.

186. ' THOUGH permitted to receive prefents,
' let him avoid a habit of taking them; fince, by
' taking many gifts, his divine light foon fades.

187. ' Let no man of fenfe, who has not fully
' informed himfelf of the law concerning gifts of
' *particular* things, accept a prefent, even though
' he pine with hunger.

188. ' The man who knows not that law, yet
                                    ' accepts

' accepts gold or gems, land, a horfe, a cow,
' food, raiment, oils, or clarified butter, becomes
' mere afhes, like wood confumed by fire:

189. ' Gold and gems burn up his nourifh-
' ment and life; land and a cow, his body; a
' horfe, his eyes; raiment, his fkin; clarified
' butter, his manly ftrength; oils, his progeny.

190. ' A twice born man, void of true devo-
' tion, and not having read the *Véda*, yet eager
' to take a gift, finks down, together with it, as
' with a boat of ftone in deep water.

191. ' Let him then, who knows not the law,
' be fearful of prefents from this or that giver;
' fince an ignorant man, even by a fmall gift,
' may become helplefs as a cow in a bog.

192. ' Let no man, apprized of this law, pre-
' fent even water to a prieft, who acts like a cat,
' nor to him, who acts like a bittern, nor to him,
' who is unlearned in the *Véda*;

193. ' Since property, though legally gained,
' if it be given to either of thofe three, becomes
' prejudicial in the next world, both to the giver
' and receiver:

194. ' As he, who tries to pafs over deep
' water in a boat of ftone, finks to the bottom,
' fo thofe two ignorant men, the receiver and the
' giver, fink to a region of torment.

195. ' A covetous wretch, who continually
' difplays the flag of virtue, a pretender, a de-
' luder of the people, is declared to be the
' man who acts like a cat; he is an injurious
' hypocrite, a detractor from the merits of all
' men.

196. ' A twice born man, with his eyes de-
' jected, morofe, intent on his own advantage,

I   fly,

‘ fly, and falfely demure, is he. who acts like a
‘ bittern.

197. ‘ Such prieſts, as live like bitterns, and
‘ ſuch as demean themſelves like cats, fall by
‘ that ſinful conduct into the hell called *Andhatá-*
‘ *miſra.*

198. ‘ LET no man, having committed ſin,
‘ perform a penance under the pretext of auſtere
‘ devotion, diſguiſing his crime under fictitious
‘ religion, and deceiving both women and low
‘ men :

199. ‘ Such impoſtors, though *Bráhmens,* are
‘ deſpiſed in the next life, and in this, by all who
‘ pronounce holy texts ; and every religious act
‘ fraudulently performed goes to evil beings.

200. ‘ He, who has no right to diſtinguiſhing
‘ marks, yet gains a ſubſiſtence by wearing falſe
‘ marks of diſtinction, takes to himſelf the ſin
‘ committed by thoſe who are entitled to ſuch
‘ marks, and ſhall again be born from the womb
‘ of a brute animal.

201. ‘ NEVER let him bathe in the pool of
‘ another man ; for he who bathes in it *without*
‘ *licence,* takes to himſelf a ſmall portion of the
‘ ſins, which the maker of the pool has com-
‘ mitted.

202. ‘ He, who appropriates to his own uſe
‘ the carriage, the bed, the ſeat, the well, the
‘ garden, or the houſe of another man, who has
‘ not delivered them to him, aſſumes a fourth
‘ part of the guilt of their owner.

203. ‘ In rivers, in ponds dug by holy perſons,
‘ and in lakes, let him always bathe ; in rivulets
‘ alſo, and in torrents.

204. ‘ A WISE man ſhould conſtantly diſcharge
                                    ‘ all

' all the moral duties, though he perform not
' conſtantly the ceremonies of religion; ſince he
' falls low, if, while he performs ceremonial acts
' only, he diſcharge not his moral duties.

205. ' NEVER let a prieſt eat part of a ſacrifice
' not begun with texts of the *Véda*, nor of one
' performed by a common ſacrificer, by a woman
' or by an eunuch:

206. ' When thoſe perſons offer the clarified
' butter, it brings misfortune to good men, and
' raiſes averſion in the deities; ſuch *oblations*,
' therefore, he muſt carefully ſhun.

207. ' Let him never eat the food of the in-
' ſane, the wrathful, or the ſick; nor that, on
' which lice have fallen; nor that, which has
' deſignedly been touched by a foot;

208. ' Nor that, which has been looked at by
' the ſlayer of a prieſt, *or by any other deadly ſinner*,
' or has even been touched by a woman in her
' courſes, or pecked by a bird, or approached by
' a dog;

209. ' Nor food which has been ſmelled by a
' cow; nor particularly that which has been pro-
' claimed *for all comers*; nor the food of aſſociated
' knaves, or of harlots; nor that which is con-
' temned by the learned in ſcripture;

210. ' Nor that of a thief or a publick ſinger,'
' of a carpenter, of an uſurer, of one who has
' recently come from a ſacrifice, of a niggardly
' churl, or of one bound with fetters;

211. ' Of one publickly defamed, of an eunuch,
' of an unchaſte woman, or of a hypocrite; nor
' any ſweet thing turned acid, nor what has been
' kept a whole night; nor the food of a ſervile
' man, nor the orts of another;

I 2 212. Nor

212. ' Nor the food of a phyfician, or of a
' hunter, or of a difhoneft man, or of an eater
' of orts; nor that of any cruel perfon; nor of
' a woman in childbed; nor of him, who rifes
' prematurely from table to make an ablution;
' nor of her whofe ten days of purification have
' not elapfed;

213. ' Nor that, which is given without due
' honour to honourable men; nor any flefh
' which has not been facrificed; nor the food of
' a woman, who has neither a hufband nor a fon;
' nor that of a foe, nor that of the whole town,
' nor that of an outcaft, nor that on which any
' perfon has fneezed;

214. ' Nor that of a backbiter, or of a falfe
' witnefs; nor of one who fells the reward of his
' facrifice; nor of a publick dancer, or a tailor;
' nor of him who has returned evil for good;

215. ' Nor that of a blackfmith, or a man of
' the tribe called *Nifháda*, nor of a ftage-player,
' nor of a worker in gold or in cane, nor of him
' who fells weapons;

216. ' Nor of thofe who train hunting dogs,
' or fell fermented liquor; nor of him who
' wafhes clothes, or who dyes them; nor of
' any malevolent perfon; nor of one who ig-
' norantly fuffers an adulterer to dwell under his
' roof;

217. ' Nor of thofe who knowingly bear
' with the paramours of their own wives, or are
' conftantly in fubjection to women; nor food
' given for the dead before ten days of purification
' have paffed; nor any food whatever, but that
' which fatisfies him.

218. ' Food given by a king, impairs his
' manly

' manly vigour ; by one of the fervile clafs,' his
' divine light ; by goldfmiths, his life ; by leather-
' cutters, his good name :

219. ' Given by *cooks and the like* mean arti-
' zans, it deftroys his offspring ; by a wafher-
' man, his mufcular ftrength ; but the food
' of knavifh affociates and harlots excludes him
' from heaven :

220. ' The food of a phyfician is purulent;
' that of a libidinous woman, feminal ; that of
' an ufurer, feculent; that of a weapon-feller,
' filthy :

221. ' That of all others, mentioned in order,
' whofe food muft never be tafted, is held equal
' by the wife to the fkin, bones, and hair of the
' dead.

222. ' Having unknowingly fwallowed the
' food of any fuch perfons, he muft faft during
' three days ; but, having eaten it knowingly, he
' muft perform the fame harfh penance, as if he
' had tafted any feminal impurity, ordure, or
' urine.

223. ' Let no learned prieft eat the dreffed
' grain of a fervile man, who performs no pa-
' rental obfequies ; but having no other means, to
' live, he may take from him raw grain, enough
' for a fingle night.

224. ' The deities, having well confidered the
' food of a niggard, who has read the fcripture,
' and that of an ufurer, who beftows gifts li-
' berally, declared the food of both to be equal
' in quality ;

225. ' But BRAHMA', advancing towards the
' gods, thus addreffed them: " Make not that
' equal, which in truth is unequal ; fince the
' food of a liberal man is purified by faith, while

I 3   that

' that of a learned mifer is defiled by his want of
' faith in what he has read."

226. ' LET each *wealthy* man continually and
' feduloufly perform facred rites, and confecrate
' pools or gardens with faith; fince thofe two
' acts, accomplifhed with faith and with riches
' honeftly gained, procure an unperifhable re-
' ward:

227. ' If he meet with fit objects of bene-
' volence, let him conftantly beftow gifts on
' them, both at facrifices and confecrations, to
' the beft of his power and with a chearful heart;

228. ' Such a gift, how fmall foever, beftowed
' on requeft without grudging, paffes to a worthy
' object, who will fecure the giver from all evil.

229. ' A giver of water obtains content; a
' giver of food, extreme blifs; a giver of *tila*,
' defired offspring; a giver of a lamp, unble-
' mifhed eyefight;

230. ' A giver of land obtains landed pro-
' perty; a giver of gems or gold, long life; a
' giver of a houfe, the moft exalted manfion; a
' giver of filver, exquifite beauty;

231. ' A giver of clothes, the fame ftation
' with CHANDRA; a giver of a horfe, the fame
' ftation with ASWI; a giver of a bull, eminent
' fortune; a giver of a cow, the manfion of
' SU'RYA;

232. ' A giver of a carriage or a bed, an ex-
' cellent confort; a giver of fafety, fupreme do-
' minion; a giver of grain, perpetual delight;
' a giver of fcriptural knowledge, union with
' GOD:

233. ' Among all thofe gifts, of water, food,
' kine, land, clothes, *tila*, gold, clarified butter,
' and

' and the reft, a gift of fpiritual knowledge is
' confequently the moft important ;

234. ' And for whatever purpofe a man be-
' ftows any gift, for a fimilar purpofe he fhall
' receive, with due honour, a fimilar reward.

235. ' Both he, who refpectfully beftows a
' prefent, and he who refpectfully accepts it, fhall
' go to a feat of blifs; but, if they act otherwife,
' to a region of horror.

236. ' LET not a man be proud of his rigorous
' devotion ; let him not, having facrificed, utter
' a falfehood ; let him not, though injured, infult
' a prieft ; having made a donation, let him never
' proclaim it :

237. ' By falfehood, the facrifice becomes
' vain ; by pride, the merit of devotion is loft ;
' by infulting priefts, life is diminifhed ; and by
' proclaiming a largefs, its fruit is deftroyed.

238. ' GIVING no pain to any creature, let
' him collect virtue by degrees, for the fake of
' acquiring a companion to the next world, as the
' white ant by degrees builds his neft ;

239. ' For, in his paffage to the next world,
' neither his father, nor his mother, nor his wife,
' nor his fon, nor his kinfmen, will remain in
' his company : his virtue alone will adhere
' to him.

240. ' Single is each man born ; fingle he
' dies ; fingle he receives the reward of his good,
' and fingle the punifhment of his evil deeds :

241. ' When he leaves his corfe, like a log
' or a lump of clay, on the ground, his kindred
' retire with averted faces ; but his virtue ac-
' companies his foul.

242. ' Continually, therefore, by degrees, let
I 4   him

' him collect virtue, for the fake of fecuring an
' infeparable companion; fince with virtue for
' his guide, he will traverfe a gloom, how hard to
' be traverfed!

243. ' A man, habitually virtuous, whofe of-
' fences have been expiated by devotion, is in-
' ftantly conveyed after death to the higher world,
' with a radiant form and a body of ethereal
' fubftance.

244. ' He, who feeks to preferve an exalted
' rank, muft conftantly form connexions with the
' higheft and beft families, but avoid the worft
' and the meaneft;

245. ' Since a prieft, who connects himfelf
' with the beft and higheft of men, avoiding the
' loweft and worft, attains eminence; but finks,
' by an oppofite conduct, to the clafs of the fer-
' vile.

246. ' He, who perfeveres in good actions, in
' fubduing his paffions, in beftowing largeffes, in
' gentlenefs of manners, who bears hardfhips pa-
' tiently, who affociates not with the malignant,
' who gives pain to no fentient being, obtains
' final beatitude.

247. ' Wood, water, roots, fruit, and food
' placed before him without his requeft, he may
' accept from all men; honey alfo, and protec-
' tion from danger.

248. ' Gold, or other alms, voluntary brought
' and prefented, but unafked and unpromifed,
' Brahma' confidered as receivable even from a
' finner:

249. ' Of him, who fhall difdain to accept
' fuch alms, neither will the manes eat the funeral
' oblations for fifteen years, nor will the fire convey
' the burnt facrifice to the gods.

250. ' A

250. ' A bed, houfes, blades of *cus'a*, perfumes,
' water, flowers, jewels, butter-milk, ground rice,
' fifh, new milk, flefh meat, and green vegetables,
' let him not proudly reject.

251. ' When he wifhes to relieve his natural
' parents or fpiritual father, his wife or others,
' whom he is bound to maintain, or when he is
' preparing to honour deities or guefts, he may
' receive gifts from any perfon, but muft not
' gratify himfelf with fuch prefents :

252. ' If his parents, however, be dead, or if
' he live without them in his own houfe, let him,
' when he feeks nourifhment for himfelf, receive
' prefents invariably from good men alone.

253. ' A labourer in tillage, a family friend, a
' herdfman, a flave, a barber, a poor ftranger of-
' fering his humble duty, are men of the fervile
' clafs, who may eat the food of their fuperiours :

254. ' As the nature of the poor ftranger is,
' as the work is, which he defires to perform, and
' as he may fhow moft refpect *to the mafter of the
' houfe*, even thus let him offer his fervice ;

255. ' For he, who defcribes himfelf to wor-
' thy men, in a manner contrary to truth, is the
' moft finful wretch in this world : he is the worft
' of thieves, a ftealer of minds.

256. ' All things have their fenfe afcertained
' by fpeech ; in fpeech they have their bafis ; and
' from fpeech they proceed : confequently, a falfi-
' fier of fpeech falfifies every thing.

257. ' WHEN he has paid, as the law directs,
' his debts to the fages, to the manes, and to the
' gods, *by reading the fcripture, begetting a fon,
' and performing regular facrifices*, he may refign
' all to his fon *of mature age*, and refide in his
' family,

' family houfe, with no employment, but that of an
' umpire.

258. ' Alone, in fome folitary place, let him
' conftantly meditate on the divine nature of the
' foul, for by fuch meditation he will attain
' happinefs.

259. ' Thus has been declared the mode, by
' which a *Bráhmen*, who keeps houfe, muft con-
' tinually fubfift, together with the rule of de-
' votion ordained for a pupil returned from his
' preceptor ; a laudable rule, which increafes the
' beft of *the three* qualities.

260. ' A prieft, who lives always by thefe
' rules, who knows the ordinances of the *Véda*,
' who is freed from the bondage of fin, fhall be
' abforbed in the divine effence.

CHAPTER THE FIFTH.

On Diet, Purification, and Women.

————

1. THE fages, having heard thofe laws delivered for the conduct of houfe-keepers, thus
addreffed the high-minded BHRĬGU, who proceeded, *in a former birth,* from the genius of fire.

2. ' How, Lord, can death prevail over *Bráh-*
' *mens,* who know the fcriptural ordinances, and
' perform their duties as they have been declared ?'

3. Then he, whofe difpofition was perfect
virtue, even BHRĬGU, the fon of MENU, thus
anfwered the great *Rĭfhis.* ' Hear from what
' fin proceeds the inclination of death, to deftroy
' the chief of the twice born :

4. ' Through a neglect of reading the *Véda,*
' through a defertion of approved ufages, through
' fupine remiffnefs *in performing holy rites,* and
' through various offences in diet, *the genius of*
' death becomes eager to deftroy them.

5. ' Garlick, onions, leeks, and mufhrooms,
' (which no twice born man muft eat) and all ve-
' getables raifed in dung.

6. ' Red gums or refins, exuding from trees,
' and juices from wounded ftems, the fruit *félu,*
' and the thickened milk of a cow within ten days
' after her calving, a prieft muft avoid with great
' care.

7. ' Rice

7. ' Rice pudding boiled with *tila*, frumenty,
' rice-milk, and baked bread, which have not
' been firft offered to fome deity, flefh meat alfo,
' the food of gods, and clarified butter, which
' have not firft been touched, while holy texts
' were recited,

8. ' Frefh milk from a cow, whofe ten days are
' not paffed, the milk of a camel, or any qua-
' druped with a hoof not cloven, that of an ewe,
' and that of a cow in heat, or whofe calf is dead
' or abfent from her,

9. ' That of any foreft beaft, except the buffalo,
' the milk of a woman, and any thing naturally
' fweet but acidulated, muft all be carefully
' fhunned :

10. ' But among fuch acids, butter-milk may
' be fwallowed, and every preparation of butter-
' milk, and all acids extracted from pure flowers,
' roots, or fruit *not cut with iron.*

11. ' Let every twice born man avoid carnivo-
' rous birds, and fuch as live in towns, and qua-
' drupeds with uncloven hoofs, except thofe al-
' lowed by the *Véda,* and the bird called *tittibha*;

12. ' The fparrow, the water bird *plava,* the
' phenicopteros, the *chacraváca,* the breed of the
' town cock, the *fárafa,* the *rajjuvála,* the wood-
' pecker, and the parot male and female;

13. ' Birds, that ftrike with their beaks, web-
' footed birds, the *côyafhti,* thofe who wound
' with ftrong talons, and thofe who dive to devour
' fifh ; let him avoid meat kept at a flaughter-
' houfe, and dried meat,

14. ' The heron, the raven, the *c'hanjana,* all
' amphibious fifh eaters, tame hogs, and fifh of
' every fort, *but thofe exprefsly permitted.*

15. ' He,

15. ' He, who eats the flesh of any animal,
' is called the eater of that animal itself; and a
' fish eater is an eater of all flesh; from fish,
' therefore, he must diligently abstain :

16. ' Yet the two fish called *pát'hina* and *róhita*,
' may be eaten *by the guests*, when offered at a re-
' past in honour of the gods or the manes ; and so
' may the *rájíva*, the *sinhatunda*, and the *fasalka*
' of every species.

17. ' Let him not eat the flesh of any solitary
' animals, nor of unknown beasts or birds, though
' by general words declared eatable, nor of any
' creature with five claws ;

18. ' The hedgehog and porcupine, the lizard
' *gódhá*, the *gandaca*, the tortoise, and the rabbit
' *or hare*, wise legislators declare lawful food
' among five toed animals ; and all quadrupeds,
' camels excepted, which have but one row of
' teeth.

19. ' The twice born man, who has intention-
' ally eaten a mushroom, the flesh of a tame hog,
' or a town cock, a leek, or an onion, or garlick,
' is degraded immediately ;

20. ' But having undesignedly tasted either of
' those six things, he must perform the penance
' *fántapana*, or the *chándráyana*, which anchorets,
' practise ; for other things he must fast a whole
' day.

21. ' One of those harsh penances, called *prá-*
' *jápatya*, the twice born man must perform an-
' nually, to purify him from the unknown taint of
' illicit food ; but he must do particular penance
' for such food intentionally eaten.

22. ' BEASTS and birds of excellent sorts may
' be slain by *Bráhmens* for sacrifice, or for the
' sustenance

‘ fuſtenance of thoſe, whom they are bound to
‘ ſupport ; ſince AGASTYA did this of old.

23. ‘ No doubt in the primeval ſacrifices by
‘ holy men, and in oblations by thoſe of the
‘ prieſtly and military tribes, the fleſh of ſuch
‘ beaſts and birds, as may be legally eaten, was
‘ preſented to the deities.

24. ‘ That which may be eaten or drunk *when
‘ freſh*, without blame, may be ſwallowed, if
‘ touched with oil, though it has been kept a
‘ whole night ; and ſo may the remains of clari-
‘ fied butter :

25. ‘ And every meſs prepared with barley or
‘ wheat, or with dreſſed milk, may be eaten by
‘ the twice born, although not ſprinkled with oil.

26. ‘ Thus has the food, allowed or forbidden
‘ to a twice born man, been comprehenſively men-
‘ tioned : I will now propound the *ſpecial* rules
‘ for eating and for avoiding fleſh meat.

27. ‘ He ſhould taſte meat, which has been
‘ hallowed for a ſacrifice with appropriated texts,
‘ and *once only*, when a prieſt ſhall deſire him, and
‘ when he is performing a legal act, or in danger
‘ of loſing life.

28. ‘ For the ſuſtenance of the vital ſpirit,
‘ BRAHMA' created all this *animal and vegetable
‘ ſyſtem* ; and all that is moveable or immoveable,
‘ that ſpirit devours.

29. ‘ Things fixed are eaten by creatures with
‘ locomotion ; toothleſs animals, by animals with
‘ teeth ; thoſe without hands, by thoſe to whom
‘ hands were given ; and the timid by the bold.

30. ‘ He, who eats *according to law*, commits
‘ no ſin, even though every day he taſtes the fleſh
‘ of ſuch animals, as may lawfully be taſted ;
‘ ſince both animals, who may be eaten, and thoſe
‘ who eat them, were equally created by BRAHMA'.

31. ‘ It

31. ' It is delivered as a rule of the gods, that
' meat must be swallowed only for the purpose
' of sacrifice; but it is a rule of gigantick de-
' mons, that it may be swallowed for any other
' purpose.

32. ' No sin is committed by him, who having
' honoured the deities and the manes, eats flesh
' meat, which he has bought, or which he has
' himself acquired, or which has been given him
' by another :

33. ' Let no twice born man, who knows the
' law, and is not in urgent distress, eat flesh with-
' out observing this rule ; for he, unable to save
' himself, will be devoured in the next world by
' those animals, whose flesh he has thus illegally
' swallowed.

34. ' The sin of him, who kills deer for gain,
' is not so heinous, with respect to *the punishment*
' *in* another life, as that of him, who eats flesh
' meat in vain, *or not previously offered as a sa-*
' *crifice :*

35. ' But the man, who, engaged *in holy rites*
' according to law, refuses to eat it, shall sink in
' another world, for twenty-one births, to the
' state of a beast.

36. ' Never let a priest eat the flesh of cattle
' unhallowed with *mantras,* but let him eat it,
' observing the primeval rule, when it has been
' hallowed with those texts of the *Véda.*

37. ' Should he have an earnest desire to taste
' flesh meat, he may gratify his fancy by forming
' the image of some beast with clarified butter
' thickened, or he may form it with dough, but
' never let him indulge a wish to kill any beast
' in vain :

38. ' As many hairs as grow on the beast, so
' many

ı

' many similar deaths shall the slayer of it, for
' his own satisfaction in this world, endure in the
' next from birth to birth.

39. ' By the self-existing in person were beasts
' created for sacrifice; and the sacrifice *was or-*
' *dained* for the increase of this universe: the
' slaughterer therefore of beasts for sacrifice is in
' truth no slaughterer.

40. ' Gramineous plants, cattle, timber-trees,
' amphibious animals, and birds, which have been
' destroyed for the purpose of sacrifice, attain in
' the next world exalted births.

41. ' On a solemn offering to a guest, at a
' sacrifice and in holy rites to the manes or to the
' gods, but on those occasions only, may cattle be
' slain: this law MENU enacted.

42. ' The twice born man, who knowing the
' meaning and principles of the *Véda*, slays cattle
' on the occasions mentioned, conveys both him-
' self and those cattle to the summit of beatitude.

43. ' Let no twice born man, whose mind is
' improved by learning, hurt animals without the
' sanction of scripture, even though in pressing
' distress, whether he live in his own house, or in
' that of his preceptor, or in a forest.

44. ' That hurt, which the scripture ordains,
' and which is done in this world of moveable and
' immoveable creatures, he must consider as no
' hurt at all; since law shone forth from *the light*
' *of* the scripture.

45. ' He, who injures animals, that are not
' injurious, from a wish to give himself pleasure,
' adds nothing to his own happiness, living or
' dead;

46. ' While he, who gives no creature willingly
' the pain of confinement or death, but seeks
                                            the

' the good of all *sentient beings* enjoys blifs without
' end.

47. ' He, who injures no animated creature,
' fhall attain without hardfhip whatever he thinks
' of, whatever he ftrives for, whatever he fixes
' his mind on.

48. ' Flefh meat cannot be procured without
' injury to animals, and the flaughter of animals
' obftruĉts the path to beatitude; from flefh meat,
' therefore, let man abftain :

49. ' Attentively confidering the formation of
' bodies, and the death or confinement of im-
' bodied fpirits, let him abftain from eating flefh
' meat of any kind.

50. ' The man who forfakes not the law, and
' eats not flefh meat, like a blood thirfty demon,
' fhall attain good will in this world, and fhall not
' be afflicted with maladies.

51. ' He, who confents to the death of an
' animal; he, who kills it; he, who diffects it;
' he, who buys it; he, who fells it; he, who
' dreffes it; he, who ferves it up; and he, who
' makes it his food; thefe are eight principals in
' the flaughter.

52. ' Not a mortal exifts more finful than he,
' who without an oblation to the manes or the
' gods, defires to enlarge his own flefh with the
' flefh of another creature.

53. ' The man, who performs annually, for a
' hundred years, an *afwamédha*, or *facrifice of a*
' *horfe*, and the man who abftains from flefh meat,
' enjoy for their virtue an equal reward.

54. ' By fubfifting on pure fruit and on roots,
' and by eating fuch grains as are eaten by her-
' mits, a man reaps not fo high a reward, as by
' carefully abftaining from animal food.

K   55. " Me

55. " Me he (*mân ſa*) will devour in the next
' world, whoſe fleſh I eat in this life :" *thus ſhould*
' *a fleſh eater ſpeak, and* thus the learned pro-
' nounce the true derivation of the word *mânſa,*
' or fleſh.

56. ' In lawfully taſting meat, in drinking
' fermented liquor, in careſſing women, there is
' no turpitude ; for to ſuch enjoyments men are
' naturally prone ; but a virtuous abſtinence from
' them produces a ſignal compenſation.

57. ' Now will I promulgate the rules of
' purification for the dead, and the modes of puri-
' fying inanimate things, as the law preſcribes
' them for the four claſſes in due order.

58. ' When a child has teethed, and when,
' after teething, his head has been ſhorn, and
' when he has been girt with his thread, and
' when, being full grown, he dies, all his kindred
' are impure : on the birth of a child the law is
' the ſame.

59. ' By a dead body, the *ſapindas* are rendered
' impure in law for ten days, or until *the fourth*
' *day, when* the bones have been gathered up, or
' for three days, or for one day only, *according to*
' *the qualities of the deceaſed :*

60. ' Now the relation of the *ſapindas,* or men
' connected by the funeral cake, ceaſes with the
' ſeventh perſon, *or in the ſixth degree of aſcent or*
' *deſcent,* and that of *ſamânôdacas,* or thoſe con-
' nected by an equal oblation of water, ends only,
' when their births and family names are no longer
' known.

61. ' As this impurity, by reaſon of a dead
' kinſman, is ordained for *ſapindas,* even thus it is
' ordained on a child-birth, for thoſe who ſeek
' abſolute purity.

62. ' Un-

62. ' Uncleanness, on account of the dead, is
' ordained for all;. but on the birth of a child,
' for the mother and father: impurity, for ten
' days after the child-birth, affects the mother
' only; but the father, having bathed, becomes
' pure.

63. ' A man, having wasted his manhood, is
' purified by bathing; but after begetting a child
' on a *parapúrvá*, he must meditate for three days
' on his impure state.

64. ' In one day and night, added to nights
' three times three, the *sapindas* are purified after
' touching the corpse; but the *samánódacas* in three
' days.

65. ' A pupil in theology, having performed
' the ceremony of burning his deceased preceptor,
' becomes pure in ten nights: he is equal, in that
' case, to the *sapindas*, who carry out the dead.

66. ' In a number of nights, equal to the
' number of months from conception, a woman
' is purified on a miscarriage; and a woman in
' her courses is rendered pure by bathing, when
' her effusion of blood has quite stopped.

67. ' For deceased male children, whose heads
' have not been shorn, purity is legally obtained
' in one night; but for those, on whom that ce-
' remony has been performed, a purification of
' three nights is required.

68. ' A dead child under the age of two years,
' let his kinsmen carry out, having decked him
' *with flowers, and bury him* in pure ground, with-
' out collecting his bones *at a future time*:

69. ' Let no ceremony with fire be performed
' for him, nor that of sprinkling water; but his
' kindred, having left him like a piece of wood
' in the forest, shall be unclean for three days.

K 2　　　　　　　70. ' For

70. ' For a child under the age of three years,
' the ceremony with water fhall not be performed
' by his kindred; but if his teeth be completely
' grown, or a name have been given him, they
' may perform it, or not, *at their option.*

71. ' A fellow ftudent in theology being dead,
' three days of impurity are ordained; and on
' the birth of a *famánódaca,* purification is required
' for three nights.

72. ' The relations of *betrothed but* unmarried
' damfels, are in three days made pure; and, in
' as many, are their paternal kinfmen purified
' *after their marriage :*

73. ' Let them eat vegetable food without
' factitious, *that is, only with native* falt; let them
' bathe for three days at intervals; let them tafte
' no flefh meat; and let them fleep apart on the
' ground.

74. ' This rule, which ordains impurity by rea-
' fon of the dead, relates to the cafe of one dying
' near his kinfmen; but, in the cafe of one dying
' at a diftance, the following rule muft be ob-
' ferved by thofe who fhare the fame cake, and
' by thofe who fhare only the fame water :

75. ' The man, who hears that a kinfman is
' dead in a diftant country, becomes unclean, if
' ten days after the death have not paffed, for the
' remainder of thofe ten days only ;

76. ' But if the ten days have elapfed, he is
' impure for three nights, and, if a year have
' expired, he is purified merely by touching water.

77. ' If, after the lapfe of ten days, he know
' the death of a kinfman, or the birth of a male
' child, he muft purify himfelf by bathing together
' with his clothes.

78. ' Should a child, whofe teeth are not
grown,

' grown, or should a *samánódaca* die in a distant
' region, the kinsman, having bathed with his
' apparel, becomes immediately pure.

79. ' If, during the ten days, another death or
' another birth intervene, a *Bráhmen* remains im-
' pure only till those ten days have elapsed.

80 ' A spiritual teacher being dead, the sages
' dec are his pupil impure for three days; but for
' a day and a night, if the son or wife of the
' teacher be deceased; such is the sacred ordi-
' nance.

81. ' For a reader of the whole *Véda*, who
' dwells in the same house, a man is unclean three
' nights; but for a maternal uncle, a pupil, an
' officiating priest, and a distant kinsman, only
' one night winged *with two days*.

82. ' On the death of a military king, in whose
' dominion he lives, *his impurity lasts* while the
' sun or the stars give light; but *it lasts* a whole
' day, on the death of a priest who has not read
' the whole *Véda*, or of a spiritual guide, who has
' read only part of it, with its *Angas*.

83. ' A man of the sacerdotal class becomes
' pure in ten days; of the warlike, in twelve;
' of the commercial, in five; of the servile, in
' a month.

84. ' Let no man prolong the days of impurity;
' let him not intermit the ceremonies to be per-
' formed with holy fires; while he performs those
' rites, even though he be a *sapinda*, he is not
' impure.

85. ' He, who has touched a *Chandála*, a wo-
' man in her courses, an outcast for deadly sin, a
' new born child, a corpse, or one who has touch-
' ed a corpse, is made pure by bathing.

86. ' If,

86. ' If, having fprinkled his mouth with
' water, and been long intent on his devotion, he
' fee an unclean perfon, let him repeat, as well as
' he is able, the folar texts of the *Véda*, and thofe
' which confer purity.

87. ' Should a *Bráhmen* touch a human bone
' moift with oil, he is purified by bathing; if it
' be not oily, by ftroking a cow, or by looking at
' the fun, having fprinkled his mouth duly with
' water.

88. ' A ftudent in theology. fhall not perform
' the ceremony of pouring water at obfequies, un-
' til he have completed his courfe of religious acts;
' but if, after the completion of them, he thus
' make an offering of water, he becomes pure in
' three nights.

89. ' For thofe, who difcharge not their pre-
' fcribed duties ; for thofe, whofe fathers were of
' a lower clafs than their mothers ; for thofe,
' who wear a drefs of religion unauthorized by the
' *Véda*; and for thofe, who *illegally* kill themfelves,
' the ceremony of giving funeral water is forbid-
' den by law ; .

90. ' And for women imitating fuch hereticks,
' as wear an unlawful drefs, and for fuch women
' as live at their own pleafure, or have caufed an
' abortion, or have ftricken their hufbands, or
' have drunk any fpirituous liquor.

91. ' A ftudent violates not the rules of his or-
' der, by carrying out, when dead, his own in ·
' ftructor in the *Védas*, who invefted him with his
' holy cord, or his teacher of particular chapters,
' or his reverend expounder of their meaning, or
' his father, or his mother.

92. ' Let men carry out a dead *Súdra* by the
' fouthern gate of the town ; but the twice born,
' in

‘ in due order, by the weftern, northern, and
‘ eaftern gates.

93. ‘ No taint of impurity can light on kings
‘ or ftudents in theology, *while employed in dif-*
‘ *charging their feveral duties,* nor on thofe who
‘ have actually begun a facrifice ; for the firft are
‘ then placed on the feat of INDRA, and the others
‘ are always equally pure with the celeftial fpirit.

94. ‘ To a king, on the throne of magnanimity,
‘ the law afcribes inftant purification, becaufe his
‘ throne was raifed for the protection of his peo-
‘ ple and the fupply of their nourifhment :

95. ‘ It is the fame with *the kinfmen of* thofe
‘ who die in battle, after the king has been flain,
‘ or have been killed by lightning, or legally by
‘ the king himfelf, or in defence of a cow, or of a
‘ prieft ; and with all thofe whom the king
‘ wifhes to be pure.

96. ‘ The corporeal frame of a king is com-
‘ pofed of particles from *Sóma,* AGNI, SÚRYA,
‘ PAVANA, INDRA, CUVE'RA, VARUNA, and
‘ YAMA, the eight guardian deities of the world :

97. ‘ By thofe guardians of men in fubftance is
‘ the king pervaded, and he cannot by law be
‘ impure ; fince by thofe tutelar gods are the
‘ purity and impurity of mortals both caufed and
‘ removed.

98. ‘ By a foldier difcharging the duties of his
‘ clafs, and flain in the field with brandifhed wea-
‘ pons, the higheft facrifice is, in that inftant,
‘ complete ; and fo is his purification : this law
‘ is fixed.

99. ‘ A prieft having performed funeral rites,
‘ is purified by touching water ; a foldier, by
‘ touching his horfe or elephant, or his arms ;
‘ a hufbandman, by touching his goad, or the hal-

‘ ter

' ter of his cattle; a fervant, by touching his
' ftaff.

100. ' This mode of purifying *fapindas*, O chief
' of the twice born, has been fully declared to
' you! learn now the purification required on the
' death of kinfmen lefs intimately connected.

101. ' A *Bráhmen*, having caried out a dead
' *Bráhmen*, though not a *fapinda*, with the affection
' of a kinfman, or any of thofe nearly related to
' him by his mother, becomes pure in three
' days;

102. ' But, if he tafte the food offered by their
' *fapindas*, he is purified in ten days; and in one
' day, if he neither partake of their food, nor dwell
' in the fame houfe.

103. ' If he voluntarily follow a corpfe, whe-
' ther of a paternal kinfman or of another, and
' afterwards bathe with his apparel, he is made
' pure by touching fire and tafting clarified
' butter.

104. ' Let no kinfman, whilft any of his own
' clafs are at hand, caufe a deceafed *Bráhmen* to be
' carried out by a *Súdra*; fince the funeral rite,
' polluted by the touch of a fervile man, obftructs
' his paffage to heaven.

105. ' Sacred learning, auftere devotion, fire,
' holy aliment, earth, the mind, water, fmearing
' with cow-dung, air, prefcribed acts of religion,
' the fun, and time, are purifiers of imbodied
' fpirits;

106. ' But of all pure things, purity in acquir-
' ing wealth is pronounced the moft excellent:
' fince he, who gains wealth with clean hands, is
' truly pure; not he, who is purified merely with
' earth and water.

107. ' By

107. ' By forgiveneſs of injuries, the learned
' are purified ; by liberality, thoſe who have neg-
' lected their duty ; by pious meditation, thoſe
' who have ſecret faults ; by devout auſterity,
' thoſe who beſt know the *Véda.*

108. ' By water and earth is purified what
' ought to be made pure ; a river, by its current ;
' a woman, whoſe thoughts have been impure, by
' her monthly diſcharge, and the chief of twice
' born men, by fixing his mind wholly on God.

109. ' Bodies are cleanſed by water ; the mind
' is purified by truth ; the vital ſpirit, by theology
' and devotion ; the underſtanding, by clear
' knowledge.

110. ' Thus have you heard me declare the
' preciſe rules for purifying animal bodies : hear
' now the modes of reſtoring purity to various
' inanimate things.

111. ' Of brilliant metals, of gems, and of every
' thing made with ſtone, the purification, ordained
' by the wiſe, is with aſhes, water, and earth.

112. ' A golden veſſel, not ſmeared, is cleanſed
' with water only ; and every thing produced in
' water, *as coral,* *ſhells or pearls,* and every ſtony
' ſubſtance, and a ſilver veſſel not enchaſed. -

113. ' From a junction of water and fire aroſe
' gold and ſilver ; and they two, therefore, are beſt
' purified by the elements whence they ſprang.

114. '. Veſſels of copper, iron, braſs, pewter,
' tin and lead, may be fitly cleanſed with aſhes,
' with acids, or with water.

115. ' The purification ordained for all ſorts of
' liquids, is by ſtirring them with *cuſa*-graſs ; for
' cloths folded, by ſprinkling them with hallowed
' water ; for wooden utenſils, by planeing them.

116. ' For

116. ' For the facrificial pots to hold clarified
' butter and juice of the moon plant, by rubbing
' them with the hand, and wafhing them, at
' the time of the facrifice :

117. ' Implements to wafh the rice, to contain,
' the oblations, to caft them into the fire, to col-
' lect, winnow, and prepare the grain, muft be
' purified with water made hot.

118. ' The purification by fprinkling is or-
' dained for grain and cloths in large quantities;
' but to purify them in fmall parcels, *which a
' man may eafily carry*, they muft be wafhed.

119. ' Leathern utenfils, and fuch as are m de
' with cane, muft generally be purified in the fame
' manner with cloths; green vegetables, roots,
' and fruit, in the fame manner with grain;

120. ' Silk and woollen ftuff, with faline earths;
' blankets from *Népála* with pounded *arifhtas*, or
' *nimba* fruit ; vefts and long drawers, with the
' fruit of the *Bilva* ; mantles of *cfhumá*, with white
' muftard feeds.

121. ' Utenfils made of fhells or horn, of bones
' or of ivory, muft be cleanfed by him who
' knows the law, as mantles of *cfhumá* are puri-
' fied, with the addition of cows urine or of water.

122. ' Grafs, firewood, and ftraw, are purified
' by fprinkling them with water; a houfe, by
' rubbing, brufhing, and fmearing with cow-dung;
' an earthen pot, by a fecond burning :

123. ' But an earthen pot, which has been
' touched with any fpirituous liquor, with urine,
' with ordure, with fpittle, with pus, or with
' blood, cannot, even by another burning, be ren-
' dered pure.

124. ' Land is cleanfed by five modes; by
                                    ' fweeping

' fweeping, by fmearing with cow-dung, by fprink-
' ling with cow's urine, by fcraping, or by letting
' a cow pafs a day and a night on it.

125. ' A thing nibbled by a bird, fmelt at by
' a cow, fhaken with a foot, fneezed on, or defiled
' by lice, is purified by earth fcattered over it.

126. ' As long as the fcent or moifture, caufed
' by any impurity, remain on the thing foiled, fo
' long muft earth and water be repeatedly ufed in
' all purifications of things inanimate.

127. ' The gods declared three pure things
' peculiar to *Bráhmens* ; what has been defiled
' without their knowledge, what, in cafes of doubt,
' they fprinkle with water; and what they com-
' mend with their fpeech.

128. ' Waters are pure, as far as a cow goes to
' quench her thirft in them, if they flow over
' clean earth, and are fullied by no impurity, but
' have a good fcent, colour, and tafte,

129. ' The hand of an artift, *employed in his art*,
' is always pure ; fo is every vendible commodity,
' when expofed to fale ; and that food is always
' clean, which a ftudent in theology has begged
' and received : fuch is the facred rule.

130. ' The mouth of a woman is conftantly
' pure ; a bird is pure on the fall of fruit, which
' he has pecked; a fucking animal, on the flowing
' of the milk ; a dog, on his catching the deer : .

131. ' The flefh of a wild beaft flain by dogs,
' MENU pronounces pure ; and that of an animal
' flain by other carnivorous creatures, or by men
' of the mixed clafs, who fubfift by hunting.

132. ' All the cavities above the navel are pure,
' and all below it, unclean ; fo are all excretions
' that fall from the body.

I ' 133. ' Gnats

· 133. ' Gnats, clear drops from the mouth of a
' speaker, a shadow, a cow, a horse, sun-beams,
' dust, earth, air and fire, must all be considered
' as clean, even when they touch an unclean
' thing.

134. ' For the cleansing of vessels, which have
' held ordure or urine, earth and water must be
' used, as long as they are needful; and the same
' for cleansing the twelve corporeal impurities :

135. ' Oily exudations, seminal fluids, blood,
' dandruff, urine, feces, ear-wax, nail-parings,
' phlegm, tears, concretions on the eyes, and
' sweat, are the twelve impurities of the human
' frame.

136. ' By the man who desires purity, one piece
' of earth, *together with water*, must be used for the
' conduit of urine, three for that of the feces; so,
' ten for one hand, *that is, the left*; then seven for
' both : *but if necessary, more must be used.*

137. ' Such is the purification of married men;
' that of students must be double; that of hermits,
' triple; that of men wholly recluse, quadruple.

138. ' Let each man sprinkle the cavities of his
' body, and taste water in due form, when he has
' discharged urine or feces; when he is going to
' read the *Véda*; and, invariably, before he takes
' his food :

139. ' First, let him thrice taste water; then,
' twice let him wipe his mouth, if he *be of a*
' *twice born class, and* desire corporeal purity ; but
' a woman or servile man may once respectively
' make that ablution.

140. ' *Súdras*, engaged in religious duties,
' must perform each month the ceremony of
' shaving their heads; their food must be the
' orts

' orts of *Bráhmens*; and their mode of purifica-
' tion, the fame with that of a *Vaifya*.

141. ' Such drops of water, as fall from the
' mouth or any part of the body, render it not
' unclean; nor hairs of the beard that enter the
' mouth; nor what adheres awhile to the teeth.

142. ' Drops, which trickle on the feet of a
' man holding water for others, are held equal to
' waters flowing over pure earth: by them he is
' not defiled.

143. ' He, who carries in any manner an in-
' animate burden, and is touched by any thing
' impure, is cleanfed by making an ablution,
' without laying his burden down.

144. ' Having vomited, or been purged, let
' him bathe and tafte clarified butter, but, if he
' have eaten already, let him only perform an ab-
' lution: for him, who has been connected with
' a woman, bathing is ordained by law.

145. ' Having flumbered, having fneezed, hav-
' ing eaten, having fpitten, having told untruths,
' having drunk water, and going to read facred
' books, let him, though pure, wafh his mouth.

146. ' This perfect fyftem of rules for purify-
' ing men of all claffes, and for cleanfing inani-
' mate things, has been declared to you: hear
' now the laws concerning women.

147. ' By a girl, or by a young woman, or
' by a woman advanced in years, nothing muft
' be done, even in her own dwelling place, ac-
' cording to her mere pleafure:

148. ' In childhood muft a female be depen-
' dent on her father; in youth, on her hufband;
' her lord being dead, on her fons; *if fhe have no*
' *fons, on the near kinfmen of her hufband; if he*
                                        ' *left*

' *left no kinſmen, on thoſe of her father* ; *if ſhe have*
' *no paternal kinſmen, on the ſovereign* : a woman
' muſt never ſeek independence.

149. ' Never let her wiſh to ſeparate herſelf
' from her father, her huſband, or her ſons ; for,
' by a ſeparation from them, ſhe expoſes both
' families to contempt.

150. ' She muſt always live with a cheerful
' temper, with good management in the affairs
' of the houſe, with great care of the houſehold
' furniture, and with a frugal hand in all her
' expences.

151. ' Him, to whom her father has given
' her, or her brother with the paternal aſſent, let
' her obſequiouſly honour, while he lives ; and,
' when he dies, let her never neglect him.

152. ' The recitation of holy texts, and the
' ſacrifice ordained by the lord of creatures, are
' uſed in marriages for the ſake of procuring
' good fortune to brides ; but the firſt gift, *or*
' *troth plighted* by the huſband, is the primary
' cauſe *and origin* of marital dominion.

153. ' When the huſband has performed the
' nuptial rites with texts from the *Véda*, he gives
' bliſs continually to his wife here below, both in
' ſeaſon and out of ſeaſon ; and he will give her
' happineſs in the next world.

154. ' Though inobſervant of approved uſages,
' or enamoured of another woman, or devoid of
' good qualities, yet a huſband muſt conſtantly
' be revered as a god by a virtuous wife.

155. ' No ſacrifice is allowed to women apart
' from their huſbands, no religious rite, no faſt-
' ing : as far only as a wife honours her lord, ſo
' far ſhe is exalted in heaven.

156. ' A

156. ' A faithful wife, who wishes to attain
' in heaven the mansion of her husband, must do
' nothing unkind to him, be he living or dead:

157. ' Let her emaciate her body, by living
' voluntarily on pure flowers, roots, and fruit;
' but let her not, when her lord is deceased, even
' pronounce the name of another man.

158. ' Let her continue till death forgiving all
' injuries, performing harsh duties, avoiding every
' sensual pleasure, and cheerfully practising the
' incomparable rules of virtue, which have been
' followed by such women, as were devoted to
' one only husband.

159. ' Many thousands of *Bráhmens*, having
' avoided sensuality from their early youth, and
' having left no issue in their families, have as-
' cended, *neverthelefs*, to heaven;

160. ' And, like those abstemious men, a vir-
' tuous wife ascends to heaven, though she have
' no child, if, after the decease of her lord, she
' devote herself to pious austerity:

161. ' But a widow, who, from a wish to bear
' children, slights her deceased husband *by marry-*
' *ing again*, brings disgrace on herself here below,
' and shall be excluded from the seat of her lord.

162. ' Issue, begotten on a woman by any
' other *than her husband*, is here declared to be
' no progeny of hers; no more than a child,
' begotten on the wife of another man, *belongs to*
' *the begetter:* nor is a second husband allowed,
' in any part of this code, to a virtuous woman.

163. ' She, who neglects her former (*púrva*)
' lord, though of a lower class, and takes another
' (*para*) of a higher, becomes despicable in this
' world, and is called *parapúrvá*, or *one who had*
' *a different husband before.*

164. ' A

164. ' A married woman, who violates the
' duty which she owes to her lord, brings infamy
' on herself in this life, and, *in the next*, shall enter
' the womb of a shakal, or be afflicted with *ele-*
' *phantiasis, and other* diseases, which punish crimes;

165. ' While she, who slights not her lord,
' but keeps her mind, speech, and body, devoted
' to him, attains his heavenly mansion, and by
' good men is called *sádhvi*, or *virtuous*.

166. ' Yes; by this course of life it is, that a
' woman, whose mind, speech, and body are
' kept in subjection, acquires high renown in this
' world, and, in the next, the same abode with
' her husband.

167. ' A twice born man, versed in sacred
' ordinances, must burn with hallowed fire and fit
' implements of sacrifice, his wife dying before
' him, if she was of his own class, and lived by
' these rules:

168. ' Having thus kindled sacred fires and
' performed funeral rites to his wife, who died
' before him, he may again marry, and again
' light the nuptial fire.

169. ' Let him not cease to perform day by
' day, according to the preceding rules, the five
' great sacraments; and having taken a lawful
' consort, let him dwell in his house during the
' second period of his life.

CHAPTER THE SIXTH.

On Devotion ; or on the Third and Fourth Orders.

———

1. ' HAVING thus remained in the order of a
' houſe-keeper, as the law ordains, let the twice
' born man, who had before completed his ſtu-
' dentſhip, dwell in a foreſt, his faith being firm
' and his organs wholly ſubdued.

2. ' When the father of a family, perceives his
' muſcles become flaccid and his hair gray, and
' ſees the child of his child, let him then ſeek
' refuge in a foreſt :

3. ' Abandoning all food eaten in towns, and all
' his houſehold utenſils, let him repair to the
' lonely wood, committing the care of his wife to
' her ſons, or accompanied by her, *if ſhe chuſe to*
' *attend him.*

4. ' Let him take up his conſecrated fire, and
' all his domeſtick implements of making oblations
' to it, and, departing from the town to the foreſt,
' let him dwell in it with complete power over his
' organs *of ſenſe and of aƈtion.*

5. ' With many ſorts of pure food, ſuch as holy
' ſages uſed to eat, with green herbs, roots, and

L   ' fruit,

' fruit, let him perform the five great facraments
' before mentioned, introducing them with due
' ceremonies.

6. ' Let him wear a black antelopes's hide, or
' a vefture of bark; let him bathe evening and
' morning; let him fuffer the hairs of his head,
' his beard, and his nails to grow continually.

7. ' From fuch food, as himfelf may eat, let
' him, to the utmoft of his power, make offerings
' and give alms; and with prefents of water, roots,
' and fruit, let him honour thofe who vifit his
' hermitage.

8. ' Let him be conftantly engaged in reading the
' Véda; patient of all extremities, univerfally be-
' nevolent, with a mind intent on the Supreme
' Being; a perpetual giver, but no receiver of
' gifts; with tender affection for all animated
' bodies.

9. ' Let him, as the law directs, make oblations
' on the hearth with three facred fires; not omit-
' ting, in due time, the ceremonies to be performed
' at the conjunction and oppofition of the moon.

10. ' Let him alfo perform the facrifice ordained
' in honour of the lunar conftellations, make the
' prefcribed offering of new grain, and folemnize
' holy rites every four months, and at the winter
' and fummer folftices.

11. ' With pure grains, the food of ancient
' fage s, growing in the vernal and autumnal fea-
' fons, and brought home by himfelf, let him feve-
' rally make, as the law ordains, the oblations of
' cakes and boiled grain;

12. ' And, having prefented to the gods, that
' pureft oblation which the wild woods produced,
' let him eat what remains, together with fome
' nativ e falt, which himfelf collected.

13. ' Let

13. ' Let him eat green herbs, flowers, roots,
' and fruit, that grow on earth or in water,
' and the productions of pure trees, and oils
' formed in fruits.

14. ' Honey and flesh meat he must avoid, and
' all sorts of mushrooms, the plant *bhústrĭna*, that
' named *sighruca*, and the fruit of the *sléshmátaca.*

15. ' In the month *Aswina* let him cast away the
' food of sages, which he before had laid up, and
' his vesture, then become old, and his herbs,
' roots, and fruit.

16. ' Let him not eat the produce of plowed
' land, though abandoned by any man *who*
' *owns it*, nor fruits and roots produced in a
' town, even though hunger oppress him.

17. ' He may eat what is mellowed by fire, and
' he may eat what is ripened by time ; and either
' let him break hard fruits with a stone, or let his
' teeth serve as a pestle.

18. ' Either let him pluck enough for a day,
' or let him gather enough for a month ; or let
' him collect enough for six months, or lay up
' enough for a year.

19. ' Having procured food, as he is able, he
' may eat it at eve or in the morning; or he
' may take only every fourth, or every eighth,
' such regular meal ;

20. ' Or, by the rules of the lunar penance, he
' may eat a mouthful more each day of the bright,
' and a mouthful less each day of the dark fort-
' night ; or he may eat only once, at the close of
' each fortnight, a mess of boiled grains :

21. ' Or he may constantly live on flowers and
' roots, and on fruit matured by time, which has
' fallen spontaneously, strictly observing the laws
' ordained for hermits.

22. ' Let

22. ' Let him flide backwards and forwards on
' the ground ; or let him ftand a whole day on
' tiptoe ; or let him continue in motion rifing and
' fitting alternately ; but at funrife, at noon, and
' at funfet, let him go to the waters and bathe.

23. ' In the hot feafon, let him fit expofed to
' five fires, *four blazing around him with the fun*
' *above* ; in the rains, let him ftand uncovered,
' *without even a mantle*, where the clouds pour *the*
' *heavieſt* ſhowers ; and in the cold feafon, let him
' wear humid vefture ; and let him increafe by
' degrees the aufterity of his devotion :

24. ' Performing his ablution at the three *Sava-*
' *nas*, let him give fatisfaction to the manes and
' to the gods ; and, enduring harſher and
' harſher mortifications, let him dry up his bodily
' frame.

25. ' Then having repofited his holy fires, as the
' law directs, in his mind, let him live without
' external fire, without a manfion, wholly filent,
' feeding on roots and fruit ;

26. ' Not folicitous for the means of gratifica-
' tion, chafte as a ftudent, fleeping on the bare
' earth, in the hants of pious hermits, without
' one felfiſh affection, dwelling at the roots of
' trees.

27. ' From devout *Bráhmens* let him receive
' alms to fupport life, or from other houfe-keep-
' ers of twice born claffes, who dwell in the
' foreſt :

28. ' Or the hermit may bring food from a
' town, having received it in a baſket of leaves,
' in his naked hand, or in a potſherd ; and then
' let him fwallow eight mouthfuls.

29. ' Thefe and other rules muft a *Bráhmen*,
' who retires to the woods, diligently practife ;
' and,

' and, for the purpofe of uniting his foul with the
' Divine Spirit, let him ftudy the various *Upa-*
' *nifhads* of fcripture, or *chapters on the effence and*
' *attributes of God,*

30. ' Which have been ftudied with reverence
' by anchorites verfed in theology, and by houfe-
' keepers, who dwelt afterwards in forefts, for the
' fake of increafing their fublime knowledge and
' devotion, and for the purification of their bodies.

31. ' Or, *if he has any incurable difeafe,* let him
' advance in a ftraight path, towards the invinci-
' ble *north eaftern* point, feeding on water and air,
' till his mortal frame totally decay, and his foul
' become united with the Supreme.

32. ' A *Bráhmen,* having fhuffled off his body
' by any of thofe modes, which great fages prac-
' tifed, and becoming void of forrow and fear,
' rifes to exaltation in the divine effence.

33. ' HAVING thus performed religious acts in
' a foreft during the third portion of his life, let
' him become a *Sannyáfi* for the fourth portion of
' it, abandoning all fenfual affections, *and wholly*
' *repofing in the Supreme Spirit* :

34. ' The man who has paffed from order to
' order, has made oblations to fire *on his refpective*
' *changes of ftate,* and has kept his members in
' fubjection, but, tired with *fo long a courfe of giving*
' alms and *making* offerings, thus repofes himfelf
' entirely on GOD, fhall be raifed, after death, to
' glory.

35. ' When he has paid his three debts *to the*
' *fages, the manes, and the gods,* let him apply his
' mind to final beatitude ; but low fhall He fall
' who prefumes to feek beatitude without hav-
' ing difcharged thofe debts :

36. ' After

36. ' After he has read the *Védas* in the form
' prescribed by law, has legally begotten a son,
' and has performed sacrifices to the best of his
' power, he *has paid his three debts, and* may then
' apply his heart to eternal bliss ;

37. ' But if a *Bráhmen* have not read the *Véda*,
' if he have not begotten a son, and if he have not
' performed sacrifices, yet shall aim at final bea-
' titude, he shall sink to a place of degradation.

38. ' Having performed the sacrifice of PRA
' JA'PETI, accompanied with a gift of all his
' wealth, *and* having reposited in his mind the sacri-
' ficial fires, a *Bráhmen* may proceed from his
' house, *that is, from the second order, or he may pro-*
' *ceed even from the first,* to the condition of a
' *Sannyásí.*

39. ' Higher worlds are illuminated with the
' glory of that man, who passes from his house
' into the fourth order, giving exemption from
' fear to all animated beings, and pronouncing
' the *mystick words of* the *Véda :*

40. ' To the *Bráhmen,* by whom not even the
' smallest dread has been occasioned by sentient
' creatures, there can be no dread from any quar-
' ter whatever, when he obtains a release from
' his mortal body.

41. ' Departing from his house, taking with him
' pure implements, *his water-pot and staff,* keeping
' silence, unallured by desire of the objects near
' him, let him enter into the fourth order.

42. ' Alone let him constantly dwell, for the
' sake of his own felicity; observing the happiness
' of a solitary man, who neither forsakes nor is
' forsaken, let him live without a companion.

43. ' Let him have no culinary fire, no domi-
'   ' cil
7

' cil ; let him, *when very hungry,* go to the town
' for food ; let him patiently bear difeafe; let his
' mind be firm ; let him ftudy to know God, and
' fix his attention on God alone.

44. ' An earthen water-pot, the roots of large
' trees, coarfe vefture, total folitude, equanimity
' toward all creatures, thefe are the characte-
' rifticks of a *Bráhmen* fet free.

45. ' Let him not wifh for death ; let him not
' wifh for life ; let him expect his appointed time,
' as a hired fervant expects his wages.

46. ' Let him advance his foot purified by
' looking down, *left he touch any thing impure*; let
' him drink water purified by ftraining with
' a cloth, *left he hurt fome infect*; let him, *if he
' chufe to fpeak,* utter words purified by truth; let
' him by all means keep his heart purified.

47. ' Let him bare a reproachful fpeech with
' patience; let him fpeak reproachfully to no
' man ; let him not, on account of this *frail and
' feverifh* body, engage in hoftility with any one
' living.

48. ' With an angry man, let him not in his turn
' be angry ; abufed, let him fpeak mildly ; nor
' let him utter a word relating to vain illufory
' things and confined within feven gates, *the five
' organs of fenfe, the heart and the intellect*; *or this
' world, with three above and three below it.*

49. ' Delighted with meditating on the Su-
' preme Spirit, fitting fixed in fuch meditation,
' without needing any thing earthly, without one
' fenfual defire, without any companion but his
' own foul, let him live in this world feeking the
' blifs of the next.

50. ' Neither by explaining omens and prodi-
L 4   ' gies,

' gies, nor by skill in astrology and palmistry, nor
' by casuistry and expositions of holy texts, let
' him at any time gain his daily support.

51. ' Let him not go near a house frequented
' by hermits, or priests, or birds, or dogs, or other
' beggars.

52. ' His hair, nails, and beard being clipped,
' bearing with him a dish, a staff, and a water-pot,
' his whole mind being fixed on GOD, let him
' wander about continually, without giving pain
' to *animal or vegetable* beings.

53. ' His dishes must have no fracture, nor
' must they be made of bright metals : the puri-
' fication ordained for them must be with water
' alone, like that of the vessels for a sacrifice.

54. ' A gourd, a wooden bowl, an earthen dish,
' or a basket made of reeds, has MENU, son of
' the Self-existing, declared fit vessels to receive
' the food of *Bráhmens* devoted to God.

55. ' Only once a day let him demand food ;
' let him not habituate him to eat much at a time ;
' for an anchorite, habituated to eat much, be-
' comes inclined to sensual gratifications.

56. ' At the time when the smoke of kitchen fires
' has ceased, when the pestle lies motionless, when
' the burning charcoal is exinguished, when
' people have eaten, and when dishes are removed,
' *that is, late in the day,* let the *Sannyási* always
' beg food.

57. ' For missing it, let him not be sorrowful ;
' nor for gaining it, let him be glad ; let him care
' only for a sufficiency to support life, but let him
' not be anxious about his utensils.

58. ' Let him constantly disdain to receive
' food after humble reverence ; since, by receiv-

' ing

' ing it in confequence of an humble falutation, a
' *Sannyáfi*, though free, becomes a captive.

59. ' By eating little and by fitting in folitary
' places, let him reftrain thofe organs which are
' naturally hurried away by fenfual defires.

60. ' By the coercion of his members, by the
' abfence of hate and affection, and by giving no
' pain to fentient creatures, he becomes fit for
' immortality.

61. ' Let him reflect on the tranfmigrations
' of men caufed by their finful deeds, on their
' downfal into a region of darknefs, and their
' torments in the manfion of YAMA ;

62. ' On their feparation from thofe whom
' they love, and their union with thofe whom
' they hate, on their ftrength overpowered by old
' age, and their bodies racked with difeafe ;

63. ' On their agonizing departure from this
' corporeal frame, their formation again in the
' womb, and the glidings of this vital fpirit
' through ten thoufand millions of uterine paf-
' fages ;

64. ' On the mifery attached to embodied fpi-
' rits from a violation of their duties, and the un-
' perifhable blifs attached to them from their
' abundant performance of all duties, religious
' and civil.

65. ' Let him reflect alfo, with exclufive appli-
' cation of mind, on the fubtil indivifable effence
' of the Supreme Spirit, and its complete exiftence
' in all beings, whether extremely high or ex-
' tremely low.

66. ' Equal minded towards all creatures, in
' what order foever *he may have been* placed, let him
' fully difcharge his duty though he bear not the

5   ' vifible

' vifible marks of his order : the vifible mark,
' *or mere name* of his order, is by no means an ef-
' fective difcharge of his duty ;

67. ' As, although the fruit of the tree *cataca*
' purify water, yet a man cannot purify water by
' merely pronouncing the name of that fruit : *he*
' *muft throw it, when pounded, into the jar.*

68. ' For the fake of preferving minute animals
' by night and by day, let him walk, though with
' pain to his own body, perpetually looking on
' the ground.

69. ' Let a *Sannyáfi,* by way of expiation for
' *the death of* thofe creatures, which he may have
' deftroyed unknowingly by day or by night,
' make fix fuppreffions of his breath, having duly
' bathed :

70. ' Even three fuppreffions of breath, made
' according to the divine rule, accompanied with
' the triverbal phrafe *(bhurbhuvah fwah)* and the
' trileteral fyllable *(óm)* may be confidered as the
' higheft devotion of a *Bráhmen* ;

71. ' For as the drofs and impurities of metal-
' lick ores are confumed by fire, thus are the finful
' acts of the human organ confumed by fuppref-
' fions of the breath, *while the myftick words, and the*
' *meafures of the* gáyatrì *are revolved in the mind.*

72. ' Let him thus, by fuch fuppreffions of
' breath, burn away his offences ; by reflecting
' intenfely on the fteps of afcent to beatitude, *let*
' *him deftroy fin* ; by coercing his members, let
' him reftrain all fenfual attachments ; by meditat-
' ing on *the intimate union of his own foul and* the
' divine effence, let him extinguifh all qualities
' repugnant to the nature of GOD.

73. ' Let him obferve, with extreme applica-
                                          ' tion

' tion of mind, the progreſs of this internal ſpirit
' through various bodies, high and low ; *a progreſs*
' hard to be diſcerned by men with unimproved
'intellects.

74. ' He, who fully underſtands the perpetual
' omnipreſence of GOD, can be led no more cap-
' tive by criminal acts ; but he, who poſſeſſes not
' that ſublime knowledge, ſhall wander again
' through the world.

75. ' By injuring nothing animated, by ſub-
' duing all ſenſual appetites, by devout rites
' ordained in the *Véda,* and by rigorous mortifi-
' cations, men obtain, even in this life, the
' ſtate of beatitude.

76. ' A manſion with bones for its rafters and
' beams ; with nerves and tendons, for cords ;
' with muſcles and blood, for mortar ; with ſkin,
' for its outward covering ; 'filled with no ſweet
' perfume, but loaded with feces and urine ;

77. ' A manſion infeſted by age and by ſor-
' row, the ſeat of malady, harraſſed with pains,
' haunted with the quality of darkneſs, and inca-
' pable of ſtanding long ; ſuch a manſion of the
' vital ſoul let its occupier always cheerfully
' quit :

78. ' As a tree leaves the bank of a river,
' *when it falls in,* or as a bird leaves the branch of
' a tree *at his pleaſure,* thus he, who leaves his
' body *by neceſſity or by legal choice,* is delivered
' from the ravening ſhark, *or crocodile* of the
' world.

79. ' Letting his good acts deſcend (by the
' law of the *Véda,)* to thoſe who love him,
' and his evil deeds, to thoſe who hate him,
' he may attain, through devout meditation, the
' eternal ſpirit.

80. ' When,

80. ' When, having well confidered the nature
' and confequence of fin, he becomes averfe
' from all fenfual delights, he then attains blifs
' in this world; blifs which fhall endure after
' death.

81. ' Thus having gradually abandoned all
' earthly attachments, and indifferent to all pairs
' of oppofite things, *as honour and difhonour, and the*
' *like,* he remains abforbed in the divine effence.

82. ' All that has now been declared, is ob-
' tained by pious meditation ; but no man who is
' ignorant of the Supreme Spirit, can gather the
' fruit of mere ceremonial acts.

83. ' Let him conftantly ftudy that part of the
' *Véda,* which relates to facrifice; that which
' treats of fubordinate deities ; that which reveals
' the nature of the fupreme GOD ; and whatever is
' declared in the *Upanifhads.*

84. ' This holy fcripture is a fure refuge, even
' for thofe who underftand not its meaning, and
' of courfe, for thofe who underftand it ; this *Véda*
' is a fure refource for thofe who feek blifs above ;
' this *is a fure refource* for thofe who feek blifs
' eternal.

85. ' That *Bráhmen,* who becomes a *Sannyáfi*
' by this difcipline, *announced* in due order, fhakes
' off fin here below, and reaches the moft
' high.

86. ' THIS *general* law has been revealed to
' you for anchorites with fubdued minds : now
' learn the particular difcipline of thofe who be-
' come reclufes according to the *Véda,* that is, *of*
' *anchorites in the firft of the four degrees.*

87. ' The ftudent, the married man, the her-
' mit, and the anchorite, are the offspring, though
' in four orders, of married men keeping houfe ;

88. ' And

88. ' And all, or 'even any of thofe orders,
' affumed in their turn, according to the facred
' ordinances, lead the *Bráhmen*, who acts by the
' preceding rules, to the higheft manfion +

89. ' But of all thofe, the houfe-keeper obferv-
' ing the regulations of the *Sruti* and *Smriti*,
' may be called the chief; fince he fupports the
' three *other orders*.

90. ' As all rivers, female and male, run to
' their determined place in the fea, thus men of all
' *other* orders, repair to their fixed place in the
' manfion of the houfe-keeper.

91. ' By *Bráhmens*, placed in thefe four orders,
' a tenfold fyftem of duties muft ever be fedu-
' loufly practifed :

92. ' Content, returning good for evil, refift-
' ance to fenfual appetites, abftinence from illicit
' gain, purification, coercion of the organs,
' knowledge of fcripture, knowledge of the
' Supreme Spirit, veracity, and freedom from
' wrath, form their tenfold fyftem of duties.

93. ' Such *Bráhmens*, as attentively read the
' ten precepts of duty, and after reading, care-
' fully practife them, attain the moft exalted
' condition.

94. ' A *Bráhmen* having practifed with organs
' under command, this tenfold fyftem of duty,
' having heard the *Upanifhads* explained, as the
' law directs, and who has difcharged his three
' debts, may become an anchorite, *in the houfe of*
' *his fon*, according to the *Véda*;

95. ' And, having abandoned all ceremonial
' acts, having expiated all his offences, having ob-
' tained a command over his organs, and having
' perfectly underftood the fcripture, he may live
' at

' at his eafe, while the houfehold affairs are
' conducted by his fon.

96. ' When he thus has relinquifhed all forms,
' is intent on his own occupation, and free from
' every other defire, when, by devoting himfelf to
' GOD, he has effaced fin, he then attains the fu-
' preme path of glory.

97. ' THIS fourfold regulation for the facer-
' dotal clafs, has thus been made known to you;
' a juft regulation, producing endlefs fruit after
' death : next, learn the duty of kings, *or the*
' *military clafs.*'

CHAPTER THE SEVENTH.

*On Government, and Publick Law ; or on the
Military Claſs.*

———

1. ' I WILL fully declare the duty of kings;
' *and ſhow* how a ruler of men ſhould conduct
' himſelf, in what manner he was framed, and
' how his ultimate reward *may be attained by him.*

2. ' By a man of the military claſs, who has
' received in due form the inveſtiture which the
' *Véda* preſcribes, great care muſt be uſed to
' maintain this whole *aſſemblage of laws.*

3. ' Since, if the world had no king, it would
' quake on all ſides through fear, the ruler of
' this *univerſe*, therefore, created a king, for the
' maintenance of this ſyſtem, both religious and
' civil,

4. ' Forming him of eternal particles drawn
' from the ſubſtance of INDRA, PAVANA, YAMA,
' SU'RYA, of AGNI and VARUNA, of CHANDRA
' and CUVE'RA :

5. ' And ſince a king was compoſed of parti-
' cles drawn from thoſe chief guardian deities, he
' conſequently ſurpaſſes all mortals in glory.

6. ' Like the ſun, he burns eyes and hearts;
' nor can any human creature on earth even gaze
' on him.

7. ' He

7. ' He *is* fire and air; he, both fun and
' moon; he, the god of criminal juftice; he,
' the genius of wealth; he, the regent of waters;
' he, the lord of the firmament.

8. ' A king, even though a child, muft not
' be treated lightly, from an idea that he is a
' mere mortal: no; he is a powerful divinity,
' who appears in a human fhape.

9. ' Fire burns only one perfon, who carelefsly
' goes too near it; but the fire of a king in wrath
' burns a whole family, with all their cattle and
' goods.

10. ' Fully confidering the bufinefs before
' him, his own force, and the place, and the time,
' he affumes in fucceffion all forts of forms, for
' the fake of advancing juftice.

11. ' He, fure, muft be the perfect effence of
' majefty, by whofe favour Abundance rifes on
' her lotos, in whofe valour dwells conqueft; in
' whofe anger, death.

12. ' He, who fhews hatred of the king,
' through delufion of mind, will certainly perifh;
' for fpeedily will the king apply his heart to that
' man's perdition.

13. ' LET the king prepare a juft compenfa-
' tion for the good, and a juft punifhment for the
' bad: the rule of ftrict juftice let him never
' tranfgrefs.

14. ' For his ufe BRAHMA' formed, in the be-
' ginning of time, the genius of punifhment, with
' a body of pure light, his own fon, even ab-
' ftract criminal juftice, the protector of all created
' things:

15. ' Through fear of that genius, all fentient
' beings, whether fixed or locomotive, are fitted
' for natural enjoyments and fwerve not from duty.

16. ' When

16. ' When the king, therefore, has fully con-
' sidered place and time, and his own ftrength,
' and the divine ordinance, let him juftly inflict
' punifhment on all thofe who act unjuftly.

17. ' Punifhment is an active ruler; he is the
' true manager of publick affairs; he is the dif-
' penfer of laws; and wife men. call him the
' fponfor of all the four orders for the difcharge
' of their feveral duties.

18. ' Punifhment governs all mahkind; punifh-
' ment alone preferves them; punifhment wakes,
' while their guards are afleep; the wife confider
' punifhment as the perfection of juftice.

19. ' When rightly and confiderately inflicted,
' it makes all the people happy; but, inflicted
' without full confideration, it wholly deftroys
' them all.

20. ' If the king were not, without indolence,
' to punifh the guilty, the ftronger would roaft
' the weaker, like fifh, on a fpit; (*or according to*
' *one reading*, the ftronger would opprefs the
' weaker, like fifh in their element;)

21. ' The crow would peck the confecrated
' offering of rice; the dog would lick the clari-
' fied butter; ownerfhip would remain with none;
' the loweft would overfet the higheft.

22. ' The whole race of men is kept in order
' by punifhment; for a guiltlefs man is hard to
' be found; through fear of punifhment, indeed,
' this univerfe is enabled to enjoy its bleffings;

23. ' Deities and demons, heavenly fongfters
' and cruel giants, birds and ferpents, are made
' capable, by juft correction, of their feveral en-
' joyments.

24. ' All claffes would become corrupt; all

M   ' barriers

' barriers would be deftroyed, there would be
' total confufion among men, if punifhment either
' were not inflicted, or were inflicted unduly :

25. ' But where punifhment, with a black hue
' and a red eye, advances to deftroy fin, there, if
' the judge difcern well, the people are undif-
' turbed.

26. ' Holy fages confider as a fit difpenfer of
' criminal juftice, that king, who invariably fpeaks
' truth, who duly confiders all cafes, who under-
' ftands the facred books, who knows the diftinc-
' tions of virtue, pleafure, and riches ;

27. ' Such a king, if he juftly inflict legal
' punifhments, greatly increafes thofe three means
' of happinefs ; but punifhment itfelf fhall deftroy
' a king, who is crafty, voluptuous, and wrathful :

28. ' Criminal juftice, the bright effence of
' majefty, and hard to be fupported by men with
' unimproved minds, eradicates a king, who
' fwerves from his duty, together with all his
' race :

29. ' Punifhment fhall overtake his caftles,
' his territories, his peopled land with all fixed
' and moveable things that exift on it : even the
' gods and the fages, *who lofe their oblations,* will
' be afflicted and afcend to the fky.

30. ' Juft punifhment cannot be inflicted by
' an ignorant and covetous king, who has no wife
' and virtuous affiftant, whofe underftanding has
' not been improved, and whofe heart is addicted
' to fenfuality :

31. ' By a king wholly pure, faithful to his
' promife, obfervant of the fcriptures, with good
' affiftants and found underftanding may punifh-
' ment be juftly inflicted.

32. ' Let

32. ' Let him in his own domains act with
' justice, chastise foreign foes with rigour, behave
' without duplicity to his affectionate friends, and
' with lenity to *Bráhmens*.

33. ' Of a king thus disposed, even though
' he subsist by gleaning, *or, be his treasure ever so*
' *small*, the fame is far spread in the world, like
' a drop of oil in water;

34. ' But of a king with a contrary disposition,
' with passions unsubdued, *be his riches ever so*
' *great*, the fame is contracted in the world, like
' clarified butter in the same element.

35. ' A king was created as the protector of
' all those classes and orders, who from the first
' to the last, discharge their several duties;

36. ' *And* all that must be done by him, for
' the protection of his people, with the assistance
' of good ministers, I will declare to you, as the
' law directs, in due order.

37. ' Let the king, having risen at early dawn,
' respectfully attend to *Bráhmens*, learned in the
' three *Védas*, and in the science of ethicks; and
' by their decision let him abide.

38. ' Constantly must he show respect to
' *Bráhmens*, who have grown old, *both in years*
' *and in piety*, who know the scriptures, who *in*
' *body and mind* are pure; for he, who honours
' the aged, will perpetually be honoured even by
' cruel demons:

39. ' From them, though he may have ac-
' quired modest behaviour *by his own good sense*
' *and by study*, let him continually learn habits
' of modesty and composure; since a king, whose
' demeanour is humble and composed, never
' perishes.

40. ' While,

40. ' While, through want of¹ such humble
' virtue, many kings have perished with all their
' possessions, and, through virtue united with
' modesty, even hermits have obtained kingdoms.

41. ' Through want of that virtuous humility
' Ve'na was utterly ruined, and so was the great
' king Nahusha, and Suda'sa, and Yavana,
' (or by a different reading, and Suda'man, the son
' of Piyavana) and Sumuc'ha, and Nimi ;

42. ' But by virtues with humble behaviour,
' Prit'hu and Menu acquired sovereignty ;
' Cuve'ra, wealth inexhaustible ; and Viswa'-
' mitra, son of Ga'dhi, the rank of a priest,
' though born in the military class.

43. ' From those who know the three Védas,
' let him learn the triple doctrine comprised in
' them, together with the primeval science of
' criminal justice and sound policy, the systems
' of logick and metaphysicks, and sublime theo-
' logical truth : from the people he must learn
' the theory of agriculture, commerce, and other
' practical arts.

44. ' Day and night must he strenuously ex-
' ert himself to gain complete victory over his
' own organs ; since that king alone, whose organs
' are completely subdued, can keep his people
' firm to their duty.

45. ' With extreme care let him shun eighteen
' vices, ten proceeding from love of pleasure,
' eight springing from wrath, and all ending in
' misery ;

46. ' Since a king, addicted to vices arising
' from love of pleasure, must lose both his wealth
' and his virtue, and, addicted to vices arising
' from anger, he may lose even his life from the
' publick resentment.

47. ' Hunt-

47. ' Hunting, gaming, sleeping by day, cen-
' suring rivals, excess with women, intoxication,
' singing, instrumental musick, dancing, and use-
' less travel, are the ten-fold set of vices produced
' by love of pleasure:

48. ' Tale bearing, violence, insidious wound-
' ing, envy, detraction, unjust seizure of property,
' reviling, and open assault, are, in like manner,
' the eight-fold set of vices to which anger gives
' birth.

49. ' A selfish inclination, which all wise men
' know to be the root of those two sets, let him
' suppress with diligence: both sets of vices are
' constantly produced by it.

50. ' Drinking, dice, women, and hunting,
' let him consider as the four most pernicious
' in the set, which love of pleasure occasions:

51. ' Battery, defamation, and injury to pro-
' perty, let him always consider as the three most
' heinous in the set, which arises from wrath;

52. ' *And* in this seven-fold assemblage of vices,
' too frequently prevailing in all kingdoms, let
' an enlightened prince consider the first, and so
' forth in order, as the most abominable in
' each set.

53. ' On a comparison between death and
' vice, the learned pronounce vice the more
' dreadful; since, after death, a vicious man sinks
' to regions lower and lower, while a man, free
' from vice, reaches heaven.

54. ' The king must appoint seven or eight
' ministers, who must be sworn *by touching a*
' *sacred image and the like*; men, whose ancestors
' were servants of kings; who are versed in the
' holy books; who are personally brave; who

M 3   ' are

‘
‚ are ſkilled in the uſe of weapons; and whoſe
lineage is noble.

55. ‘ Even an act´ eaſy in itſelf is hard ſome-
‘ times to be performed by a ſingle man, eſpe-
‘ cially if he has no aſſiſtant near: how much
‘ harder *muſt it be to perform alone the buſineſs of* a
‘ kingdom with great revenues!

56. ‘ Let him perpetually conſult with thoſe
‘ miniſters on peace and war, on his forces, on
‘ his revenues, on the protection of his people,
‘ and on the means of beſtowing aptly the wealth
‘ which he has acquired:

57. ‘ Having aſcertained the ſeveral opinions
‘ of his counſellors, *firſt* apart and *then* collectively,
‘ let him do what is moſt beneficial for him in
‘ publick affairs.

58. ‘ To one learned *Bráhmen*, diſtinguiſhed
‘ among them all, let the king impart his momen-
‘ tous counſel, relating to ſix *principal* articles.

59. ‘ To him, with full confidence, let him
‘ intruſt all tranſactions; and with him, having
‘ taken his final reſolution, let him begin all his
‘ meaſures.

60. ‘ He muſt likewiſe appoint other officers;
‘ men of integrity, well informed, ſteady, ha-
‘ bituated to gain wealth, by honourable means,
‘ and tried by experience.

61. ‘ As many officers as the due performance
‘ of his buſineſs requires, not ſlothful men, *but*
‘ *active*, able, and well inſtructed, ſo many, and no
‘ more, let him appoint.

62. ‘ Among thoſe let him employ the brave,
‘ the ſkilful, the well born, and the honeſt, in his
‘ mines *of gold or gems*, and in other ſimilar works
‘ *for amaſſing wealth*; but the puſillanimous, in
‘ the receſſes of his palace.

63. ‘ Let

63. ' Let him likewife appoint an ambaſſador,
' verſed in all the *Siſtras*, who underſtands hints,
' external ſigns and actions, *whoſe hand and heart*
' *are* pure, whoſe abilities are great, and whoſe
' birth was illuſtrious :

64. ' That royal ambaſſador is applauded moſt,
' who is generally beloved, pure within and with-
' out, dextrous in buſineſs, and endued with an
' excellent memory ; who knows countries and
' times, is handſome, intrepid and eloquent.

65. ' The forces of the realm muſt be im-
' mediately regulated by the commander in chief;
' the actual infliction of puniſhment, by the of-
' ficers of criminal juſtice ; the treaſury and the
' country, by the king himſelf; peace and war,
' by the ambaſſador;

66. ' For it is the ambaſſador alone who unites,
' who alone disjoints the united ; that is, he tranſ-
' acts the buſineſs, by which kingdoms are at
' variance or in amity.

67. ' In the tranſaction of affairs let the ambaſ-
' ſador comprehend the viſible ſigns and hints, and
' diſcover the acts, of the foreign king, by the
' ſigns, hints, and acts of his confidential ſervants,
' and the meaſures, which that king wiſhes to
' take by *the character and conduct of* his miniſters.

68. ' Thus, having learned completely *from*
' *his ambaſſador* all the deſigns of the foreign
' prince, let the king ſo apply his vigilant care,
' that he bring no evil on himſelf.

69. ' Let him fix his abode in a diſtrict contain-
' ing open champaigns ; abounding with grain ;
' inhabited chiefly by the virtuous ; not infected
' with maladies ; beautiful to the ſight ; ſurround-
' ed by ſubmiſſive *mountaineers, foreſters, or other*

' neigh-

' neighbours; a country in which the subjects
' may live at ease.

70. ' There let him reside in a capital, having,
' by way of a fortress, a desert *rather more than*
' *twenty miles round it,* or a fortress of earth, a
' fortress of water, or of trees, a fortress of armed
' men, or a fortress of mountains.

71. ' With all possible care let him secure a
' fortress of mountains; for, among those just
' mentioned, a fortress of mountains has many
' transcendent properties.

72. ' In the three first of them live wild beasts,
' vermin, and aquatick animals; in the three last,
' apes, men, and gods, in order as they are named:

73. ' As enemies hurt them not in the shelter
' of their several abodes, thus foes hurt not a
' king who has taken refuge in his *durga,* or *place*
' *of difficult access.*

74. ' One bowman, placed on a wall, is a
' match in war for a hundred enemies; and a
' hundred, for ten thousand; therefore is a fort
' recommended.

75. ' Let that fort be supplied with weapons,
' with money, with grain, with beasts, with *Bráh-*
' *mens,* with artificers, with engines, with grass,
' and with water.

76. ' In the centre of it let him raise his own
' palace, well finished in all its parts, completely
' defended, habitable in every season, brilliant *with*
' *white stucco,* surrounded with water and trees:

77. ' Having prepared it for his mansion, let
' him chuse a consort of the same class with him-
' self, endued with all the bodily marks of excel-
' lence, born of an exalted race, captivating his
' heart, adorned with beauty and the best qualities.

78. ' HE must appoint also a domestick priest,
' and

' and retain a performer of facrifices, who may
' folemnize the religious rites of his family, and
' thofe performed with three facred fires.

79. ' Let the king make facrifices, accom-
' panied with gifts of many different kinds; and
' for the full difcharge of his duty, let him give
' the *Bráhmens* both legal enjoyments and mo-
' derate wealth.

80. ' His annual revenue he may receive from
' his whole dominion through his collectors; but
' let him in this world obferve the divine ordi-
' nances; let him act as a father to his people.

81. ' Here and there he muft appoint many
' forts of intelligent fupervifors, who may infpect
' all the acts of the officers engaged in his bufi-
' nefs.

82. ' To *Bráhmens* returned from the manfions
' of their preceptors, let him fhow due refpect;
' for that is called a precious unperifhable gem,
' depofited by kings with the facerdotal clafs:

83. ' It is a gem, which neither thieves or foes
' take away; which never perifhes: kings muft,
' therefore, depofit with *Bráhmens* that indeftruc-
' tible jewel *of refpectful prefents.*

84. ' An oblation in the mouth, *or hand,* of a
' *Bráhmen,* is far better than offerings to holy fire:
' it never drops: it never dries: it is never
' confumed.

85. ' A gift to one not a *Bráhmen* produces
' fruit of a middle ftandard; to one who calls
' himfelf a *Bráhmen,* double; to a well read
' *Bráhmen,* a hundred thoufand fold; to one who
' has read all the *Védas,* infinite.

86. ' Of a gift made with faith in the *Sáftra,*
' to a perfon highly deferving it, the giver fhall
' indubitably

' indubitably gain the fruit after death, be the
' prefent fmall or great.

87. ' A KING, while he protects his people,
' being defied by an enemy of equal, greater, or
' lefs force, muft by no means turn his face from
' battle, but muft remember the duty of his mi-
' litary clafs :

88. ' Never to recede from combat, to protect
' the people, and to honour the priefts, is the
' higheft duty of kings and enfures their felicity.

89. ' Thofe rulers of the earth, who, defirous
' of defeating each other, exert their utmoft
' ftrength in battle, without ever averting their
' faces, afcend after death directly to heaven.

90. ' LET no man, engaged in combat, fmite
' his foe with *fharp* weapons concealed *in wood*,
' nor with arrows mifchievoufly barbed, nor with
' poifoned arrows, nor with darts blazing with fire;

91. ' Nor let him *in a car or on horfeback* ftrike
' his enemy alighted on the ground ; nor an ef-
' feminate man ; nor one who fues for life with
' clofed palms ; nor one whofe hair is loofe *and*
' *obftructs his fight*; nor one, who fits down *fa-*
' *tigued*; nor one, who fays, " I am thy captive ;"

92. ' Nor one, who fleeps ; nor one, who has
' loft his coat of mail ; nor one, who is naked ;
' nor one, who is difarmed ; nor one, who is a
' fpectator, but not a combatant ; nor one, who
' is fighting with another man :

93. ' Calling to mind the duty of honourable
' men, let him never flay one, who has broken
' his weapon ; nor one, who is afflicted *with pri-*
' *vate forrow* ; nor one, who has been grievoufly
' wounded ; nor one, who is terrified ; nor one,
' who turns his back,

94. ' The

94. ' The foldier, indeed, who fearing and
' turning his back, happens to be flain by his
' foes in an engagement, fhall take upon himfelf
' all the fin of his commander, whatever it be ;

9:. ' And the commander fhall take to himfelf
' *the fruit of* all the good conduct, which the fol-
' dier, who turns his back and is killed, had pre-
' vioufly ftored up for a future life.

96. ' Cars, horfes, elephants, umbrellas, habi-
' liments, *except the jewels which may adorn them,*
' grain, cattle, women, all forts of liquids and
' metals, except gold and filver, are the lawful
' prizes of the man who takes them in war ;

97. ' But of thofe prizes, the captors muft
' lay the moft valuable before the king ; fuch is
' the rule in the *Véda,* concerning them ; and the
' king fhould diftribute among the whole army
' what has not been feparately taken.

98. ' Thus has been declared the blamelefs
' primeval law for military men ; from this law a
' king muft never depart, when he attacks his foes
' in battle.

99. ' What he has not gained *from his foe,* let
' him ftrive to gain ; what he has acquired, let
' him preferve with care ; what he preferves, let
' him augment ; and what he has augmented, let
' him beftow on the deferving.

100. ' This is the four-fold rule, which he muft
' confider as the fure means of attaining the great
' object of man, *happiness* ; and let him practife
' it fully without intermiffion, without indolence :

101. ' what he has not gained, let him ftrive
' to gain by military ftrength ; what he has ac-
' quired, let him preferve by careful infpection ;
' what he has preferved, let him augment by

ı   ' legal

' legal modes of increafe ; and what he has aug-
' mented, let him difpenfe with juft liberality.

102. ' Let his troops be conftantly exercifed;
' his prowefs conftantly difplayed ; what he
' ought to fecure, conftantly fecured; and the
' weaknefs of his foe, conftantly inveftigated.

103. ' By a king, whofe forces are always ready
' for action, the whole world may be kept in awe ;
' let him then, by a force always ready, make all
' creatures living his own.

104. ' Let him act on all occafions without
' guile, and never with infincerity ; but, keeping
' himfelf ever on his guard, let him difcover the
' fraud intended by his foe.

105. ' Let not his enemy difcern his vulne-
' rable part, but the volunerable part of his enemy
' let him well difcern : like a tortoife, let him
' draw in his members under *the fhell of* conceal-
' ment, and diligently let him repair any breach
' that may be made in it.

106. ' Like a heron, let him mufe on gaining
' advantages ; like a lion, let him put forth his
' ftrength ; like a wolf, let him creep towards his
' prey ; like a hare, let him double to fecure his
' retreat.

107. ' When he thus has prepared himfelf for
' conqueft, let him reduce all oppofers to fubmif-
' fion by negotiation and three other expedients,
' *namely, prefents, divifion, and force of arms :*

108. ' If they cannot be reftrained by the three
' firft methods, then let him firmly, but gradu-
' ally, bring them to fubjection by military force.

109. ' Among thofe four modes of obtain-
' ing fuccefs, the wife prefer negotiation and war
' for the exaltation of kingdoms.

110. ' As

110. ' As a hufbandman plucks up weeds and
' preferves his corn, thus let a king deftroy his
' opponents and fecure his people.

111. ' That king, who, through weaknefs of
' intelleƈt, rafhly oppreffes his people, will, to-
' gether with his family, be deprived both of
' kingdom and life :

، 112. ' As by the lofs of bodily fuftenance, the
' lives of animated beings are deftroyed, thus,
' by the diftrefs of kingdoms, are deftroyed even
' the lives of kings.

113. ' For the fake of proteƈting his domini-
' ons, let the king perpetually obferve the follow-
' ing rules; for, by proteƈting his dominions, he
' will increafe his own happinefs.

114. ' Let him place, as the proteƈtors of his
' realm, a company of guards, commanded by an
' approved officer, over two, three, five, or a
' hundred diftriƈts, *according to their extent*.

115. ' Let him appoint a lord of one ·own with
' its diftriƈt, a lord of ten towns, a lord of twenty,
' a lord of a hundred, and a lord of a thoufand.

116. ' Let the lord of one town certify of his
' own accord to the lord of ten towns any *robberies*,
' *tumults, or other* evils, which arife in his dif-
' triƈt, *and which he cannot fupprefs* ; and the lord
' of ten, to the lord of twenty :

117. ' Then let the lord of twenty towns no-
' tify them to the lord of a hundred ; and let the
' lord of a hundred tranfmit the information him-
' felf to the lord of a thoufand townfhips.

118. ' Such food, drink, wood, and other ar-
' ticles, as by law fhould be given each day to the
' king by the inhabitants of the townfhip, let the
' lord of one town receive *as his perquifite :*

119. ' Let

110. ' Let the lord of ten towns enjoy the
' produce of two plough-lands, *or as much ground*
' *as can be tilled with two ploughs, each drawn by*
' *six bulls* ; the lord of twenty, that of five plough-
' lands ; the lord of a hundred, that of a village
' or small town ; the lord of a thousand, that of a
' large town.

120. ' The affairs of those *townships*, either
' jointly or separately transacted, let another mi-
' nister of the king inspect ; who should be well
' affected, and by no means remiss.

121. ' In every large town or city, let him ap-
' point one superintendent of all affairs, elevated in
' rank, formidable in power, distinguished as a
' planet among stars :

122. ' Let that governor from time to time
' survey all the rest in person, and by means of his
' emissaries, let him perfectly know their conduct
' in their several districts.

123. ' Since the servants of the king, whom he
' has appointed guardians of districts, are generally
' knaves, who seize what belongs to other men,
' from such knaves let him defend his people :

124. ' Of such evil minded servants, as wring
' wealth from subjects attending them on business,
' let the king confiscate all the possessions, and
' banish them from his realm.

125. ' For women, employed in the service of
' the king, and for his whole set of menial ser-
' vants, let him daily provide a maintenance,
' in proportion to their station and to their
' work :

126. ' One *pana* of copper must be given *each*
' *day* as wages to the lowest servant, with two
' cloths *for apparel* every half year, and a *dróna* of
                                                  ' grain

‘ grain every month ; to the higheft *muft be given*
‘ *wages in the ratio of* fix *to one.*

127. ‘ HAVING afcertained the rates of pur-
‘ chafe and fale, *the length of* the way, the expen-
‘ ces of food and of condiments, the charges of
‘ fecuring the goods carried, and the neat profits
‘ of trade, let the king oblige traders to pay taxes
‘ *on their faleable commodities :*

128. ‘ After full confideration, let a king fo
‘ levy thofe taxes continually in his dominions,
‘ that both he and the merchant may receive a
‘ juft compenfation for their feveral acts.

129. ‘ As the leech, the fuckling calf, and
‘ the bee, take their natural food by little and
‘ little, thus muft a king draw from his domi-
‘ nions an annual revenue.

130. ‘ Of cattle, of gems, of gold and filver,
‘ *added each year to the capital ftock,* a fiftieth part
‘ may be taken by the king ; of grain an eighth
‘ part, a fixth, or a twelfth, *according to the dif-*
‘ *ference of the foil, and the labour neceffary to cul-*
‘ *tivate it.*

131. ‘ He may alfo take a fixth part of the
‘ clear annual increafe of trees, flefh meat, honey,
‘ clarified butter, perfumes, medical fubftances,
‘ liquids, flowers, roots, and fruit,

132. ‘ Of gathered leaves, potherbs, grafs,
‘ utenfils made with leather or cane, earthen pots,
‘ and all things made of ftone.

133. ‘ A king, even though dying *with want,*
‘ muft not receive any tax from a *Brâhmen* learned
‘ in the *Védas,* nor fuffer fuch a *Brâhmen,* refiding
‘ in his territories, to be afflicted with hunger :

134. ‘ Of that king, in whofe dominion a learned
‘ *Brâhmen* is afflicted with hunger, the whole
‘ kingdom

' kingdom will in a fhort time be afflicted with
' famine.

13:. ' The king, having afcertained his know-
' ledge of fcripture and good morals, muft allot
' him a fuitable maintenance, and protect him on
' all fides, as a father protects his own fon :

~   136. ' By that religious duty, which fuch a *Bráh-*
' *men* performs each day, under the full protection
' of the fovereign, the life, wealth, and dominions
' of his protector fhall be greatly increafed.

137. ' Let the king order a mere trifle to be
' paid, in the name of the annual tax, by the
' meaner inhabitants of his realm, who fubfifts
' by petty traffick :

138. ' By low handicrafts-men, artificers, and
' fervile men, who fupport themfelves by labour,
' the king may caufe work to be done for a day
' in each month.

139. ' Let him not cut up his own root *by tak-*
' *ing no revenue,* nor the root of other men by
' excefs of covetoufnefs; for by cutting up his
' own root *and theirs,* he makes both himfelf and
' them wretched.

140. ' Let him, confidering the *diverfity of* cafes,
' be *occafionally* fharp, and *occafionally* mild, fince
' a king, duly fharp and mild, becomes univer-
' fally approved.

141. ' When tired of overlooking the affairs
' of men, let him affign the ftation *of fuch an in-*
' *fpector* to a principal minifter, who well knows
' his duty, who is eminently learned whofe paf-
' fions are fubdued, and whofe birth is exalted.

142. ' Thus muft he protect his people, dif-
' charging, with great exertion, and without
' languor, all thofe duties, which the law requires
' him to perform.

143. ' That

143. ' That monarch, whofe fubjects are car-
' ried from his kingdom by ruffians, while they
' call aloud for protection, and he barely looks
' on them with his minifters,, is a dead, and not
' a living king.

144. ' The higheft duty of a military man is
' the defence of his people, and the king who
' receives the confideration juft mentioned, is
' bound to difcharge that duty.

145. ' Having rifen in the laft watch of the
' night, his body being pure, and his mind at-
' tentive, having made oblations to fire, and fhown
' due refpect to the priefts, let him enter his hall
' decently fplendid :

146. ' Standing there, let him gratify his fub-
' jects, before he difmifs them, *with kind looks and*
' *words* ; and, having difmiffed them all, let him
' take fecret council with his principal minifters:

147. ' Afcending up the back of a mountain,
' or going privately to a terrace, a bower, a foreft,
' or a lonely place, without lifteners, let him con-
' fult with them unobferved.

148. ' That prince, of whofe weighty fecrets all
' affemblies of men are ignorant, fhall attain do-
' minion over the whole earth, though *at firft* he
' poffefs no treafure.

149. ' At the time of confultation, let him re-
' move the ftupid, the dumb, the blind and the
' deaf, talking birds, decripit old men, women,
' and infidels, the difeafed and the maimed ;

150. ' Since thofe, who are difgraced *in this*
' *life, by reafon of fins formerly committed*, are apt to
' betray fecret council ; fo are talking birds ; and
' fo above all are women : them he muft for that
' reafon diligently remove.

N   151. ' At

151. ' At noon or at midnight, when his fa-
' tigues have ceafed, and his cares are difperfed,
' let him deliberate, with thofe minifters or alone,
' on virtue, lawful pleafure, and wealth ;

152. ' On the means of reconciling the acqui-
' fition of them, when they oppofe each other ;
' on beftowing his daughters in marriage, and on
' preferving his fons *from evil by the beſt education* ;

153. ' On fending ambaſſadors and meſſengers ;
' on the probable events of his meafures ; on the
' behaviour *of his women* in the private apart-
' ments ; and on the acts even of his own emiſ-
' faries.

154. ' On the whole eightfold bufinefs of
' kings, *relating to the revenue, to their expences,*
' *to the good or bad conduct of their miniſters, to*
' *legiſlation in dubious cafes, to civil and criminal*
' *juſtice, and to expiations for crimes,* let him reflect
' with the greateſt attention ; on his five forts of
' fpies, *or active and artful youths, degraded ancho-*
' *rets, diſtreſſed huſbandmen, decayed merchants, and*
' *fictitious penitents, whom he muſt pay and fee pri-*
' *vately* ; on the good will or enmity of his neigh-
' bours, and on the ſtate of the circumjacent
' countries.

155. ' On the conduct of that foreign prince,
' who has moderate ſtrength *equal to one ordinary*
' *foe, but no match for two* ; on the defigns of
' him, who is willing and able to be a conqueror ;
' on the condition of him, who is pacifick, *but a*
' *match even for the former unallied* ; and on that
' of his *natural* enemy let him feduloufly me-
' ditate :

156. ' Thofe *four powers,* who, in one word,
' are the root or *principal ſtrength* of the countries
7   ' round

' round him, added to eight others, *who are called*
' *the* branches, *and are as many degrees of allies*
' *and opponents varioufly diftinguifhed,* are declared
' to be twelve chief objects *of the royal con-*
' *fideration ;*

157. ' And five other heads, namely, their
' minifters, their territories, their ftrong holds,
' their treafuries, and their armies, being applied
' to each *of thofe twelve,* there are in all, *together*
' *with them,* feventy-two *foreign* objects *to be care-*
' *fully inveftigated.*

158. ' Let the king confider as hoftile to him,
' the power immediately beyond him, and the
' favourer of that power ; as amicable, the power
' next beyond his *natural* foe ; and as neutral,
' the powers beyond that *circle :*

159. ' All thofe *powers* let him render fubfer-
' vient to his interefts by mild meafures and the
' other *three* expedients *before mentioned,* either fe-
' parate or united, but principally by valour and
' policy *in arms and negotiation.*

160. ' Let him conftantly deliberate on the fix
' meafures of a military prince, *namely*, waging
' war, and making peace or alliance, marching to
' battle, and fitting encamped, diftributing his
' forces, and feeking the protection of a more
' powerful monarch :

161. ' Having confidered the pofture of affairs,
' let him occafionally apply to it the meafure of
' fitting inactive, or of marching to action, of
' peace, or of war, of dividing his force, or of
' feeking protection.

162. ' A king muft know, that there are two
' forts of alliance and war ; two, of remaining en-
' camped, and of marching ; two likewife, of

N 2   ' dividing

' dividing his army, and of obtaining protection
' from another power.

163. ' The two forts of alliance, attended with
' prefent and future advantages, are held to be
' thofe, when he acts in conjunction with his ally,
' and when he acts apart from him.

164. ' War is declared to be of two forts;
' when it is waged for an injury to himfelf, and
' when it is waged for an injury to his ally, with a
' view to harafs the enemy both in feafon and out
' of feafon.

165. ' Marching is of two forts, when deftruc-
' tive acts are done at his own pleafure by himfelf
' apart, or when his ally attends him.

166. ' The two forts of fitting encamped are,
' *firft*, when he has been gradually weakened by
' the Divine Power, or by the operation of paft
' fins, and, *fecondly*, when, to favour his ally, he
' remains in his camp.

167. ' A detachment commanded by the king
' in perfon, and a detachment commanded by a
' general officer, for the purpofe of carrying fome
' important point, are declared by thofe, who will
' know the fix meafures, to be the two modes of
' dividing his army.

168. ' The two modes of feeking protection,
' that his powerful fupport may be proclaimed in
' all countries, are, *firft*, when he wifhes to be
' fecure from apprehended injury, and, *next*, when
' his enemies actually affail him.

169. ' When the king knows with certainty,
' that at fome future time his force will be greatly
' augmented, and when, at the time prefent, he
' fuftains little injury, let him then have recourfe
' to peaceful meafures ;

170. ' But, when he fees all his fubjects confi-
' derably firm in ftrength, and feels himfelf highly
                                                        ' exalted

' exalted in power, let him protect his dominions
' by war.

171. ' When he perfectly knows his own
' troops to be cheerful and well supplied, and
' those of his enemy quite the reverse, let him
' eagerly march against his foes;

172. ' But when he finds himself weak in
' beasts of burden and in troops, let him then sit
' quiet in camp, using great attention, and paci-
' fying his enemy by degrees.

173. ' When a king sees his foe stronger in all
' respects than himself, let him detach a part of
' his army, *to keep the enemy amused*, and secure
' his own safety *in an inaccessible place*;

174. ' But when he is in all places assailable
' by the hostile troops, let him speedily seek the
' protection of a just and powerful monarch.

175. ' Him, who can keep in subjection both
' his own subjects and his foes, let him constantly
' sooth by all sorts of attentive respect, as he
' would honour his father, natural or spiritual:

176. ' But if, even in that situation, he find
' such protection a cause of evil, let him alone,
' though weak, wage vigorous war without fear.

177. ' By all these expedients let a politick
' prince act with such wisdom, that neither allies,
' neutral powers, nor foes, may gain over him
' any great advantage.

178. ' Perfectly let him consider the state of
' his kingdom, both actually present and probably
' future, with the good and bad parts of all his
' actions:

179. ' That king shall never be overcome by
' his enemies, who foresees the good and evil, to
' ensue from his measures; who, on present oc-
' casions, takes his resolution with prudent speed,

N 3   ' and

' and who weighs the various events of his paſt
' conduct.

180. ' Let him ſo arrange all his affairs, that
' no ally, neutral prince, or enemy, may obtain
' any advantage over him: this, in a few words,
' is the ſum of political wiſdom.

181. 'WHEN the king begins his march againſt
' the domains of his foe, let him gradually ad-
' vance, in the following manner, againſt the
' hoſtile metropolis.

182. ' Lêt him ſet out on his expedition in the
' fine month *Márgasîrſha,* or about the month of
' *Phálguna* and *Chaitra,* according to *the number*
' *of* his forces, *that he may find autumnal or vernal*
' *crops in the country invaded by him:*

183. ' Even in other ſeaſons, when he has a
' clear proſpect of victory, and when any diſaſter
' has befallen his foe, let him advance with the
' greater part of his army.

184. ' Having made a due arrangement of
' affairs in his own dominions, and a diſpoſition
' fit for his enterprize, having provided all things
' neceſſary for his continuance in the foreign
' realms, and having ſeen all his ſpies diſpatched
' with propriety,

185. ' Having ſecured the three ſorts of ways,
' *over water, on plains, and through foreſts,* and
' placed his ſix-fold army, *elephants, cavalry, cars,*
' *infantry, officers,* and *attendants,* in complete
' military form, let him proceed by fit journeys
' toward the metropolis of his enemy:

186. ' Let him be much on his guard againſt
' every ſecret friend in the ſervice of the hoſtile
' prince, and againſt emiſſaries, who go and re-
' turn; for in ſuch friends he may find very
' dangerous foes.

187. ' On

187. ' On his march let him form his troops
' either like a ftaff, or in an even column; like a
' wain, or in a wedge with the apex foremoft; like
' a boar, or in a rhomb with the van and rear
' narrow and the centre broad; like a Macara or
' fea monfter, that is, in a double triangle with apices
' joined; like a needle, or in a long line; or like
' the bird of Vishnu, that is, in a rhomboid with
' the wings far extended:

188. ' From whatever fide he apprehends
' danger, to that fide let him extend his troops;
' and let him always conceal himself in the midft
' of a fquadron, formed like a lotos flower.

189. ' Let him caufe his generals and the chief
'• commander under himfelf, to act in all quarters;
' and from whatever fide he perceives a defign of
' attacking him, to that fide let him turn his front.

190. ' On all fides let him ftation troops of
' foldiers, in whom he confides, diftinguifhed by
' known colours and other marks; who are ex-
' cellent both in fuftaining a charge and in charg-
' ing, who are fearlefs and incapable of defertion.

191. ' Let him at his pleafure order a few men
' to engage in a clofe phalanx, or a large number
' of warriours in loofe ranks; and, having formed
' them in a long line like a needle, or in three di-
' vifions like a thunderbolt, let him give orders
' for battle.

192. ' ' On a plain, let him fight with his armed
' cars and horfes; on watery places, with manned
' boats and elephants; on ground full of trees
' and fhrubs, with bows; on cleared ground, with
' fwords and targets, and other weapons,

193. ' Men born in Curucfhétra, near Indrap-
' reft'ha, in Matfya, or Viráta, in Panchála, or
' Cányacubja, and in Súraféna, in the diftrict of
N 4   ' Mat'hurà

' *Mat'hurà*, let him caufe to engage in the van;
' and men, *born in other countries*, who are tall
' and light.

194. ' Let him, when he has formed his
' troops in array, encourage them *with fhort ani-*
' *mated fpeeches*; and then let him try them com-
' pletely : let him know likewife how his men feve-
' rally exert themfelves, while they charge the foe.

195. ' If he block up his enemy, let him fit
' encamped, and lay wafte the hoftile country ;
' let him continually fpoil the grafs, water, and
' wood of the adverfe prince.

196. ' Pools, wells, and trenches, let him de-
' ftroy : let him harafs the foe by day, and alarm
' him by night.

197. ' Let him fecretly bring over to his party
' all fuch *leaders* as he can fafely bring over; let
' him be informed of all that his enemies are
' doing ; and, when a fortunate moment is of-
' fered by heaven, let him give battle, pufhing
' on to conqueft and abandoning fear :

198. ' Yet he fhould be more fedulous to re-
' duce his enemy by negotiation, by well applied
' gifts, and by creating divifions, ufing either all
' or fome of thofe methods, than by hazarding at
' any time a decifive action,

199. ' Since victory or defeat are not furely
' forefeen on either fide, when two armies engage
' in the field : let the king then, *if other expedients*
' *prevail*, avoid a pitched battle :

200. ' But, fhould there be no means of ap-
' plying the three *before-mentioned* expedients, let
' him, after due preparation, fight fo valiantly,
' that his enemy may be totally routed.'

201. ' HAVING conquered a country, let him
' refpect the deities adored in it, and their vir-
' tuous

' tuous priefts; let him alfo diftribute largeffes
' *to the people*, and caufe a full exemption from
' terrour to be loudly proclaimed.

202. ' When he has perfectly afcertained the
' conduct and intentions of all the vanquifhed, let
' him fix in that country a prince of the royal
' race, and give him precife inftructions.

203. ' Let him eftablifh the laws of the con-
' quered nation as declared *in their books*; and let
' him gratify the new prince with gems, *and other*
' *precious gifts.*

204. ' The feizure of defirable property, though
' it caufe hatred, and the donation of it, though
' it caufe love, may be laudable or blameable on
' different occafions:

205. ' All this *conduct of human affairs* is con-
' fidered as dependent on acts afcribed to the
' deity, and on acts afcribed to men; now the
' operations of the deity cannot be known by any
' intenfenefs of thought, but thofe of men may be
' clearly difcovered.

206. ' OR the victor, confidering an ally, ter-
' ritory, and wealth as the triple fruit of conqueft,
' may form an alliance with the vanquifhed prince,
' and proceed in union with him, ufing diligent
' circumfpection.

207. ' He fhould pay due attention to the
' prince who fupported his caufe, and to any
' other prince of the circumjacent region, who
' checked that fupporter, fo that both from a well-
' wifher and from an opponent, he may fecure the
' fruit of his expedition.

208. ' By gaining wealth and territory a king
' acquires not fo great an increafe of ftrength, as
' by obtaining a firm ally, who, though weak,
' may hereafter be powerful.

209. ' That

209. ' That ally, though feeble, is highly es-
' timable, who knows the whole extent of his
' duties, who gratefully remembers benefits,
' whose people are satisfied, *or, who has a gentle*
' *nature,* who loves his friend, and perseveres in
' his good resolutions.

210. ' Him have the sages declared an enemy
' hard to be subdued, who is eminently learned,
' of a noble race, personally brave, dextrous in
' management, liberal, grateful, and firm.

211. ' Good nature, knowledge of mankind,
' valour, benignity of heart, and inceffant libe-
' rality, are the assemblage of virtues which adorn
' a neutral prince, *whose amity must be courted.*

212. ' Even a salubrious and fertile country,
' where cattle continually increase, let a king
' abandon, without hesitation, for the sake of pre-
' serving himself:

213. ' Against misfortune let him preserve his
' wealth; at the expence of his wealth let him
' preserve his wife; but let him at all events pre-
' serve himself even at the hazard of his wife and
' his riches.

214. ' A wise prince, who finds' every sort of
' calamity rushing violently upon him, should
' have recourse to all just expedients, united or
' separate:

215. ' Let him consider the business to be ex-
' pedited, the expedients collectively, and himself
' who must apply them; and taking refuge com-
' pletely in those three, let him strenuously labour
' for his own prosperity.

216. ' Having consulted with his ministers,
' in the manner before prescribed on all this *mass*
' *of publick affairs;* having used exercise *becoming*
' *a warriour,* and having bathed *after it,* let the
                                        ' king

' king enter at noon his private apartments for
' the purpofe of taking food.

217. ' There let him eat lawful aliment, pre-
' pared by fervants attached to his perfon, who
' know the difference of times and are incapable
' of perfidy, after it has been proved innocent *by*
' *certain experiments,* and hallowed by texts of the
' *Véda,* repulfive of poifon.

2 8. ' Together with all his food let him fwal-
' low fuch medical fubftances as refift venom ;
' and let him conftantly wear with attention fuch
' gems as are known to repel it.

219. ' Let his females, well tried and attentive,
' their drefs and ornaments having been exa-
' mined, *left fome weapon fhould be concealed in them,*
' do him humble fervice with fans, water, and
' perfumes :

220. ' Thus let him take diligent care, when
' he goes out in a carriage or on horfeback, when
' he lies down to reft, when he fits, when he
' takes food, when he bathes, anoints his body
' *with odorous effences,* and puts on all his habili-
' ments.

221. ' After eating, let him divert himfelf with
' his women in the receffes of his palace ; and,
' having idled a reafonable time, let him again
' think of publick affairs :

222. When he has dreffed himfelf completely,
' let him once more review his armed men, with
' all their elephants, horfes, and cars, their accou-
' trements and weapons.

223. ' At funfet, having performed his religious
' duty, let him privately, but well armed, in his
' interior apartment, hear what has been done by
' his reporters and emiffaries :

224. ' Then,

224. 'Then, having difmiffed thofe informers,
' and returning to another fecret chamber, let him
' go, attended by women, to the inmoft recefs of
' his manfion for the fake of his evening meal;

225. ' There, having a fecond time eaten a lit-
' tle, and having been recreated with mufical
' ftrains, let him take reft early, and rife refrefhed
' from his labour.

226. ' This perfect fyftem of rules let a king,
' free from illnefs, obferve; but when really af-
' flicted with difeafe, he may intruft all thefe affairs
' to his officers.'

CHAPTER THE EIGHTH.

On *Judicature*; and on *Law, Private and Criminal.*

———

1. ' A KING, defirous of infpecting judicial pro-
' ceedings muft enter his court of juftice, com-
' pofed and fedate in his demeanour, together
' with *Bráhmens* and counfellors, who know how
' to give him advice:

2. ' There, either fitting or ftanding, holding
' forth his right arm, without oftentation in his
' drefs and ornaments, let him examine the affairs
' of litigant parties.

3. ' Each day let him decide caufes one after
' another, under the eighteen *principal* titles of
' law, by arguments and rules drawn from local
' ufages, and from written codes:

4. ' Of thofe *titles*, the firft is debt, on loans
' for confumption; *the fecond*, depofits, and loans
' for ufe; *the third*, fale without ownerfhip; *the
' fourth*, concerns among partners; *the fifth*, fub-
' traction of what has been given;

5. ' *The fixth*, non-payment of wages or hire;
' *the feventh*, non-performance of agreements;
' *the eighth*, refciffion of fale and purchafe; *the
' ninth*, difputes between mafter and fervant;

6. ' *The tenth*, contefts on boundaries; *the
eleventh*

' *eleventh and twelfth*, affault and flander; *the*
' *thirteenth*, larceny; *the fourteenth*, robbery and
' other violence; *the fifteenth*, adultery;

7. ' *The fixteenth*, altercation between man and
' wife, and their feveral duties; *the feventeenth*,
' the law of inheritance; *the eighteenth*, gaming with
' dice and with living creatures: thefe eighteen
' titles of law are fettled as the ground work of
' all judicial procedure in this world.

8. ' Among men, who contend for the moft
' part on the titles juft mentioned, *and on a few*
' *mifcellaneous heads not comprifed under them*, let
' the king decide caufes juftly, obferving prime-
' val law;

9. ' But when he cannot infpect fuch affairs in
' perfon, let him appoint, for the infpection of
' them, a *Bráhmen* of eminent learning:

10. ' Let that chief judge, accompanied by
' three affeffors, fully confider all caufes brought
' before the king; and, having entered the court
' room, let him fit or ftand, *but not move back-*
' *wards and forwards*.

11. ' In whatever country three *Bráhmens*,
' particularly fkilled in the three feveral *Védas*, fit
' together with the very learned *Bráhmen* ap-
' pointed by the king, the wife call that *affembly*
' the court of BRAHMA' *with four faces*.

12. ' WHEN juftice, having been wounded by
' iniquity, approaches the court, and the judges
' extract not the dart, they alfo fhall be wounded
' by it.

13. ' Either the court muft not be entered *by*
' *judges, parties, and witneffes*, or law and truth
' muft be openly declared: that man is criminal,
' who either fays nothing, or fays what is falfe
' or unjuft.

14. ' Where

14. ' Where juftice is deftroyed by iniquity,
' and truth by falfe evidence, the judges, who
' bafely look on, *without giving redrefs*, fhall alfo
' be deftroyed.

15. ' Juftice being deftroyed, will deftroy;
' being preferved, will preferve: it muft never
' therefore be violated. " Beware, *O judge*, left
" juftice being overturned, overturn *both* us and
" thyfelf."

16. ' The divine form of juftice is reprefented
' as *Vrĭſha*, or *a bull*, and the gods confider him,
' who violates juftice, as a *Vrĭſhala*, or one who
' flays a bull: let the king, therefore, and his
' judges beware of violating juftice.

17. ' The only firm friend, who follows men
' even after death, is juftice; all others are ex-
' tinct with the body.

18. ' Of injuftice *in decifions*, one quarter falls
' on the party in the caufe; one quarter, on his
' witneffes; one quarter, on all the judges; and
' one quarter on the king;

19. ' But where he, who deferves condemna-
' tion fhall be condemned, the king is guiltlefs,
' and the judges free from blame: an evil deed
' fhall recoil on him who committed it.

20. ' A *Bráhmen* fupported only by his clafs,
' and one barely reputed a *Bráhmen*, but without
' performing any facerdotal acts, may, at the king's
' pleafure, interpret the law to him: *fo may the*
' *two middle claffes*; but a *Súdra*, in no cafe what-
' ever.

21. ' Of that king, who ftupidly looks on,
' while a *Súdra* decides caufes, the kingdom it-
' felf fhall be embarraffed, like a cow in deep
' mire.

22. ' The

22. ' The whole territory, which is inhabited
' by a number of *Súdras*, overwhelmed with
' atheifts, and deprived of *Bráhmens*, muft fpeedily
' perifh, afflicted with death and difeafe.

23. ' Let the king *or his judge*, having feated
' himfelf on the bench, his body properly clothed,
' and his mind attentively fixed, begin with doing
' reverence to the deities, who guard the world ;
' and then let him enter on the trial of caufes :

24. ' Underftanding what is expedient or in-
' expedient, but confidering only what is law or
' not law, let him examine all difputes between
' parties, in the order of their feveral claffes.

25. ' By external figns let him fee through the
' thoughts of men ; by their voice, colour, coun-
' tenance, limbs, eyes, and action :

26. ' From the limbs, the look, the motion
' of the body, the gefticulation, the fpeech, the
' changes of the eye and the face, are difcovered
' the internal workings of the mind.

27. ' THE property of a ftudent and of an infant,
' whether by defcent or otherwife, let the king
' hold in his cuftody, until the owner fhall have
' ended his ftudentfhip, or until his infancy fhall
' have ceafed *in his fixteenth year*.

28. ' Equal care muſt be taken of barren
' women, of women without fons, *whofe hufbands*
' *have married other wives*, of women without
' kindred, or whofe hufbands are in diftant places,
' of widows true to their lords, and of women
' afflicted with illnefs.

29. ' Such kinfmen, as *by any pretence*, ap-
' propriate the fortunes of women during their
' lives, a juft king muft punifh with the feverity
' due to thieves.

30. ' Three

30. ' Three years let the king detain the pro-
' perty of which no owner appears, *after a diſtinct*
' *proclamation:* the owner appearing within the
' three years, may take it; but, after that term,
' the king may confiſcate it.

31. ' He, who ſays " This is mine," muſt be
' duly examined; and if, *before he inſpect it*, he
' declare its form, number, and other circum-
' ſtances, the owner muſt have his property;

32. ' But if he ſhow not at what place and
' time it was loſt, and ſpecify not its colour,
' ſhape, and dimenſions, he ought to be amerced:

33. ' The king may take a ſixth part of the
' property ſo detained by him, or a tenth, or a
' twelfth, remembering the duty of good kings.

34. ' Property loſt *by one man*, and found *by*
' *another*, let the king ſecure, by committing it
' to the care of truſt-worthy men; and thoſe,
' whom he ſhall convict of ſtealing it, let him
' cauſe to be trampled on by an elephant.

35. ' From the man who ſhall ſay with truth,
" This property, which has been kept, belongs
" to me," the king may take a ſixth or twelfth
' part, *for having ſecured it*;

36. ' But he who ſhall ſay ſo falſely, may be
' fined either an eighth part of his own property,
' or elſe in ſome ſmall proportion, to the value
' of the goods falſely claimed, a juſt calculation
' having been made.

37. ' A learned *Bráhmen*, having found a
' treaſure formerly hidden, may take it without
' any deduction; ſince he is the lord of all;

38. ' But of a treaſure anciently repoſited un-
' der ground, which *any other ſubject* or the king
' has diſcovered, the king may lay up half in his
' treaſury, having given half to the *Bráhmens*.

O   39. ' Of

39. ' Of old hoards, and precious minerals in
' the earth, the king is entitled to half by reafon
' of his general protection, and becaufe he is the
' lord paramount of the foil.

40. ' To men of all claffes, the king muft
' reftore their property, which robbers have
' feized; fince a king, who takes it for himfelf,
' incurs the guilt of a robber.

41. ' A king who knows the revealed law,
' muft enquire into the particular laws of claffes,
' the laws *or ufages* of diftricts, the cuftoms of
' traders, and the rules of certain families, and
' eftablifh their peculiar laws, *if they be not re-*
' *pugnant to the law of* God ;

42. ' Since all men, who mind their own
' cuftomary ways of proceeding, and are fixed in
' the difcharge of their feveral duties, become
' united by affection with the people at large,
' even though they dwell far afunder.

43. ' Neither the king himfelf, nor his officers
' muft ever promote litigation ; nor ever neglect
' a law fuit inftituted by others.

44. ' As a hunter traces the lair of a *wounded*
' beaft by the drops of blood; thus let a king
' inveftigate the true point of juftice by deliberate
' arguments :

45. ' Let him fully confider the nature of
' truth, the ftate of the cafe, and his own perfon;
' and next, the witneffes, the place, the mode,
' and the time ; firmly adhering to all the rules
' of practice :

46. '' What has been practifed by good men and
' by virtuous *Bráhmens,* if it be not inconfiftent
' with the legal cuftoms of provinces or diftricts,
' of claffes and families, let him eftablifh.

47. ' When

47. ' When a creditor sues before him for the
' recovery of his right from a debtor, let him
' cause the debtor to pay what the creditor shall
' prove due.

48. ' By whatever lawful means a creditor
' may have gotten possession of his own property,
' let the king ratify such payment by the debtor,
' though obtained even by compulsory means :

49. ' By the mediation of friends, by suit in
' court, by artful management, or by distress, a
' creditor may recover the property lent; and
' fifthly, by legal force.

50. ' That creditor, who recovers his right
' from his debtor, must not be rebuked by the
' king for retaking his own property.

51. ' In a suit for a debt, which the defendant
' denies, let him award payment to the creditor
' of what, by good evidence, he shall prove due,
' and exact a small fine, *according to the circum-*
' *stances of the debtor.*

52. ' On the denial of a debt, which the de-
' fendant has in court been required to pay, the
' plaintiff must call a witness who was present at
' the place of the loan, or produce other evidence,
' *as a note and the like.*

53. ' The plaintiff, who calls a witness not
' present at the place *where the contract was made,*
' or, having knowingly called him, disclaims him
' as his witness; or who perceives not, that he
' asserts confused and contradictory facts ;

54. ' Or who, having stated what he designs
' to prove, varies afterwards from his case ; or
' who, being questioned on a fact which he had
' before admitted, refuses to acknowledge that
' very fact :

55. ' Or

55. ' Or who has converfed with the witneffes
' in a place unfit for fuch converfation ; or who
' declines anfwering a queftion properly put; or
' who departs from the court ;

56. ' Or who, being ordered to fpeak, ftands
' mute; or who proves not what he has alledged;
' or who knows not what is capable or incapa-
' ble of proof; *fuch a plaintiff* fhall fail in that
' fuit.

57. ' Him who has faid " I have witneffes,"
' and being told to produce them, produces them
' not, the judge muft on this account declare
' nonfuited.

58. ' If the plaintiff delay to put in his plaint,
' he may, *according to the nature of the cafe*, be
' corporally punifhed or juftly amerced ; and if
' the defendant plead not within three fortnights,
' he is by law condemned.

59. ' In the double of that fum, which the
' defendant falfely denies, or on which the com-
' plainant falfely declares, fhall thofe two men,
' wilfully offending againft juftice, be fined by
' the king.

60. ' When a man has been brought into
' court by a fuitor for property, and, being called
' on to anfwer, denies the debt, the caufe fhould
' be decided by the *Bráhmen* who reprefents the
' king, having heard three witneffes at leaft.

61. ' WHAT fort of witneffes muft be pro-
' duced by creditors *and others* on the trial
' of caufes, I will comprehenfively declare ; and
' in what manner thofe witneffes muft give true
' evidence.

62. ' Married houfe-keepers, men with male
' iffue, inhabitants of the fame diftrict, either of
' the

' the military, the commercial, or the fervile clafs,
' are-competent, when called by the party, to give
' their evidence ; not any perfons indifcriminately,
' except in *fuch* cafes of urgency *as will foon be*
' mentioned.

63. ' Juft and fenfible men of all the *four* claffes
' may be witneffes on trials ; men, who know
' their whole duty, and are free from covetoufnefs :
' but men of an oppofite character the judge muft
' reject.

64. ' Thofe muft not be admitted who have a
' pecuniary intereft ; nor familiar friends ; nor
' menial fervants; nor enemies ; nor men for-
' merly perjured ; nor perfons grievoufly dif-
' eafed ; nor thofe who have committed henious
' offences.

65. ' The king cannot be made a witnefs ; nor
' *cooks and the like* mean artificers ; nor public
' dancers nor fingers ; nor a prieft of deep learn-
' ing in fcripture ; nor a ftudent in theology ; nor
' an anchoret fecluded from all worldly con-
' nexions ;

66. ' Nor one wholy dependent ; nor one of
' bad fame ; nor one who follows a cruel occu-
' pation ; nor one who acts openly againft the
' law ; nor a decripit old man ; nor a child ; nor
' one man only, *unlefs he be diftinguifhed for virtue* ;
' nor a wretch of the loweft mixed clafs ; nor one
' who has loft the organs of fenfe ;

67. ' Nor one extremely grieved ; nor one in-
' toxicated ; nor a madman ; nor one tormented
' with hunger or thirft ; nor one oppreffed by
' fatigue ; nor one excited by luft ; nor one in-
' flamed by wrath ; nor one who has been con-
' victed of theft.

O 3

68. ' Women

68. ' Women fhould regularly be witneffes for
' women ; twice born men, for men alike twice
' born ; good fervants and mechanicks, for fer-
' vants and mechanicks ; and thofe of the loweft
' race, for thofe of the loweft ;

69. ' But any perfon whatever, who has pofitive
' knowledge *of tranfactions* in the private apart-
' ments of a houfe, or in a foreft, or at a time
' of death, may give evidence between the
' parties :

70. ' On failure *of witneffes duly qualified*, evi-
' dence may, *in fuch cafes*, be given by a woman, by
' a child, or by an aged man, by a pupil, by a
' kinfman, by a flave, or by a hired fervant ;

71. ' Yet of children, of old men, and of the
' difeafed, who are all apt to fpeak untruly, the
' judge muft confider the teftimony as weak ; and
' *much more*, that of men with difordered minds :

72. ' In all cafes of violence, of theft and
' adultery, of defamation and affault, he muft not
' examine too ftrictly the competence of wit-
' neffes.

73. ' If there be contradictory evidence, let the
' king decide by the plurality of credible wit-
' neffes ; if equality in number, by fuperiority in
' virtue ; if parity in virtue, by the teftimony of
' fuch twice born men as have beft performed
' publick duties.

74. ' Evidence of what has been feen, or of what
' has been heard, *as flander and the like*, given by
' thofe who faw or heard it, is admiffable ; and a
' witnefs who fpeaks truth in thofe cafes, neither
' deviates from virtue nor lofes his wealth :

75. ' But a witnefs, who knowingly fays any
' thing, before an affembly of good men, differ-
' ent from what he had feen or heard, fhall fall
' headlong

' headlong, after death, into a region of horrour,
' and be debarred from heaven.

76. ' When a man fees or hears any thing,
' without being then called upon to atteft it, yet if
' he be *afterwards* examined as a witnefs, he muft
' declare it, exactly as *it was* feen, *and* as *it was*
' heard.

77. ' One man, untainted with covetoufnefs *and*
' *other vices*, may *in fome cafes* be the fole witnefs,
' and will have more weight than many women,
' becaufe female underftandings are apt to waver;
' or than many other men who have been tar-
' nifhed with crimes.

78. ' What witneffes declare naturally *or with-*
' *out bias*, muft be received on trials; but what
' they improperly fay, from fome unnatural bent,
' is inapplicable to the purpofes of juftice.

79. ' THE witneffes being affembled in the
' middle of the court-room, in the prefence of
' the plaintiff and the defendant, let the judge
' examine them, after having addreffed them *all*
' *together* in the following manner:

80. '' What ye know to have been tranfacted
'' in the matter before us, between the parties re-
'' ciprocally, declare at large and with truth; for
'' your evidence in this caufe is required.''

81. ' A witnefs, who gives teftimony with
' truth, fhall attain exalted feats of beatitude
' above, and the higheft fame here below: fuch
' teftimony is revered by BRAHMA' himfelf;

82. ' The witnefs who fpeaks falfely, fhall be
' faft bound, *under water,* in the *fnaky* cords of
' VARUNA, and be wholly deprived of power *to*
' *efcape torment*, during a hundred tranfmigrations:
' let mankind, therefore, give no falfe teftimony.

83. ' By

83. ' By truth is a witnefs cleared of fin ; by
' truth is juftice advanced : truth muft, therefore,
' be fpoken by witneffes of every clafs.

84. '· The foul itfelf is its own witnefs ; the
' foul itfelf is its own refuge ; offend not thy
' confcious foul, the fupreme internal witnefs of
' men !

85. ' The finful have faid in their hearts :
" None fees us." Yes ; the gods diftinctly fee
' them ; and fo does the fpirit within their breafts.

86. ' The guardian deities of the firmament, of
' the earth, of the waters, of the human heart,
' of the moon, of the fun, and of fire, of pu-
' nifhment after death, of the winds, of night, of
' both twilights, and of juftice, perfectly know
' the ftate of all fpirits clothed with bodies.

87. ' In the forenoon let the the judge, being
' purified, feverally call on the twice born, being
' purified alfo, to declare the truth, in the pre-
' fence of *fome image, a fymbol* of the divinity, and
' of *Bráhmens,* while the witneffes turn their faces
' either to the north or to the eaft.

88. ' To a *Bráhmen* he muft begin with faying,
" Declare ;" to a *Cfhatriya,* with faying " De-
" clare the truth ;" to a *Vaifya,* with comparing
' perjury to the crime of ftealing kine, grain, or
' gold ; to a *Súdra,* with comparing it *in fome or all*
' *of the following fentences,* to every crime that men
' can commit.

89. " WHATEVER places of torture have been
" prepared for the flayer of a prieft, for the mur-
" derer of a woman or of a child, for the injurer
" of a friend, and for an ungrateful man, thofe
" places are ordained for a witnefs who gives falfe
" evidence.

90. " The

90. " The fruit of every virtuous act, which
" thou haft done, O good man, fince thy birth,
" fhall depart from thee to dogs, if thou deviate
" in fpeech from the truth.

91. " O friend to virtue, that Supreme Spirit,
" which thou believeft one and the fame with
" thyfelf, refides in thy bofom perpetually, and is
" an all-knowing infpector of thy goodnefs or
" of thy wickednefs.

92. " If thou beeft not at variance, *by fpeaking*
" *falfely*, with YAMA, or the fubduer of all ; with
" VAIVASWATA, or the punifher ; with that great
" divinity who dwells in thy breaft ; go not *on a*
" *pilgrimage* to the river *Gangà*, nor to the plains
" of CURU, *for thou haft no need of expiation.*

93. " Naked and fhorn, tormented with hun-
" ger and thirft, and deprived of fight, fhall the
" man who gives falfe evidence, go with a
" potfherd to beg food at the door of his enemy.

94. " Headlong, in utter darknefs, fhall the
" impious wretch tumble into hell, who, being
" interrogated in a judicial inquiry, anfwers one
" queftion falfely,

95. " He, who in a court of juftice gives an
" imperfect account of any tranfaction, or afferts
" a fact of which he was no eye-witnefs, fhall re-
" ceive pain *inftead of pleafure*, and refemble a man,
" who eats fifh *with eagernefs* and fwallows the
" fharp bones.

96. " The gods are acquainted with no better
" mortal in this world, than the man, of whom
" the intelligent fpirit, which pervades his
" body, has no diftruft, when he prepares to give
" evidence.

97. " Hear, honeft man, from a juft enumera-
" tion

" tion in order, how many kinfmen, in evidence
" of different forts, a falfe witnefs kills *or incurs*
" *the guilt of killing :*

98. " He kills five by falfe teftimony concern-
" ing cattle in general; he kills ten by falfe tef-
" timony concerning kine; he kills a hundred
" by falfe evidence concerning horfes; and a
" thoufand by falfe evidence concerning the hu-
" man race :

· 99. " By fpeaking falfely in a caufe concerning
" gold, he kills the born and the unborn; by
" fpeaking falfely concerning land, he kills
" every thing animated : beware then of fpeaking
" falfely in a caufe concerning land !

100. " The fages have held falfe evidence con-
" cerning water, and the poffeffion or enjoyment
" of women, equal to falfe evidence concerning
" land; and it is equally criminal in caufes con-
" cerning *pearls and other* precious things formed
" in water, and concerning all things made of
" ftone.

101. " Marking well all the murders which are
" comprehended in the crime of perjury, declare
" thou the whole truth with precifion, as *it was*
" heard, *and* as *it was* feen by thee."

102. ' *Bráhmens* who tend herds of cattle, who
' trade, who practife mechanical arts, who profefs
' dancing and finging, who are hired fervants or
' ufurers, let the judge exhort and examine as if
' they were *Súdras.*

103. ' In fome cafes, a giver of falfe evidence
' from a pious motive, even though he know the
' truth, fhall not lofe a feat in heaven; fuch evi-
' dence wife men call the fpeech of the gods.

104. ' Whenever the death of a man, *who had*
' *not*

‘ *not been a grievous offender*, either of the servile,
‘ the commercial, the military, or the sacerdotal
‘ class, would be occasioned by true evidence,
‘ *from the known rigour of the king, even though*
‘ *the fault arose from inadvertence or errour*, false-
‘ hood may be spoken : it is even preferable to
‘ truth.

105. ‘ Such *witnesses* must offer, as oblations to
‘ SARASWATI', cakes of rice and milk addressed
‘ to the goddess of speech ; and thus will they
‘ fully expiate that venial sin of benevolent false-
‘ hood :

106. ‘ Or such a *witness* may pour clarified
‘ butter into the holy fire, according to the sacred
‘ rule, hallowing it with the texts called *cúshmándá*,
‘ or with those which relate to VARUNA, begin-
‘ ing with *ud* ; or with the three texts appropriated
‘ to the water gods.

107. ‘ A MAN who labours not under illness,
‘ yet comes not to give evidence in cases of loans
‘ and the like, within three fortnights *after due*
‘ *summons*, shall take upon himself the whole debt,
‘ and pay a tenth part of it as a fine *to the king*.

108. ‘ The witness, who has given evidence,
‘ and to whom, within seven days after, *a misfor-*
‘ *tune* happens *from* disease, fire, or the death of
‘ a kinsman, shall be condemned to pay the debt
‘ and a fine.

109. ‘ IN cases, where no witness can be
‘ had, between two parties opposing each other,
‘ the judge may acquire a knowledge of the truth,
‘ by the oath of the parties ; *or* if he cannot *other-*
‘ *wise* perfectly ascertain it.

110. ‘ By the *seven* great *Ríshis*, and by the
‘ deities themselves, have oaths been taken, for
‘ the

' the purpose of judicial proof; and even
' VASISHT'HA, *being accused by* VISWA'MITRA *of*
' *murder*, took an oath before the *king* SUDA'MAN,
' son of PIYAVANA.

111. ' Let no man of sense take an oath in
' vain, *that is, not in a court of justice*, on a trifling
' occasion ; for the man, who takes an oath in
' vain, shall be punished in this life and in the
' next :

112. ' To women, however, at a time of dal-
' liance, or on a proposal of marriage, in the
' case of grass or fruit eaten by a cow, of wood
' taken for a sacrifice, or of a promise made for
' the preservation of a *Bráhmen*, it is no deadly sin
' to take a light oath.

113. ' Let the judge cause a priest to swear by his
' veracity ; a soldier by his horse or elephant,
' and his weapons ; a merchant by his kine, grain,
' and gold ; a mechanick, or servile man, by *im-*
' *precating on his own head, if he speak falsely*, all
' possible crimes ;

114. ' Or, *on great occasions*, let him cause the
' party to hold fire, or to dive under water, or
' severally to touch the heads of his children
' and wife :

115. ' He, whom the blazing fire burns not,
' whom the water soon forces not up, or meets with
' no speedy misfortune, must be held veracious in
' his testimony on oath.

116. ' Of the sage VASTA, whom his younger
' *half* brother formerly attacked, *as the son of a*
' *servile woman*, the fire, which pervades the
' world, burned not even a hair, by reason of his
' perfect veracity.

117. ' WHENEVER false evidence has been
' given in any suit, the king must reverse the
' judgement ;

' judgement ; and whatever has been done, muft
' be confidered as undone.

118. ' Evidence, given from covetoufnefs,
' from diftraction of mind, from terrour, from
' friendfhip, from luft, from wrath, from ignorance,
' and from inattention, muft be held invalid.

119. ' THE diftinctions of punifhment for a
' falfe witnefs, from either of thofe motives, I will
' propound fully and in order.

120. ' If he fpeak falfely through covetoufnefs,
' he fhall be fined a thoufand *panas*; if through
' diftraction of mind, *two hundred and fifty*, or the
' loweft amercements ; if through terrour, two
' mean amercements ; if through friendfhip, four
' times the loweft ;

121. ' If through luft, ten times the loweft
' amercement ; if through wrath, three times the
' next *or middlemoft* ; if through ignorance, two
' hundred complete ; if through inattention, a
' hundred only.

122. ' Learned men have fpecified thefe pu-
' nifhments, *which were* ordained by fage legifla-
' tors for perjured witneffes, with a view to prevent
' a failure of juftice and to reftrain iniquity.

123. ' Let a juft prince banifh men of the three
' *lower* claffes, if they give falfe evidence, having
' firft levied the fine ; but a *Bráhmen* let him only
' banifh.

124. ' MENU, fon of the Self-exiftent, has named
' ten places of punifhment, which are appropriated
' to the three *lower* claffes ; but a *Bráhmen* muft
' depart from the realm unhurt *in any one of*
' *them :*

125. ' The part of generation, the belly, the
' tongue, the two hands, and fifthly, the two feet,
the

' the eye, the nose, both ears, the property, and, *in*
' *a capital cafe*, the whole body.

126. ' Let the king, having confidered and af-
' certained the frequency of a fimilar offence, the
' place and time, the ability of the criminal *to pay*
' *or fuffer*, and the crime itfelf, caufe punifhment
' to fall on thofe alone who deferve it.

127. ' Unjuft punifhment deftroys reputation
' during life, and fame after death ; it even ob-
' ftructs, in the next life, the path to heaven :
' unjuft punifhment, therefore, let the king by all
' means avoid.

128. ' A king who inflicts punifhment on fuch
' as deferve it not, and inflicts no punifhment on
' fuch as deferve it, brings infamy on himfelf,
' while he lives, and fhall fink, when he dies, to a
' region of torment.

129. ' Firft, let him punifh by gentle admoni-
' tion ; afterwards, by harfh reproof ; thirdly, by
' deprivation of property; after that, by corpo-
' ral pain :

130. ' But, when even by corporal punifhment
' he cannot reftrain fuch offenders, let him apply
' to them all the four modes with rigour.

131. ' THOSE names of copper, filver, and
' gold weights, which are commonly ufed among
' men, for the purpofe of worldly bufinefs, I will
' now comprehenfively explain.

132. ' The very fmall mote, which may be dif-
' cerned in a fun-beam paffing through a lattice,
' is the leaft vifible quantity, and men call it a
' *trafarenu* :

133. ' Eight of thofe *trafarenus* are fuppofed
' equal in weight to one minute poppy-feed ; three
' of thofe feeds are equal to one black muftard-feed ;
' and three of thofe leaft, to a white muftard-feed :

134. ' Six

134. ' Six white muſtard-ſeeds are equal to a
' middle ſized barley-corn; three ſuch barley-
' corns to one *raĉticà*, or ſeed of the *Gunjà*; five
' *raĉticas* of gold are one *máſha*, and ſixteen ſuch
' *máſhas* one *ſuverna*:

135. ' Four *ſuvernas* make a *pala*; ten *palas*
' a *dharana*; but two *raĉticas* of ſilver weighed
' together, are conſidered as one *máſhaca*;

136. ' Sixteen of thoſe *máſhacas* are a ſilver
' *dharana*, or *purána*; but a *carſha*, or eighty
' *raĉticas* of copper, is called a *pana* or *cárſhápana*.

137. ' Ten *dharanas* of ſilver are known by the
' name of a *ſatamána*; and the weight of four
' *ſuvernas* has alſo the appellation of a *niſhca*.

138. ' Now two hundred and fifty *panas* are
' declared to be the firſt *or loweſt* amercement;
' five hundred of them are conſidered as the
' mean; and a thouſand as the higheſt.

139. ' A DEBT being admitted by the de-
' fendant, he muſt pay five in the hundred, *as a*
' *fine to the king*; but, if it be denied *and proved*,
' twice as much : this law was enaĉted by MENU.

140. ' A LENDER of money may take, in ad-
' dition to his capital, the intereſt allowed by
' VASISHT'HA, *that is*, an eightieth part of a
' hundred, *or one and a quarter* by the month, *if*
' *he have a pledge*;

141. ' Or, *if he have no pledge*, he may take
' two in the hundred *by the month*, remembering
' the duty of good men : for, by *thus* taking
' two in the hundred, he becomes not a ſinner
' for gain.

142. ' He may thus take, *in proportion to the*
' *riſk, and* in the direĉt order of the claſſes, two
' in the hundred *from a prieſt*; three *from a ſoldier*,
four

' four *from a merchant*; and five *from a mechanick*
' *or fervile man*, but never more, as intereft by
' the month.

143. ' If he take a beneficial pledge, *or a pledge*
' *to be ufed for his profit*, he muft have no other
' intereft on the loan ; nor, after a great length
' of time, *or when the profits have amounted to the*
' *debt*, can he give or fell fuch a pledge, *though*
' *he may affign it in pledge to another.*

144. ' A pledge *to be kept only* muft not be
' ufed by force, *that is, againft confent* : the pawner
' fo ufing it muft give up his whole intereft, or
' muft fatisfy the pawner, *if it be fpoiled or worn*
' *out*, by paying him the original price of it ;
' otherwife, he commits a theft of the pawn.

145. ' Neither a pledge *without limit*, nor a
' depofit, are loft to the owner by lapfe of time :
' they are both recoverable, though they have
' long remained with the bailee.

146. ' A milch cow, a camel, a riding horfe,
' *a bull, or other beaft* which has been fent to be
' tamed for labour, and other things ufed with
' friendly affent, are not loft, *by length of time*, to
' the owner.

147. ' *In general,* whatever chattel the owner
' fees enjoyed by others for ten years, while,
' though prefent, he fays nothing, that chattel he
' fhall not recover:

148. ' If he be neither an idiot, nor an infant
' under the full age of fifteen years, and if the
' chattel be adverfely poffeffed in a place where
' he may fee it, his property in it is extinct by
' law, and the adverfe poffeffor fhall keep it.

149. ' A pledge, a boundary of land, the
' property of an infant, a depofit either open or

in

' in a cheft fealed, female flaves, the wealth of
' a king, and of a learned *Bráhmen*, are not loft
' in confequence of adverfe enjoyment.

150. ' The fool, who fecretly ufes a pledge
' without, *though not againft* the affent of the
' owner, fhall give up half of his intereft, as a
' compenfation for fuch ufe.

151. ' INTEREST on money received at once,
' *not month by month, or day by day, as it ought,*
' muft never be more than enough to double the
' debt, *that is, more than the amount of the princi-*
' *pal paid at the fame time:* on grain, on fruit, on
' wool or hair, on beafts of burden, *lent to be paid*
' *in the fame kind of equal value,* it muft not be
' more than enough to make the debt quintuple.

152. ' Stipulated intereft beyond the legal rate,
' and different from the *preceding* rule, is invalid;
' and the wife call it an ufurous way *of lending:*
' the lender is entitled, *at moft,* to five in the
' hundred.

153. ' Let no lender *for a month, or for two or*
' *three months at a certain intereft,* receive *fuch*
' intereft beyond the year; nor any intereft,
' which is unapproved; nor intereft upon intereft
' *by previous agreement;* nor monthly intereft ex-
' ceeding in time the amount of the principal;
' nor intereft exacted from a debtor, *as the price*
' *of the rifk, when there is no publick danger or dif-*
' *trefs;* nor immoderate profits from a pledge to
' be ufed by way of intereft.

154. ' He, who cannot pay the debt *at the*
' *fixed time,* and wifhes to renew the contract,
' may renew it in writing, *with the creditor's af-*
' *fent,* if he pay all the intereft then due;

155. ' But if *by fome unavoidable accident,* he
' cannot pay the whole intereft, he may infert, *as*

' *principal*

‘ *principal* in the renewed contract, so much of the
‘ interest accrued as he ought to pay.

156. ‘ A lender at interest on *the risk of* safe
‘ carriage, who has agreed on the place and time,
‘ shall not receive such interest, if *by accident* the
‘ goods are not carried to the place, or within
‘ the time :

157. ‘ Whatever interest *or price of the risk*
‘ shall be settled *between the parties*, by men well
‘ acquainted with sea voyages or journeys by land,
‘ with times and with places, such interest shall
‘ have legal force.

158. ‘ THE man who becomes surety, for the
‘ appearance of a debtor in this world, and pro-
‘ duces him not, shall pay the debt out of his
‘ own property ;

159. ‘ But money due by a surety, or idly
‘ promised *to musicians and actresses*, or lost at
‘ play, or due for spirituous liquors, or what re-
‘ mains unpaid of a fine or toll, the son *of the surety*
‘ *or debtor* shall not *in general* be obliged to pay :

160. ‘ Such is the rule in cases of a surety for
‘ appearance *or good behaviour*; but if a surety
‘ for payment should die, the judge may compel
‘ even his heirs to discharge the debt.

161. ‘ On what account then is it, that after
‘ the death of a surety other than for payment,
‘ the creditor may *in one case* demand the debt
‘ *of the heir*, all the affairs of the deceased being
‘ known and proved ?

162. ‘ If the surety had received money from
‘ the debtor, and had enough to pay the debt,
‘ the son of him who so received it, shall dis-
‘ charge the debt out of his *inherited* property :
‘ this is a sacred ordinance.

163. ‘ A contract made by a person intoxicated
‘ or

' or infane, or grievoufly difordered, or wholly
' dependent, by an infant or a decrepit old man,
' or *in the name of another*, by a perfon without
' authority, is utterly null.

164. ' That plaint can have no effect though
' it may be fupported by evidence, which con-
' tains a caufe of action inconfiftent with pofitive
' law or with fettled ufage.

165. ' When the judge difcovers a fraudulent
' pledge or fale, a fraudulent gift and acceptance,
' or in what ever other cafe he detects fraud, let
' him annul the whole tranfaction.

166. ' If the debtor be dead, and if the money
' borrowed was expended for the ufe of his fa-
' mily, it muft be paid by that family, divided
' or undivided, out of their own eftate.

167. ' Should even a flave make a contract
' *in the name of his abfent mafter* for the behoof of
' the family, that mafter, whether in his own
' country or abroad, fhall not refcind it.

168. ' What is given by force *to a man who
' cannot accept it legally*, what is by force enjoyed,
' by force caufed to be written, and all other
' things done by force *or againft free confent*, MA-
' NU has pronounced void.

169. ' Three are troubled by means of others,
' *namely*, witneffes, fureties, and infpectors of
' caufes; and four collect wealth flowly, with
' benefit to others, a *Bráhmen*, a money-lender,
' a merchant, and a king.

170. ' Let no king, how indigent foever, take
' any thing which ought not to be taken; nor
' let him, how wealthy foever, decline taking
' that which he ought to take, be it ever fo fmall :

171. ' By taking what ought not to be taken,

' and

' and by refuſing what ought to be received, the
' king betrays his own weakneſs, and is loſt both
' in this world and in the next;

172. ' But by taking his due, by adminiſtering
' juſtice, and by protecting the weak, the king
' augments his own force, and is exalted in the
' next world and in this.

173. ' Therefore, let the king, like Yama,
' reſigning what may be pleaſing or unpleaſing
' to himſelf, live by the ſtrict rules of Yama,
' his anger being repreſſed, and his organs kept
' in ſubjection.

174. ' That evil-minded king, who, through
' infatuation, decides cauſes with injuſtice, his
' enemies, *through the diſaffection of his people,*
' quickly reduce to a ſtate of dependence;

175. ' But him, who ſubduing both luſt and
' wrath, examines cauſes with juſtice, his people
' naturally ſeek, as rivers the ocean.

176. ' The debtor who complains before the
' king, that his creditor has recovered the debt
' by his own legal act, *as before-mentioned,* ſhall be
' compelled by the king to pay a quarter of the
' ſum *as a fine,* and the creditor ſhall be left in
' poſſeſſion of his own.

177. ' Even by perſonal labour ſhall the debtor
' pay what is adjudged, if he be of the ſame claſs
' with the creditor, or of a lower; but a debtor
' of a higher claſs muſt pay it *according to his in-*
' *come,* by little and little.

178. ' By this ſyſtem of rules let the king
' decide, with equal juſtice, all diſputes between
' men oppoſing each other, having aſcertained
' the truth by evidence or the oaths of the parties.

179. ' A sensible man ſhould make a depoſit
' with

‘ with some person of high birth, and of good
‘ morals, well acquainted with law, habitually
‘ veracious, having a large famil,, wealthy and
‘ venerable.

180. Whatever thing, and in whatever manner
‘ a person shall deposit in the hands of another,
‘ the same thing, and in the same manner, ought
‘ to be received back by the owner; as the de-
‘ livery *was*, so *must be* the receipt.

181. ‘ He, who restores not to the depositor, on
‘ his request, what has been deposited, may first
‘ be tried by the judge *in the following manner*, the
‘ depositor himself being absent.

182. ‘ On failure of witnesses, let the judge ac-
‘ tually deposit gold, *or precious things*, with the
‘ defendant, by the artful contrivance of spies, who
‘ have passed the age of child-hood, and whose
‘ persons are engaging:

183. ‘ Should the defendant restore that depo-
‘ sit in the manner and shape ‘in which it was
‘ bailed *by the spies*, there is nothing in his hands,
‘ for which others can justly accuse him

184. ‘ But if he restore not the gold, or
‘ *precious things*, as he ought, to those emissaries,
‘ let him be apprehended and compelled to pay
‘ the value of both deposits ; this is a settled rule.

185. ‘ A deposit, whether sealed up or not,
‘ should never be redelivered, while the depositor
‘ is alive, to his heir apparent or presumptive :
‘ both sorts of deposits, indeed, are extinct, or can-
‘ not be demanded by the heir, if the depositor die,
‘ *in that case* ; but not, unless he die, *for should the*
‘ *heir apparent keep them, the depositor himself may*
‘ *sue the bailee :*

186. ‘ But, if a depositary by his own free act
‘ shall deliver a deposit to the heir of a deceased

P 3   ‘ bailor,

' bailor, he muſt not be haraſſed *with claims of a*
' *ſimilar kind*, either by the king, or by that heir;

187. ' And, *if ſimilar claims be made*, the king
' muſt decide the queſtions after friendly admoni-
' tion, *without having recourſe to artifice* ; for the
' honeſt diſpoſition of the man being proved, the
' judge muſt proceed with mildneſs.

188. ' Such is the mode of aſcertaining the right
' in all theſe caſes of a depoſit : in the caſe of a
' depoſit ſealed up, the bailee ſhall incur no cen-
' ſure *on the redelivery*, unleſs he have *altered the*
' *ſeal or* taken out ſomething.

189. ' If a depoſit be ſeized by thieves *or deſ-*
' *troyed by vermine*, or waſhed away by water, or
' conſumed by fire, the bailee ſhall not be obliged
' to make it good, unleſs he took part of it for
' himſelf.

190. ' The defendant, who denies a depoſit, and
' the plaintiff who aſſerts it, let the king try by all
' ſorts of expedients, and by the modes of ordeal
' preſcribed in the *Véda*.

191. ' He who reſtores not a thing really de-
' poſited, and he, who demands what he never
' bailed, ſhall both, *for a ſecond offence*, be pu-
' niſhed as thieves, *if gold, pearls, or the like be*
' *demanded* ; or, *in the caſe of a trifling demand*, ſhall
' pay a fine equal to the value of the thing claimed :

192. ' For the firſt offence, the king ſhould
' compel a fraudulent depoſitary, without any dif-
' tinction betweeen a depoſit under ſeal or open,
' to pay a fine equal to its value.

193. ' That man, who, by falſe pretences, gets
' into his hands the goods of another, ſhall, toge-
' ther with his accomplices, be puniſhed by vari-
' ous degrees of whipping or mutilation, or even
' by death.

194. ' Regularly,

194. ' *Regularly*, a depofit fhould be produced,
' the fame in kind and quantity as it was bailed,
' by the fame and to the fame perfon, by whom
' and from whom it was received, and before the
' fame company, *who were witneffes to the depofit* :
' he who produces it, in a different manner, ought
' to be fined ;

195. ' But a thing, privately depofited, fhould
' be privately reftored by and to the perfon, by
' and from whom it was received : as the bailment
' *was*, fo *fhould be* the delivery, *according to a rule*
' *in the* Véda.

196. ' Thus let the king decide caufes concern-
' ing a depofit, or a friendly loan for ufe, without
' fhowing rigour to the depofitary.

197. ' HIM, who fells the property of another
' man, without the affent of the owner, the judge
' fhall not admit as a competent witnefs, but fhall
' treat as a thief, who pretends that he has com-
' mitted no theft :

198. ' If, indeed he be a near kinfman of the
' owner, he fhall be fined fix hundred *panas* ; but,
' if he be neither his kinfman or a claimant under
' him, he commits an offence equal to larceny.

199. ' A gift or fale, thus made by any other
' than the true owner, muft, by a fettled rule, be
' confidered, in judicial proceedings, as not made.

200. ' Where occupation *for a time* fhall be
' proved, but no fort of title fhall appear, *the fale*
' *cannot be fupported :* title, not occupation, is
' effential to its fupport; *and* this rule *alfo* is fixed.

201. ' He who has received a chattel, by pur-
' chafe in open market, before a number of men,
' juftly acquires the abfolute property, by having
' paid the price of it, *if he can produce the vendor* ;

202. ' But

202. ' But if the vendor be not producible, and
' the vendee prove the publick sale, the latter must
' be dismissed by the king, without punishment ;
' and the former owner, who lost the chattel, may
' take it back, *on paying the vendee half its value.*

203. ' One commodity mixed with another,
' shall never be sold as *unmixed* ; nor a bad com-
' modity as good ; nor less *than agreed on* ; nor
' any thing kept at a distance or concealed, *lest*
' *some defect in it should be discovered.*

204. ' If after one damsel has been shown, another
' be offered to the bridegroom, *who had purchased*
' *leave to marry her from her next kinsman,* he may
' become the husband of both for the same price ;
' this law MENU ordained.

205. ' The kinsman, who gives a damsel in
' marriage, having first openly told her blemishes,
' whether she be insane, or disordered with ele-
' phantiasis, or defiled by connexion with a man,
' shall suffer no punishment.   :

206. ' If an officiating priest, actually engaged
' in a sacrifice, abandon his work, a share only,
' in proportion to his work done, shall be given to
' him by his partners in the business, *out of their*
' *common pay :*

207. ' But if he discontinue his work *without*
' *fraud,* after the time of giving the sacrificial fees,
' he may take his full share, and cause what re-
' mains to be performed by another priest.

208. ' Where, on the performance of solemn
' rites, a specifick fee is ordained for each part of
' them, shall he alone, who performs that part,
' receive the fee, or shall all the priests take the
' perquisites jointly ?

209. ' *At some holy rites,* let the reader of the
' *Yajurvéda* take the car, and the *Brahmá,* or su-
I   ' perintending

' perintending prieft, the horfe ; or, *on another*
' *occafion*, let the reader of the *Rigvéda* take the'
', horfe, and the chanter of the *Sámavéda* receive
' the carriage, in which the purchafed materials
' of the facrifice had been brought.

210. ' *A hundred cows being diftributable among*
' *fixteen priefts*, the four chief *or firft fet*, are en-
' titled to *near* half, *or forty eight* ; the next four
' to half of that number ; the third fet, to a third
' part of it; and the fourth fet, to a quarter :

211. ' According to this rule, *or in proportion*
' *to the work*, muft allotments of fhares be given
' to men here below, who; *though* in conjunction,
' perform their feveral parts of the bufinefs.

212. ' SHOULD money or goods be given, *or*
' *promifed as a gift*, by one man to another who
' afks it for fome religious act, the gift fhall be
' void, if that act be not afterwards performed :

213. ' If the money be delivered, and the re-
' ceiver, through pride or avarice, refufe *in that*
' *cafe* to return it, he fhall be fined one *fuverna* by
' the king, as a punifhment for his theft.

214. ' Such, as here declared, is the rule or-
' dained for withdrawing what has been given :
' I will, next, propound the law for non-payment
' of wages.

215. ' THAT hired fervant or workman, who,
' not from any diforder but from infolence, fails
' to perform his work according to his agreement,
' fhall be fined eight *racticas*, and his wages or
' hire fhall not be paid.

216. ' But, if he be really ill, and, when reftored
' to health, fhall perform his work according to
' his original bargain, he fhall receive his pay
' even for a very long time ;

217. ' Yet,

217. ' Yet, whether he be fick or well, if the
' work ftipulated be not performed *by another for*
' *him or by himfelf*, his whole wages are forfeited,
' though the work want but a little of being
' complete.

218. ' This is the general rule concerning work
' undertaken for wages or hire: next I will fully
' declare the law concerning fuch men as break
' their promifes.

219. ' THE man, among the traders and other
' inhabitants of a town or diftrict, who breaks a
' promife through avarice, though he had taken
' an oath to perform it, let the king banifh from
' his realm :

220. ' Or, *according to circumftances*, let the
' judge, having arrefted the promife-breaker, con-
' demn him to pay fix *nifhcas*, or four *fuvernas*, or
' one *fatamána* of filver, or all three *if he deferve*
' *fuch a fine*.

221. ' Among all citizens, and in all claffes, let
' a juft king obferve this rule for impofing fines on
' men who fhall break their engagements.

222. ' A MAN who has bought or fold any
' thing in this world, *that has a fixed price, and is*
' *not perifhable, as land or metals*, and wifhes to
' refcind the contract, may give or take back fuch
' a thing within ten days ;

223. ' But, after ten days, he fhall neither give
' nor take it back : the giver or the taker, *except*
' *by confent*, fhall be fined by the king fix hundred
' *panas*.

224. ' The king himfelf fhall take a fine of
' ninety-fix *panas* from him who gives a blemifhed
' girl *in marriage, for a reward*, without avowing
' her blemifh ;

5   225. ' But

225. ' But the man, who, through malignity,
' fays of a damfel, that fhe is no virgin, fhall be
' fined a hundred *panas*, if he cannot prove her
' defilement.

226. ' The holy nuptial texts are applied folely
' to virgins, and no where on earth to girls who
' have loft their virginity ; fince thofe women are
' *in general* excluded from legal ceremonies :

227. ' The nuptial texts are a certain rule
' in regard to wedlock, and the bridal contract is
' known by the learned to be complete *and irrevo-*
' *cable*, on the feventh ftep *of the married pair, hand*
' *in hand, after thofe texts have been pronounced.*

228. ' By this law, in all bufinefs whatever here
' below, muft the judge confine, within the path
' of rectitude, a perfon inclined to refcind his
' contract of fale and purchafe.

229. ' I now will decide exactly, according to
' principles of law, the contefts ufually arifing from
' the fault of fuch as own herds of cattle, and of
' fuch as are hired to keep them.

230. ' By day the blame falls on the herdfman ;
' by night on the owner, *if the cattle be fed and*
' *kept* in his own houfe ; but, if the place of their
' food and cuftody be different, the keeper incurs
' the blame.

231. ' That hired fervant, whofe wages are
' paid with milk, may, with the affent of the
' owner, milk the beft cow out of ten : fuch are
' the wages of herdfmen, unlefs they be paid in a
' different mode.

232. ' The herdfman himfelf fhall make good
' the lofs of a beaft, which through his want of
' due care, has ftrayed, has been deftroyed by
' reptiles, or killed by dogs, or has died by falling
' into a pit ;

233. ' But

233. ' But he fhall not be compelled' to make
' it good, when robbers have carried it away, if,
' after frefh proclamation and purfuit, he give
' notice to his mafter in a proper place and ıeafon.

234. '.When cattle die, let him carry to his
' mafter their ears, their hides, their tails, the
' fkin below their navels, their tendons, and the
' liquor exuding from their foreheads: let him
' alfo point out their limbs.

235. ' A flock of goats or of fheep being at-
' tacked by wolves, and the keeper not going *to
' repel the attack*, he fhall be refponfible for every
' one of them, which a wolf fhall violently kill ;

236. ' But, if any one of them, while they
' graze together near a wood, and the fhepherd
' keeps them in order, fhall be fuddenly killed
' by a wolf fpringing on it, he fhall not in that cafe
' be refponfible.

237. ' On all fides of a village or fmall town
' let a fpace be left for pafture, in breadth either
' four hundred cubits, or three cafts of a large
' ftick ; and thrice that fpace round a city or con-.
' fiderable town :

238. ' Within that pafture ground, if cattle do
' any damage to grain in a field uninclofed with
' a hedge, the king fhall not punifh the herdf-
' man.

239. ' Let the owner of the field inclofe it with
' a hedge *of thorny plants*, over which a camel
' could not look ; and let him ftop every gap,
' through which a dog or a boar could thruft
' his head.

240. ' Should cattle, attended by a herdfman,
' do mifchief near a highway, in an inclofed field
' or near the village, he fhall be fined a hundred
' *panas* ;

' *panas* ; but againſt cattle which have no keeper,
' let the owner of the field ſecure it.

24 . ' In other fields, the *owner of* cattle *doing*
' *miſchief* ſhall be fined one *pana* and a quarter ;
' but, in all places, the value of the *damaged*
' grain muſt be paid : ſuch is the fixed rule con-
' cerning a huſbandman.

242. ' For damage by a cow before ten days
' have paſſed ſince her calving, by bulls kept for
' impregnation, and by cattle conſecrated to the
' deity, whether attended or unattended, MENU
' has ordained no fine.

243. ' If land be injured, by the fault of the
' farmer himſelf, *as if he fails to ſow it in due time*,
' he ſhall be fined ten times as much as the *king's*
' ſhare *of the crop, that might otherwiſe have been*
' *raiſed* ; but only five times as much, if it was
' the fault of his ſervants without his knowledge.

244. ' Theſe rules let a juſt prince obſerve in
' all caſes of tranſgreſſion by maſters, their cattle,
' and their herdſmen.

245. ' IF a conteſt ariſe between two villages,
' *or landholders*, concerning a boundary, let the
' king, *or his judge*, aſcertain the limits in the
' month of *Jyaiſht'ha*, when the land-marks are
' ſeen more diſtinctly.

246. ' *When boundaries firſt are eſtabliſhed*, let
' ſtrong trees be planted on them, *Vatas, Pippalas*,
' *Paláſas, Sálmalis, Sálas* or *Tálas* ; or ſuch trees
' *(like the* Udumbara *or* Vajradru) as abound in
' milk ;

247. ' Or cluſtering ſhrubs, or *Vénus* of differ-
' ent ſorts, or *Sami*-trees, and creepers, or *Saras*,
' and clumps of *Cubjacas* : and mounds of earth
' ſhould be raiſed on them, ſo that the land-mark
' may not eaſily periſh :

248. ' Lakes

248. ' Lakes and wells, pools and ftreams,
' ought alfo to be made on the common limits,
' and temples dedicated to the gods.

249. ' The perfons concerned, reflecting on
' the perpetual trefpaffes committed by men here
' below through ignorance of boundaries, fhould
' caufe other land-marks to be concealed *under*
' *ground :*

250. ' Large pieces of ftone, bones, tails of
' cows, bran, afhes, potfherds, dried cow-dung,
' bricks and tiles, charcoal, pebbles and fand,

251. ' And fubftances of all forts, which the
' earth corrodes not even in a long time, fhould
' be placed *in jars* not appearing *above ground* on
' the common boundary.

252. ' By fuch marks, or by the courfe of a
' ftream, and long continued poffeffion, the judge
' may afcertain the limit between the lands of two
' parties in litigation :

253. ' Should there be a doubt, even on the
' infpection of thofe marks, recourfe muft be had,
' for the decifion of fuch a conteft, to the declara-
' tions of witneffes.

254. ' Thofe witneffes muft be examined con-
' cerning the land-marks, in the prefence of all
' the townfmen or villagers, or of both the con-
' tending parties :

255. ' What the witneffes, thus affembled and
' interrogated, fhall pofitively declare con cering
' the limits, muft be recorded in writing, together
' with all their names.

256. ' Let them, putting earth on their heads,
' wearing chaplets of red flowers and clad in red
' mantles, be fworn by *the reward of* all their
' feveral good actions to give correct evidence
' concerning the metes and bounds.

257. ' Veracious

257. ' Veracious witneffes, who give evidence
' as the law requires, are abfolved from their fins;
' but fuch as give it unjuftly, fhall each be fined
' two hundred *panas.*

258. ' If there be no witneffes, let four men,
' who dwell on all the four fides of the two vil-
' lages, make a decifion concerning the boundary,
' being duly prepared, *like the witneffes,* in the
' prefence of the king.

259. ' If there be no fuch neighbours on all
' fides, nor any men, nor any men whofe an-
' ceftors had lived there fince the villages were
' built, nor other inhabitants of towns, who can
' give evidence on the limits, the judge muft ex-
' amine the following men, who inhabit the woods;

260. ' Hunters, fowlers, herdfmen, fifhers,
' diggers for roots, catchers of fnakes, gleaners,
' and other forefters :

261. ' According to their declaration, when
' they are duly examined, let the king with pre-
' cifion order land-marks to be fixed on the boun-
' dary line between the two villages.

262. ' As to the bounds of arable fields, wells
' or pools, gardens and houfes, the teftimony of
' next neighbours on every fide muft be confidered
' as the beft means of decifion :

263. ' Should the neighbours fay any thing
' untrue, when two men difpute about a land-
' mark, the king fhall make each of thofe wit-
' neffes pay the middlemoft of the three ufual
' amercements.

264. ' He, who by means of intimidation, fhall
' poffefs himfelf of a houfe, a pool, a field, or
' a garden, fhall be fined five hundred *panas*; but
' only two hundred, if he trefpaffed through ig-
' norance *of the right.*

265. ' If

265. ' If the boundary cannot be *otherwise* af-
' certained, let the king, knowing what is juſt,
' *that is, without partiality, and* conſulting the
' future benefit of both parties, make a bound-line
' between their lands: this is a ſettled law.

266. ' Thus has the rule been propounded for
' deciſions concerning land-marks: I next will
' declare the law concerning defamatory words.

267. ' A SOLDIER, defaming a prieſt, ſhall be
' fined a hundred *panas*; a merchant, *thus offend-*
' *ing*, an hundred and fifty, or two hundred; but,
' *for ſuch an offence*, a mechanick or ſervile man
' ſhall be whipped.

268. ' A prieſt ſhall be fined five hundred, if
' he ſlander a ſoldier; twenty-five if a merchant';
' and twelve if he ſlander a man of the ſervile
' claſs.

269. ' For abuſing one of the ſame claſs, a
' twice born man, ſhall be fined only twelve; but
' for ribaldry not to be uttered, even that *and*
' *every fine* ſhall be doubled.

270. ' A once born man, who inſults the twice
' born with groſs invectives, ought to have his
' tongue ſlit; for he ſprang from the loweſt part
' *of* BRAHMA' ;

271. ' If he mention their names and claſſes
' with contumely, *as if he ſay,* " *Oh* DE'VADAT-
' TA, *thou refuſe of* Bráhmens," an iron ſtyle,
' ten fingers long; ſhall be thruſt red hot into his
' mouth.

272. ' Should he, through pride, give in-
' ſtruction to prieſts concerning their duty, let
' the king order ſome hot oil to be dropped into
' his mouth and his ear.

273. ' He, who falſely denies through inſolence,
' the

' the sacred knowledge, the country, the class, or
' the corporeal inveftiture *of a man, equal in rank,*
' fhall be compelled to pay a fine of two hundred
' *panas.*

274. ' If a man call another ,blind with one
' eye, or lame, or defective in any, fimilar way,
' he fhall pay the fmall fine of one *pana,* even
' though he fpeak truth.

275. ' He fhall be fined a hundred, who de-
' fames his mother, his father, his wife, his
' brother, his fon, or his preceptor ; and he who
' gives not his preceptor the way.

276. ' For *mutual* abufe by a prieft and a
' foldier, this fine muft be impofed by a learned
' king; the loweft amercement on the prieft,
' and the middlemoft on the foldier.

277. ' Such exactly, *as before-mentioned,* muft
' be the punifhment of a merchant and a me-
' chanick in refpect of their feveral claffes, except
' the flitting of the tongue : this is a fixed rule of
' punifhment.

278. ' THUS fully has the law been declared
' for the punifhment of defamatory fpeech : I
' will next propound the eftablifhed law concern-
' ing affault and battery.

279. ' With whatever member a low born
' man fhall affault or hurt a fuperiour, even that
' member of his muft be flit, *or cut more or lefs*
' *in proportion to the injury :* this is an ordinance
' of MENU.

280. ' He, who raifes his hand or a ftaff againft
' another, fhall have his hand cut; and he who
' kicks another in wrath, fhall have an incifion
' made in his foot.

281. ' A man of the loweft clafs, who fhall
' infolently place himfelf on the fame feat with

Q   ' one

' one of the higheſt, ſhall either be baniſhed with
' a mark on his hinder parts, or the king ſhall
' cauſe a gaſh to be made on his buttock :

282. ' Should he ſpit on him through pride,
' the king ſhall order both of his lips to be gaſhed;
' ſhould he urine on him, his penis; ſhould he
' break wind againſt him, his anus.

283. ' If he ſeize the *Bráhmen* by the locks,
' or by the feet, or by the beard, or by the
' throat, or by the ſcrotum, let the king with-
' out heſitation cauſe inciſions to be made in his
' hands.

284. ' If any man ſcratch the ſkin *of his equal*
' *in claſs,* or fetch blood *from him,* he ſhall be
' fined a hundred *panas;* if he wound a muſcle,
' ſix *niſhcas;* but, if he break a bone, let him be
' inſtantly baniſhed.

285. ' ACCORDING to the uſe and value of all
' great trees, muſt a fine be ſet for injuring them :
' this is an eſtabliſhed rule.

286. ' IF a blow, attended with much pain,
' be given either to human creatures or cattle,
' the king ſhall inflict on the ſtriker a puniſhment
' as heavy as the preſumed ſuffering.

287. ' In all caſes of hurting a limb, wound-
' ing, or fetching blood, the aſſailant ſhall pay
' the expence of a perfect cure ; or, *on his failure,*
' both full damages and a fine to the ſame
' amount.

288. ' HE, who injures the goods of another,
' whether acquainted or unacquainted with the
' owner of them, ſhall give ſatisfaction to the
' owner, and pay a fine to the king equal to the
' damage.

289. ' If injury be done to leather or to
leathern

' leathern bags, or utenfils made of wood or clay,
' the fine fhall be five times their value.'

290. ' THE wife reckon ten occafions, in re-
' gard to a carriage, its driver, and its owner, on
' which the fine is remitted; on other occa-
' fions a fine is ordained by law:

291. ' The nofe-cord or bridle being cut, *by*
' *fome accident without negligence,* or the yoke being
' fnapped, on a fudden overturn, or running againft
' any thing *without fault,* the axle being broken,
' or the wheel cracked;

292. ' On the breaking of the thongs, of the
' halter, or of the reins, and when the driver has
' called aloud to make way, *on thefe occafions* has
' MENU declared that no fine fhall be fet:

293. ' But, where a carriage has been over-
' turned by the unfkilfulnefs of the driver, there,
' in the cafe of any hurt, the mafter fhall be fined
' two hundred *panas.*

294. ' If the driver be fkilful, *but negligent,* the
' driver alone fhall be fined; and thofe in the car-
' riage fhall be fined each a hundred, if the driver
' be clearly unfkilful.

295. ' Should a driver, being met in the way
' by another carriage or by cattle, kill any animal
' *by his negligence,* a fine fhall, without doubt,
' be impofed *by the following rule:*

296. ' For killing a man, a fine, equal to that
' for theft, fhall be inftantly fet; half that amount,
' for large brute animals, as for a bull or cow,
' an elephant, a camel, or a horfe;

297. ' For killing very young cattle, the fine
' fhall be two hundred *panas;* and fifty, for ele-
' gant quadrupeds or beautiful birds, as *antelopes,*
' *parrots, and the like;*

298. ' For

298. ' For an afs, a goat, or a fheep, the fine
' muft be five filver *máfhas* ; and one *máfha* for
' killing a dog or a boar.

299. ' A WIFE, a fon, a fervant, a pupil, and
' a *younger* whole brother, may be corrected,
' when they commit faults, with a rope, or the
' fmall fhoot of a cane ;

300. ' But on the back part only of their
' bodies, and not on a noble part by any means :
' he who ftrikes them otherwife than by this rule,
' incurs the guilt, *or fhall pay the fine* of a thief.

301. ' This law of affault and battery has been
' completely declared : I proceed to declare the
' rule for the fettled punifhment of theft.

302. ' IN reftraining thieves and robbers, let
' the king ufe extreme diligence; fince, by
' reftraining thieves and robbers, his fame and
' his domain are increafed.

303. ' Conftantly, no doubt, is that king to be
' honoured, who beftows exemption from fear ;
' fince he performs, *as it were*, a perpetual facri-
' fice, giving exemption from fear, as a conftant
' facrificial prefent.

304. ' A fixth part of *the reward for* virtuous
' deeds, performed by the whole people, belongs
' to the king, who protects them ; but, if he
' protect them not, a fixth part of their iniquity
' lights on him :

305. ' Of *the reward for* what every fubject
' reads in the *Véda*, for what he facrifices, for
' what he gives in charity, for what he performs
' in worfhip, the king juftly takes a fixth part in
' confequence of protection.

306. ' A king, who acts with juftice in defend-
' ing all creatures, and flays only thofe who ought
' to

' to be flain, performs, *as it were*, each day a
' facrifice with a hundred thoufand gifts ;

307 ' But a king, who gives no fuch protec-
' tion, yet receives taxes in kind or in value, mar-
' ket duties and tolls, the fmall daily prefents for
' his houfehold, and fines for offences, falls directly,
' *on his death*, to a region of horrour.

308. ' That king, who gives no protection,
' yet takes a fixth part of the grain as his revenue,
' wife men have confidered as a prince who draws
' to him the foulnefs of all his people.

309. ' Be it known, that a monarch who pays
' no regard to the fcriptures, who denies a future
' ftate, who acts with rapacity, who protects not
' his people, yet fwallows up their poffeffions,
' will fink low indeed *after death*.

310. ' WITH great care and by three methods
' let him reftrain the unjuft; by imprifonment, by
' confinement in fetters, and by various kinds of
' corporal punifhment ;

311. ' Since, by reftraining the bad, and by
' encouraging the good, kings are perpetually
' made pure, as the twice born are purified by fa-
' crificing.

312. ' A KING who feeks benefit to his own
' foul, muft always forgive parties litigant, chil-
' dren, old men, and fick perfons, who inveigh
' againft him.

313. ' He, who forgives perfons in pain, when
' they abufe him, fhall, on that account, be exalted
' in heaven ; but he, who excufes them not,
' through the pride of dominion, fhall for that
' reafon fink into hell.

314. ' The ftealer *of gold from a prieft* muft run
' haftily to the king, with loofened hair, pro-

Q 3   ' claiming

' claiming the theft ; *and adding*; " Thus have I
' finned, punifh me."

. 315. ' He muft bear on his fhoulder a peftle of
' ftone, or a club of *c'hadira*-wood, or a javelin
' pointed at both ends, or an iron mace :

3 6. ' Whether the king ftrike him with it, or
' difmifs him unhurt, the thief is then abfolved
' from the crime ; but the king, if he punifh him
' not, fhall incur the guilt of the thief.

317. ' The killer of a prieft, *or deftroyer of an*
' *embryo*, cafts his guilt on the *willing* eater of his
' provifions ; an adulterous wife, on her *negligent*
' hufband ; a bad fcholar and facrificer, on their
' *ignorant* preceptor ; and a thief, on the *forgiving*
' prince.

318. ' But men who have committed offences,
' and have received from kings the punifhment
' due to them, go pure to heaven, and become as
' clear as thofe who have done well.

319. ' He, who fteals the rope or the water-pot
' from a well, and he, who breaks down a ciftern,
' fhall be fined a *máfha* of gold ; and that, *which*
' *he has taken or injured* he muft reftore to its
' former condition.

32 . ' Corporal punifhment fhall be inflicted
' on him who fteals more than ten *cumbhas* of
' grain; (a *cumbha* is twenty *drónas*, and a *dróna*
' two hundred *palas* :) for lefs he muft be fined
' eleven times as much, and fhall pay to the
' owner the amount of his property.

3 . ' So fhall corporal punifhment be inflicted
' for ftealing commodities ufually fold by weight,
' or more than a hundred head of cattle, or gold,
' or filver, or coftly apparel ;

322. ' For ftealing more than fifty *palas*, it is
' enacted

' enacted that a hand shall be amputated; for less,
' the king shall set a fine eleven times as much as
' the value.

323. ' For stealing men of high birth, and wo-
' men above all, and the most precious gems,
' *as diamonds or rubies*, the thief deserves capital
' punishment.

324. ' For stealing large beasts, weapons, or
' medicines, let the king inflict *adequate* punish-
' ment, considering the time and the act.

325. ' For taking kine belonging to priests, and
' boring their nostrils, or for stealing their other
' cattle, the offender shall instantly lose half of
' one foot.

326. ' For stealing thread, raw-cotton, mate-
' rials to make spirituous liquor, cow-dung, mo-
' lasses, curds, milk, butter-milk, water, or grass,

327. ' Large canes, baskets of canes, salt of
' every kind, earthen pots, clay or ashes,

328. ' Fish, birds, oil, or clarified butter,
' flesh-meat, honey, or any thing, *as leather, born,*
' *or ivory*, that came from a beast,

329. ' Or other things not precious, or spiri-
' tuous liquors, rice dressed with clarified but-
' ter, or other messes of boiled rice, the fine
' must be twice the value of the commodity
' stolen.

330. ' For stealing *as much as a man can carry*
' of flowers, green corn, shrubs, creepers, small
' trees, or other vegetables, enclosed by a hedge,
' the fine shall be five *racticas* of gold or silver;

331. ' But for corn, pot-herbs, roots, and fruit,
' unenclosed by a fence, the fine is an hundred
' *panas*, if there be no sort of relation *between the*
' *taker and the owner*; or half a hundred if there
' be such relation.

Q 4   332. ' If

332. ' If the taking be violent, and in the fight
' of the owner, it is robbery; if privately in his
' abfence, it is only theft, and *it is confidered as*
' *theft*, when a man, having received any thing,
' refufes to give it back.

333. ' On him who fteals the before-mentioned
' things, when they are prepared for ufe, let the
' king fet the loweft amercement *of the three*;
' and *the fame* on him who fteals only fire from
' the temple.

334. ' With whatever limb a thief commits
' the offence by any means in this world, *as if*
' *he break a wall with his hand or his foot*, even
' that limb fhall the king amputate for the pre-
' vention of a fimilar crime.

335. ' NEITHER a father, nor a preceptor, nor
' a friend, nor a mother, nor a wife, nor a fon,
' nor a domeftick prieft, muft be left unpunifhed
' by the king, if they adhere not with firmnefs to
' their duty.

336. ' WHERE another man of lower birth
' would be fined one *pana*, the king fhall be fined
' a thoufand, *and he fhall give the fine to the*
' *priefts, or caft it into the river*: this is a facred
' rule.

337. ' But the fine of a *Súdra* for theft fhall
' be eight-fold; that of a *Vaifya*, fixteen-fold;
' that of a *Cfhatriya*, two and thirty-fold.

338. ' That of a *Bráhmen*, four and fixty-fold;
' or a hundred-fold complete, or even twice four
' and fixty-fold; each of them knowing the na-
' ture of his offence.

339. ' The taking of roots and fruit from a
' large tree, *in a field or a foreft* unenclofed, or of
' wood for a facrificial fire, or of grafs to be eaten
' by cows, MENU has pronounced no theft.

340. ' A

340. ' A PRIEST who willingly receives any
' thing, either for facrificing or for inftructing,
' from the hand of a man who had taken what
' the owner had not given, fhall be *punifhed* even
' as the thief.

341. ' A twice born man who is travelling,
' and whofe provifions are fcanty, fhall not be
' fined for taking only two fugar canes, or two
' efculent roots, from the field of another man.

342. ' He who ties the unbound, or loofes
' the bound *cattle of another*, and he who takes a
' flave, a horfe, or a carriage *without permiffion*,
' fhall be punifhed as for theft.

343. ' A king, who by *enforcing* thefe laws
' reftrains men from committing theft, acquires
' in this world fame, and in the next beatitude.

344. ' LET not the king who ardently de-
' fires a feat with INDRA, and wifhes for glory,
' which nothing can change or diminifh, endure
' for a moment the man who has committed
' atrocious violence, as by robbery, arfon, or
' homicide.

345. ' He who commits great violence, muft
' be confidered as a more grievous offender than
' a defamer, a thief, or a ftriker with a ftaff:

346. ' That king who endures a man convict-
' ed of fuch atrocity, quickly goes to perdition,
' and incurs publick hate.

347. ' Neither on account of friendfhip, nor
' for the fake of great lucre, fhall the king difmifs
' the perpetrators of violent acts, who fpread
' terrour among all creatures.

348. ' THE twice born may take arms when
' their duty is obftructed by force; and when in
' fome evil time a difafter has befallen the twice-
' born claffes;

349. ' And

349. ' And in their own defence; and in a
' war for juft caufe ; and in defence of a woman
' or a prieft ; he who kills juftly, commits no
' crime.

350. ' Let a man without hefitation flay ano-
' ther, *if he cannot otherwife efcape*, who affails him
' with intent to murder, whether young or old,
' or his preceptor, or a *Bráhmen* deeply verfed in
' the fcripture.

351. ' By killing an affaffin, who attempts to
' kill, whether in public or in private, no crime
' is committed by the flayer : fury recoils upon
' fury.

352. ' MEN who commit overt-acts of adul-
' terous inclinations for the wives of others, let
' the king banifh from his realm, having pu-
' nifhed them with fuch bodily marks as excite
' averfion;

353. ' Since adultery caufes, to the general
' ruin, a mixture of claffes among men : thence
' arifes violation of duties ; and thence is the root
' of felicity quite deftroyed.

354. ' A man before noted for fuch an offence,
' who converfes in fecret with the wife of ano-
' ther, fhall pay the firft of the three ufual amerce-
' ments ;

355. ' But a man, not before noted, who thus
' converfes with her for fome reafonable caufe,
' fhall pay no fine ; fince in him there is no
' tranfgreffion.

356. ' He, who talks with the wife of another
' man at a place of pilgrimage, in a foreft or a
' grove, or at the confluence of rivers, incurs the
' guilt of an adulterous inclination :

357. ' To fend her flowers or perfumes, to
' fport and jeft with her, to touch her apparel and
      ' ornaments,

' ornaments, to fit with her on the fame couch,
' are held adulterous acts on his part;

358. ' To touch a married woman on *her*
' *breafts or* any *other* place, which ought not to be
' touched, or, being touched unbecomingly by
' her, to bear it complacently, are adulterous acts
' with mutual affent.

359. ' A man of the fervile clafs, who com-
' mits actual adultery with the wife of a prieft,
' ought to fuffer death : the wives, indeed, of all
' the four claffes muft ever be moft efpecially
' guarded.

360. ' Mendicants, encomiafts, men prepared
' for a facrifice, and *cooks and other* artifans, are
' not prohibited from fpeaking to married women.

361. ' Let no man converfe, after he has been
' forbidden, with the wives of others : he, who
' thus converfes, *after a hufband or father has* for-
' bidden *him*, fhall pay a fine of one *fuverna.*

362. ' Thefe laws relate not to the wives of
' publick dancers or fingers, or of fuch bafe men
' as live by intrigues of their wives; men, who
' either carry women to others, or, lying con-
' cealed at home, permit them to hold a culpable
' intercourfe :

363. ' Yet he, who has a private connexion with
' fuch women, or with fervant-girls kept by one
' mafter, or with female anchorets *of an heretical*
' *religion*, fhall be compelled to pay a fmall fine.

364. ' He, who vitiates a damfel without her
' confent, fhall fuffer corporal punifhment in-
' ftantly ; but he, who enjoys a willing damfel,
' fhall not be corporally punifhed, if his clafs be
' the fame with hers.

365. ' From a girl, who makes advances to
a man

‘ a man of a high clafs, let not the king take the
‘ fmalleft fine ; but her, who firft addreffes a low
‘ man, let him conftrain to live in her houfe
‘ well guarded.

366. ‘ A low man, who makes love to a dam-
‘ fel of high birth, ought to be punifhed corpo-
‘ rally ; but he who addreffes a maid of equal
‘ rank, fhall give the nuptial prefent *and marry*
‘ *her*, if her father pleafe.

367. ‘ Of the man, who through infolence
‘ forcibly contaminates a damfel, let the king in-
‘ ftantly order two fingers to be amputated, and
‘ condemn him to pay a fine of fix hundred
‘ *panas :*

368. ‘ A man of equal rank, who defiles a con-
‘ fenting damfel, fhall not have his fingers am-
‘ putated, but fhall pay a fine of two hundred
‘ *panas*, to reftrain him from a repetition of his
‘ offence.

369. ‘ A damfel polluting another damfel, muft
‘ be fined two hundred *panas*, pay the double
‘ value of her nuptial prefent, and receive ten
‘ lafhes with a whip ;

370. ‘ But a woman, polluting a damfel, fhall
‘ have her head inftantly fhaved, and two of her
‘ fingers chopped off ; and fhall ride, mounted on
‘ an afs, *through the publick ftreet.*

371. ‘ Should a wife, proud of her family
‘ and the great qualities of her kinfmen, actually
‘ violate the duty which fhe owes to her lord,
‘ let the king condemn her to be devoured by
‘ dogs in a place much frequented ;

372. ‘ And let him place the adulterer on an
‘ iron bed well heated, under which the execu-
‘ tioners fhall throw logs continually, till the
‘ finful wretch be there burned *to death.*

373. ‘ Of

373. ' Of a man once convicted, and a year
' after guilty *of the same crime*, the fine muſt be
' doubled: *ſo it muſt* if he be connected with
' the daughter of an outcaſt or with a *Chándálí*
' woman.

374. ' A mechanick or ſervile man, having an
' adulterous connexion with a woman of a twice
' born claſs, whether guarded at home or un-
' guarded, *ſhall thus be puniſhed*; if ſhe was un-
' guarded, *he* ſhall loſe the part *offending*, and his
' whole ſubſtance ; if guarded, *and a prieſteſs*,
' every thing, *even his life.*

375. ' *For adultery with a guarded prieſteſs*, a
' merchant ſhall forfeit all his wealth after impri-
' ſonment for a year ; a ſoldier ſhall be fined a
' thouſand *panas*, and be ſhaved with *the* urine *of*
' *an aſs :*

376. ' But, if a merchant or a ſoldier commit
' adultery with a woman of the ſacerdotal claſs,
' whom her huſband guards not at home, the king
' ſhall only fine the merchant five hundred, and
' the ſoldier a thouſand :

377. ' Both of them, however, if they commit
' that offence with a prieſteſs *not only* guarded, *but*
' *eminent for good qualities*, ſhall be puniſhed like
' men of the ſervile claſs, or be burned in a fire
' of dry graſs or reeds.

378. ' A *Bráhmen*, who carnally knows a
' guarded woman without her free will, muſt be,
' fined a thouſand *panas*, but only five hundred if
' he knew her with her free conſent.

379. ' Ignominious tonſure is ordained, in-
' ſtead of capital puniſhment, for an adulterer of.
' the prieſtly claſs, where the puniſhment of other
' claſſes may extend to loſs of life.

380. ' Never

380. ' Never shall the king slay a *Bráhmen*
' though convicted of all possible crimes : let him
' banish the offender from his realm, but with all
' his property secure, and his body unhurt :

381. ' No greater crime is known on earth
' than slaying a *Bráhmen*; and the king, therefore,
' must not even form in his mind an idea of kill-
' ing a priest.

382. ' If a merchant converse criminally with
' a guarded woman of the military, or a soldier
' with one of the mercantile class, they both de-
' serve the same punishment as in the case of a
' priestess unguarded :

383. ' But a *Bráhmen*, who shall commit adul-
' tery with a guarded woman of those two classes,
' must be fined a thousand *panas*; and, for the
' like offence with a guarded woman of the servile
' class, the fine of a soldier or a merchant shall
' also be one thousand.

384. ' For adultery with a woman of the mi-
' litary class, if unguarded, the fine of a merchant
' is five hundred ; but a soldier, *for the converse of*
' *that offence*, must be shaved with urine, or pay
' the fine *just mentioned*.

385. ' A priest shall pay five hundred *panas* if
' he connect himself criminally with an unguarded
' woman of the military, commercial, or servile
' class; and a thousand *for such a connexion with* a
' woman of vile *mixed* breed.

386. ' THAT king, in whose realm lives no
' thief, no adulterer, no defamer, no man guilty
' of atrocious violence, and no committer of af-
' saults, attains the mansion of SACRA.

387. ' By suppressing those five in his dominion,
' he gains royalty paramount over men of the
' fame

' fame kingly rank, and fpreads his fame through
' the world.

388. ' THE facrificer who forfakes the officiat-
' ing prieft, and the officiating prieft who aban-
' dons the facrificer, each being able to do his
' work, and guilty of no grievous offence, muft
' each be fined a hundred *panas*.

389. ' A mother, a father, a wife, and a fon,
' fhall not be forfaken : he, who forfakes either of
' them, unlefs guilty of a deadly fin, fhall pay
' fix hundred *panas* as a fine to the king.

390. ' LET not a prince, who feeks the good
' of his own foul, *haftily and alone* pronounce the
' law, on a difpute concerning any legal obfer-
' vance, among twice born men in their feveral
' orders ;

391. ' *But* let him, after giving them due ho-
' nour according to their merit, and, at firft, hav-
' ing foothed them by mildnefs, apprife them of
' their duty with the affiftance of *Bráhmens*.

392. ' THE prieft who gives an entertainment
' to twenty men of the three firft claffes, without
' inviting his next neighbour, and his neighbour,
' next but one, if both be worthy of an invitation,
' fhall be fined one *máfha* of filver.

393. ' A *Bráhmen* of deep learning in the *Véda*
' who invites not another *Bráhmen*, both learned
' and virtuous, to an entertainment *given on fome*
' *occafion* relating to his wealth, *as the marriage of*
' *his child, and the like*, fhall be made to pay him
' twice the value of the repaft, and be fined a
' *máfha* of gold.

394. ' NEITHER a blind man, nor an idiot, nor
' a cripple, nor a man full feventy years old, nor
' one who confers great benefits on priefts of emi-

3 ' nent

' nent learning, fhall be compelled by any *king* to
' pay taxes.

395. ' Let the king always do honour to a
' learned theologian, to a man either fick or
' grieved, to a little child, to an aged or indigent
' man, to a man of exalted birth, and to a man of
' diftinguifhed virtue.

396. ' Let a wafherman wafh *the* clothes *of his*
' *employers* by little and little, *or piece by piece, and*
' *not haftily,* on a fmooth board of *Sálmali*-wood:
' let him never mix *the* clothes *of one perfon* with
' *the* clothes *of another,* nor fuffer any *but the owner*
' to wear them.

397. ' Let a weaver who has received ten
' *palas* of cotton thread, give them back increafed
' to eleven *by the rice water and the like ufed in*
' *weaving:* he who does otherwife, fhall pay a
' fine of twelve *panas.*

398. ' As men verfed in cafes of tolls, and ac-
' quainted with all marketable commodities, fhall
' eftablifh the price of faleable things, let the king
' take a twentieth part of *the profit on fales at* that
' price.

399. ' Of the trader, who, through avarice,
' exports commodities, of which the king juftly
' claims the pre-emption, or on which he has
' laid an embargo, let the fovereign confifcate the
' whole property.

400. ' Any feller or buyer, who *fraudulently*
' paffes by the toll office at *night, or* any *other* im-
' proper time, or who makes a falfe enumeration
' *of the articles bought,* fhall be fined eight times
' as much as their value.

401. ' Let the king eftablifh rules for the fale
' and purchafe of all marketable things, having
' duly confidered whence they come, *if imported* ;
                                        ' and,

' and, *if exported*, whither they muſt be ſent ;
' how long they have been kept ; what may be
' gained by them; and what has been expended
' on them.

402. ' Once in five nights, or at the cloſe of
' every half month, *according to the nature of the*
' *commodities*, let the king make a regulation for
' market prices in the preſence of thoſe *experi-*
' *enced men :*

403. ' Let all weights and meaſures be well
' aſcertained by him ; and once in ſix months let
' him re-examine them.

404. ' The toll at a ferry is one *paña* for an
' empty cart ; half a *pana*, for a man with a load ;
' a quarter, for a beaſt uſed in agriculture, or for
' a woman ; and an eighth, for an unloaded man.

405. ' Waggons filled with goods packed up,
' ſhall pay toll in proportion to their value; but
' for empty veſſels and bags, and for *poor* men ill-
' apparelled, a very ſmall toll ſhall be demanded.

406. ' For a long paſſage, the freight muſt be
' proportioned to places and times ; but this
' muſt be underſtood of paſſages up and down
' rivers : at ſea there can be no ſettled freight.

407. ' A woman, who has been two months
' pregnant, a religious beggar, a foreſter in the
' third order, and *Bráhmens, who are* ſtudents in
' theology, ſhall not be obliged to pay toll for
' their paſſage.

408. ' Whatever ſhall be broken in a boat, by
' the fault of the boatmen, ſhall be made good by
' thoſe men collectively, each paying his portion.

409. ' This rule, ordained for ſuch as paſs
' rivers in boats, relates to the culpable neglect of
' boatmen on the water : in the caſe of inevitable
' accident, there can be no damages recovered.

R

410. ' THE

410. ' THE king should order each man of the
' mercantile class to practise trade, or money-
' lending, or agriculture and attendance on cattle;
' and each man of the servile class to act in the
' service of the twice born.

411. ' Both him of the military, and him of the
' commercial class, if distressed for a livelihood,
' let some wealthy *Bráhmen* support, obliging them
' without harshness to discharge their several duties.

412. ' A *Bráhmen*, who, by his power and
' through avarice, shall cause twice born men,
' girt with the sacrificial thread, to perform ser-
' vile acts, *such as washing his feet*, without their
' consent, shall be fined by the king six hundred
' *panas*;

413. ' But a man of the servile class whether
' bought or unbought, he may compel to perform
' servile duty; because such a man was created
' by the Self-existent for the purpose of serving
' *Bráhmens*:

414. ' A *Súdra*, though emancipated by his
' master, is not released from a state of servitude;
' for of a state which is natural to him, by whom
' can he be divested?

415. ' THERE are servants of seven sorts; one
' made captive under a standard *or in battle*, one
' maintained in consideration of service, one born
' of a female slave in the house, one sold, or
' given, or inherited from ancestors, and one en-
' slaved by way of punishment *on his inability to
' pay a large fine*.

416. ' Three persons, a wife, a son, and a slave,
' are declared by law to have *in general* no wealth
' exclusively their own: the wealth, which they
' may earn, is *regularly* acquired for the man to
' whom they belong.

417. ' A

417. ' A *Bráhmen* may feize without hefitation,
' *if he be diftreffed for a fubfiftence*, the goods of his
' *Súdra* flave; for as that flave can have no pro-
' perty, his mafter may take his goods.

418. ' With vigilant care fhould the king ex-
' ert himfelf in compelling merchants and mecha-
' nicks to perform their refpective duties; for
' when fuch men fwerve from their duty, they
' throw this world into confufion.

419. ' Day by day muft the king, *though en-*
' *gaged in forenfick bufinefs*, confider the great ob-
' jects of publick meafures, and inquire into the
' ftate of his carriages, *elephants, horfes, and cars*, his
' conftant revenues and neceffary expences, his
' mines *of precious metals or gems*, and his treafury :

420. ' Thus, bringing to a conclufion all thefe
' weighty affairs, and removing *from his realm and*
' *from himfelf* every taint of fin, a king reaches the
' fupreme path of beatitude.'

CHAPTER THE NINTH.

On the fame; and on the Commercial and
Servile Claffes.

═══════

1. ' I NOW will propound the immemorial
' duties of man and woman, who muft both re-
' main firm in the legal path, whether united or
' feparated.

2. ' Day and night muft women be held by
' their protectors in a ftate of dependence; but
' in *lawful and innocent* recreations, though rather
' addicted to them, they may be left at their own
' difpofal.

3. ' Their fathers protect them in child-hood;
' their hufbands protect them in youth; their
' fons protect them in age : a woman is never fit
' for independence.

4. ' Reprehenfible is the father, who gives not
' his daughter in marriage at the proper time;
' and the hufband, who approaches not his wife
' in due feafon; reprehenfible alfo is the fon,
' who protects not his mother after the death of
' her lord.

5. ' Women muft, above all, be reftrained from
' the fmalleft illicit gratification; for, not being

' thus

' thus reſtrained, they bring ſorrow on both fa-
' milies :

6. ' Let huſbands conſider this as the ſupreme
' law, ordained for all claſſes ; and let them,
' how weak ſoever, diligently keep their wives
' under lawful reſtrictions ;

7. ' For he who preſerves his wife *from vice*,
' preſerves his offspring *from ſuſpicion of baſtardy*,
' his ancient uſages *from neglect*, his family *from*
' *diſgrace*, himſelf *from anguiſh*, and his duty *from*
' *violation.*

8. ' The huſband, after conception by his wife,
' becomes himſelf an embryo, and is born a
' ſecond time here below ; for which reaſon the
' wife is called *jáyá*, ſince by her *(jáyaté)* he is
' born again :

9. ' Now the wife brings forth a ſon endued
' with ſimilar qualities to thoſe of the father ;
' ſo that with a view to an excellent offspring,
' he muſt vigilantly guard his wife.

10. ' No man, indeed, can wholly reſtrain
' women by violent meaſures ; but, by theſe
' expedients, they may be reſtrained :

11. ' Let the huſband keep his wife employed in
' the collection and expenditure of wealth, in puri-
' fication and female duty, in the preparation of
' daily food, and the ſuper-intendence of houſe-
' hold utenſils.

12. ' By confinement at home, even under
' affectionate and obſervant guardians, they are
' not ſecure ; but thoſe women are truly ſecure,
' who are guarded by their own good inclina-
' tions.

13. ' Drinking *ſpirituous liquor*, aſſociating with
' evil perſons, abſence from her huſband, ram-
                                        ' bling

' bling abroad, unfeasonable sleep, and dwelling
' in the house of another, are six faults which
' bring infamy on a married woman :

14. ' Such *women* examine not beauty, nor pay
' attention to age ; whether *their lover be* hand-
' some or ugly, they think it is enough that he is
' a man, and pursue their pleasures.

15. ' Through their passion for men, their
' mutable temper, their want of settled affection,
' and their perverse nature, (let them be guarded
' in this world ever so well) they soon become
' alienated from their husbands.

16. ' Yet should their husbands be diligently
' careful in guarding them ; though they well
' know the disposition with which the lord of
' creation formed them :

17. ' MENU allotted to such women a love
' of their bed, of their seat, and of ornament,
' impure appetites, wrath, weak flexibility, desire
' of mischief, and bad conduct.

18. ' Women have no business with the texts
' of the *Véda* ; thus is the law fully settled :
' having therefore no evidence *of law*, and no
' *knowledge of* expiatory texts, sinful women must
' be as foul as falsehood itself ; and this is a fixed
' rule.

19. ' To this effect, many texts, which may
' show their true disposition, are chanted in the
' *Védas :* hear now their expiation for sin.

20. " That pure blood, which my mother
" defileth by adulterous desire, frequenting the
" houses of other men, and violating her duty
" to her lord, that blood may my father purify !"
' Such is the tenour of the holy text, *which her*
' *son, who knows her guilt, must pronounce for her* ;

21. ' And

21. ' *And* this expiation has been declared for
' every unbecoming thought, which enters her
' mind, concerning infidelity to her hufband,
' fince that is *the beginning of* adultery.

22. ' Whatever be the qualities of the man
' with whom a woman is united by lawful mar-
' riage, fuch qualities even fhe affumes; like a
' river *united* with the fea.

23. ' ACSHAMA'LA', a woman of the loweft
' birth, being thus united to VASISHT'HA, and
' SA'RANGÍ, being united to MANDAPA'LA, were
' entitled to very high honour :

24. ' Thefe and other females of low birth,
' have attained eminence in this world by the
' refpective good qualities of their lords.

25. ' Thus has the law, ever pure, been pro-
' pounded for the civil conduct of men and wo-
' men : hear next the laws concerning children,
' by obedience to which may happinefs be at-
' tained in this and the future life.

26. ' WHEN good women united with hufbands
' in expectation of progeny, eminently fortunate
' and worthy of reverence, irradiate the houfes
' of their lords, between them, and goddeffes of
' abundance, there is no diverfity whatever.

27. ' The production of children, the nurture
' of them when produced, and the daily fuper-
' intendence of domeftick affairs are peculiar to
' the wife :

28. ' From the wife alone proceed offspring,
' good houfehold management, folicitous atten-
' tion, moft exquifite careffes, and that heavenly
' beatitude which fhe obtains for the manes of
' anceftors, and for *the hufband* himfelf.

29. ' She who deferts not her lord, but keeps
' in

' in subjection to him her heart, her speech, and
' her body, shall attain his mansion in heaven; and,
' by the virtuous in this world, be called *Sádhwì,*
' *or good and faithful* ;

30. ' But a wife, by disloyalty to her huf-
' band, shall incur disgrace in this life, and be
' born *in the next* from the womb of a shakal, or
' be tormented with horrible diseases, which pu-
' nish vice

31. ' LEARN now that excellent law, univer-
' sally salutary, which was declared concerning
' issue, by great and good sages, formerly born.

32. ' They consider the male issue of a woman
' as the son of the lord; but, on the subject of
' that lord, a difference of opinion is mentioned
' in the *Véda* ; some giving that name to the real
' procreator of the child, and others applying it
' to the married possessor of the woman.

33. ' The woman is considered in law as the
' field, and the man as the grain : now vegetable
' bodies are formed by the united operation of the
' seed and the field.

34. ' In some cases the prolifick power of the
' male is chiefly distinguished ; in others, the re-
' ceptacle of the female ; but, when both are
' equal in dignity, the offspring is most highly
' esteemed :

35. ' In general, as between the male and fe-
' male powers of procreation, the male is held
' superiour ; since the offspring of all procreant
' beings is distinguished by marks of the male
' power.

36. ' Whatever be the quality of seed, scattered
' in a field prepared in due season, a plant of the
' same quality springs in that field, with peculiar
' visible properties.

37. ' Certainly

37. ' Certainly this earth is called the primeval
' womb of many beings; but the seed exhibits
' not in its vegetation any properties of the womb.

38. ' On earth here below, even in the same
' ploughed field, seeds of many different forms,
' having been sown by husbandmen in the proper
' season, vegetate according to their nature :

39. ' Rice plants, mature in sixty days, and
' those which require transplantation, *mudga, tila,*
' *másha,* barley, leaks, and sugar-canes, all spring
' up according to the seeds.

40. ' That one plant should be sown, and ano-
' ther produced cannot happen : whatever seed
' may be sown, even that produces its proper stem.

41. ' Never must it be sown in another man's
' field by him, who has natural good sense, who
' has been well instructed, who knows the *Véda*
' and its *Angas,* who desires long life :

42. ' They who are acquainted with pastimes,
' have preserved, on this subject, holy strains
' chanted by every breeze, *declaring,* that " seed
" must not be sown in the field of another man."

43. ' As the arrow of that hunter is vain, who
' shoots it into the wound which another had made
' just before in the antelope, thus instantly pe-
' rishes the seed which a man throws into the
' soil of another :

44. ' Sages, who know former times, consider
' this earth *(Prit'hiví)* as the wife of king PRĬTHU;
' and thus they pronounce cultivated land to be
' the property of him who cut away the wood, *or*
' *who cleared and tilled it*; and the antelope, of the
' first hunter, who mortally wounded it.

45. ' Then only is a man perfect, when he
' consists of *three persons united,* his wife, himself,
' and his son; and thus have learned *Bráhmens*
                                    ' announced

' announced this *maxim :* " The husband is even
" one person with his wife," *for all domestick and*
' *religious, not for all civil purposes.*

46. ' Neither by sale nor desertion can a wife be
' released from her husband : thus we fully ac-
' knowledge the law enacted of old by the Lord
' of creatures.

47. ' Once is the partition of an inheritance
' made ; once is a damsel given in marriage ; and
' once does a man say " I give :" these three
' are, by good men, done once for all *and ir-*
' *revocably.*

48. ' As with cows, mares, female camels,
' slave-girls, milch buffalos, she goats, and
' ewes, it is not the owner of the *bull, or other*
' father, who owns the offspring, even thus is it
' with the wives of others.

49. ' They who have no property in the field,
' but having grain in their possession, sow it in soil
' owned by another, can receive no advantage
' whatever from the corn, which may be pro-
' duced :

50. ' Should a bull beget a hundred calves on
' cows not owned by his master, those calves be-
' long solely to the proprietors of the cows ; and
' the strength of the bull was wasted :

51. ' Thus men, who have no marital pro-
' perty in women, but sow in the fields owned
' by others, may raise up fruit to the husbands ;
' but the procreator can have no advantage
' from it.

52. ' Unless there be a special agreement be-
' tween the owners of the land and of the seed,
' the fruit belongs clearly to the land-owner, for
' the receptacle is more important than the seed :

' 53. ' But

53. ' But the owners of the feed 'and of the foil
' may be confidered in this world as joint owners
' of the crop, which they agree, by fpecial com-
' pact in confideration of the feed, to divide
' between them.

54. ' Whatever man owns a field, if feed, con-
' veyed into it by water or wind, fhould germinate,
' the plant belongs to the land-owner ; the mere
' fower takes not the fruit.

55. ' Such is the law concerning the offspring
' of cows, and mares, of female camels, goats,
' and fheep, of flave girls, hens, and milch buf-
' falos, *unlefs there be a fpecial agreement.*

56. ' THUS has the comparative importance of
' the foil and the feed been declared to you : I will
' next propound the law concerning women, who
' have no iffue *by their hufbands.*

57. ' The wife of an elder brother is confidered
' as mother-in-law to the younger ; and the wife
' of the younger as daughter-in-law to the elder :

58. ' The elder brother, amoroufly approach-
' ing the wife of the younger, and the younger,
' careffing the wife of the elder, are both degraded,
' even though authorized *by the hufband or fpiritual*
' *guide,* except when fuch wife has no iffue.

59. ' On failure of iffue by the hufband, *if he*
' *be of the fervile clafs,* the defired offspring may be
' procreated, either by his brother or fome other
' *fapinda,* on the wife, who has been duly au-
' thorized :

60. ' Sprinkled with clarified butter, filent in
' the night, let the kinfman thus appointed beget
' one fon, but a fecond by no means, on the
' widow *or childlefs wife :*

61. ' Some fages, learned in the laws concern-
'ing

' ing women, thinking it poffible, that the great
' object of that appointment may not be obtained
' *by the birth of a fingle fon*, are of opinion, that the
' wife and appointed kinfman may legally pro-
' create a fecond.

62. ' The firft object of the appointment being
' attained according to law, both *the brother and
the widow* muft live together like a father and a
' daughter by affinity.

63. ' Either brother, appointed for this pur-
' pofe, who deviates from the ftrict rule, and acts
' from carnal defire, fhall be degraded, as having
' defiled the bed of his daughter-in-law or of his
' father.

64. ' By men of twice born claffes no widow,
' *or childlefs wife*, muft be authorized to conceive
' by any other than her lord, for they, who au-
' thorize her to conceive by any other, violate the
' primeval law.

65. ' Such a commiffion *to a brother or other
near kinfman* is no where mentioned in the nuptial
' texts of the *Véda*; nor is the marriage of a
' widow even named in the laws concerning
' marriage.

66. ' This practice, fit only for cattle, is repre-
' hended by learned *Bráhmens*; yet it is declared
' to have been the practice even of men, while
' Ve'na had fovereign power:

67. ' He, poffeffing the whole earth, and *thence
only called* the chief of fage monarchs, gave rife
' to a confufion of claffes, when his intellect be-
' came weak through luft.

68. ' Since his time the virtuous difapprove of
' that man, who, through delufion of mind, di-
' rects a widow *to receive the careffes of another* for
' the fake of progeny.

69. The

69. ' The damfel, *indeed*, whofe hufband fhall
' die after troth verbally plighted, *but before con-*
' *fummation*, his brother fhall take in marriage ac-
' cording to this rule :

70. ' Having efpoufed her in due form of law,
' fhe being clad in a white robe, and pure in her
' moral conduct, let him approach her once in
' each proper feafon, and until iffue *be had.*

71. ' LET no man of fenfe, who has once
' given his daughter to a fuitor, give her again to
' another ; for he, who gives away his daughter,
' whom he had before given, incurs the guilt and
' fine of fpeaking falfely in a caufe concerning
' mankind.

72. ' EVEN though a man have married a
' young woman in legal form, yet he may aban-
' don her, if he find her blemifhed, afflicted with
' difeafe, or previoufly deflowered, and given to
' him with fraud :

73. ' If any man give a faulty damfel in
' marriage, without difclofing her blemifh, the
' hufband may annul that act of her ill-minded
' giver.

74. ' SHOULD a man have bufinefs abroad, let
' him affure a fit maintenance to his wife, and
' then refide *for a time* in a foreign country ; fince
' a wife, even though virtuous, may be tempted
' to act amifs, if fhe be diftreffed by want of
' fubfiftence :

75. ' While her hufband, having fettled her
' maintenance, refides abroad, let her continue
' firm in religious aufterities ; but, if he leave her
' no fupport, let her fubfift by *fpinning and other*
' blamelefs arts.

76. ' If he live abroad on account of fome
7   ' facred

' facred duty, let her wait for him eight years;
' if on account of knowledge or fame, fix ; if on
' account of pleafure, three : *after thofe terms have*
' *expired fhe muft follow him.*

77. ' FOR a whole year let a hufband bear with
' his wife, who treats him with averfion ; but,
' after a year, let him deprive her of her feparate
' property, and ceafe to cohabit with her.

78. ' She, who neglects her lord, though
' addicted to gaming, fond of fpirituous liquors,
' or difeafed, muft be deferted for three months,
' and deprived of her ornaments and houfehold
' furniture :

79. ' But fhe who is averfe from a mad huf-
' band, or a deadly finner, or an eunuch, or one
' without manly ftrength, or one afflicted with
' fuch maladies as punifh crimes, muft neither
' be deferted nor ftripped of her property.

80. ' A WIFE, who drinks any fpirituous li-
' quors, who acts immorally, who fhows hatred
' *to her lord,* who is *incurably* difeafed, who is mif-
' chievous, who waftes his property, may at all
' times be fuperfeded by another wife.

81. ' A barren wife may be fuperfeded by ano-
' ther in the eighth year : fhe, whofe children are
' all dead, in the tenth ; fhe, who brings forth *only*
' daughters, in the eleventh; fhe, who fpeaks
' unkindly, without delay ;

82. ' But fhe, who, though afflicted with ill-
' nefs, is beloved and virtuous, muft never be
' difgraced, though fhe may be fuperfeded by
' another wife with her own confent.

83. ' If a wife, legally fuperfeded, fhall depart
' in wrath from the houfe, fhe muft either in-
' ftantly be confined, or abandoned in the pre-
' fence of the whole family :

84. ' But

84. ' But she, who having been forbidden,
' addicts herself to intoxicating liquor even at
' jubilees, or mixes in crowds at theatres, must be
' fined six *racticas* of gold.

85. ' WHEN twice born men take wives, both
' of their own class and others, the precedence,
' honour and habitation of those wives, must be
' settled according to the order of their classes :

86. ' To all such married men, the wives of
' the same class only (not wives of a different
' class by any means) must perform the duty of
' personal attendance, and the daily business re-
' lating to acts of religion ;

87. ' For he who foolishly causes those duties
' to be performed by any other than his wife of
' the same class, when she is near at hand, has
' been immemorially considered as a mere *Chán-*
' *dala* begotten on a *Bráhmeni.*

88. ' To an excellent and handsome youth of
' the same class, let every man give his daughter
' in marriage, according to law ; even though
' she have not attained her age *of eight years :*

89. ' *But* it is better that the damsel, though
' marriageable, should stay at home till her death,
' than that he should ever give her in marriage
' to a bridegroom void of excellent qualities.

90. ' Three years let a damsel wait, though
' she be marriageable ; but, after that term, let
' her chuse for herself a bridegroom of equal
' rank :

91. ' If not being given in marriage, she chuse
' her bridegroom, neither she, nor the youth
' chosen, commits any offence ;

92. ' But a damsel, thus electing her husband,
' shall not carry with her the ornaments which
                                              ' she

' fhe received from her father, nor thofe given
' by her mother, or brethren: if fhe carry
' them away fhe commits theft. ,

93. ' He who takes to wife a damfel of full
' age, fhall not give a nuptial prefent to her fa-
' ther; fince the father loft his dominion over
' her, by detaining her at a time when fhe might
' have been a parent.

94. ' A man aged thirty years, may marry a
' girl of twelve, *if he find one* dear to his heart;
' or a man of twenty-four years a damfel of
' eight: but if *he finifh his ftudentfhip earlier and*
' *the duties of his next order* would otherwife be
' impeded, let him marry immediately.

95. ' A wife given by the gods *who are named*
' *in the bridal texts,* let the hufband receive and
' fupport conftantly, if fhe be virtuous, though he
' married her not from inclination: fuch conduct
' will pleafe the gods.

96. ' To be mothers were women created;
' and to be fathers, men; religious rites therefore
' are ordained in the *Véda* to be performed *by the*
' *hufband* together with the wife.

97. ' If a nuptial gratuity has actually been
' given to a damfel, and he, who gave it fhould
. ' die *before marriage*, the damfel fhall be married
' to his brother if fhe confent;

98. ' But even a man of the fervile clafs ought
' not to receive a gratuity when he gives his
' daughter in marriage; fince a father who
' takes a fee *on that occafion*, tacitly fells his
' daughter.

99. ' Neither ancients nor moderns who were
' good men, have ever given a damfel in mar-
.' riage after fhe had been promifed to another
' man;

100. ' Nor, even in former creations, have we
' heard *the virtuous approve* the tacit fale of a
' daughter for a price, under the name of a nuptial
' gratuity.

101. " Let mutual fidelity continue till death:"
' this, in few words, may be confidered as the fu-
' preme law between hufband and wife.

102. ' Let a man and woman, united by mar-
' riage, conftantly beware, left at any time dif-
' united, they violate their mutual fidelity.

103. ' Thus has been declared to you the law,
' abounding in the pureft affection, for the con-
' duct of man and wife ; together with the prac-
' tice of raifing up offspring *to a hufband of the*
' *fervile clafs* on failure *of iffue by him begotten* :
' learn now the law of inheritance.

104. ' AFTER the death of the father and the
' mother, the brothers being affembled, may di-
' vide among themfelves the paternal *and ma-*
' *ternal* eftate; but they have no power over it,
' while their parents live, *unlefs the father chufe*
' *to diftribute it.*

105. ' The eldeft brother may take entire
' poffeffion of the patrimony ; and the others
' may live under him as *they lived* under their
' father, *unlefs they chufe to be feparated.*

106. ' By the eldeft, at the moment of his
' birth, the father having begotten a fon, dif-
' charges his debt to his own progenitors ; the
' eldeft fon, therefore, ought *before partition* to
' manage the whole patrimony :

107. ' That fon alone, by whofe birth he dif-
' charges his debt, and through whom he attains
' immortality, was begotten from a fenfe of duty :
' all the reft are confidered by the wife as begotten
' from love of pleafure.

108. ' Let

108. ' Let the father alone support his sons;
' and the firſt-born, his younger brothers, and let
' them behave to the eldeſt according to law, as
' children *ſhould behave* to their father.

109. ' The firſt-born, *if virtuous*, exalts the
' family, or, *if vitious*, deſtroys it : the firſt-born
' is in this world the moſt reſpectable; and the
' good never treat him with diſdain.

110. ' If an elder brother act as an elder
' brother ought, he is *to be revered* as a mother,
' as a father; and, even if he have not the be-
' haviour of a good elder brother, he ſhould be
' reſpected as a *maternal uncle, or other* kinſman.

111. ' Either let them thus live together, or;
' if they deſire *ſeparately to perform* religious rites,
' let them live apart; ſince religious duties are
' multiplied in ſeparate houſes, their ſeparation is,
' therefore, legal *and even laudable.*

112. ' The portion deducted for the eldeſt is
' a twentieth part *of the heritage*, with the beſt of
' all the chattels ; for the middlemoſt, half of that,
' *or a fortieth* ; for the youngeſt, a quarter of it, *or*
' *an eightieth.*

113. ' The eldeſt and youngeſt reſpectively
' take their juſt mentioned portions ; and if there
' be more than one between them, each of the
' intermediate ſons has the mean portion, *or the*
' *fortieth.*

114. ' Of all the goods collected let the firſt-
' born, *if he be tranſcendently learned and virtuous*,
' take the beſt article, whatever is moſt excellent
' in its kind, and the beſt of ten *cows or the like* :

115. ' But among brothers equally ſkilled in
' performing their ſeveral duties, there is no de-
' duction of the beſt in ten, *or the moſt excellent*

chattel;

' *chattel*; though some trifle, as a mark of greater
' veneration, should be given to the first-born.

116. ' If a deduction be thus made, let equal
' shares of the residue be ascertained *and received*;
' but, if there be no deduction, the shares must
' be distributed in this manner:

117. ' Let the eldest have a double share, and
' the next born, a share and a half, *if they clearly
' surpass the rest in virtue and learning*; the younger
' sons must have each a share: *if all be equal in
' good qualities, they must all take share and share
' alike.*

118. ' To the *unmarried* daughters *by the same
' mother*, let their brothers give portions out of
' their own allotments respectively, *according to
' the classes of their several mothers*: let each give
' a fourth part of his own distinct share; and
' they who refuse to give it shall be degraded.

119. ' Let them never divide *the value of* a
' single goat or sheep, or a single beast with
' uncloven hoofs: a single goat or sheep *remain-
' ing after an equal distribution*, belongs to the first-
' born.

120. ' Should a younger brother, *in the manner
' before mentioned*, have begotten a son on the wife
' of his *deceased* elder brother, the division must
' then be made equally *between that son who re-
' presents the deceased, and his natural father*: thus
' is the law settled.

121. ' The representative is not *so far* wholly
' substituted by law in the place of the *deceased*
' principal, *as to have the portion of an elder son*;
' and the principal became a father in consequence
' of the procreation *by his younger brother*; the son,
' therefore, is entitled by law to an equal share,
' *but not to a double portion.*

122. ' A

122. ' A younger son being born of a first mar-
' ried wife, after an elder son had been born of a
' wife last married, *but of a lower class*, it may be
' a doubt in that case, how the division shall be
' made :

123. ' Let the son born of the elder wife, take
' one most excellent bull deducted from the in-
' heritance ; the next excellent bulls are for those
' who *were born first, but* are inferior on account of
' their mothers *who were married last*.

124. ' A son, indeed, who was first born, and
' brought forth by the wife first married, may
' take, *if learned and virtuous*, one bull and fifteen
' cows ; and the other sons may then take, each
' in right of his several mother : such is the fixed
' rule.

125. ' As between sons, born of wives equal in
' their class, *and* without *any other* distinction,
' there can be no seniority in right of the mother ;
' but the seniority ordained by law is according to
' the birth.

126. ' The right of invoking INDRA by the
' texts, called *swabráhmanyá*, depends on actual
' priority of birth ; and of twins also, *if any such
' be conceived* among *different* wives, the eldest is
' he, who was first actually born.

127. ' HE, who has no son, may appoint his
' daughter in this manner to raise up a son for him,
' *saying*, " the male child, who shall be born
'' from her in wedlock, shall be mine for the pur-
'' pose of performing my obsequies."

128. ' In this manner DACSHA himself, lord
' of created beings, anciently appointed all his
' *fifty* daughters to raise up sons to him, for the
' sake of multiplying his race :

129. ' He

129. ' He gave ten to Dherma, thirteen to
' Casyapa, twenty-seven to Sóma king *of Bráh-*
' *mens and medical plants,* after doing honour to
' them with an affectionate heart.

130. ' The son of a man is even as himself;
' and as the son, such is the daughter *thus ap-*
' *pointed:* how then, *if he have no son,* can any in-
' herit his property, but a daughter who is closely
' united with his own soul ?

131. ' Property, given to the mother on her
' marriage, is inherited by her *unmaried* daughter;
' and the son of a daughter, *appointed in the manner*
' *just mentioned,* shall inherit the whole estate of
' her father, who leaves no son *by himself begotten :*

132. ' The son, however, of *such* a daughter,
' who succeeds to all the wealth of her father
' dying without a son, must offer two funeral
' cakes, one to his own father, and one to the
' father of his mother.

133. ' Between a son's son and the son of *such*
' a daughter, there is no difference in law ; since
' their father and their mother both sprang from
' the body of the same man :

134. ' But a daughter having been oppointed
' to produce a son forher father, and a son, *begotten*
' *by himself,* being afterwards born, the division of
' the heritage must in that case be equal; since
' there is no right of primogeniture for a woman.

135. ' Should a daughter, thus appointed to
' raise up a son for her father, die by any accident
' without a son, the husband of that daughter
' may, without hesitation, possess himself of her
' property.

136. ' By that male child, whom a daughter
' thus appointed, either by an implied intention
' or

' or a plain declaration, ſhall produce from an
' huſband of an equal claſs, the maternal grand-
' father becomes in law the father of a ſon: let
' that ſon give the funeral cake and poſſeſs the
' inheritance.

137. ' By a ſon, a man obtains victory over all
' people; by a ſon's ſon, he enjoys immortality;
' and, afterward, by the ſon of that granſdon, he
' reaches the ſolar abode.

138. ' Since the ſon *(tráyaté)* delivers his father
' from the hell named *put,* he was, therefore
' called *puttra* by BRAHMA' himſelf:

139. ' Now between the ſons of his ſon and of
' his daughter *thus appointed,* there ſubſiſts in this
' world no difference, for even the ſon of *ſuch* a
' daughter delivers him in the next, like the ſon
' of his ſon.

140. ' Let the ſon of ſuch a daughter offer the
' firſt funeral cake to his mother; the ſecond to her
' father; the third to her paternal grandfather.

141. ' OF the man, to whóm a ſon has been
' given, *according, to a ſubſequent law,* adorned
' with every virtue, that ſon ſhall take *a fifth or
' ſixth part of* the heritage, though brought from
' a different family.

142. ' A given ſon muſt never claim the family
' and eſtate of his natural father: the funeral cake
' follows the family and eſtate; but of him who
' has given away his ſon, the funeral oblation is
' extinct.

143. ' THE ſon of a wife, not authorized to
' have iſſue by another, and the ſon begotten, by
' the brother of the huſband, on a wife who has
' a ſon then living, are both unworthy of the heri-
' tage; one being the child of an adulterer, and
' the other produced through mere luſt.

144. ' Even

144. ' Even the fon of a wife duly authorized,
' not begotten according to the law *already*
' *propounded*, is unworthy of the paternal eftate;
' for he was procreated by an outcaft :

145. ' But the fon *legally* begotten on a wife, au-
' thorized for the purpofe *before mentioned*, may
' inherit *in all refpects, if he be virtuous and learned*,
' as a fon begotten by the hufband; fince, *in that*
' *cafe*, the feed and the produce belong of right to
' the owner of the field.

146 ' He, who keeps the *fixed and moveable*
' eftate of his *deceafed* brother, maintains the
' widow, and raifes up a fon to that brother, muft
' give that fon, *at the age of fifteen*, the whole of
' his brother's *divided* property.

147. ' Should a wife, even though legally au-
' thorized, produce a fon by the brother, or any
' other *fapinda*, of her hufband, that fon, if begot-
' ten with *amorous embraces, and tokens of* impure
' defire, the fages proclaim bafe-born and incapa-
' ble of inheriting.

148. ' This law, *which has preceded*, muft be
' underftood of a diftribution among fons begotten
' on women of the fame clafs : hear now the
' law concerning *fons by* feveral women of differ-
' ent claffes.

149. ' If there be four wives of a *Bráhmen* in
' the direct order of the claffes, and fons are pro-
' duced by them all, this is the rule of partition
' *among them :*

150. ' The chief fervant in hufbandry, the bull
' kept for impregnating cows, the riding horfe or
' carriage, the *ring and other* ornaments, and the
' principal meffuage, fhall be deducted from the
' inheritance and given to the *Bráhmen-*fon,
                                    ' together

' together with a larger share by way of pre-
' eminence.

151. ' Let the *Bráhmen* take three shares of the
' residue; the son of a *Cshatriyá* wife, two shares;
' the son of the *Vaisyá* wife, a share and a half;
' and the son of the *Súdra* wife may take one share.

152. ' Or, *if no deduction be made,* let some per-
' son learned in the law divide the whole collected
' estate into ten parts, and make a legal distribu-
' tion by this *following* rule:

153. ' Let the son of the *Bráhmaní* take four
' parts; the son of the *Cshatriyá* three; let the
' son of the *Vaisyá* have two parts; let the son of
' the *Súdra* take a single part, *if he be virtuous.*

154. ' But whether the *Bráhmen* have sons, or
' have no sons, *by wives of the three first classes,* no
' more than a tenth part must be given to the son
' of a *Súdra.*

155. ' The son of a *Bráhmen,* a *Cshatriya,* or a
' *Vaisya* by a woman of the servile class, shall
' inherit no part of the estate, *unless he be virtuous;*
' *nor jointly with other sons, unless his mother was*
' *lawfully married:* whatever his father may give
' him, let that be his own.

156. ' All the sons of twice born men, pro-
' duced by wives of the same class, must divide
' the heritage equally, after the younger brothers
' have given the first-born his deducted allot-
' ment.

157. ' For a *Súdra* is ordained a wife of his
' own class, *and* no other: all produced by her
' shall have equal shares, though she have a hun-
' dred sons.

158. ' OF the twelve sons of men, whom
' MENU, sprung from the Self-existent, has named,
' six

' fix are kinfman and heirs; fix not heirs, *except to*
' *their own fathers*, but kinfmen.

159. ' The fon begotten by a man himself *in*
' *lawful wedlock*, the fon of his wife begotten *in*
' *the manner before defcribed*, a fon given *to him*,
' a fon made *or adopted*, a fon of concealed birth,
' *or whofe real father cannot be known*, and a fon
' rejected *by his natural parents*, are the fix kinf-
' men and heirs:

·160. ' The fon of a young woman *unmarried*,
' and the fon of a pregnant bride, a fon bought,
' a fon by a twice married woman, a fon felf-
' given, and a fon by a *Súdra*, are the fix kinfmen,
' but not heirs *to collaterals*.

161. ' Such advantage, as a man would gain,
' who fhould attempt to pafs deep water in a
' boat made of woven reeds, the father obtains,
' who paffes the gloom of death, leaving only
' contemptible fons, *who are the eleven, or at leaft*
' *the fix laft mentioned.*

16 . ' If the two heirs of one man be the fon
' of his own body and a fon of his wife by a kinf-
' man, *the former of whom was begotten after his*
' *recovery from an illnefs thought incurable*, each of
' the fons, exclufively of the other, fhall fucceed
' to the whole eftate of his natural father.

163. ' The fon of his own body is the fole heir
' to his eftate, but, that all evil may be removed,
' let him allow a maintenance to the reft;

164. ' And, when the fon of the body has taken
' an account of the paternal inheritance, let
' him give a fixth part of it to the fon of the
' wife begotten by a kinfman, *before his father's*
' *recovery*; or a fifth part, *if that fon be eminently*
' *virtuous.*

165. ' The fon of the body, and the fon of the
' wife,

' wife, may fucced *immediately* to the paternal
' eſtate *in the manner juſt mentioned*; but the ten
' other ſons can only ſucceed in order to the fa-
' mily duties, and to their ſhare of the inheritance,
' *thoſe laſt named being excluded by any one of the*
' *preceding*.

166. ' HIM, whom a man has begotten on his
' own wedded wife, let him know to be the firſt
' in rank, as the ſon of his body.

167. · He who was begotten, according to law,
' on the wife of a man deceaſed, or impotent, or
' diſordered, after due authority given to her, is
' called the lawful ſon of the wife.

168. ' He, whom his father, or mother *with*
' *her huſbands aſſent*, gives to another as his ſon,
' provided that the donee have no iſſue, if the boy
' be of the ſame claſs and affectionately diſpoſed,
' is conſidered as a ſon given, *the gift being con-*
' *firmed* by *pouring* water.

169. ' He is conſidered as a ſon made *or adopted*,
' whom a man takes as his own ſon, the boy being
' equal in claſs, endued with filial virtues, ac-
' quainted with *the* merit *of performing obſequies*
' *to his adopter*, and with *the* ſin *of omitting them*.

170. ' In whoſe manſion ſoever a male child
' ſhall be brought forth *by a married woman, whoſe*
' *huſband has long been abſent*, if the real father
' cannot be diſcovered, *but if it be probable that*
' *he was of an equal claſs*, that child belongs to the
' lord of the *unfaithful* wife, and is called a ſon of
' concealed birth in his manſion.

171. ' A boy, whom a man receives as his own
' ſon, after he has been deſerted *without juſt cauſe*
' by his parents, or by either of them, *if one be*
' *dead*, is called a ſon rejected.

172. ' A

172. ' A fon, whom the daughter of any man
' privately brings forth in the houfe of her father,
' if fhe *afterwards* marry her lover, is defcribed as
' a fon begotten on an unmarried girl.

173. ' If a pregnant young woman marry,'
' whether her pregnancy be known or unknown,
' the male child in her womb belongs to the bride-
' groom, and is called a fon received with his
' bride.

174. ' He is called a fon bought, whom a man,
' for the fake of having a fon *to perform his obfe-*
' *quies,* purchafes from his father and mother,
' whether the boy be equal or unequal *to himfelf*
' *in good qualities, for in clafs all adopted fons muft*
' *be equal.*

175. ' He, whom a woman, either forfaken by
' her lord or a widow, conceived by a fecond
' hufband, whom fhe took by. her own defire,
' *though againft law,* is called the fon of a woman
' twice married :

176. ' If, *on her fecond marriage,* fhe be ftill a
' virgin, or if fhe left her hufband under the age
' of puberty and return to him at his full age, fhe
' muft again perform the nuptial ceremony *either*
' with her fecond, *or her young and deferted,*
' hufband.

177. ' He, who has loft his parents, or been
' abandoned *by them* without juft caufe, and offers
' himfelf to a man *as his fon* is called a fon felf-
' given.

178. ' A fon, begotten through luft on a *Súdra*
' by a man of the prieftly clafs, is even as a corpfe,
' though alive, and is thence called in law a living
' corpfe :

179. ' But a fon begotten by a man of the fer-
' vile clafs on his female flave, or on the female

5   ' flave

' flave of his male flave, may take a fhare of the
' heritage, if permitted *by the other fons :* thus is'
' the law eftablifhed.

180. ' Thefe eleven fons (the fon of the wife
' and the reft, as enumerated) are allowed by wife
' legiflators to be fubftitutes *in order* for fons ,of
' the body, for the fake of preventing a failure of
' obfequies ;

181. ' Though fuch, as are called fons for that
' purpofe, but were produced from the manhood
' of others, belong in truth to the father, from
' whofe manhood they feverally fprang, and to no
' other, *except by a juft fiction of law.*

182. ' Iғ among feveral brothers of the whole
' blood, one have a fon born, Menu pronounces
' them all fathers of a male child by means of
' that fon ; *fo that if fuch nephew would be the*
' *heir, the uncles have no power to adopt fons :*

183. ' *Thus*, if, among all the wives of the fame
' hufband, one bring forth a male child, Menu
' has declared them all, by means of that fon,
' to be mothers of male iffue.

184. ' On failure of the beft, *and* of the *next*
' beft, *among thofe twelve fons*, let the inferiour
' in order take the heritage ; but if there be
' many of equal rank, let all be fharers of the
' eftate.

185. ' Not brothers, nor parents, but fons, *if*
' *living, or their male iffue*, are heirs to the de-
' ceafed, but of him, who leaves no fon, *nor a*
' *wife, nor a daughter*, the father fhall take the
' inheritance ; and *if he leave neither father nor*
' *mother*, the brothers.

186. ' To three *anceſtors* muft water be given
' at their obfequies; for three *(the father, his*
' *father, and the paternal grandfather)* is the funeral
' cake

' cake ordained : the fourth *in defcent* is the giver
' *of oblations to them and their heir, if they die with-*
' *out nearer defcendants* ; but the fifth has no' con-
' cern *with the gift of the funeral cake.*

187. ' To the neareft *fapinda, male or female,*
' after him in the third degree, the inheritance
' *next* belongs, then on failure of *fapindas* and of
' their iffue, the *famánódaca,* or diftant kinfman,
' fhall be the heir ; or the fpiritual preceptor, or
'·the pupil, *or the fellow ftudent of the deceafed :*

188. ' On failure of all thofe, the lawful heirs
' are fuch *Bráhmens* as have read the three *Védas,*
' as are pure *in body and mind,* as have fubdued
' their paffions ; *and they muft confequently offer the*
' *cake :* thus the rites of obfequies cannot fail.

189. ' The property of a *Bráhmen* fhall never
' be taken *as an efcheat* by the king ; this is a
' fixed law : but the wealth of the other claffes,
' on failure of all heirs, the king may take.

190. ' If the widow of a man, who died with-
' out a fon, raife up a fon to him by one of his
' kinfmen, let her deliver to that fon, *at his full*
' *age,* the collected eftate of the deceafed, whatever
' it be.

191. ' If two fons, begotten by two *fucceffive*
' *hufbands, who are both dead,* contend for their
' property, then in the hands of their mother,
' let each take, exclufively of the other, his own
' father's eftate.

192. ' On the death of the mother, let all the
' uterine brothers and the uterine fifters, *if un-*
' *married,* equally divide the maternal eftate : *each*
' *married fifter fhall have a fourth part of a brother's*
' *allotment.*

193. ' Even to the daughters of thofe daugh-
' ters, it is fit that fomething fhould be given,
                                                    ' from

‘ from the affets of their maternal grandmother,
‘ on the fcore of natural affection.

194. ‘ WHAT was given before the nuptial
‘ fire, what was given on the bridal proceffion,
‘ what was given in token of love, and what was
‘ received from a brother, a mother, or a father,
‘ are confidered as the fix-fold *feparate* property
‘ of a *married* woman:

195. ‘ What fhe received after marriage from
‘ the family of her hufband, and what her affec-
‘ tionate lord may have given her, fhall be in-
‘ herited, even if fhe die in his life-time, by her
‘ children.

196. ‘ It is ordained, that the property of a
‘ woman, married by the ceremonies called *Bráh-*
‘ *ma, Daiva, Arfha, Gándharva,* or *Prájápatya,*
‘ fhall go to her hufband, if fhe die without iffue;

197. ‘ But her wealth given on the marriage
‘ called *A fura,* or on either of the *two* others, is
‘ ordained, on her death without iffue, to become
‘ the property of her father and mother.

198. ‘ If a widow, *whofe hufband had other*
‘ *wives of different claffes,* fhall have received
‘ wealth at any time, *as a gift* from her father,
‘ *and fhall die without iffue,* it fhall go to the daugh-
‘ ter of the *Bráhmanì* wife, or to the iffue of that
‘ daughter.

199. ‘ A woman fhould never make a hoard
‘ from the goods of her kindred, *which are* com-
‘ mon to *her and* many; or even from the pro-
‘ perty of her lord, without his affent.

200. ‘ Such ornamental apparel, as women
‘ wear during the lives of their hufbands, the
‘ heirs of thofe hufbands fhall not divide among
‘ themfelves: they, who divide it among them-
‘ felves, fall deep *into fin.*

7 201. ‘ Eunuchs

201. ' Eunuchs, and outcasts, persons born
' blind or deaf, madmen, idiots, the dumb, and
' such as have lost the use of a limb, are excluded
' from a share of the heritage ;

202. ' But it is just, that the heir, who knows
' his duty, should give all of them food and rai-
' ment *for life* without stint, according to the best
' of his power : he, who gives them nothing, sinks
' assuredly *to a region of punishment.*

203. ' If the eunuch and the rest should at any
' time desire to marry, *and if the wife of the eunuch*
' *should raise up a son to him by a man legally ap-*
' *pointed, that son and* the issue of such, as have
' children, shall be capable of inheriting.

204. ' After the death of the father, if the
' eldest brother acquire *wealth by his own efforts*
' *before partition*, a share of that *acquisition* shall
' go to the younger brothers, if they have made
' a due progress in learning;

205. ' And if all of them, being unlearned,
' acquire property *before partition* by their own
' labour, there shall be an equal division of that
' property *without regard to the first born*; for it
' was not the wealth of their father : this rule is
' clearly settled.

206. ' Wealth, however, acquired by learning,
' belongs exclusively to any one *of them, who ac-*
' *quired it*; so does any thing given by a friend,
' received on account of marriage, or presented
' as a mark of respect to a guest.

207. ' If any one of the brethren has a com-
' petence from his own occupation, and wants not
' the property *of his father*, he may debar himself
' from his own share, some trifle being given him
' as a consideration, *to prevent future strife.*

208. ' What

208. ' What a brother has acquired by labour
' or fkill, without ufing the patrimony, he fhall
' not give up without his affent; for it was gained
.' by his own exertion :

209. ' And if a fon, by his own efforts, recover
' *a debt or property unjuftly detained*, which could
' not be recovered before *by his father*, he fhall
' not, unlefs by his free will, put it into parcenary
' with his brethren, fince in fact it was acquired
' by himfelf.

210. ' If brethren, once divided and living
' again together as parceners, make a fecond par-
' tition, the fhares muft in that cafe be equal;
' and the firft born fhall have no right of deduc-
' tion.

211. ' Should the eldeft or youngeft of feveral
' brothers be deprived of his fhare *by a civil death*
' *on his entrance into the fourth order*, or fhould any
' one of them die, his *vefted intereft in a* fhare fhall
' not wholly be loft ;

212. ' But, *if he leave neither fon, nor wife,*
' *nor daughter, nor father, nor mother*, his uterine
' brothers and fifters, and fuch brothers as were
' re-united after a feparation, fhall affemble and
' divide his fhare equally.

213. ' Any eldeft brother, who, from avarice,
' fhall defraud his younger brother, fhall forfeit
' *the honours of* his primogeniture, be deprived
' of his own fhare, and pay a fine to the king.

214. ' All thofe brothers who are addicted to
' any vice, lofe their title to the inheritance: the
' firft born fhall not appropriate it to himfelf, but
' fhall give fhares to the youngeft, *if they be not*
' *vitious.*

215. ' If among undivided brethren *living* with
' their father, there be a common exertion for

T　　　　　　　　' common

' common gain, the father ſhall never make an
' unequal diviſion among them, *when they divide
' their families.*

216. ' A ſon, born after a diviſion *in the life-
' time of his father,* ſhall alone inherit the pa-
' trimony, or ſhall have a ſhare of it with the
' divided brethren, if they return and unite them-
' ſelves with him.

217. ' Of a ſon, dying childleſs *and leaving no
' widow,* the *father and* mother ſhall take the
' eſtate; and the mother alſo being dead, the pa-
' ternal *grandfather and* grandmother ſhall take
' the heritage, *on failure of brothers and nephews.*

218. ' When all the debts and wealth have
' been juſtly diſtributed according to law, any
' property, that may afterwards be diſcovered,
' ſhall be ſubject to a ſimilar diſtribution.

219. ' Apparel, carriages, or riding horſes,
' and ornaments *of ordinary value, which any of
' the heirs had uſed by conſent before partition,*
' dreſſed rice, water *in a well or ciſtern,* female
' ſlaves, family prieſts, or ſpiritual counſellors,
' and paſtue ground for cattle, the wife have
' declared indiviſible, *and ſtill to be uſed as be-
' fore.*

220. ' Thus have the laws of inheritance, and
' the rule for the conduct of ſons (whether
' the ſon of the wife or others) been expounded
' to you in order: learn at preſent the law con-
' cerning games of chance.

221. ' GAMING, either with inanimate or with
' animated things, let the king exclude wholly
' from his realm: both thoſe modes of play cauſe
' deſtruction to princes.

222. ' Such play with dice *and the like,* or by
' matches *between rams and cocks,* amounts to open
'　　　　　　　　　　　　　　　　　　' theft;

' theft; and the king muft ever be vigilant in
' fuppreffing both *modes of play :*

223. ' Gaming with lifelefs things is known
' among men by the name of *dy'ta*; but *famá-*
' *hwaya* fignifies a match between living creatures.

224. ' Let the king punifh corporally at dif-
' cretion both the gamefter and the keeper of a
' gaming-houfe, whether they play with inanimate
' or animated things; and men of the fervile clafs,
' who wear the *ftring and other* marks of the
' twice born.

225. ' Gamefters, publick dancers, and fingers,
' revilers of fcripture, open hereticks, men who
' perform not the duties of their feveral claffes,
' and fellers of fpirituous liquors, let him inftantly
' banifh from the town :

226. ' Thofe wretches, lurking like unfeen
' thieves in the dominion of a prince, continually
' harafs his good fubjects with their vitious conduct.

227. ' Even in a former creation was this *vice*
' *of* gaming found a great provoker of enmity :
' let no fenfible man, therefore, addict himfelf to
' play even for his amufement :

228. ' On the man addicted to it, either pri-
' vately or openly, let punifhment be inflicted at
' the difcretion of the king.

229. ' A MAN of the military, commercial, or
' fervile clafs, who cannot pay a fine, fhall dif-
' charge the debt by his labour : a prieft fhall dif-
' charge it by little and little.

230. ' For women, children, perfons of crazy
' intellect, the old, the poor, and the infirm, the
' king fhall order punifhment with a fmall whip,
' a twig, or a rope.

231. ' THOSE minifters who are employed in
' publick affairs, and, inflamed by the blaze of

T 2   wealth,

' wealth, mar the bufinefs of any perfon con-
' cerned, let the king ftrip of all their property.

232. ' Such as forge royal edicts, caufe diffen-
' fions among the great minifters, or kill women,
' priefts, or children, let the king put to death;
' and fuch as adhere to his enemies.

233. ' Whatever bufinefs has at any time been
' tranfacted conformably to law, let him confider
' as finally fettled, and refufe to unravel;

234. ' But whatever bufinefs has been con-
' cluded illegally by his minifters or by a judge,
' let the king himfelf re-examine; and let him
' fine them each a thoufand *panas*.

235. ' The flayer of a prieft, a foldier, or
' merchant drinking arak, or a prieft drinking
' arak, mead, or rum, he who fteals the gold of
' a prieft, and he who violates the bed of his *na-*
' *tural or fpiritual* father, are all to be confidered
' refpectively as offenders in the higheft degree,
' *except thofe whofe crimes are not fit to be named :*

236. ' On fuch of thofe four, as have not actual-
' ly performed an expiation, let the king legally
' inflict corporal punifhment, together with a fine.

237. ' For violating the paternal bed, let *the*
' *mark of* a female part be impreffed *on the fore-*
' *head with hot iron*; for drinking fpirits a vint-
' ner's flag; for ftealing facred gold, a dog's foot;
' for murdering a prieft, *the figure of* a headlefs
' corpfe:

238. ' With none to eat with them, with none
' to facrifice with them, with none to read with
' them, with none to be allied by marriage to
' them, abject and excluded from all focial duties,
' let them wander over this earth:

239. ' Branded with *indelible* marks, they fhall
' be deferted by their paternal and maternal relations,

5

" lations, treated by none with affection, received
' by none with refpect: fuch is the ordinance of
' MENU.

240. ' *Criminals of* all the claffes, having per-
' formed an expiation, as ordained by law, fhall
' not be marked on the forehead, but condemned
' to pay the higheft fine:

241. ' For crimes by a prieft, *who had a good*
' *character before his offence,* the middle fine fhall
' be fet on him; or, *if his crime was premeditated,*
' he fhall be banifhed from the realm, *taking* with
' *him* his effects and his family;

242. ' But men of the other claffes, who have
' committed thofe crimes, *though without preme-*
' *ditation,* fhall be ftripped of all their poffeffions;
' and, if their offence was premeditated, fhall be
' corporally, or even capitally punifhed, *according*
' *to circumftances.*

243. ' LET no virtuous prince appropriate the
' wealth of a criminal in the higheft degree, for
' he who appropriates it through covetoufnefs,
' is contaminated with the fame guilt:

244. ' Having thrown fuch a fine into the
' waters, let him offer it to VARUNA; or let him
' beftow it on fome prieft of eminent learning in
' the fcriptures:

245. ' VARUNA is the lord of punifhment; he
' holds a rod even over kings; and a prieft who
' has gone through the whole *Véda,* is *equal to* a
' fovereign of all the world.

246. ' Where the king abftains from receiving
' *to his own ufe* the wealth of fuch offenders, there
' children are born in due feafon and enjoy long
' lives;

247. ' *There* the grain of hufbandmen rifes
' abundantly, as it was refpectively fown; there

' no

'no younglings die, nor is one deformed animal
'born.

248. 'SHOULD a man of the bafeft clafs, with
'preconceived malice, give pain to *Bráhmens*, let
'the prince corporally punifh him by various
'modes, that may raife terrour.

249. 'A king is pronounced equally unjuft in
'releafing the man who deferves punifhment, and
'in punifhing the man who deferves it not: he
'is juft who always inflicts the punifhment or-
'dained by law.

250. 'Thefe eftablifhed rules for adminiftering
'juftice between two litigant parties, have been
'propounded at length under eighteen heads.

251. 'THUS fully performing all duties re-
'quired by law, let a king feek, *with juftice*, to
'poffefs regions yet unpoffeffed, and, when they are
'in his poffeffion, let him govern them well.

252. 'His realm being completely arranged
'and his fortreffes amply provided, let him ever
'apply the moft diligent care to eradicate *bad men*,
'*refembling* thorny weeds, as the law directs.

253. 'By protecting fuch as live virtuoufly,
'and by rooting up fuch as live wickedly, thofe
'kings, whofe hearts are intent on the fecurity of
'their people, fhall rife to heaven.

254. 'Of that prince, who takes a revenue with-
'out reftraining rogues, the dominions are thrown
'into diforder, and himfelf fhall be precluded
'from a celeftial abode;

255. 'But of him, whofe realm, by the ftrength
'of his arm, is defended and free from terrour,
'the dominions continually flourifh, like trees
'duly watered.

256. 'LET the king, whofe emiffaries are his
'eyes, difcern well the two forts of rogues, the
'open

ɪ

' open and the concealed, who deprive other men
' of their wealth:

257. ' Open rogues are they who fubfift by
' cheating in various marketable commodities;
' and concealed rogues are they who fteal and
' rob in forefts and the like fecret places.

258. ' Receivers of bribes, extorters of money
' by threats, debafers of metals, gamefters, fortune-
' tellers, impofters, and profeffors of palmiftry;

259. ' Elephant-brakers, and quacks, not per-
' forming what they engage to perform, pretended,
' artifts, and fubtil harlots;

260. ' Thefe and the like thorny weeds, over-
' fpreading the world, let the king difcover with a
' quick fight, and others who act ill in fecret;
' worthlefs men, yet bearing the outward figns of
' the worthy.

261. ' Having detected them by the means of
' trufty perfons difguifed, who *pretend to* have the
' fame occupation with them, and of fpies placed
' in feveral ftations, let him bring them by ar-
' tifice into his power:

262. ' Then, having fully proclaimed their re-
' fpective criminal acts, let the king inflict punifh-
' ment legally, according to the crimes proved;

263. ' Since, without certain punifhment, it is
' impoffible to reftrain the delinquency of fcoun-
' drels with depraved fouls, who fecretly prowl
' over this earth.

264. ' Much frequented places, cifterns of
' water, bake-houfes, the lodgings of harlots,
' taverns and victualling fhops, fquares where four
' ways meet, large well known trees, affemblies,
' and publick fpectacles;

265. ' Old court-yards, thickets, the houfes of
' artifts, empty manfions, groves, and gardens;

T 4 266. ' Thefe

266. ‘ Thefe and the like places let the king
‘ guard, for the prevention of robberies, with
‘ foldiers both ftationary and patrolling, as well as
‘ with fecret watchmen.

267. ‘ By the means of able fpies, once thieves,
‘ *but reformed*, who well knowing the various
‘ machinations of rogues, affociate with them and
‘ follow them, let the king deteƈt and draw them
‘ forth :

268. ‘ On pretexts of dainty food and gratifica-
‘ tions, or of feeing fome wife prieft, *who could en-*
‘ *fure their fuccefs*, or on pretence of *mock battles*
‘ *and the like* feats of ftrength, let the fpies procure
‘ an affembly of thofe men.

269. ‘ Such as refufe to go forth on thofe occa-
‘ fions, deterred by *former punifhments*, *which* the
‘ king *had inflicted*, let him *feize* by force, *and* put
‘ to death, *on proof of their guilt*, with their friends
‘ and kinfmen, paternal and maternal, *if proved to*
‘ *be their confederates*.

270. ‘ Let not a juft prince kill a man con-
‘ viƈted of fimple theft, unlefs taken with the
‘ mainer or with implements of robbery; but any
‘ thief, taken with the mainer or with fuch im-
‘ plements, let him deftroy without hefitation ;

271. ‘ And let him flay all thofe, who give rob-
‘ bers food in towns, or fupply them with imple-
‘ ments, or afford them fhelter.

272. ‘ Should thofe men, who were appointed
‘ to guard any diftriƈts, or thofe of the vicinity,
‘ who were employed for that purpofe, be neutral
‘ in attacks by robbers *and inaƈtive in feizing them*,
‘ let him inftantly punifh them as thieves.

273. ‘ Him, who lives *apparently* by the rules
‘ of his clafs, but *really* departs from thofe rules,
                                                    ‘ let

‘ let the king feverely punifh by fine, as a wretch
‘ who violates his duty.

274. ‘ They who give no affiftance on the
‘ plundering of a town, on the forcible breaking of
‘ a dike, or on feeing a robbery on the highway,
‘ fhall be banifhed with their cattle and utenfils.

275. ‘ Men, who rob the king’s treafure, or ob-
‘ ftinately oppofe his commands, let him deftroy
‘ by various modes of juft punifhment ; and thofe
‘ who encourage his enemies.

276. ‘ Of robbers who break a wall or partition,
‘ and commit theft in the night, let the prince or-
‘ der the hands to be lopped off, and themfelves
‘ to be fixed on a fharp ftake.

277. ‘ Two fingers of a cutpurfe, *the thumb and
‘ the index*, let him caufe to be amputated on his
‘ firft conviction ; on the fecond, one hand and
‘ one foot; on the third, he fhall fuffer death.

278. ‘ Such as give thieves fire, fuch as give
‘ them food, fuch as give them arms and apart-
‘ ments, and fuch as knowingly receive a thing
‘ ftolen, let the king punifh as *he would punifh* a
‘ thief.

279. ‘ The breaker of a *dam to fecure a* pool,
‘ let him punifh by long immerfion under water,
‘ or by keen corporal fuffering; or the offender
‘ fhall repair it, but muft pay the higheft mulct.

280. ‘ Thofe, who break open the treafury, or
‘ the arfenal, or the temple of a deity, and thofe
‘ who carry off royal elephants, horfes, or cars, let
‘ him, without hefitation, deftroy.

281. ‘ He, who fhall take away the water of
‘ an ancient pool, or fhall obftruct a watercourfe,
‘ muft be condemned to pay the loweft ufual
‘ amercement.

282. ‘ He,

282. ' HE, who fhall drop his ordure on the
' king's highway, except in cafe of neceffity, fhall
' pay two *panas* and immediately remove the filth ;

283. ' But a perfon in urgent neceffity, a very
' old man, a pregnant woman, and a child, only
' deferves reproof, and fhall clean the place them-
' felves : this is a fettled rule.

284. ' ALL phyficians and furgeons acting
' unfkilfully in their feveral profeffions, muft
' pay for *injury to* brute animals the loweft, but
' for *injury to* human creatures the middle amerce-
' ment.

285. ' THE breaker of a foot bridge, of a pub-
' lick flag, of a palifade, and of idols *made of clay*,
' fhall repair what he has broken, and pay a mulct
' of five hundred *panas*.

286. ' FOR mixing impure with pure commo-
' dities, for piercing fine gems, *as diamonds or
' rubies*, and for boring *pearls or inferiour gems*
' improperly, the fine is the loweft of the three ;
' *but damages muft always be paid.*

287. ' THE man, who fhall deal unjuftly
' with purchafers at a fair price *by delivering goods
' of lefs value*, or fhall fell, at a high price, *goods of
' ordinary value*, fhall pay, *according to circumftances,*
' the loweft or the middle amercement.

288. ' LET the king place all prifons near a
' publick road, where offenders may be feen
' wretched or disfigured.

289. ' HIM who breaks down a *publick* wall,
' him who fills up a *publick* ditch, him who
' throws down a *publick* gate, the king fhall fpeedily
' banifh.

290. ' FOR all facrifices to deftroy innocent
' men, the punifhment is a fine of two hundred
' *panas* ; and for machinations with *poifonous* roots,
                                        ' and

‘ and for the various *charms and* witcheries *in-*
‘ *tended* to kill, by perfons not effecting their
‘ purpofe.

291. ‘ THE feller of bad grain for good, or of
‘ good feed placed at the top *of the bag, to conceal*
‘ *the bad below*, and the deftroyer of known land-
‘ marks, mult fuffer fuch corporal punifhment as
‘ will disfigure them ;

292. ‘ But the moft pernicious of all deceivers
‘ is a goldfmith, who commits frauds : the king
‘ fhall order him to be cut piecemeal with razors.

293. ‘ FOR ftealing implements of hufbandry,
‘ weapons, and prepared medicines, let the king
‘ award punifhment according to the time and ac-
‘ cording to their ufe.

294. ‘ THE king, and his council, his metro-
‘ polis, his realm, his treafure, and his army,
‘ together with his ally, are the feven members
‘ of his kingdom ; *whence* it is called *Septánga :*

295. ‘ Among thofe feven members of a king-
‘ dom, let him confider the ruin of the firft, and
‘ fo forth in order, as the greateft calamity ;

296. ‘ Yet, in a feven-parted kingdom here
‘ below, there is no fupremacy among the feveral
‘ parts, from any pre-eminence in ufeful qualities :
‘ but all the parts muft reciprocally fupport each
‘ other, like the three ftaves of a holy mendicant :

297. ‘ In thefe and thofe acts, *indeed*, this and
‘ that member may be diftinguifhed ; *and* the
‘ member by which any affair is tranfacted, has
‘ the pre-eminence in that particular affair.

298. ‘ WHEN the king employs emiffaries,
‘ when he exerts power, when he regulates pub-
‘ lic bufinefs, let him invariably know both his
‘ own ftrength and that of his enemy,

299. ‘ With

299. ' With all *their several* diftreffes and vices :
' let him then begin his operations, having maturely
' confidered the greater and lefs importance *of*
' *particular acts :*

300. ' Let him, *though frequently difappointed,*
' renew his operations, how fatigued foever, again
' and again ; fince fortune always attends the man,
' who, *having begun well,* ftrenuoufly renews his
' efforts.

301. 'ALL the ages, called *Satya,* Trétá, Dwápara,
' and *Cali,* depend on the conduct of the king;
' who is declared *in turn* to reprefent each of
' thofe ages :

302. ' Sleeping, he is the *Cali* age ; waking,
' the *Dwápara* ; exerting himfelf in action, the
' Trétá ; living virtuoufly, the *Satya.*

303. ' Of INDRA, of SU'RYA, of PAVANA, of
' YAMA, of VARUNA, of CHANDRA, of AGNI,
' and of PRÏT'HIVÌ, let the king emulate the
' power and attributes.

304. ' As INDRA fheds plentiful fhowers during
' the four rainy months, thus let him, acting like
' the regent of clouds, rain juft gratifications over
' his kingdom :

305. ' As SU'RYA with ftrong rays draws up
' the water during eight months, thus let him,
' performing the function of the fun, gradually
' draw from his realm the legal revenue :

306. ' As PAVANA, when he moves, pervades
' all creatures, thus let him, imitating the regent
' of wind, pervade *all places* by his concealed
' emiffaries :

307. ' As YAMA, at the appointed time, pu-
' nifhes friends and foes, *or thofe who revere, and*
' *thofe who contemn him,* thus let the king, refem-
' bling

' bling the judge of departed fpirits, punifh of-
' fending fubjects :

308. ' As Varuna moſt affuredly binds the
' guilty in fatal cords, thus let him, reprefenting
' the genius of water, keep offenders in clofe
' confinement :

309. ' When the people are no lefs delighted
' on feeing the king, than on feeing the full moon,
' he appears in the character of Chandra :

310. ' Againſt criminals let him ever be ardent
' in wrath, let him be fplendid in glory, let him
' confume wicked miniſters, thus emulating the
' functions of Agni, regent of fire.

311. ' As PriT'hiví fupports all creatures
' equally, thus a king, fuſtaining all fubjects, re-
' fembles in his office the goddefs of earth.

312. ' Engaged in thefe duties and in others,
' with continual activity, let the king, *above all*
' *things,* reſtrain robbers, both in his own territories
' and in thofe of other princes, *from which they*
' *come, or in which they feek refuge.*

313. ' Let him not, although in the greateſt
' diſtrefs *for money,* provoke *Bráhmens* to anger
' *by taking their property*; for they, once enraged,
' could immediately *by facrifices and imprecations*
' deſtroy him with his troops, elephants, horfes
' and cars.

314. ' Who without perifhing could provoke
' thofe holy men, by whom, *that is, by whofe an-*
' *ceſtors, under* Brahma', the all-devouring fire
' was created, the fea with waters not drinkable,
' and the moon with its wane and increafe ?

315. ' What prince could gain wealth by op-
' preffing thofe, who, if angry, could frame other
' worlds and regents of worlds, could give being
' to new gods and mortals ?

316. ' What

316. ' What man, defirous of life, would injure
' thofe, by the aid of whom, *that is, by whofe ob-*
'*lations,* worlds and gods perpetually fubfift ;
' thofe who are rich in the learning of the *Véda?*

317. ' A *Bráhmen,* whether learned or ignorant,
' is a powerful divinity ; even as fire is a powerful
' divinity, whether confecrated or popular.

318. ' Even in places for burning the dead,
' the bright fire is undefiled ; and, when prefented
' with clarified butter at *fubfequent* facrifices, blazes
' again with extreme fplendour :

319. ' Thus though *Bráhmens* employ themfelves
' in all forts of mean occupation, they muft in-
' variably be honoured ; for they are fomething
' tranfcendently divine.

320. ' Of a military man, who raifes his arm
' violently on all occafions againft the prieftly
' clafs, the prieft himfelf fhall be the chaftifer ;
' fince the foldier originally proceeded from the
' *Bráhmen.*

321. ' From the waters arofe fire ; from the
' prieft, the foldier ; from ftone, iron : their all-
' penetrating force is ineffectual in the places
' whence they refpectively fprang.

322. ' The military clafs cannot profper with-
' out the facerdotal, nor can the facerdotal be
' raifed without the military : both claffes by
' cordial union, are exalted in this world and in
' the next.

323. ' SHOULD the king *be near his end through*
' *fome incurable difeafe, he* muft beftow on the
' priefts all his riches accumulated from legal fines;
' and, having duly committed his kingdom to his
' fon, let him feek death in battle, *or, if there be*
' *no war, by abftaining from food.*

324. ' Thus conducting himfelf, *and* ever firm
' in

' in difcharging his royal duties, let the king em-
' ploy all his minifters in acts beneficial to his
' people.

325. ' Thefe rules for the conduct of a military
' man having been propounded, let mankind next
' hear the rules for the commercial and fervile
' claffes in due order.

326. ' LET the *Vaifya*, having been girt with
' his proper facrificial thread, and having married
' an equal wife, be always attentive to his bufinefs
of agriculture and trade, and to that of keeping
' cattle ;

327. ' Since the Lord of created beings, having
' formed herds, and flocks, intrufted them to the
care of the *Vaifya*, while he intrufted the whole
' human fpecies to the *Bráhmen* and the *Cfhatriya* :

328. ' Never muft a *Vaifya* be difpofed to fay,
" I keep no cattle ;" nor, he being willing to keep
' them, muft they by any means be kept by men
' of another clafs.

329. ' Of gems, pearls, and coral, of iron,
' of woven cloth, of perfumes and of liquids, let
' him well know the prices both high and low :

330. ' Let him be fkilled likewife in *the time
' and manner of* fowing feeds, and in the bad
' or good qualities of land ; let him alfo perfectly
' know the correct modes of meafuring and
' weighing,

331. ' The excellence or defects of commodi-
' ties, the advantages and difadvantages of differ-
' ent regions, the probable gain or lofs on vendi-
' ble goods, and the means of breeding cattle
' with large augmentation :

332. ' Let him know the juft wages of fervants,
' the various dialects of men, the beft way of
' keeping

' keeping goods, and *whatever elſe belongs to* pur-
' chaſe and ſale.

333. ' Let him apply the moſt vigilant care to
' augment his wealth by *performing* his duty ; and,
' with great ſolicitude, let him give nouriſhment
' to all ſentient creatures.

334. ' SERVILE attendance on *Bráhmens* learned
' in the *Véda*, chiefly on ſuch as keep houſe and
' are famed for virtue, is of itſelf the higheſt duty
' of a *Súdra*, and leads him to future beatitude :

335. ' Pure *in body and mind*, humbly ſerving
' the three higher claſſes, mild in ſpeech, never
' arrogant, ever ſeeking refuge in *Bráhmens* prin-
' cipally, he may attain the moſt eminent claſs *in*
' *another tranſmigration.*

336. ' THIS clear ſyſtem of duties has been
' promulgated for the four claſſes ; when they are
' not in diſtreſs for ſubſiſtence ; now learn in
' order their ſeveral duties in times of neceſſity.'

CHAPTER THE TENTH.

On the mixed Classes; and on Times of Distress.

———————

1. ' LET the three twice born classes, remain-
' ing firm in their several duties, carefully read
' the *Véda*; but a *Bráhmen* must explain it to
' them, not *a man of* the other two *classes*: this
' is an established rule.

2. ' The *Bráhmen* must know the means of
' subsistence ordained by law for all the classes,
' and must declare them to the rest: let him
' likewise act in conformity *to law*.

3. ' From priority of birth, from superiority of
' origin, from a more exact knowledge of scrip-
' ture, and from a distinction in the sacrificial
' thread, the *Bráhmen* is the lord of all classes.

4. ' The three twice born classes are the sacer-
' dotal, the military, and the commercial; but
' the fourth, or servile, is once born, *that is, has*
' *no second birth from the* gáyatrì, *and wears no*
' *thread*: nor is there a fifth pure class.

5. ' IN all classes they, and they only, who are
' born, in a direct order, of wives equal in class,

U   ' and

‘ and virgins at the time of marriage, are
‘ to be confidered as the fame in clafs *with their*
‘ *fathers:*

6. ‘ Sons, begotten by twice born men, on wo-
‘ men of the clafs next immediately below them,
‘ wife legiflators call fimilar, *not the fame,* in clafs
‘ *with their parents,* becaufe they are degraded
‘ *to a middle rank between both,* by the lownefs of
‘ their mothers: *they are named in order* Múrdháb-
‘ hifhicta, Máhifhya, *and* Carana, *or* Cáyaft’ha;
‘ *and their feveral employments are teaching military*
‘ *exercifes; mufick, aftronomy, and keeping herds; and*
‘ *attendance on princes.*

7. ‘ Such is the primeval rule for the fons of
‘ women one degree lower *than their hufbands:*
‘ for the fons of women two or three degrees
‘ lower, let this rule of law be known.

8. ‘ From a *Bráhmen,* on a wife of the *Vaifya*
‘ clafs, is born a fon called *Ambafht’ha,* or
‘ *Vaidya,* on a *Súdrá* wife a *Nifháda,* named alfo
‘ *Párafava:*

9. ‘ From a *Cfhatriya,* on a wife of the *Súdra*
‘ clafs, fprings a creature called *Ugra,* with a na-
‘ ture partly warlike and partly fervile, ferocious
‘ in his manners, cruel in his acts.

10. ‘ The fons of a *Bráhmen* by *women of* three
‘ *lower* claffes, of a *Cfhatriya* by *women of* two,
‘ and of a *Vaifya* by one *lower* clafs, are called
‘ *Apafadáb,* or degraded *below their fathers.*

11. ‘ From a *Cfhatriya,* by a *Bráhmení* wife,
‘ fprings a *Súta* by birth; from a *Vaifya,* by a
‘ military or facerdotal wife, fpring a *Mágadha* and
‘ a *Vaidéha.*

12. ‘ From a *Súdra,* on women of the com-
‘ mercial, military, and prieftly claffes, are born
                                                    ‘ fons

‘ fons of a mixed breed, called *A'yógava*, *Cſhattrĭ*,
‘ and *Chandála*, the loweſt of mortals.

13. ‘ As the *Ambaſht'ha* and *Ugra*, born in a
‘ direct order, with one claſs between *thoſe of their*
‘ *parents*, are confidered in law, ſo are the *Cſhattrĭ*,
‘ and the *Vaidéha*, born in an inverſe order *with one*
‘ *intermediate claſs*; *and all four may be touched*
‘ *without impurity*.

14. ‘ Thoſe fons of the twice born, who are
‘ begotten on women without an interval *(An-*
‘ *tara)* between the claſſes mentioned in order,
‘ the wiſe call *Anantaras*, giving them a *diſ-*
‘ *tinct* name from the lower degree of their
‘ mothers.

15. ‘ From a *Bráhmen*, by a girl of the *Ugrá*
‘ tribe, is born an *A'vrĭta*; by one of the *Ambaſt'ha*
‘ tribe, an *A'bhíra*; by one of the *A'yógava* tribe,
‘ a *Dhigvana*.

16. ‘ The *A'yógava*, the *Cſhattrĭ*, and the *Chan-*
‘ *dála*, the loweſt of men, ſpring from a *Súdra* in
‘ an inverſe order *of the claſſes*, and are *therefore*
‘ all three excluded *from the performance of obſequies*
‘ *to their anceſtors:*

17. ‘ From a *Vaiſya* the *Mágadha* and *Vaidéha*,
‘ from a *Cſhatriya* the *Súta* only, are born in an
‘ inverſe order; and they are three other ſons ex-
‘ cluded *from funeral rites to their fathers.*

18. ‘ The ſon of a *Niſháda* by a woman of the
‘ *Súdra* claſs, is by tribe a *Puccaſa*; but the ſon
‘ of a *Súdra* by a *Niſhádí* woman, is named *Cuc-*
‘ *cutaca*.

19. ‘ One born of a *Cſhattrĭ* by an *Ugrá*, is
‘ called *Swapáca*; and one begotten by a *Vaidéha*
‘ on an *Ambaſhthí* wife is called *Véna*.

20. ‘ Thoſe, whom the twice born beget on
‘ women of equal claſſes, but who perform not

the

' the proper ceremonies *of assuming the thread, and*
' *the like,* people denominate *Vrátyas,* or excluded
' from the *gáyatrì.*

21. ' From such an outcaft *Bráhmen* fprings a
' fon of a finful nature, *who in different countries*
' *is* named a *Bhúrjacantaca,* an *A'vantya,* a *Vátad-*
' *hána,* a *Puſhpadha* and a *Saic'ha :*

22. ' From such an outcaft *Cſhatriya* comes a
' fon called a *J'halla,* a *Malla,* a *Nich'hivi,* a *Nata,*
' a *Carana,* a *C'haſa,* and a *Dravira :*

23. ' From such an outcaft *Vaiſya* is born a fon
' called *Sudhanwan, Chárya, Caruſha, Vijanman,*
' *Maitra,* and *Satwata.*

24. ' By intermixtures of the claffes, by their
' marriages with women who ought not to be
' married, and by their omiffion of prefcribed
' duties, impure claffes have been formed.

25. ' THOSE men of mingled births, who were
' born in the inverfe order of claffes, and who
' intermarry among themfelves, I will now com-
' pendioufly defcribe.

26. ' The *Súta,* the *Vaidêha,* and the *Chandála,*
' that loweft of mortals, the *Mágadha,* the *Cſhattrï*
' by tribe, and the *A'yógava.*

27. ' Thefe fix beget fimilar fons on women of
' their own claffes, or on women of the fame clafs
' with their mothers ; and they produce the like
' from women of the two higheft claffes, *and of*
' *the loweft :*

28. ' As a twice born fon may fpring from a
' *Bráhmen,* by women of two claffes out of
' three, *a fimilar fon,* when there is no interval,
' and *an equal fon* from a woman of his own
' clafs, it is thus in the cafe of the low tribes in
' order.

29. ' Thofe

29. ' Thofe fix beget, on women of their own
' tribes, reciprocally, very many defpicable and
' abject races even more foul than their begetters.

30. ' Even as a *Súdra* begets, on a *Bráhmeni*
' woman, a fon more vile than himfelf, thus any
' other low man begets, on *women of* the four
' claffes, a fon yet lower.

31. ' The fix low claffes, marrying inverfely,
' beget fifteen yet lower tribes, the bafe producing
' ftill bafer ; *and in a direct order they produce fifteen*
' *more.*

32. ' A *Dafyu,* or outcaft of any pure clafs,
' begets, on an *A'yógavi* woman, a *Sairindhra,* who
' fhould know how to attend and to drefs his
' mafter ; though not a flave, he muft live by
' flavifh work, and may alfo gain fubfiftence by
' catching wild beafts in toils :

33. ' A *Vaidéha* begets on her a fweet-voiced
' *Maitréyaca,* who, ringing a bell at the appear-
' ance of dawn, continually praifes great men :

34. ' A *Nifháda* begets on her a *Márgava* or
' *Dáfa,* who fubfifts by his labour in boats, and
' is named *Caiverta* by thofe who dwell in *A'ryá-*
' *verta,* or the land of the venerable.

35. ' Thofe three of a bafe tribe are feverally
' begotten on *A'yógavi* women, who wear the
' clothes of the deceafed and eat reprehenfible food.

36. ' From a *Nifháda* fprings, *by a woman of the*
' Vaidéha *tribe,* a *Cárávara,* who cuts leather, and
' from a *Vaidéha* fpring, *by women of* the Cárávará
' *and* Nifháda *cafts,* an *Andhra* and a *Méda,* who
' muft live without the town

37. ' From a *Chandála,* by a *Vaidéhi* woman,
' comes a *Pándufópáca,* who works with cane and
' reeds ; and from a *Nifháda,* an *Ahindica,* who
' acts as a jailor.

U 3   38. ' From

38. ' From a *Chandála*, by a *Puccasì* woman,
' is born a *Sópáca*, who lives by punishing cri-
' minals condemned by the king, a sinful wretch
' ever despised by the virtuous.

39. ' A *Niṣhádì* woman, by a *Chandála*, pro-
' duces a son called *Antyavaṣáyin*, employed in
' places for burning the dead, contemned even
' by the contemptible.

40. ' These, among various mixed classes,
' have been described by their several fathers and
' mothers; and, whether concealed or open, they
' may be known by their occupations.

41. ' Six sons, *three* begotten on women of the
' same class, and *three* on women of lower classes,
' must perform the duties of twice born men;
' but those who are *born in an inverse order, and*
' called low born, are equal, in respect of duty, to
' mere *Súdras*.

42. ' By the force of extreme devotion and of
' exalted fathers, all of them may rise *in time* to
' high birth, as, *by the reverse*, they may sink to a
' lower state, in every age among mortals in this
' inferiour world.

43. ' THE following races of *Cṣhatriyas*, by
' their omiṣſion of holy rites, and by ſeeing no
' *Bráhmens*, have gradually ſunk among men, to
' the loweſt of the four claſſes:

44. ' *Paund'racas, Odras*, and *Draviras; Cám-
' bójas, Yavanas*, and *Sacas; Páradas, Pahlavas*,
' *Chinas, Cirátas, Deradas*, and *C'haſas*.

45. ' All thoſe tribes of men, who ſprang from
' the mouth, the arm, the thigh, and the foot of
' BRAHMÁ, *but* who became outcaſts *by having*
' *neglected their duties*, are called *Daſyus*, or *plun-*
' *derers*, whether they ſpeak the language of
' *Mléchch'has*, or that of *A'ryas*.

46. ' THOSE

46. ' THOSE fons of the twice born who are
' faid to be degraded, and who are confidered as
' low born, fhall fubfift only by fuch employments,
' as the twice born defpife.

47. ' *Sútas* muft live by managing horfes and
' by driving cars ; *Ambafht'has,* by curing dif-
' orders ; *Vaidéhas,* by waiting on women ; *Má-*
' *gadhas,* by travelling with merchandize ;

48. ' *Nifhádas,* by catching fifh ; an *A'yógava,*
' by the work of a carpenter ; a *Méda,* an *Andhra,*
' and (the fons of a *Bráhmen* by wives of the *Vai-*
' *déba* and *Ugra* claffes, refpectively called) a *Chun-*
' *chu* and a *Madgu,* by flaying beafts of the foreft ;

49. ' A *Cfhattri,* an *Ugra,* and a *Puccafa,* by
' killing or confining fuch animals as live in holes:
' *Dhigvanas,* by felling leather ; *Vénas,* by ftriking
' mufical inftruments ;

50. ' Near large publick trees, in places for
' burning the dead, on mountains, and in groves,
' let thofe tribes dwell, generally known, and en-
' gaged in their feveral works.

51. ' THE abode of a *Chandálu* and a *Swapáca*
' muft be out of the town ; they muft not have
' the ufe of entire veffels ; their fole wealth muft
' be dogs and affes :

52. ' Their clothes muft be the mantles of the
' deceafed ; their difhes for food, broken pots ;
' their ornaments, rufty iron ; continually muft
' they roam from place to place :

53. ' Let no man, who regards his duty reli-
' gious and civil, hold any intercourfe with them ;
' let their tranfactions be confined to themfelves,
' and their marriages only between equals :

54. ' Let food be given to them in potfherds,
' but not by the hands of the giver ; and let them
' not walk by night in cities or towns :

U 4

55. ' By

55. ' By day they may walk about for the
' purpofe of work, diftinguifhed by the king's
' badges ; and they fhall carry out the corpfe of
' every one who dies without kindred : fuch is
' the fixed rule.

56. ' They fhall always kill thofe who are to
' be flain by the fentence of the law, and by the
' royal warrant ; and let them take the clothes of
' the flain, their beds, and their ornaments.

57. ' HIM, who was born of a finful mother,
' *and confequently* in a low clafs, but is not openly
' known, who, though worthlefs in truth, bears
' the femblance of a worthy man, let people dif-
' cover by his acts :

58. ' Want of virtuous dignity, harfhnefs of
' fpeech, cruelty, and habitual negleĉt of pre-
' fcribed duties, betray, in this world, the fon of a
' criminal mother.

59. ' Whether a man of debafed birth affume
' the charaĉter of his father or of his mother, he
' can at no time conceal his origin :

60. ' He, whofe family had been exalted, but
' whofe parents were criminal in marrying, has a
' bafe nature, according as the offence *of his mother*
' was great or fmall.

61. ' In whatever country fuch men are born,
' as deftroy the purity of the four claffes, that
' country foon perifhes, together with the natives
' of it.

62. ' Defertion of life, without reward, for the
' fake of preferving a prieft or a cow, a woman
' or a child, may caufe the beatitude of thofe bafe-
' born tribes.

63. ' Avoiding all injury *to animated beings,*
' veracity, abftinence from theft, *and from unjuft*
' *feizure of property,* cleanlinefs, and command
' over

' over the bodily organs, form the compendious
' fyftem of duty which MENU has ordained for
' the four claffes.

64. SHOULD the tribe fprung from a *Bráhmen*
' by a *Súdra* woman, produce *a fucceffion of children*
' by the marriages of its women with other *Brá-*
' *mens*, the low tribe fhall be raifed to the higheft
' in the feventh generation.

65. ' As the fon of a *Súdra* may *thus* attain the
' rank of a *Bráhmen*, and as the fon of a *Bráhmen*
' may fink to a level with *Súdras*, even fo muft it
' be with him who fprings from a *Cfhatriya*; even
' fo with him who was born of a *Vaifya*.

66. ' IF there be a doubt, as to the preference
' between him who wa**s** begotten by a *Bráhmen*
' for his pleafure, *but not in wedlock*, on a *Súdra*
' woman, and him who was begotten by a *Súdra*
' on a *Bráhmenì*,

67. ' Thus is it removed: he, who was be-
' gotten by an exalted man on a bafe woman,
' may, by his good acts, become refpectable; but
' he, who was begotten on an exalted woman by
' a bafe man, muft himfelf continue bafe:

68. ' Neither of the two (as the law is fixed)
' fhall be girt with a facred ftring; not the former,
' becaufe his mother was low; nor the fecond,
' becaufe the order of the claffes was inverted.

69. ' As good grain, fpringing from good foil,
' is in all refpects excellent, thus a man, fpringing
' from a refpectable father by a refpectable mo-
' ther, has a claim to the whole inftitution of the
' twice born.

70. ' Some fages give a preference to the
' grain; others to the field; and others confider
' both field and grain; on this point the decifion
' follows;

71. ' Grain,

71. ' Grain, caft into bad ground, wholly
' perifhes, and a good field, with no grain fown in
' it, is a mere heap of clods ;

72. ' But fince, by the virtue of eminent fa- ·
' thers, even the fons of wild animals, *as* Rĭfh-
' yafringa, *and others*, have been transformed into
' holy men revered and extolled, the paternal fide,
' therefore, prevails.

73. ' BRAHMA' himfelf, having compared a
' *Súdra*, who performs the duties of the twice-
' born, with a twice born man, who does the acts
' of a *Súdra*, faid : " Thofe two are neither equal
" nor unequal," *that is, they are neither equal in*
' *rank, nor unequal in bad conduct.*

74. ' LET fuch *Bráhmens* as are intent on the
' means of attaining the fupreme godhead, and
' firm in their own duties, completely perform, in
' order, the fix following acts :

75. ' Reading the *Védas*, and teaching *others*
' to read them, facrificing, and affifting *others* to
' facrifice, giving *to the poor, if themfelves have*
' *enough*, and accepting *gifts from the virtuous, if*
' *themfelves are poor*, are the fix prefcribed acts of
' the firft born clafs ;

76. ' But, among thofe fix acts of a *Bráhmen*,
' three are his *means of* fubfiftence ; affifting to
' facrifice, ˌteaching the *Védas*, and receiving gifts
' from a pure-handed giver. ˌ

77. ' Three acts of duty ceafe with the *Bráh-*
' *men*, and belong not to the *Cfhatriya*; teaching
' the *Védas*, officiaing at a facrifice, and, thirdly,
' receiving prefents :

78. ' Thofe *three* are alfo, by the fixed rule of
' law, forbidden to the *Vaifya* ; fince MENU, the
' lord of all men, prefcribed not thofe acts to the
' two *claffes, military and commercial.*

79. ˌ The

79. ' The means of subsistence, peculiar to the
' *Cshatriya*, are bearing arms, either held for strik-
' ing or missile, to the *Vaisya*, merchandize, at-
' tending on cattle, and agriculture : but, *with a*
' *view to the next life*, the duties of both are alms-
' giving, reading, sacrificing.

80. ' Among the several occupations *for gaining*
' *a livelihood* ; the most commendable respectively
' for the sacerdotal, military, and mercantile
' classes, are teaching the *Véda*, defending the
' people, and commerce, or keeping herds and
' flocks.

81. ' Yet a *Bráhmen*, unable to subsist by his
' duties just mentioned, may live by the duty of
' a soldier ; for that is the next in rank.

82. ' If it be asked, how he must live, should
' he be unable to get a subsistence by either of
' those employments ; *the answer is*, he may sub-
' sist as a mercantile man, applying himself *in per-*
' *son* to tillage and attendance on cattle :

83. ' But a *Bráhmen* and a *Cshatriya*, obliged
' to subsist by the acts of a *Vaisya*, must avoid with
' care, *if they can live by keeping herds*, the business
' of tillage, which gives great pain *to sentient crea-*
' *tures*, and is dependant on *the labour of* others,
' *as bulls and so forth.*

84. ' Some are of opinion, that agriculture is
' excellent ; but it is a mode of subsistence which
' the benevolent greatly blame ; 'for the iron-
' mouthed pieces of wood not only wound the
' earth, but the creatures dwelling in it.

85. ' If, through want of a virtuous livelihood,
' they cannot follow laudable occupations, they
' may then gain a competence of wealth by selling
' commodities usually sold by merchants, avoiding
' what ought to be avoided.

86. ' They

86. ' They muſt avoid ſelling liquids of all
' ſorts, dreſſed grain, ſeeds of *tila*, ſtones, ſalt,
' cattle, and human creatures;

87. ' All woven cloth dyed red, cloth made of
' *ſana*, of *cſhumá* bark, and of wool, even though
' not red; fruit, roots, and medicinal plants;

88. ' Water, iron, poiſon, fleſh-meat, the
' moon-plant, and perfumes of any ſort; milk,
' honey, butter-milk, clarified butter, oil of *tila*,
' wax, ſugar, and blades of *cuſa*-graſs;

89. ' All beaſts of the foreſt, *as deer and the
' like*; ravenous beaſts, birds, *and fiſh*; ſpirituous
' liquors, *níli*, or indigo, and *lácſhá*, or lac; and
' all beaſts with uncloven hoofs.

90. ' But the *Bráhmen* huſbandman may at
' pleaſure ſell pure *tila*-ſeeds for the purpoſe of
' holy rites, if he keep them not long *with a hope
' of more gain*, and ſhall have produced them by
' his own culture:

91. ' If he apply ſeeds of *tila* to any purpoſe
' but food, anointing, and ſacred oblations, he
' ſhall be plunged, in the ſhape of a worm, to-
' gether with his parents, into the ordure of
' dogs.

92. ' By ſelling fleſh-meat, *lácſhá*, or ſalt,
' a *Bráhmen* immediately ſinks low, by ſelling
' milk three days, he falls to a level with a *Súdra*;

93. ' And by ſelling the other forbidden com-
' modities with his own free will, he aſſumes in
' this world, after ſeven nights, the nature of a
' mere *Vaiſya*.

94. ' Fluid things may, however, be bartered
' for other fluids, but not ſalt for any thing liquid;
' ſo may dreſſed grain for grain undreſſed, and *tila*-
' ſeeds for grain in the huſk, equal weights or
' meaſures being given and taken.

95. ' A

95. ' A MILITARY man, in diftrefs, may fub-
' fift by all thefe means, but at no time muft
' he have recourfe to the higheft, *or facerdotal*
' function.

96. ' A man of the loweft clafs, who, through
' covetoufnefs, lives by the acts of the higheft, let
' the king ftrip of all his wealth and inftantly
' banifh :

97. ' His own office, though defectively per-
' formed, is preferable to that of another, though
' performed completely ; for he, who *without ne-*
' *ceffity* difcharges the duties of another clafs,
' immediately forfeits his own.

98. ' A MERCANTILE man, unable to fubfift
' by his own duties, may defcend even to the
' fervile acts of a *Súdra*, taking care never to do
' what ought never to be done : but, when he has
' gained a competence, let him depart from
' fervice.

99. ' A MAN of the fourth clafs, not finding
' employment by waiting on the twice born, while
' his wife and fon are tormented with hunger,
' may fubfift by handicrafts :

100. ' Let him principally follow thofe mecha-
' nical occupations, *as joinery and mafonry*, or thofe
' various practical arts, *as painting and writing*, by
' following of which he may ferve the twice born.

101. ' SHOULD a *Bráhmen*, afflicted and pining
' through want of food, choofe rather to remain fix-
' ed in the path of his own duty, than to adopt the
' practice of *Vaifyas*, let him act in this manner :

102. ' The *Bráhmen*, having fallen into diftrefs,
' may receive gifts from any perfon whatever,
' for by no facred rule can it be fhown, that ab-
' folute purity can be fullied.

103. ' From

103. ' From interpreting the *Véda*, from offici-
' ating at facrifices, or from taking prefents, though
' in modes generally difapproved, no fin is com-
' mitted by priefts *in diftrefs* ; for they are as pure
' as fire or water.

104. ' He who receives food, when his life
' could not otherwife be fuftained, from any man
' whatever, is no more tainted by fin than the
' fubtil ether by mud :

105. ' Aji′garta, dying with hunger, was
' going to deftroy his own fon (*named* Su′nah-
' s′e′p′ha) *by felling him for fome cattle*, yet he was
' guilty of no crime, fince he only fought a re-
' medy againft famifhing :

106. ' Va′made′va who well knew right and
' wrong, was by no means rendered impure,
' though defirous, when oppreffed *with hunger*,
' of eating the flefh of dogs for the prefervation
' of his life :

107. ' Bharadwa′ja, eminent in devotion,
' when he and his fon were almoft ftarved in a
' dreary foreft, accepted feveral cows from the
' carpenter Vrĭdhu :

108. ' Viswa′mitra too, than whom none
' better knew the diftinctions between virtue and
' vice, refolved, when he was perifhing with hun-
' ger, to eat the haunch of a dog, which he had
' received from a Chanda′la.

109. ' Among *the* acts *generally difapproved*,
' *namely*, accepting prefents *from low men*, affifting
' *them* to facrifice, and explaining the fcripture *to*
' *them*, the receipt of prefents is the meaneft *in*
' *this world*, and the moft blamed in a *Bráhmen*
' after his prefent life ;

110. ' Becaufe affifting to facrifice and explain-
                                        ' ing

' ing the scripture, are two acts always performed
' for those, whose minds have been improved *by*
' *the sacred initiation* ; but gifts are also received
' from a servile man of the lowest class.

111. ' The guilt incurred by assisting *low men*
' to sacrifice, and by teaching *them* the scripture,
' is removed by repetitions of the *gáyatrì* and ob-
' lations to fire ; but that, incurred by accepting
' gifts *from them*, is expiated only by abandoning
' the gifts and by rigorous devotion.

112. ' It were better for a *Bráhmen*, who could
' not maintain himself, to glean ears and grains,
' after harvest, from *the field of* any person what-
' ever : gleaning whole ears would be better than
' accepting a present, and picking up single grains
' would be still more laudable.

113. ' *Bráhmens*, who keep house, and are in
' want of any metals, *except gold and silver*, or of
' articles *for good uses*, may ask the king for them,
' if he be of the military class ; but a king, *known*
' *to be avaricious and* unwilling to give, must not
' be solicited.

114. ' The foremost, *in order*, of these things
' may be received more innocently than that which
' follows it : a field untilled, a tilled field, cows,
' goats, sheep, precious metals or gems, new grain,
' dressed grain.

115. ' THERE are seven virtuous means of ac-
' quiring property ; succession, occupancy or dona-
' tion, and purchase or exchange, *which are al-*
' *lowed to all classes* ; conquests, *which is peculiar*
' *to the military class* ; lending at interest, husban-
' dry or commerce, *which belong to the mercantile*
' *class* ; and acceptance of presents, *by the sacer-*
' *dotal class*, from respectable men.

116. ' Learning,

116. ' Learning, *except that contained in the*
' *scriptures,* art, *as mixing perfumes and the like,*
' work for wages, menial service, attendance on
' cattle, traffick, agriculture, content with little,
' alms, and receiving high interest on money, are
' ten modes of subsistence *in times of distress.*

117. ' Neither a priest nor a military man,
' *though distressed,* must receive interest on loans,
' but each of them, if he please, may pay *the* small
' interest *permitted by law, on borrowing* for some
' pious use, to the sinful man *who demands it.*

118. ' A MILITARY king, who takes even a
' fourth part *of the crops of his realm* at a time of
' urgent necessity, *as of war or invasion,* and pro-
' tects his people to the utmost of his power,
' commits no sin:

119. ' His peculiar duty is conquest, and he
' must not recede from battle ; so that while he
' defends by his arms the merchant and husband-
' man, he may levy the legal tax *as the price of*
' *protection.*

120. ' The tax on the mercantile class, *which*
' *in times of prosperity must be only a twelfth part of*
' *their crops, and a fiftieth of their personal profits,*
' may be an eighth of their crops *in a time of distress,*
' *or a sixth, which is the medium,* or even a *fourth*
' *in great publick adversity* ; but a twentieth of
' their *gains on* money, and other moveables, is
' the highest *tax:* serving men, artisans, and me-
' chanicks must assist by their labour, *but at no*
' *time pay taxes.*

121. ' IF a *Súdra* want a subsistence, *and cannot*
' *attend a priest,* he may serve a *Cshatriya* ; or, *if*
' *he cannot wait on a soldier by birth,* he may gain
' his livelihood by serving an opulent *Vaisya.*

122. ' To

122. ' To him, who ferves *Bráhmens* with a
' view to a heavenly reward, or even with a view
' to both *this life and the next*, the union of the
' word *Bráhmen* with his *name of fervant* will af-
' furedly bring fuccefs.

123. ' Attendance on *Bráhmens* is pronounced
' the beft work of a *Súdra :* whatever elfe
' he may perform will comparatively avail him
' nothing.

124. ' They muft allot him a fit maintenance
' according to their own circumftances, after con-
' fidering his ability, his exertions, and the
' number of thofe whom he muft provide with
' nourifhment :

125. ' What remains of their dreffed rice muft
' be given to him ; and apparel which they have
' worn, and the refufe of their grain, and their
' old houfehold furniture.

126. ' THERE is no guilt in a man of the fer-
' vile clafs *who eats leeks and other forbidden vege-*
' *tables :* he muft not have the facred inveftiture :
' he has no bufinefs with *the* duty *of making obla-*
' *tions to fire and the like* ; but there is no prohibi-
' tion againft *his offering dreffed grain as a facrifice,*
' *by way of difcharging* his own duty.

127. ' Even *Súdras*, who are anxious to per-
' form their entire duty, and, knowing what they
' fhould perform, imitate the practice of good
' men *in the houfehold facraments*, but without any
' holy text, *except thofe containing praife and faluta-*
' *tion*, are fo far from finning, that they acquire
' juft applaufe :

128. ' As a *Súdra*, without injuring another
' man, performs the *lawful* acts of the twice
' born, even thus, without being cenfured, he
' gains exaltation in this world and in the next.

X 129. ' No

129. ' No *superfluous* collection of wealth muſt
' be made by a *Súdra*, even though he has power
' *to make it*, ſince a ſervile man, who has amaſſed
' riches, *becomes proud, and, by his inſolence or ne-*
' *glect*, gives pain even to *Bráhmens*.

130. ' SUCH, as have been fully declared, are
' the ſeveral duties of the four claſſes in diſtreſs
' for ſubſiſtence ; and, if they perform them ex-
' actly, they ſhall attain the higheſt beatitude.

131. ' Thus has been propounded the ſyſtem
' of duties, religious and civil, ordained for all
' claſſes : I next will declare the pure law of ex-
' piation for ſin.'

CHAPTER THE ELEVENTH.

On Penance and Expiation.

———

1. ' HIM, who intends to marry for the fake of
' having iffue ; him, who wifhes to make a fa-
' crifice ; him, who travels ; him, who has given
' all his wealth at a facred rite ; him, who defires
' to maintain his preceptor, his father, or his mo-
' ther ; him, who needs a maintenance for him-
' felf, when he firft reads the *Véda*; and him,
' who is afflicted with illnefs ;

2. ' Thefe nine *Bráhmens* let mankind confider
' as virtuous mendicants, called *fnátacas*; and,
' to relieve their wants, let gifts *of cattle or gold*
' be prefented to them, in proportion to their
' learning :

3. ' To thefe moft excellent *Bráhmens* muft
' rice alfo be given, with holy prefents *at oblations*
' *to fire, and within the confecrated circle*; but the
' dreffed rice, which others are to receive, muft be
' delivered on the outfide of the facred hearth :
' *gold and the like may be given any where.*

4. ' On fuch *Bráhmens* as well know the *Véda*,
' let the king beftow, as it becomes him, jewels
' of all forts, and the folemn reward for officiating
' at the facrifice.

X 2

5. ' HE,

5. ' HE, who has a wife, and, having begged
' money *to defray his nuptial expences*, marries an-
' other woman, fhall have no advantage but fen-
' fual enjoyment: the offspring belongs to the
' beftower of the gift.

6. ' LET every man, according to his ability,
' give wealth to *Bráhmens* detached from the
' world and learned in fcripture: fuch a giver
' fhall attain heaven after this life.

7. ' HE alone is worthy to drink the juice of
' the moon-plant, who keeps a provifion of grain
' fufficient to fupply thofe, whom the law com-
' mands him to nourifh, for the term of three
' years or more;

8. ' But a twice-born man, who keeps a lefs
' provifion of grain, yet prefumes to tafte the
' juice of the moon-plant, fhall gather no fruit
' from that facrament, even though he tafte it
' at the firft, *or folemn, much lefs at any occafional*
' ceremony.

9. ' HE, who beftows gifts on ftrangers, *with a*
' *view to worldly fame*, while he fuffers his family
' to live in diftrefs, though he has power *to fup-*
' *port them*, touches his lips with honey, but
' fwallows poifon; fuch virtue is counterfeit:

10. ' Even what he does for the fake of his
' future fpiritual body, to the injury of thofe
' whom he is bound to maintain, fhall bring him
' ultimate mifery both in this life and in the next.

11. ' SHOULD a facrifice, performed by any
' twice born facrificer, and by a *Bráhmen* efpe-
' cially, be imperfect from the want of fome
' ingredient, during the reign of a prince who
' knows the law,

12. ' Let him take that article, for the com-
　　　　　　　　　　　　' pletion

' pletion of the facrifice, from the houfe of any
' *Vaifya*, who poffeffes confiderable herds, but
' neither facrifices, nor drinks the juice of the
' moon-plant :

13. ' If fuch a *Vaifya* be not near, he may take
' two or three fuch neceffary articles, at pleafure,
' from the houfe of a *Súdra* ; fince a *Súdra* has
' no bufinefs with folemn rites.

14. ' Even from the houfe of a *Bráhmen* or a
' *Cfhatriya*, who poffeffes a hundred cows, but has
' no confecrated fire, or a thoufand cows, but
' performs no facrifice *with the moon-plant*, let a
' prieft, without fcruple, take *the articles wanted.*

15. ' From another *Bráhmen*, who continually
' receives prefents but never gives, let him take
' fuch ingredients of the facrifice, if not beftowed
' *on requeft* : fo fhall his fame be fpread abroad,
' and his habits of virtue increafe.

16. ' Thus, likewife, may a *Bráhmen*, who has
' not eaten at the time of fix meals, *or has fafted*
' *three whole days*, take at the time of the feventh
' meal, *or on the fourth morning*, from the man
' who behaves bafely *by not offering him food*
' enough to fupply him till the morrow :

17. ' He may take it from the floor, where
' the grain is trodden out of the hufk; or from
' the field, or from the houfe, or from any place
' whatever ; but, if the owner afk *why he takes it*,
' the caufe of the taking muft be declared.

18. ' The wealth of a virtuous *Bráhmen* muft
' at no time be feized by a *Cfhatriya*; but, having
' no other means *to complete a facrifice*, he may
' take the goods of any man who acts wickedly,
' and of any who performs not his religious duties:

19. ' He who takes property from the bad, *for*
' *the purpofe before-mentioned*, and beftows it on the

X 3   ' good,

' good, transforms himself into a boat, and car-
' ries both *the good and the bad* over *a sea of ca-*
' *lamities.*

20. ' Wealth, poffeffed by men for the per-
' formance of facrifices, the wife call the property
' of the gods; but the wealth of men, who
' perform no facrifice, they confider as the pro-
' perty of demons.

21. ' Let no pious king fine the man *who*
' *takes by ftealth, or by force, what he wants to make*
' *a facrifice perfect* ; fince it is the king's folly,
' that caufes the hunger or wants of a *Bráhmen :*

22. ' Having reckoned up the perfons, whom
' the *Bráhmen* is obliged to fupport, having af-
' certained his divine knowledge and moral con-
' duct, let the king allow him a fuitable main-
' tenance from his own houfehold ;

23. ' And, having appointed him a mainte-
' nance, let the king protect him on all fides ; for
' he gains from the *Bráhmen* whom he protects,
' 'a fixth part of *the reward for* his virtue.

24. ' Let no *Bráhmen* ever beg a gift from a
' *Súdra;* for, if he perform a facrifice after fuch
' begging, he fhall, in the next life, be born a
' *Chandála.*

25. ' The *Bráhmen* who begs any articles for
' a facrifice, and difpofes not of them all for that
' purpofe, fhall become a kite or a crow for a
' hundred years.

26. ' Any evil-hearted wretch, who, through
' covetoufnefs, fhall feize the property of the gods
' or of *Bráhmens,* fhall feed in another world on
' the orts of vultures.

27. ' The facrifice *Vaifwánarí* muft be conftantly performed on the firft day of the new
year, or on the new moon of *Chaitra,* as an
' expiation

' expiation for having omitted, *through mere for-*
' *getfulnefs,* the appointed facrifices of cattle and
' the rites of the moon-plant :

28. ' But a twice born man, who, without
' neceffity, does an act allowed only in a cafe of
' neceffity, reaps no fruit from it hereafter : thus
' has it been decided.

29. ' By the *Vifwédévas,* by the *Sádhyas,* and
' by eminent *Rǐfhis* of the facerdotal clafs, the
' fubftitute was adopted for the principal act,
' when they were apprehenfive of dying in times
' of imminent peril ;

30. ' But no reward is prepared in a future
' ftate for that ill-minded man, who, when able
' to perform the principal facrifice, has recourfe
' to the fubftitute.

31. ' A Priest, who well knows the law,
' needs not complain to the king of any grievous
' injury ; fince, even by his own power, he may
' chaftife thofe who injure him :

32. ' His own power, *which depends on himfelf*
' *alone,* is mightier than the royal power, *which*
' *depends on other men :* by his own might, there-
' fore, may a *Bráhmen* coerce his foes.

33. ' He may ufe, without hefitation, the
' powerful charms revealed to At'harvan, and
' *by him* to Angiras ; for fpeech is the weapon
' of a *Bráhmen :* with that he may deftroy his
' oppreffors.

34. ' A foldier may avert danger from himfelf
' by the ftrength of his arm ; a merchant and a
' mechanick, by their property ; but the chief of
' the twice born, by holy texts and oblations
' to fire.

35. ' A prieft, who performs his duties, who
' juftly corrects *his children and pupils,* who advifes

' expiations for sin, and who loves all animated
' creatures, is truly called a *Bráhmen :* to him let
' no man say any thing unpropitious, nor use any
' offensive language.

36. ' Let not a girl, nor a young woman, *mar-*
' *ried or unmarried,* nor a man with little learning,
' nor a dunce, perform an oblation to fire ; nor a
' man diseafed, nor one uninvested *with the facri-*
' *ficial string;*

37. ' Since any of those persons, who make
' such an oblation, shall fall into a region of tor-
' ture, together with him who suffers his hearth
' to be used : he alone, who perfectly knows the
' sacred ordinances, and has read all the *Védas,*
' must officiate at an oblation to holy fire.

38. ' A *Bráhmen* with abundant wealth, who
' presents not the priest that hallows his fire, with
' a horse consecrated to PRAJA'PATI, becomes
' equal to one who has no fire hallowed. :

39. ' Let him, who believes the scripture, and
' keeps his organs in subjection, perform all other
' pious acts ; but never in this world let him offer
' a sacrifice with trifling gifts to the officiating
' priest :

40. ' The organs of sense and action, reputa-
' tion *in this life,* a heavenly mansion *in the next,*
' life *itself,* a great name *after death,* children *and*
' cattle, are all destroyed by a sacrifice offered
' with trifling presents : let no man, therefore,
' sacrifice without liberal gifts.

41. ' THE priest who keeps a sacred hearth,
' but voluntarily neglects *the morning and evening*
' *oblations to* his fires, must perform, *in the manner*
' *to be described,* the penance *chándráyana* for one
' month ; since that *neglect* is equally sinful with
' the slaughter of a son.

42. ' They

42. ' They who receive property from a *Súdra*,
' for the performance of rites to confecrated fire,
' are contemned, as minifters of the bafe, by all
' fuch as pronounce texts of the *Véda*:

43. ' Of thofe ignorant priefts, who ferve the
' holy fire for the wealth of a *Súdra*, the giver
' fhall always tread on the foreheads, and thus
' pafs over miferies *in the gloom of death*.

44. ' EVERY man, who does not an act pre-
' fcribed, or does an act forbidden, or is guilty
' of excefs, *even* in *legal* gratifications of the fenfes,
' muft perform an expiatory penance.

45. ' Some of the learned confider an expiation
' as confined to involuntary fin; but others, from
' the evidence of the *Véda*, hold it effectual even
' in the cafe of a voluntary offence:

46. ' A fin, involuntarily committed, is re-
' moved by repeating certain texts of the fcrip-
' ture; but a fin committed intentionally, through
' ftrange infatuation, by harfh penances of dif-
' ferent forts.

47. ' IF a twice-born man, by the will of GOD
' in this world, or from his natural birth, have
' any corporeal mark of an expiable fin committed
' in this or a former ftate, he muft hold' no in-
' tercourfe with the virtuous, while his penance
' remains unperformed.

48. ' Some evil-minded perfons, for fins com-
' mitted in this life, and fome for bad actions in
' a preceding ftate, fuffer a morbid change in
' their bodies:

49. ' A ftealer of gold from a *Bráhmen* has
' whitlows on his nails; a drinker of fpirits, black
' teeth; the flayer of a *Bráhmen*, a marafmus; the
' violator of his *guru's* bed, a deformity in the
' generative organs;

50. ' A

50. ' A malignant informer, fetid ulcers in his
' noſtrils; a falſe detractor, ſtinking breath; a
' ſtealer of grain, the defect of ſome limb; a'
' mixer *of bad wares with good,* ſome redundant
' member;

51. ' A ſtealer of dreſſed grain, dyſpepſia; a
' ſtealer of holy words, *or an unauthorized reader*
' *of the ſcriptures,* dumbneſs; a ſtealer of clothes,
' leproſy; a horſe-ſtealer, lameneſs;

52. ' The ſtealer of a lamp, total blindneſs;
' the miſchievous extinguiſher of it, blindneſs in
' one eye; a delighter in hurting ſentient crea-
' tures, perpetual illneſs; an adulterer, windy
' ſwellings in his limbs:

53. ' Thus, according to the diverſity of ac-
' tions, are born men deſpiſed by the good,
' ſtupid, dumb, blind, deaf, and deformed.

54. ' Penance, therefore, muſt invariably be
' performed for the ſake of expiation; ſince they,
' who have not expiated their ſins, will again
' ſpring to birth with diſgraceful marks.

- 55. ' KILLING a *Bráhmen,* drinking forbidden
' liquor, ſtealing gold from a prieſt, adultery
' with the wife of a father, natural or ſpiritual,
' and aſſociating with ſuch as commit thoſe of-
' fences, wiſe legiſlators muſt declare to be crimes
' in the higheſt degree, *in reſpect of thoſe after men-*
' *tioned, but leſs than inceſt in a direct line, and ſome*
' *others.*

56. ' FALSE boaſting of a high tribe, malignant
' information, before the king, of a criminal *who*
' *muſt ſuffer death,* and falſely accuſing a ſpiritual
' preceptor, are crimes *in the ſecond degree, and*
' nearly equal to killing a *Bráhmen.*

57. ' Forgetting the texts of ſcripture, ſhowing
' contempt of the *Véda,* giving falſe evidence
' *with-*

' *without a bad motive*, killing a friend *without malice*,
' eating things prohibited, or, *from their manifest*
' *impurity*, unfit to be tasted, are six crimes nearly
' equal to drinking spirits ; *but perjury and homi-*
' *cide require, in atrocious cases, the harsheft expiation.*

58. ' To appropriate a thing deposited *or lent*
' *for a time*, a human creature, a horse, precious
' metals, a field, a diamond, or any other gem,
' is nearly equal to stealing the gold of a *Bráhmen.*

59. ' Carnal commerce with sisters by the same
' mother, with little girls, with women of the
' lowest mixed class, or with the wives of a friend,
' or of a son, the wife must consider as nearly
' equal to a violation of the paternal bed.

60. ' SLAYING a bull or cow, sacrificing what
' ought not to be sacrificed, adultery, selling
' oneself, deserting a preceptor, a mother, a fa-
' ther, or a son, omitting to read the scripture,
' and neglect of the fires *prescribed by the* Dher-
' maſáſtra *only*,

61. ' The marriage of a younger brother be-
' fore the elder, and that elder's omiſſion to marry
' before the younger, giving a daughter to either
' of them, and officiating at their nuptial ſacrifice,

62. ' Defiling a damſel, uſury, want of perfect
' chaſtity in a ſtudent, ſelling a holy pool or
' garden, a wife, or a child,

63. ' Omitting the ſacred inveſtiture, abandon-
' ing a kinſman, teaching the *Véda* for hire, learn-
' ing it from a hired teacher, ſelling commodities
' that ought not to be ſold,

64. ' Working in mines of any ſort, engaging
' in *dykes, bridges, or other* great mechanical works,
' ſpoiling medicinal plants *repeatedly*, ſubſiſting by
' *the harlotry of* a wife, offering ſacrifices and
' preparing charms to deſtroy *the innocent*,

65. ' Cutting

65. ' Cutting down green trees for firewood,
' performing holy rites with a selfish view merely,
' and eating prohibited food *once without a previous*
' *design,*

66. ' Neglecting to keep up the consecrated
' fire, stealing *any valuable thing besides gold,* non-
'-payment of *the three* debts, application to the
' books of a false religion, and excessive attention
' to musick or dancing,

67. ' Stealing grain, base metals, or cattle,
' familiarity, *by the twice born,* with women who
' have drunk inebriating liquor, killing *without*
' *malice* a woman, *a Súdra, a Vaisya,* or a *Cshatriya,*
' and denying a future state of rewards and pu-
' nishments, are all crimes in the third degree,
' *but higher or lower according to circumstances.*

68. ' GIVING pain to a *Bráhmen,* smelling at
' any spirituous liquor or any thing *extremely fetid*
' *and* unfit to be smelt, cheating, and unnatural
' practices with a male, are considered as causing
' a loss of class.

69. ' To kill an ass, a horse, a camel, a deer,
' an elephant, a goat, a sheep, a fish, a snake, or
' a buffalo, is declared an offence which degrades
' the killer to a mixed tribe.

70. ' ACCEPTING presents from despicable
' men, illegal traffick, attendance on a *Súdra*
' master, and speaking falsehood, must be con-
' sidered as causes of exclusion from social repasts.

71. KILLING an insect, small or large, a worm,
' or a bird, eating what has been brought *in the*
' *same basket* with spirituous liquor, stealing fruit,
' wood, or flowers, and great perturbation of
' mind on trifling occasions, are offences which
' cause defilement.

72. ' You

72. ' You fhall now be completely inftructed
' in thofe penances, by which all the fins juft'
' mentioned are expiable.

73. ' IF a *Bráhmen* have killed a man of the'
' facerdotal clafs, *without malice prepenfe, the flayer*
' *being far fuperiour to the flain in good qualities,* he'
' muft himfelf make a hut in a foreft and dwell in
' it twelve whole years, fubfifting on alms for the'
' purification of his foul, placing near him, as a'
' token *of his crime, the fkull of the flain, if he can*
' *procure it,* or, *if not, any human fkull.* The time
' *of penance for the three lower claffes muft be twenty-*
' *four, thirty-fix,* and *forty-eight years.*

74. ' Or, *if the flayer be of the military clafs,* he'
' may voluntarily expofe himfelf as a mark to
' archers, who know *his intention* ; or, *according to*
' *circumftances,* may caft himfelf head-long thrice,'
' or even till he die, into blazing fire.

75. ' Or, *if he be a king, and flew a prieft with-*
' *out malice or knowledge of his clafs,* he may per-
' form, *with prefents of great wealth,* one of the
' following facrifices ; an *Afwamédha,* or a *Swerjit,*'
' or a *Gofava,* or an *Abhijit,* or a *Vifwajit,* or a'
' *Trivrit,* or an *Agnifhtut.*

76. ' Or, to expiate the guilt of killing a prieft
' *without knowing him and without defign,* the killer
' may walk *on a pilgrimage* a hundred *yójanas,* re-
' peating any one of the *Védas,* eating barely
' enough to fuftain life, and keeping his organs in
' perfect fubjection ;

77. ' Or, *if in that cafe the flayer be unlearned,*
' *but rich,* he may give all his property to fome
' *Bráhmen* learned in the *Véda,* or a fufficiency of
' wealth for his life, or a houfe and furniture to
' *hold while he lives :*

78. ' Or,

78. ' Or, eating only such wild grains as are
' offered to the gods, he may walk to *the head of*
' the river *Saraswatì* againſt the courſe of the
' ſtream ; or, ſubſiſting on very little food, he
' may thrice repeat the whole collection of *Védas,*
' or the *Rïch, Yajuſh,* and *Sáman.*

79. ' Or, his hair being ſhorn, he may dwell
' near a town, or on paſture ground for cows,
' or in ſome holy place, or at the root of a ſacred
' tree, taking pleaſure in doing good to cows and
' to *Bráhmens :*

80. ' There, for the preſervation of a cow or
' a *Bráhmen,* let him inſtantly abandon life ; ſince
' the preſerver of a cow or a *Bráhmen* atones for
' the crime of killing a prieſt :

81. ' Or, by attempting at leaſt three times
' forcibly to recover *from robbers* the property of a
' *Bráhmen,* or by recovering it in one of its attacks,
' or even by loſing his life in the attempt, he
' atones for his crime.

82. ' Thus continually firm in religious auſte-
' rity, chaſte as a ſtudent in the firſt order, with
' his mind intent on virtue, he may expiate the
' guilt of *undeſignedly* killing a *Bráhmen,* after the
' twelfth year has expired.

83. ' Or, *if a virtuous* Bráhmen *unintentionally kill*
' *another, who had no good quality,* he may atone for
' his guilt by proclaiming it in an aſſembly of
' prieſts and military men, at the ſacrifice of a
' horſe, and by bathing with other *Bráhmens* at the
' cloſe of the ſacrifice :

84. ' *Bráhmens* are declared to be the baſis, and
' *Cſhatriyas* the ſummit of the legal ſyſtem : he,
' therefore, expiates his offence by fully proclaim-
' ing it in ſuch an aſſembly.

85. ' From

85. ' From his high birth alone, a *Bráhmen* is
' an object of veneration even to deities ; his de-
' clarations to mankind are decisive evidence ;
' and the *Véda* itself confers on him that character.

86. ' Three at least, who are learned in the
' *Véda*, should be assembled to declare the proper
' expiation for the sin *of a priest, but, for the three*
' *other classes, the number must be doubled, tripled, and*
' *quadrupled :* what they declare shall be an atone-
' ment for sinners, since the words of the learned
' give purity.

87. ' Thus a *Bráhmen*, who has performed one
' of the preceding expiations, *according to the cir-*
' *cumstances of the homicide and the characters of the*
' *persons killed and killing*, with his whole mind fixed
' on GOD, purifies his soul, and removes the guilt
' of slaying a man of his own class :

88. ' He must perform the same penance for
' killing an embryo, *the sex of which was* unknown,
' but whose parents were *sacerdotal*, or a military
' or a commercial man employed in a sacrifice, or
' a *Bráhmeni* woman, who has bathed after tem-
' porary uncleanness ;

89. ' And *the same* for giving false evidence *in*
' *a cause concerning land or gold, or precious commodi-*
' *ties*, and for accusing his preceptor unjustly, and
' for appropriating a deposit, and for killing the
' wife of a priest, *who keeps a consecrated fire*, or
' for slaying a friend.

90. ' Such is the atonement ordained for killing
' a priest *without malice* ; but for killing a *Bráh-*
' *men* with malice prepense, this is no expia-
' tion : *the term of twelve years must be doubled, or,*
' *if the case was atrocious, the murderer must actually*
' *die in flames or in battle.*

3   91. ' ANY

91. ' ANY twice born man, who has *intention-*
' *ally* drunk fpirit of rice, through perverfe delu-
' fion of mind, may drink more fpirit in flame,
' and atone for his offence by feverely burning
' his body ;

92. ' Or he may drink boiling hot, until he
' die, the urine of a cow, or pure water, or milk,
' or clarified butter, or juice expreffed from
' cow dung :

93. ' Or, *if he tafted it unknowingly,* he may
' expiate the fin of drinking fpirituous liquor, by
' eating only fome broken rice or grains of *tila,*
' from which oil has been extracted, once every
' night for a whole year, wrapped in coarfe vef-
' ture of hairs from a cow's tail, *or fitting un-*
' *clothed in his houfe,* wearing his locks and beard
' uncut, and putting out the flag of a tavern-
' keeper.

94. ' Since the fpirit of rice is *diftilled from the*
' *Mala, or* filthy refufe of the grain, and fince
' *Mala* is alfo a name for fin, let no *Bráhmen,*
' *Cfhatriya* or *Vaifya* drink that fpirit.

95. ' Inebriating liquor may be confidered as
' of three *principal* forts : that extracted from
' dregs of fugar, that extracted from bruifed rice,
' and that extracted from the flowers of the *Mad-*
' *húca :* as one, fo *are* all ; they fhall not be tafted
' by the chief of the twice born.

96. ' Thofe liquors, and *eight* other forts,
' with the flefh of animals, and *Afava,* the moft
' pernicious beverage, *prepared with narcotick drugs,*
' are fwallowed at the juncates of *Yacfhas, Rac-*
' *fhafhas,* and *Pifachas :* they fhall not, therefore,
' be tafted by a *Bráhmen* who feeds on clarified
' butter offered to gods.

97. ' A *Bráh-*

98. ' When the divine fpirit, *or the light of holy*
' *knowledge*, which has been infufed into his body,
' has once been fprinkled with any intoxicating
' liquor, even his prieftly character leaves him,
' and he finks to the low degree of a *Súdra*.

99. ' Thus have been promulgated the various
' modes of expiation for drinking fpirits : I will
' next propound the atonement for ftealing the
' gold of a prieft *to the amount of a* fuverna.

100. ' He, who has purloined the gold of a
' *Bráhmen*, muft haften to the king, and proclaim
' his offence ; adding, " Inflict on me the punifh-
" ment due to my crime."

101. ' Then fhall the king himfelf, taking
' from him an iron mace, *which the criminal muft*
' *bear on his fhoulder*, ftrike him with it once ;
' and by that ftroke, *whether he die or be only left*
' *as dead*, the thief is releafed from fin : a *Bráh-*
' *men*, by rigid penance alone, *can expiate that of-*
' *fence* ; *another twice born man may alfo perform*
' *fuch a penance* at his election.

102. ' The twice born man, who defires to
' remove, by auftere devotion, the taint caufed
' by ftealing gold, muft perform in a foreft, co-
' vered with a mantle of rough bark, the penance
' *before ordained* for him, who, *without malice per-*
' *penfe*, has killed a *Bráhmen*.

103. ' By thefe expiations may the twice
' born atone for the guilt of ftealing gold from
' a prieft ; but the fin of adultery with the wife
' of a father, *natural or fpiritual*, they muft expiate
' by the following penances.

104. ' He, who *knowingly and actually* has
' defiled the wife of his father, *fhe being of the*
' *fame clafs*, muft extend himfelf on a heated

X ' iron.

‘ iron bed, loudly proclaiming his guilt; and,
‘ there embracing the red hot iron image of a
‘ woman, he shall atone for his crime by death:

105. ‘ Or, having himself amputated his penis
‘ and scrotum, and holding them in his fingers,
‘ he may walk in a direct path toward the south-
‘ west, or the region of NIRRĬTI, until he fall
‘ dead on the ground:

106. ‘ Or, *if he had mistaken her for another*
‘ *woman*, he may perform, for a whole year, with
‘ intense application of mind, the penance *prá-*
‘ *jápatya*, with part of a bed, *or a human bone,*
‘ in his hand, wrapped in vesture of coarse bark,
‘ letting his hair and beard grow, and living in a
‘ deserted forest:

107. ‘ Or, *if she was of a lower class and a*
‘ *corrupt woman*, he may expiate the sin of violat-
‘ ing the bed of his father, by continuing the
‘ penance *chándráyana* for three months, always
‘ mortifying his body by eating only forest herbs,
‘ or wild grains boiled in water.

108. ‘ By the preceding penances, may sinners
‘ of the two higher degrees atone for their guilt;
‘ and the less offenders may expiate theirs by the
‘ following austerities.

109. ‘ HE, who has committed the smaller
‘ offence of killing a cow, *without malice*, must
‘ drink, for the first month, barley corns boiled
‘ soft in water; his head must be shaved en-
‘ tirely; and, covered with the hide *of the slain*
‘ *cow*, he must fix his abode on her late pasture
‘ ground:

110. ‘ He may eat a moderate quantity *of*
‘ *wild grains*, but without any factitious salt, for
‘ the next two months at the time of each fourth
                                                ‘ repast,

2

' repaſt, *on the evening of every ſecond day*; regu-
' larly bathing in the urine of cows, and keeping
' his members under controul:

111. ' All day he muſt wait on the herd, and
' ſtand quaffing the duſt raiſed *by their hoofs*;
' at night, having ſervilely attended and ſtroked
' and ſaluted them, he muſt ſurround them with
' a fence, and ſit near *to guard* them:

112. ' Pure and free from paſſion, he muſt
' ſtand, while they ſtand; follow them, when
' they move together; and lie down by them,
' when they lie down:

113. ' Should a cow be ſick or terrified by
' tigers or thieves, or fall, or ſtick in mud, he
' muſt relieve her by all poſſible means:

114. ' In heat, in rain, or in cold, or while
' the blaſt furiouſly rages, let him not ſeek his
' own ſhelter, without firſt ſheltering the cows to
' the utmoſt of his power:

115. ' Neither in his own houſe, or field, or
' floor for treading out grain, nor in thoſe of any
' other perſon, let him ſay a word of a cow, who
' eats *corn or graſs*, or of a calf who drinks *milk:*

116. ' By waiting on a herd, according to theſe
' rules, for three months, the ſlayer of a cow
' atones for his guilt;

117. ' *But*, his penance being performed, he
' muſt give ten cows and a bull, or, his ſtock
' not being ſo large, muſt deliver all he poſſeſſes,
' to ſuch as beſt know the *Véda*.

118. ' THE preceding penances, or that called
' *chándráyana*, muſt be performed for the abſo-
' lution of all twice born men, who have com-
' mitted ſins of the lower *or third* degree; except
' thoſe, who have incurred the guilt of an *ava-*
' *círna*;

Y 2　　　119. ' But

119. ' But he, who has become *Avacirni*, muſt
' ſacrifice *a black* or a one-eyed aſs, by way of a
' meat-offering to NIRRĪTI, *patroneſs of the ſouth-*
' *weſt*, by night, in a place where four ways meet:

120. ' Let him daily offer to her, in fire, the
' fat of that aſs, and, at the cloſe *of the ceremony*,
' let him offer clarified butter, with the holy text
' *Sem* and ſo forth, to PAVANA, to INDRA, to
' VRĪHASPATI, and to AGNI, *regents of wind,*
' *clouds, a planet, and fire.*

121. ' A voluntary effuſion, *naturally or other-*
' *wiſe*, of that which may produce a man, by a
' twice born youth, during the time of his ſtudent-
' ſhip, *or before marriage,* has been pronounced
' *avacirna*, or a violation of the rule preſcribed
' *for the firſt order*, by ſages who knew the whole
' ſyſtem of duty, and uttered the words of the
' *Véda*.

122. ' To the four *deities of purification*, MA'-
' RUTA, INDRA, VRĪHASPATI, AGNI, goes all the
' divine light, which the *Véda* had imparted, from
' the ſtudent, who commits the foul ſin *avacirna*;

123. ' But, this crime having actually been
' committed, he muſt go begging to ſeven houſes,
' clothed only with the hide of the *ſacrificed* aſs,
' and openly proclaiming his act:

124. ' Eating a ſingle meal begged from them,
' at the regular time of the day, *that is, in the*
' *morning or evening*, and bathing *each day* at the
' three *ſavanas*, he ſhall be abſolved from his guilt
' at the end of one year.

125. ' HE, who has voluntarily committed
' any ſin, which cauſes a loſs of claſs, muſt per-
' form the *tormenting* penance, *thence* called *ſánta-*
' *pana*; or the *prájápatya*, if he offended involun-
' tarily.

126. 'For sins, which degrade to a mixed
' class, or exclude from society, the sinner must
' have recourse to the *lunar* expiation *chândráyana*
' for one month: to atone for acts which occa-
' sion defilement, he must swallow nothing for
' three days but hot barley cruel.

127. 'For killing *intentionally* a *virtuous* man
' of the military class, the penance must be a
' fourth part of that ordained for killing a priest;
' for killing a *Vaisya*, only an eighth; for killing
' a *Súdra*, who had been constant in *discharging* his
' duties, a sixteenth part:

128. 'But, if a *Bráhmen* kill a *Cshatriya* with-
' out malice, he must, after a full performance of
' his religious rites, give the priests one bull to-
' gether with a thousand cows;

129. 'Or he may perform for three years the
' penance for slaying a *Bráhmen*, mortifying his
' organs of sensation and action, letting his hair
' grow long, and living remote from the town,
' with the root of a tree for his mansion.

130. 'If he kill *without malice* a *Vaisya*, who
' had a good moral character, he may perform
' the same penance for one year, or give the
' priests a hundred cows and a bull:

131. 'For six months must he perform this
' whole penance, if, *without intention*, he kill a
' *Súdra*; or he may give ten white cows and a
' bull to the priests.

132. 'If he kill, *by design*, a cat, or an ichneu-
' mon, the bird *chásha*, or a frog, a dog, a lizard,
' an owl, or a crow, he must perform the *ordinary*
' penance required for the death of a *Súdra*, that
' is, the *chándráyana*:

133. 'Or, if he kill one of them undesignedly, he
' may drink nothing but milk for three *days and*
' nights,

' nights, or *each night* walk a *yógan*, or *thrice*
' bathe in a river, or silently repeat the text on
' the divinity of water; *that is, if he be disabled by*
' *real infirmity from performing the first mentioned*
' *penances, he may have recourse to the next in order.*

'134. ' A *Bráhmen*, if he kill a snake, must give
' *to some priest* a hoe, *or iron-headed stick*; if an
' eunuch, a load of rice straw, and a *másha* of
' lead;

135. ' If a boar, a pot of clarified butter; if
' the bird *tittiri*, a *dróna* of *tila*-seeds; if a parrot,
' a steer two years old; if the water-bird *craun-*
' *cha*, a steer aged three years:

136. ' If he kill *a goose, or* a phenicopteros, a
' *heron, or* cormorant, a bittern, a peacock, an
' ape, a hawk, or a kite, he must give a cow to
' some *Bráhmen*:

137. ' If he kill a horse, he must give a man-
' tle; if an elephant, five black bulls; if a goat
' or a sheep, one bull; if an ass, a calf one year
' old:

138. ' If he kill a carnivorous wild beast, he
' must give a cow with abundance of milk; if a
' wild beast not carnivorous, a fine heifer; and
' a *ráctica* of gold, if he slay a camel:

139. ' If he kill a woman *of any class* caught
' in adultery, he must give, as an expiation, in the
' direct order of the four classes, a leathern pouch,
' a bow, a goat, and a sheep.

140. ' Should a *Bráhmen* be unable to expiate
' by gifts the sin of killing a snake and the rest,
' he must atone for his guilt by performing, on
' each occasion, the penance *prájápatya.*

141. ' For the slaughter of a thousand small
' animals which have bones, or for that of bone-
' less animals enow to fill a cart, he must per-
                                            form

' form the *chándráyana,* or common penance for
' killing a *Súdra;*

142. ' But, for killing boned animals, he muſt
' alſo give ſome trifle, *as a* pana *of copper,* to a
' *Bráhmen:* for killing thoſe without bones, he
' may be abſolved by holding his breath, *at the*
' *cloſe of his penance,* while he thrice repeats the *gá-*
' *yatrì* with its *head,* the *pranava,* and the *vyáhritis.*

143. ' For cutting *once without malice* trees
' yielding fruit, ſhrubs with many crowded ſtems,
' creeping or climbing plants, or ſuch as grow
' again when cut, if they were in bloſſom *when he*
' *hurt them,* he muſt repeat a hundred texts of the
' *Véda.*

144. ' For killing inſects of any ſort bred in
' rice or other grains, or thoſe bred in honey *or*
' *other* fluids, or thoſe bred in fruit or flowers,
' eating clarified butter is a full expiation.

145. If a man cut, *wantonly and* for no good
' purpoſe, ſuch graſſes as are cultivated, or ſuch
' as riſe in the foreſt ſpontaneouſly, he muſt wait
' on a cow for one day, nouriſhed by milk alone.

146. ' By theſe penances may mankind atone
' for the ſin of injuring ſentient creatures, whether
' committed by deſign or through inadvertence:
' hear now what penances are ordained for eating
' or drinking what ought not to be taſted.

147. ' HE, who drinks undeſignedly any ſpirit
' *but that of rice,* may be abſolved by a new in-
' veſtiture with the ſacrificial ſtring: even for
' drinking intentionally *the weaker ſorts of ſpirit,*
' a penance extending to death muſt not (as the
' law is now fixed) be preſcribed.

148. ' For drinking water which has ſtood in
' a veſſel, where ſpirit of rice or any other ſpi-
' rituous liquor had been kept, he muſt ſwallow
Y 4   ' nothing

' nothing for five *days and* nights, but the plant
' *sanc'hapuſhpi* boiled in milk:

149. ' If he touch any ſpirituous liquor, or
' give any away, or accept any in due form, *or*
' *with thanks*, or drink water left by a *Súdra*, he
' muſt ſwallow nothing for three *days and* nights,
' but *cuſa*-graſs boiled in water.

150. ' Should a *Bráhmen*, who has once taſted
' the holy juice of the moon-plant, even ſmell
' the breath of a man who has been drinking
' ſpirits, he muſt remove the taint by thrice
' repeating the *gáyatrì*, while he ſuppreſſes his
' breath in water, and by eating clarified butter
' *after that ceremony.*

151. ' IF any of the three twice born claſſes
' have taſted unknowingly human ordure or urine,
' or any thing that has touched ſpirituous liquor,
' they muſt, *after a penance*, be girt anew with
' the ſacrificial thread;

152. ' But, in ſuch new inveſtiture of the twice
' born, the partial tonſure, the zone, the ſtaff, the
' petition of alms, and the ſtrict rules of abſti-
' nence, need not be renewed.

153. ' SHOULD one of them eat the food of
' thoſe perſons, with whom he ought never to
' eat, or food left by a woman or a *Súdra*, or any
' prohibited fleſh, he muſt drink barley gruel only
' for ſeven *days and* nights.

154. ' If a *Bráhmen* drink ſweet liquors turned
' acid, or aſtringent juices from impure fruits, he
' becomes unclean as long as thoſe fluids remain
' undigeſted.

155. ' Any twice born man, who *by accident*
' has taſted the dung or urine of a tame boar, an
' aſs, a camel, a ſhakal, an ape, or a crow, muſt
' perform the penance *chándráyána.*

156. ' If

156. ' If he tafte dried flefh meat, or mufh-
' rooms rifing from the ground, or any thing
' brought from a flaughter houfe, though he knew
' not whence it came, he muft perform the fame
' penance.

157. ' For *knowingly* eating the flefh of carni-
' vorous beafts, of town boars, of camels, of
' gallinaceous birds, of human creatures, of crows,
' or of affes, the penance *taptacrich'hra*, or *burning
' and fevere*, is the only atonement.

158. ' A *Bráhmen*, who, before he has com-
' pleted his theological ftudies, eats food at
' monthly obfequies *to one anceftor*, muft faft three
' days *and nights*, and fit in water a day:

159. ' But a ftudent in theology, who at any
' time *unknowingly* taftes honey or flefh, muft per-
' form the loweft penance, or the *prájápatya*, and
' proceed to finifh his ftudentfhip.

160. ' Having eaten what has been left by a
' cat, a crow, a moufe, a dog, or an ichneumon,
' or what has even been touched by a loufe, he
' muft drink, *boiled in water*, the plant *brahmafu-
' verchalá*.

161. ' By the man, who feeks purity of foul,
' no forbidden food muft be tafted: what he
' has undefignedly fwallowed, he muft inftantly
' vomit up, or muft purify himfelf with fpeed by
' legal expiations.

162. ' Such, as have been declared, are the
' various penances for eating prohibited food:
' hear now the law of penance for an expiation
' of theft.

163. ' THE chief of the twice born, having
' voluntarily ftolen fuch property, as grain, raw
' or dreffed, from the houfe of another *Bráhmen*,
                                          ' fhall

' shall be abfolved on performing the penance
' *prájápatya* for a whole year;

164. ' But the penance *chándráyana* muft be
' performed for ftealing a man, woman, or child,
' for feizing a field, or a houfe, or for taking the
' waters of an enclofed pool or well.

165. ' Having taken goods of little value from
' the houfe of another man, he muft procure
' abfolution by performing the penance *fántapana*;
' having firft reftored, *as the penitent thief always
' muft*, the goods that he ftole.

166. ' For taking what may be eaten, or what
' may be fipped, a carriage, a bed, or a feat,
' roots, flowers, or fruit, an atonement may be
' made by fwallowing the five pure things pro-
' duced by a cow, *or milk, curds, butter, urine,
' dung*:

167. ' For ftealing grafs, wood, or trees, rice
' in the hufk, molaffes, cloth or leather, fifh, or
' other animal food, a ftrict faft muft be kept
' three *days and three* nights.

168. ' For ftealing gems, pearls, coral, copper,
' filver, iron, brafs, or ftone, nothing but broken
' rice muft be fwallowed for twelve days;

169. ' And nothing but milk for three days,
' if cotton or filk, or wool had been ftolen, or a
' beaft either with cloven or uncloven hoofs, or
' a bird, or perfumes, or medicinal herbs, or
' cordage.

170. ' By thefe penances may a twice born
' man atone for the guilt of theft; but the fol-
' lowing aufterities only can remove the fin of
' carnally approaching' thofe, who muft not be
' carnally approached.

171. ' HE, who has wafted his manly ftrength
' with fifters by the fame womb, with the wives
                                        ' of

' of his friend or of his fon, with girls under the
' age of puberty, or with women of the loweft
' claffes, muft perform the penance ordained for
' defiling the bed of a preceptor:

172. ' He, who has carnally known the daugh-
' ter of his paternal aunt, *who is almoft equal to* a
' fifter, or the daughter of his maternal aunt, or
' the daughter of his maternal uncle, *who is* a near
' kinfman, muft perform the *chándráyana,* or *lunar*
' *penance*;

173. ' No man of fenfe would take one of
' thofe three as his wife: they fhall not be taken
' in marriage by reafon of their confanguinity;
' and he, who marries any one of them, falls
' deep *into fin.*

174. ' He, who has wafted what might have
' produced a man, with female brute animals,
' with a woman during her courfes, or in any
' but the natural part, or in water, muft perform
' the penance *fántapana: for a beaftial act with a*
' *cow the penance muft be far more fevere.*

175. ' A twice born man, dallying lafcivioufly
' with a male *in any place or at any time,* or with
' a female in a carriage drawn by bullocks, or in
' water, or by day, *fhall be degraded, and* muft
' bathe himfelf *publickly* with his apparel.

176. ' Should a *Bráhmen* carnally know a wo-
' man of the *Chandála* or *Mléch'ha* tribes, or tafte
' their food, or accept a gift from them, he lofes
' his own clafs; *if he acted unknowingly,* or, *if*
' *knowingly,* finks to a level *with them.*

177. ' A wife, exceffively corrupt, let her
' hufband confine to one apartment, and compel
' her to perform the penance ordained for a man
' who has committed adultery:

178. ' If,

178. ' If, having been folicited by a man of
' her own clafs, fhe again be defiled, her expiation
' muſt be the penance *prájápatya* added to the
' *chándráyána.*

179. ' The guilt of a *Bráhmen*, who has dallied
' a whole night with a *Chándálì* woman, he may
' remove in three years by fubfifting on alms,
' and inceſſantly repeating the *gáyatrì* with other
' myſterious texts.

180. ' Theſe penances have been declared for
' finners of four forts, *thoſe who hurt ſentient crea-*
' *tures, thoſe who eat prohibited food, thoſe who*
' *commit theft, and thoſe who are guilty of laſcivi-*
' *ouſneſs:* hear now the preſcribed expiation for
' fuch as hold any intercourſe with degraded
' offenders.

181. ' HE, who aſſociates himſelf for one year
' with a fallen finner, falls like him ; not by fa-
' crificing, reading the *Véda*, or contracting af-
' finity with him, *ſince by thoſe acts he loſes his*
' *claſs immediately*, but even by uſing the fame
' carriage or feat, or by taking his food at the
' fame board :

182. ' That man who holds an intercourſe
' with any one of thoſe degraded offenders, muſt
' perform, as an atonement for fuch intercourſe,
' the penance ordained for that finner himſelf.

183. ' The *ſapindas* and *ſamánódacas* of a man
' degraded, *for a crime in the firſt degree*, muſt
' offer a libation of water to his manes, *às if*
' *he were naturally dead*, out of the town, in
' the evening of fome inauſpicious day, *as the*
' *ninth of the moon*, his paternal kinſman, his
' officiating prieſt, and his ſpiritual guide being
' preſent.

184. ' A female flave muſt kick down with
' her

' her foot an old pot filled with water, *which had*
' *for that purpose been placed toward the south,* as
' if it were an oblation for the dead ; and all the
' kinfmen, in the nearer and remoter degrees,
' muft remain impure for a day and a night :

185. ' They muft thenceforth defift from fpeak-
' ing to him, from fitting in his company, from
' delivering to him any inherited or other pro-
' perty, and from every civil or ufual attention,
' *as inviting him on the firft day of the year, and the*
' *like.*

186. ' His right of primogeniture, *if he was*
' *an elder brother,* muft be with-holden from him,
' and whatever perquifites arife from priority of
' birth : a younger brother, excelling him in vir-
' tue, muft appropriate the fhare of the firft-born.

187. ' But, when he has performed his due
' penance, his kinfmen and he muft throw down
' a new veffel full of water, after having bathed
' together in a pure pool :

188. ' Then muft he caft that veffel into the
' water ; and, having entered his houfe, he may
' perform, as before, all the acts incident to his
' relation by blood.

189. ' The fame ceremony muft be performed
' by the kindred even of women degraded, for
' whom clothes, dreffed rice, and water muft be
' provided ; and they muft dwell *in huts* near the
' family houfe.

190. ' With finners, whofe expiations are un-
' performed, let not a man tranfact bufinefs of
' any kind; but thofe, who have performed their
' expiations, let him at no time reproach :

191. ' Let him not, however, live with thofe
' who have flain children, or injured their bene-
' factors, or killed fuppliants for protection, or
' put

' put women to death, even though such offenders
' have been legally purified.

192. ' THOSE men of the twice born classes,
' to whom the *gáyatrì* has not been repeated and
' explained, according to law, the assembly must
' cause to perform three *prájápatya* penances, and
' *afterwards* to be girt with the sacrificial string;

193. ' And the same penance they must pre-
' scribe to such twice born men, as are anxious to
' atone for some illegal act, or a neglect of the *Véda*.

194. ' IF priests have accepted any property
' from base hands, they may be absolved by re-
' linquishing the presents, by repeating mysterious
' texts, and by acts of devotion:

195. ' By three thousand repetitions of the
' *gáyatrì* with intense application of mind, and by
' subsisting on milk only for a whole month in
' the pasture of cows, a *Bráhmen*, who has re-
' ceived any gift from a bad man, *or a bad gift*
' *from any man*, may be cleared from sin.

196. ' When he has been mortified by ab-
' stinence, and has returned from the pasturage,
' let him bend low to the other *Bráhmens*, who
' must thus interrogate him: " Art thou really
" desirous, good man, of re-admission to an equa-
" lity with us ?"

197. ' If he answer in the affirmative, let him
' give some grass to the cows, and in the place,
' made pure by their having eaten on it, let the
' men of his class give their assent to his re-
' admission.

19 . ' HE, who has officiated at a sacrifice for
' outcasts, or burned the corpse of a stranger, or
' performed rites to destroy the innocent, or
' made the impure sacrifice, called *Ahína*, may
' expiate his guilt by three *prájápatya* penances.

199. ' A TWICE

199. ' A TWICE BORN man, who has rejected
' a fuppliant for his protection, or taught the *Véda*
' on a forbidden day, may atone for his offence by
' fubfifting a whole year on barley alone.

200. ' HE, who has been bitten by a dog, a
' fhakal, or an afs, by any carnivorous animal fre-
' quenting a town, by a man, a horfe, a camel, or
' a boar, may be purified by ftopping his breath
' during one repetition of the *gáyatrì.*

201. ' To eat only at the time of the fixth
' meal, *or on the evening of every third day*, for a
' month, to repeat a *Sanhità* of the *Védas*, and to
' make *eight* oblations to fire, accompanied with
' *eight* holy texts, are always an expiation for
' thofe, who are excluded from fociety at repafts.

202. ' SHOULD a *Bráhmen* voluntarily afcend a
' carriage borne by camels or drawn by affes, or
' defignedly bathe quite naked, he may be ab-
' folved by one fuppreffion of breath, while he re-
' peats, in his mind, the moft holy text.

203. ' HE, who has made any excretion, be-
' ing greatly preffed, either without water *near*
' *him*, or in water, may be purified by bathing
' in his clothes out of town, and by touching a
' cow.

204. ' FOR an omiffion of the acts, which the
' *Véda* commands to be conftantly performed,
' and for a violation of the duties prefcribed to a
' houfekeeper, the atonement is fafting *one day.*

205. ' HE, who fays hufh or pifh to a *Bráh-*
' *men*, or thou *to a fuperiour*, muft *immediately*
' bathe, eat nothing for the reft of the day, and
' appeafe him by clafping his feet with refpectful
' falutation.

206. ' FOR ftriking a *Bráhmen* even with a
' blade of grafs, or tying him by the neck with a
' cloth,

‘ cloth, or overpowering him in argument, and
‘ adding contemptuous words, the offender muſt
‘ ſoothe him by falling proſtrate.

207. ‘ An aſſaulter of a *Bráhmen*, with intent
‘ to kiłł, ſhall remain in hell a hundred years;
‘ for actually ſtriking him *with the like intent*, a
‘ thouſand :

208. ‘ As many ſmall pellets of duſt as the
‘ blood of a *Bráhmen* collects on the ground, for
‘ ſo many thouſand years muſt the ſhedder of that
‘ blood be tormented in hell.

209. ‘ For a ſimple aſſault, the firſt *or common*
‘ penance muſt be performed ; for a battery, the
‘ *third or* very ſevere penance ; but for ſhedding
‘ blood, *without killing*, both of thoſe penances.

210. ‘ To remove the ſins, for which no par-
‘ ticular penance has been ordained, the aſſembly
‘ muſt award a fit expiation, conſidering the ability
‘ of the ſinner *to perform it*, and the *nature of*
‘ *the* ſin.

211. ‘ Those penances, by which a man may
‘ atone for his crimes, I now will deſcribe to you;
‘ penances, which have been performed by deities,
‘ by holy ſages, and by forefathers *of the human*
‘ *race.*

212. ‘ When a twice born man performs the
‘ *common* penance, *or that* of Praja'pati, he muſt,
‘ for three days, eat only in the morning; for
‘ three days, only in the evening; for three days,
‘ food unaſked *but preſented to him* ; and for three
‘ more days, nothing.

213. ‘ Eating *for a whole day* the dung and
‘ urine of cows mixed with curds, milk, clarified
‘ butter, and water boiled with *cuſa*-graſs, and
‘ then faſting entirely for a *day and a* night, is the
‘ penance

' penance called *Sántapaná*, either from the de-
' vout man SANTAPANA, or from *tormenting*.

214. ' A twice born man performing the pe-
' nance, called very severe, *in respect of the common*,
' must eat, as before, a single mouthful, *or a ball*
' *of rice as large as a hen's egg* for three times
' three days; and for the last three days, must
' wholly abstain from food.

215. ' A *Bráhmen*, performing the ardent pe-
' nance, must swallow nothing but hot water, hot
' milk, hot clarified butter, and hot steam, each
' of them for three days succeffively, performing
' an ablution and mortifying all his members.

216. ' A total fast for twelve days *and nights*,
' by a penitent with his organs controlled and his
' mind attentive, is the penance named *paráca*,
' which expiates all *degrees of* guilt.

217. ' If he diminish his food by one mouthful
' *each day*, during the dark fortnight, *eating fifteen*
' *mouthfuls on the day of the oppofition*, and increafe
' it, *in the fame proportion*, during the bright fort-
' night, *fafting entirely on the day of the conjunction*,
' and perform an ablution regularly at funrife,
' noon, and funfet, this is the *chándráyana*, or the
' lunar penance:

218. ' Such is the *penance* called ant-fhaped *or*
' *narrow in the middle*; but, if he perform the
' barley-fhaped *or broad in the middle*, he must
' obferve the fame rule, beginning with the bright
' half month, and keeping under command his
' organs of action and fenfe.

219. ' To perform the lunar penance of an
' anchoret, he must eat only eight mouthfuls of
' foreft grains at noon, *for a whole month*, taking
' care to fubdue his mind.

220. ' If a *Bráhmen* eat only four mouthfuls at

Z　　　　　　' funrife

'sunrise, and four at sunset, *for a month,* keeping
'his organs controlled, he performs the lunar
'penance of children.

221. 'He, who, for a whole month, eats no
'more than thrice eighty mouthfuls of wild
'grains, *as he happens* by any means *to meet with*
'*them,* keeping his organs in subjection, shall at-
'tain the same abode with the regent of the moon:

222. 'The eleven *Rudras,* the twelve *A'dityas,*
'the eight *Vasus,* the *Maruts,* or genii of the
'winds, and the seven great *Rishis,* have per-
'formed this lunar penance as a security from
'all evil.

223. 'The oblation *of clarified butter* to fire
'must every day be made by *the penitent* himself,
'accompanied with the mighty words, *earth, sky,*
'*heaven*; he must perfectly abstain from injury
'to sentient creatures, from falsehood, from wrath,
'and from all crooked ways.

224. 'Or, thrice each day and thrice each
'night for a month, the penitent may plunge into
'water, clothed in his mantle, and at no time con-
'versing with a woman, a *Súdra,* or an outcast.

225. 'LET him be always in motion, sitting
'and rising alternately; or, if unable *to be thus*
'*restless,* let him sleep low *on the bare ground*;
'chaste as a student of the *Véda,* bearing the sa-
'cred zone and staff, showing reverence to his
'preceptor, to the gods, and to priests;

226. 'Perpetually must he repeat the *gáyatrì,*
'and other pure texts to the best of his know-
'ledge: thus in all penances for absolution from
'sin, must he vigilantly employ himself.

227. 'By these expiations are twice born men
'absolved, whose offences are publickly known,
'*and are mischievous by their example*; but for

2   'sins

' fins not public'k, the affembly of priefts muft
' award them penances, with holy texts and ob-
' lations to fire.

228. ' By open confeffion, by repentance, by
' devotion, and by reading the fcripture, a finner
' may be releafed from his guilt; or by alms-
' giving, in cafe of his inability *to perform the other*
' *acts of religion.*

229. ' In proportion as a man, who has com-
' mitted a fin, fhall truly and voluntarily confefs
' it, fo far he is difengaged from that offence, like
' a fnake from his flough;

230. ' And, in proportion as his heart fincerely
' loathes his evil deed, fo far fhall his vital fpirit
' be freed from the taint of it.

231. ' If he commit fin, and actually repent,
' that fin fhall be removed from him; but if he
' merely fay, " I will fin thus no more," he can
' only be releafed by an actual abftinence from
' guilt.

232. ' Thus revolving in his mind the cer-
' tainty of retribution in a future ftate, let him
' be conftantly good in thoughts, words, and
' action.

233. ' If he defire complete remiffion of any
' foul act which he has committed, either ig-
' norantly or knowingly, let him beware of com-
' mitting it again: *for the fecond fault his penance*
' *muft be doubled.*

234. ' If, having performed any expiation, he
' feel not a perfect fatisfaction of confcience, let
' him repeat the fame devout act, until his con-
' fcience be perfectly fatisfied.

235. ' All the blifs of deities and of men is
' declared by fages, who difcern the fenfe of the

Z 2   ' *Véda,*

' *Véda*, to have in devotion its cauſe, in devotion
' its continuance, in devotion its fullneſs.

236. ' Devotion is *equal to the performance of*
' *all duties* ; *it is* divine knowledge in a *Bráhmen* ;
' it is defence of the people in a *Cſhatriya* ; de-
' votion is *the* buſineſs *of trade and agriculture* in
' a *Vaiſya* ; devotion is dutiful ſervice in a *Súdra*.

237. ' Holy ſages, with ſubdued paſſions, feed-
' ing only on food, roots, and air, by devotion
' alone are enabled to ſurvey the three worlds,
' *terreſtrial, ethereal, and celeſtial*, peopled with
' animal creatures, locomotive and fixed.

238. ' Perfect health, or unfailing medicines,
' divine learning, and the various manſions of
' deities, are acquired by devotion alone : their
' efficient cauſe is devotion.

239. ' Whatever is hard to be traverſed, what-
' ever is hard to be acquired, whatever is hard to
' be viſited, whatever is hard to be performed, all
' this may be accompliſhed by true devotion ;
' for the difficulty of devotion is the greateſt
' of all.

240. ' Even ſinners in the higheſt degree, and
' of courſe the other offenders, are abſolved from
' guilt by auſtere devotion well practiſed.

241. ' *Souls, that animate* worms, and inſects,
' ſerpents, moths, beaſts, birds, and vegetables,
' attain heaven by the power of devotion.

242. ' Whatever ſin has been conceived in the
' hearts of men, uttered in their ſpeech, or com-
' mitted in their bodily acts, they ſpeedily burn
' it all away by devotion, if they preſerve devo-
' tion as their beſt wealth.

243. ' Of a prieſt, whom devotion has purified,
' the divine ſpirits accept the ſacrifices, and grant
' the deſires with ample increaſe.

ɪ   244. ' Even

244. ' Even BRAHMA', lord of creatures, by
' devotion enacted this code of laws; and the
' sages by devotion acquired a knowledge of the
' *Védas*.

245. ' Thus the gods themselves, obferving
' in this universe the incomparable power of de-
' votion, have proclaimed aloud the tranfcendent
' excellence of pious aufterity.

246. ' By reading each day as much as poffible
' of the *Véda*, by performing the *five* great fa-
' craments, and by forgiving all injuries, even fins
' of the higheft degree fhall be foon effaced:

247. ' As fire confumes in an inftant, with his
' bright flame, the wood that has been placed on
' it, thus, with the flame of knowledge, a *Bráh-*
' *men*, who underftands the *Véda*, confumes all fin.

248. ' Thus has been declared, according to
' law, the mode of atoning for open fins: now
' learn the mode of obtaining abfolution for fecret
' offences.

249. ' SIXTEEN fuppreffions of the breath,
' *while the holieft of texts is repeated* with the three
' mighty words, and the triliteral fyllable, con-
' tinued each day for a month, abfolve even the
' flayer of a *Bráhmen* from his hidden faults.

250. ' Even a drinker of fpirituous liquor is
' abfolved by repeating each day the text *apa* ufed
' by the fage CAUTSA, or that beginning with
' *preti* ufed by VASISHT'HA, or that called *má-*
' *bitra*, or that, of which the firft word is *fuddha-*
' *vatyah*.

251. ' By repeating *each day, for a month*, the
' text *áfyavámíya*, or the hymn *Sivafancalpa*, the
' ftealer of gold from a prieft becomes inftantly
' pure.

252. ' He, who has violated the bed of his

Z 3   ' pre-

' preceptor, is cleared *from secret faults* by repeat-
' ing *sixteen times a day* the text *havishyantiya,* or
' that beginning with *na tamanhah,* or by revolv-
' ing in his mind the *sixteen* holy verses, called
' *Paurusha.*

253. ' The man, who desires to expiate *his*
' hidden sins, great and small, must repeat *once a*
' day, for a year, the text *ava,* or the text *yat-
' cinchida.*

254. ' He, who has accepted an illegal present,
' or eaten prohibited food, may be cleansed in
' three days by repeating the text *taratsamandiya.*

255. ' Though he have committed many secret
' sins, he shall be purified by repeating, for a
' month, the text *sômâraudra,* or the three texts
' *áryamna,* while he bathes in a sacred stream.

256. ' A grievous offender must repeat the
' seven verses, beginning with INDRA, for half a
' year ; and he, who has defiled water with any
' impurity, must sit a whole year subsisting by
' alms.

257. ' A twice born man, who shall offer
' clarified butter for a year, with *eight* texts ap-
' propriated to *eight* several oblations, or with the
' text *na mé,* shall efface a sin even of an extreme-
' ly high degree.

258. ' He, who had committed a crime of the
' first degree, shall be absolved, if he attend a
' herd of kine for a year, mortify his organs, and
' continually repeat the texts beginning with *pá-
' vamáni,* living solely on food given in charity :

259. ' Or, if he thrice repeat a *Sanhitá* of the
' *Védas,* or *a large portion of them with all the*
' mantras *and* bráhmanas, dwelling in a forest with
' subdued organs, and purified by three *parácas,*
' he

' he fhall be fet free from all fins how heinous
' foever.

260. ' Or he fhall be releafed from all deadly
' fins, if he faft three days, with his members
' mortified, and twice a day plunge into water,
' thrice repeating the text *aghamarſhana* :

261. ' As the facrifice of a horſe, the king of
' facrifices, removes all fin, thus the text *agha-*
' *marſhana* deſtroys all offences.

262. ' A prieſt, who ſhould retain in his me-
' mory the whole *Rigvéda*, would be abfolved
' from guilt, even if he had flain the inhabitants
' of the three worlds, and had eaten food from the
' fouleſt hands.

263 ' By thrice repeating the *mantras* and
' *bráhmanas* of the *Rïch*, or thoſe of the *Yajuſh*,
' or thoſe of the *Sáman*, with the *upaniſhads*, he
' ſhall perfectly be cleanſed from every poſſible
' taint:

264. ' As a clod of earth, caſt into a great lake,
' finks in it, thus is every finful act fubmerged in
' the triple *Véda*.

265. ' The divifions of the *Rïch*, the feveral
' branches of the *Yajuſh*, and the manifold ſtrains
' of the *Sáman*, muſt be confidered as forming the
' triple *Véda*: he knows the *Véda*, who knows
' them collectively.

266. ' The primary triliteral fyllable, in which
' the three *Védas* themſelves are compriſed, muſt
' be kept fecret, as another triple *Véda*: he knows
' the *Véda*, who *diſtinctly* knows *the myſtick fenſe of*
' *that word.*'

Z 4

CHAPTER THE TWELFTH.

On Tranfmigration and Final Beatitude.

———

1. ' O THOU, who art free from fin,' *faid the devout fages*, ' thou haft declared the whole fyftem
' of duties ordained for the four claffes of men:
' explain to us now, from the firft principles, the
' ultimate retribution for their deeds.'

2. BHRĬGU, whofe heart was the pure effence of virtue, who proceeded from MENU himfelf, thus addreffed the great fages: ' Hear the in-
' fallible rules for *the fruit of* deeds in this uni-
' verfe.

3. '. ACTION, either mental, verbal, or cor-
' poreal, bears good or evil fruit, *as itfelf is good*
' *or evil*; and from the actions of men proceed
' their various tranfmigrations in the higheft, the
' mean, and the loweft degree :

4. ' Of that three-fold action, connected with
' bodily functions, difpofed in three claffes, and
' confifting of ten orders, be it known in this
' world, that the heart is the inftigator.

5. ' Devifing means to appropriate the wealth
' of other men, refolving on any forbidden deed,

                                                  ' and

‘ and conceiving notions of atheifm or mate-
‘ rialifm, are the three bad acts of the mind:

6. ‘ Scurrilous language, falfehood, indifcri-
‘ minate backbiting, and ufelefs tattle, are the
‘ four bad acts of the tongue:

7. ‘ Taking effects not given, hurting fentient
‘ creatures without the fanction of law, and cri-
‘ minal intercourfe with the wife of another, are
‘ the three bad acts of the body; *and all the ten*
‘ *have their oppofites, which are good in an equal*
‘ *degree.*

8. ‘ A rational creature has a reward or a
‘ punifhment for mental acts, in his mind; for
‘ verbal acts, in his organs of fpeech; for corpo-
‘ real acts, in his bodily frame.

9. ‘ For finful acts moftly corporeal, a man
‘ fhall affume *after death* a vegetable or mineral
‘ form; for fuch acts moftly verbal, the form of
‘ a bird or a beaft; for acts moftly mental, the
‘ loweft of human conditions:

10. ‘ He, whofe firm underftanding obtains a
‘ command over his words, a command over his
‘ thoughts, and a command over his whole body,
‘ may juftly be called a *tridandì,* or *triple com-*
‘ *mander; not a mere anchoret, who bears three*
‘ *vifible ftaves.*

11. ‘ The man, who exerts this triple felf-
‘ command with refpect to all animated creatures,
‘ wholly fubduing both luft and wrath, fhall by
‘ thofe means attain beatitude.

12. ‘ THAT fubftance, which gives a power of
‘ motion to the body, the wife call *cfhétrajnya,* or
‘ *jívátman,* the vital fpirit; and that body, which
‘ thencè derives active functions, they name *bhú-*
‘ *tátman,* or *compofed of elements:*

13. ‘ Another internal fpirit, called *mahat,* or
‘ *the*

' *the great soul,* attends the birth of all creatures
' imbodied, and thence, in all mortal forms, is
' conveyed a perception either pleafing or painful.

14. ' Thofe two, the vital fpirit and reafonable
' foul, are clofely united with *five* elements, but
' connected with the fupreme fpirit, or divine
' effence, which pervades all beings high and low:

15. ' From the fubftance of that *fupreme fpirit,*
' are diffufed, *like fparks from fire,* innumerable
' vital fpirits, which perpetually give motion to
' creatures exalted and bafe.

16. ' By the vital fouls of thofe men, who
' have committed fins *in the body reduced to afhes,*
' another body, compofed of *nerves with* five
' fenfations, in order to be fufceptible of torment,
' fhall certainly be affumed after death;

17. ' And, being intimately united with thofe
' minute nervous particles, according to their dif-
' tribution, they fhall feel, in that new body,
' the pangs inflicted in each cafe by the fentence
' of YAMA.

18. ' When the vital foul has gathered the
' fruit of fins, which arife from a love of fenfual
' pleafure, but muft produce mifery, and, when
' its taint has thus been removed, it approaches
' again thofe two moft effulgent effences, *the in-*
' *tellectual foul and the divine fpirit :*

19. ' They two, clofely conjoined, examine
' without remiffion the virtues and vices of that
' fenfitive foul, according to its union with which
' it acquires pleafure or pain in the prefent and
' future worlds.

20. ' If the vital fpirit had practifed virtue
' for the moft part, and vice in a fmall degree,
' it enjoys delight in celeftial abodes, clothed
' with

' with a body formed of pure elementary par-
'. ticles ;

21. ' But, if it had generally been addicted to
'. vice, and feldom attended to virtue, then fhall
' it be deferted by thofe pure elements, and, *hav-*
'. *ing a coarfer body of fenfible nerves*, it feels the
'. pains to which YAMA fhall doom it :

22. ' Having endured thofe torments according
'. to the fentence of YAMA, and its taint being
' almoft removed, it again reaches thofe five pure
' elements in the order of their natural diftribu-
' tion.

23. ' Let each man, confidering with his in-
' tellectual powers thefe migrations of the foul,
' according to its virtue or vice, *into a region of*
'* *blifs or pain*, continually fix his heart on virtue.

24 ' BE it known, that the three qualities of
'. the rational foul are a tendency to goodnefs, to
'. paffion, and to darknefs; and, endued with one
' or more of them, it remains inceffantly attached
' to all thefe created fubftances :

25. ' When any one of the *three* qualities pre-
' dominates in a mortal frame, it renders the
': imbodied fpirit eminently diftinguifhed for that
' quality.

26. ' Goodnefs is declared to be true know-
' ledge; darknefs, grofs ignorance ; paffion, an
' emotion of defire or averfion : fuch is the com-
' pendious defcription of thofe qualities, which
' attend all fouls.

27. ' When a man perceives, in the reafonable
' foul, a difpofition tending to virtuous love, un-
' clouded with any malignant paffion, clear as the
': pureft light, let him recognife it as the quality
' of goodnefs :

28. ' A temper of mind, which gives uneafinefs
' and

' and produces difaffection; let him confider as
' the adverfe quality of paffion, ever agitating
' imbodied fpirits :

29. ' That indiftinct, inconceivable, unaccount-
' able difpofition of a mind naturally fenfual, and
' clouded with infatuation, let him know to be
' the quality of darknefs.

30. ' Now will I declare at large the various
' acts, in the higheft, middle, and loweft degrees,
' which proceed from thofe three difpofitions of
' mind.

31. ' Study of fcripture, auftere devotion, fa-
' cred knowledge, corporeal purity, command
' over the organs, performance of duties, and
' meditation on the divine fpirit, accompany the
' good quality of the foul :

32. ' Interefted motives for acts *of religion or*
' *morality*, perturbation of mind on flight occa-
' fions, commiffion of acts forbidden by law, and
' habitual indulgence in felfifh gratifications, are
' attendant on the quality of paffion :

33. ' Covetoufnefs, indolence, avarice, detrac-
' tion, atheifm, omiffion of prefcribed acts, a
' habit of foliciting favours, and inattention to
' neceffary bufinefs, belong to the dark quality.

34. ' Of thofe three qualities, as they appear
' in the three times, *paft, prefent, and future*, the
' following in order *from the loweft* may be con-
' fidered as a fhort *but certain* criterion.

35. ' Let the wife confider, as belonging to
' the quality of darknefs, every act, which a man
' is afhamed of having done, of doing, or of
' going to do :

36. ' Let them confider, as proceeding from
' the quality of paffion, every act, by which a
' man feeks exaltation and celebrity in this world,
' though

‘ though he may not be much afflicted, if he fail
‘ of attaining his object :

37. ‘ To the quality of goodnefs belongs every
‘ act, by which he hopes to acquire divine know-
‘ ledge, which he is never afhamed of doing, and
‘ which brings placid joy to his confcience.

38. ‘ Of the dark quality, as defcribed, the
‘ principal object is pleafure ; of the paffionate,
‘ worldly profperity ; but of the good quality,
‘ the chief object is virtue : the laft mentioned
‘ *objects* are fuperiour in dignity.

39. ‘ Such tranfmigrations, as the foul procures
‘ in this univerfe by each of thofe qualities, I now
‘ will declare in order fuccinctly.

40. ‘ Souls, endued with goodnefs, attain al-
‘ ways the ftate of deities ; thofe filled with am-
‘ bitious paffions, the condition of men ; and
‘ thofe immerfed in darknefs, the nature of beafts :
‘ this is the triple order of tranfmigration.

41. ‘ Each of thofe three tranfmigrations, caufed
‘ by the feveral qualities, muft alfo be confidered
‘ as three-fold, the loweft, the mean, and the
‘ higheft, according to as many diftinctions of
‘ acts and of knowledge.

42. ‘ Vegetable and mineral fubftances, worms,
‘ infects, and reptiles, fome very minute, fome
‘ rather larger, fifh, fnakes, tortoifes, cattle,
‘ fhakals, are the loweft forms, to which the dark
‘ quality leads :

43. ‘ Elephants, horfes, men of the fervile clafs,
‘ and contemptible *Mléch'has*, or *barbarians*, lions,
‘ tigers, and boars, are the mean ftates procured
‘ by the quality of darknefs :

44. ‘ Dancers and fingers, birds, and deceitful
‘ men, giants and blood-thirfty favages, are the
‘ higheft conditions, to which the dark quality can
‘ afcend.   45. ‘ *Jhallas*,

45. ' *J'hallas*, or cudgel players, *Mallas*, or
' boxers and wreftlers, *Natas*, or actors, thofe
' who teach the ufe of weapons, and thofe who are
' addicted to gaming or drinking, are the loweft
' forms occafioned by the paffionate quality :

46. ' Kings, men of the fighting clafs, domeftick
' priefts of kings, and men fkilled in the war of
' controverfy, are the middle ftates caufed by the
' quality of paffion :

47. ' *Gandharvas*, or aerial muficians, *Guhyacas*
' and *Yacfhas*, or fervants and companions of
' CUVE'RA, genii attending fuperiour gods, as the
' *Vidyádharas* and others, together with various
' companies of *Apfarafes* or nymphs, are the
' higheft of thofe forms, which the quality of
' paffion attains.

48. ' Hermits, religious mendicants, other
' *Bráhmens*, fuch orders of demigods as are wafted
' in airy cars, genii of the figns and lunar man-
' fions, and *Daityas*, or the offspring of DITI,
' are the loweft of ftates procured by the quality
' of goodnefs :

49. ' Sacrificers, holy fages, deities of the
' lower heaven, genii of the *Védas*, regents of ftars
' *not in the paths of the fun and moon*, divinities of
' years, *Pitrïs* or progenitors of mankind, and the
' demigods named *Sádhyas*, are the middle forms,
' to which the good quality conveys *all fpirits*
' *moderately endued with it* :

50. ' BRAHMA' with four faces, creators of
' worlds *under him, as* MARÍCHI *and others*, the
' genius of virtue, the divinities prefiding over (*two*
' *principles of nature in the philofophy of* CAPILA)
' *mahat*, or the *mighty*, and *avyacta*, or *unperceived*,
' are the higheft conditions, to which, by the
' good quality, fouls are exalted.

51. ' This

51. ' This triple fyftem of tranfmigrations, in
' which each clafs has three orders, according to
' actions of three kinds, and which comprifes all
' animated beings, has been revealed in its full
' extent:

5 . ' Thus, by indulging the fenfual appetites,
' and by neglecting the performance of duties,
' the bafeft of men, ignorant of facred expiations,
' affume the bafeft forms.

53. ' WHAT particular bodies the vital fpirit
' enters in this world, and in confequence of what
' fins here committed, now hear at large and in
' order.

54. ' Sinners, in the firft degree, having paffed
' through terrible regions of torture for a great
' number of years, are condemned to the following
' births, at the clofe of that period, *to efface all re-*
' *mains of their fin.*

55. ' The flayer of a *Bráhmen* muft enter *ac-*
' *cording to the circumftances of his crime* the body
' of a dog, a boar, an afs, a camel, a bull, a goat,
' a fheep, a ftag, a bird, a *Chandála,* or a *Puccafa.*

56. ' A prieft, who has drunk fpirituous liquor,
' fhall migrate into the form of a fmaller or larger
' worm or infect, of a moth, of a fly feeding on
' ordure, or of fome ravenous animal.

57. ' He, who fteals the gold of a prieft, fhall
' pafs a thoufand times into the bodies of fpiders,
' of fnakes and cameleons, of *crocodiles and other*
' aquatick monfters, or of mifchievous blood-
' fucking demons.

58. ' He, who violates the bed of his *natural*
' *or fpiritual* father, migrates a hundred times into
' the form of graffes, of fhrubs with crowded
' ftems, or of creeping and twining plants, of
' *vultures and other* carnivorous animals, of *lions*
' *and*

' and other beasts with sharp teeth, or of *tigers and*
' *other* cruel brutes.

59. ' They who hurt any sentient beings, are
' born *cats and other* eaters of raw flesh ; they who
' taste what ought not to be tasted, maggots or
' small flies ; they who steal *ordinary things*, de-
' vourers of each other : theywho embrace very
' low women, become restless ghosts.

60. ' He who has held intercourse with de-
' graded men, or been criminally connected with
' the wife of another, or stolen *common things* from
' a priest, shall be changed into a spirit called
' *Brahmarácshasa.*

61. ' The wretch, who through covetousness
' has stolen *rubies or other* gems, pearls, or coral,
' or precious things, of which there are many sorts,
' shall be born *in the tribe of goldsmiths, or* among
' *birds called* hémacáras, *or gold makers.*

62. ' If a man steal grain in the husk, he shall
' be born a rat ; if a yellow mixed metal, a gan-
' der ; if water, a *plava*, or diver ; if honey, a
' great stinging gnat ; if milk, a crow ; if ex-
' pressed juice, a dog ; if clarified butter, an ich-
' neumon weasel ;

63. ' If he steal flesh meat, a vulture ; if any
' sort of fat, the water-bird *madgu* ; if oil, a blatta,
' or oil-drinking beetle ; if salt, a cicada or cricket;
' if curds, the bird *valúca;*

64. ' If silken clothes, the bird *tittiri* ; if wo-
' ven flax, a frog ; if cotton cloth, the water bird
' *crauncha* ; if a cow, the lizard *gódhá* ; if molasses,
' the bird *vágguda;*

65. If exquisite perfumes, a musk-rat ; if pot-
' herbs, a peacock ; if dressed grain in any of its
' various forms, a porcupine ; if raw grain, a
' hedge-hog ;

66. ' If

66. ' If he steal fire, the bird *vaca* ; if a house-
' hold utensil, an ichneumon fly ; if dyed cloth, the
' bird *chacora*;

67. ' If a deer or an elephant, he shall be born
' a wolf; if a horse, a tiger; if roots or fruit, an ape;
' if a woman, a bear ; if water from a jar, the bird
' *chátaca*; if carriages, a camel ; if small cattle, a
' goat.

68. ' That man, who designedly takes away the
' property of another, or eats any holy cakes not
' first presented *to the deity* at a solemn rite, shall
' inevitably sink to the condition of a brute.

69. ' Women, who have committed similar
' thefts, incur a similar taint, and shall be paired
' with those male beasts in the form of their
' females.

70. ' IF any of the four classes omit, without
' urgent necessity, the performance of their several
' duties, they shall migrate into sinful bodies, and
' become slaves to their foes.

71. ' Should a *Bráhmen* omit his peculiar duty,
' he shall be changed into a demon called *Ulcá-*
' *muc'ha* or *with a mouth like a firebrand,* who de-
' vours what has been vomited ; a *Cshatriya* into
' a demon called *Catapútana*, who feeds on ordure
' and carrion ;

72. ' A *Vaisya*, into an evil being called *Mai-*
' *trácshajyótica*, who eats purulent carcasses ; and
' a *Súdra*, who neglects his occupations, becomes
' a foul imbodied spirit called *Chailásaca*, who
' feeds on lice.

73. ' As far as vital souls, addicted to sensu-
' ality, indulge themselves in forbidden pleasures,
' even to the same degree shall the acuteness of
' their senses be raised *in their future bodies, that*
' *they may endure analogous pains*;

74. ' And

74. ' And, in confequence of their folly, they
' fhall be doomed, as often as they repeat their cri-
' minal acts, to pains more and more intenfe in
' defpicable forms on this earth.

75. ' They fhall firft have a fenfation of agony
' in *Tamifra* or *utter darknefs*, and in other feats
' of horrour ; in *Afipatravana*, or *the fword-leaved*
' *foreft*, and in different places of binding faft and
' of rending :

76. ' Multifarious tortures await them : they
' fhall be mangled by ravens and owls, fhall fwal-
' low cakes boiling hot ; fhall walk over inflamed
' fands, and fhall feel the pangs of being baked
' like the veffels of a potter :

77. ' They fhall affume the forms of beafts con-
' tinually miferable, and fuffer alternate afflictions
' from extremities of cold and of heat, furrounded
' with terrours of various kinds :

78. ' More than once fhall they lie in different
' wombs ; and, after agonizing births, be con-
' demned to fevere captivity, and to fervile atten-
' dance on creatures like themfelves :

79. ' Then fhall follow feparations from kindred
' and friends, forced refidence with the wicked,
' painful gains and ruinous loffes of wealth ;
' friendfhips hardly acquired, and at length
' changed into enmities,

80. ' Old age without refource, difeafes at-
' tended with anguifh, pangs of innumerable forts,
' and, laftly, unconquerable death.

81. ' With whatever difpofition of mind a
' man fhall perform in this life any act *religious*
' *or moral*, in a future body endued with the fame
' quality, fhall he receive his retribution.

82. ' Thus has been revealed to you the fyftem

‘ of punifhments for evil deeds : next learn thofe
‘ acts of a *Bráhmen* which lead to eternal blifs.

83. ‘ Studying and comprehending the *Véda*,
‘ practifing pious aufterities, acquiring divine
‘ knowledge *of law and philofophy*, command over
‘ the organs of fenfe and action, avoiding all injury
‘ to fentient creatures, and fhowing reverence to
‘ a *natural and fpiritual* father, are the chief
‘ branches of duty which enfure final happinefs.’

84. ‘ Among all thofe good acts performed in
‘ this world, *faid the fages,* is no fingle act held
‘ more powerful than the reft in leading men to
‘ beatitude ?’

85. ‘ Of all thofe duties, *anfwered* BHRĬGU, the
‘ principal is to acquire from the *Upanifhads* a
‘ true knowledge of one fupreme GOD ; that is
‘ the moft exalted of all fciences, becaufe it en-
‘ fures immortality :

86. ‘ In this life, indeed, as well as the next,
‘ the ftudy of the *Véda*, to acquire a knowledge of
‘ GOD, is held the moft efficacious of thofe fix
‘ duties in procuring felicity to man ;

87. ‘ For in the knowledge and adoration of
‘ one GOD, which the *Véda* teaches, all the rules
‘ of good conduct, *before-mentioned* in order, are
‘ fully comprifed.

88. ‘ The ceremonial duty, prefcribed by the
‘ *Véda*, is of two kinds ; *one* connected with this
‘ world, and caufing profperity on earth ; *the
‘ other* abftracted from it, and procuring blifs in
‘ heaven.

89. ‘ A religious act, proceeding from felfifh
‘ views in this world, *as a facrifice for rain,* or in
‘ the next, *as a pious oblation in hope of a future
‘ reward,* is declared to be concrete and interefted ;
‘ but

' but an act performed with a knowledge of GOD,
' and without felf-love, is called abftract and dif-
' interefted.

90. ' He, who frequently performs interefted
' rites, attains an equal ftation with the regents of
' the lower heaven : but he, who frequently per-
' forms difinterefted acts of religion, becomes for
' ever exempt from *a body compofed of* the five ele-
' ments :

: 91. ' Equally perceiving the fupreme foul in
' all beings, and all beings in the fupreme foul, he
' facrifices his own fpirit by fixing it on the fpirit
' of GOD, and approaches the nature of that fole
' divinity who fhines by his own effulgence.

92. ' Thus muft the chief of the twice born,
' though he neglect the ceremonial rites mentioned
' in the *Sáftras*, be diligent alike in attaining
' a knowledge of GOD, and in repeating the
' *Véda :*

93. ' Such is the advantageous privilege of
' thofe, who have a double birth *from their natu-*
' *ral mothers and from the* gáyatrì *their fpiritual*
' *mother*, efpecially of a *Bráhmen* ; fince the twice
' born man, by performing this duty, but not
' otherwife, may foon acquire endlefs felicity.

94. ' To patriarchs, to deities, and to man-
' kind, the fcripture is an eye giving conftant
• light; nor could the *Véda Sáftra* have been made
' by human faculties ; nor can it be meafured by
' human reafon *unaffifted by revealed gloffes and com-*
' *ments :* this is a fure propofition.

95. ' Such codes of law as are not grounded
' on the *Véda*, and the various heterodox theories
' of men, produce no good fruit after death ;
' for they all are declared to have their bafis on
' darknefs.

96. ' All

96. ' All fyftems which are repugnant to the
' *Véda*, muft bave been compofed by mortals, and
' fhall foon perifh : their modern date proves
' them vain and falfe.

97. ' The three worlds, the four claffes of men,
' and their four diftinct orders, with all that has
' been, all that is, and all that will be, are made
' known by the *Véda :*

98. ' The nature of found, of tangible and vifi-
' ble fhape, of tafte, and of odour, the fifth object
' of fenfe, is clearly explained in the *Véda* alone,
' together with the three qualities of mind, the
' births attended with them, and the acts which
' they occafion.

99. ' All creatures are fuftained by the prime-
' val *Véda Sáftra*, which the wife therefore hold
' fupreme, becaufe it is the fupreme fource of prof-
' perity to this creature, man.

100. ' Command of armies, royal authority,
' power of inflicting punifhment, and fovereign
' dominion over all nations, he only well deferves,
' who perfectly underftands the *Véda Sáftra.*

101. ' As fire with augmented force burns up
' even humid trees, thus he, who well knows
' the *Véda*, burns out the taint of fin, which has
' infected his foul.

102. ' He who completely knows the fenfe of
' the *Véda Sáftra*, while he remains in any one of
' the four orders, approaches the divine nature,
' even though he fojourn in this low world.

103. ' They who have read many books, are
' more exalted than fuch as have feldom ftudied
' they who retain what they have read, than for-
' getful readers ; they who fully underftand,
' than fuch as only remember ; and they who
                                                   ' perform

' perform their known duty, than fuch men as
' barely know it.

104. ' Devotion and facred knowledge are the
' beſt means by which a *Bráhmen* can arrive at
' beatitude : by devotion he may deſtroy guilt ;
' by facred knowledge he may acquire immortal
' glory.

105. ' Three modes of proof, ocular demon-
' ſtration, logical inference, and the authority of
' thofe various books, which are deduced from the
' *Véda,* muſt be well underſtood by that man who
' feeks a diſtinct knowledge of all his duties.

106. ' He alone comprehends the ſyſtem of
' duties, religious and civil, who can reafon, by
' rules of logic agreeable to the *Véda,* on the
' general heads of that ſyſtem, as revealed by the
' holy fages.

107. ' Thefe rules of conduct, which lead to
' fupreme blifs, have been exactly and compre-
' henfively declared : the more fecret learning of
' this *Mánava Sáſtra* ſhall now be difclofed.

108. ' If it be aſked, how the law ſhall be af-
' certained, when particular cafes are not com-
' prifed *under any of the general rules, the an-*
' *fwer is this:* " That, which well inſtructed
" *Bráhmens* propound, ſhall be held inconteſtable
" law."

109. ' Well inſtructed *Bráhmens* are they who
' can adduce ocular proof from the fcripture it-
' felf, having ſtudied, as the law ordains, the *Vé-*
' *das* and their extended branches, or *Védangas,*
' *Mímánſá, Nyáya, Dherma ſáſtra, Puránas:*

110 ' A point of law, *before not exprefsly re-*
' *vealed,* which ſhall be decided by an aſſembly of
' ten fuch virtuous *Bráhmens* under one chief, or,
' *if ten be not procurable,* of three fuch, under one
' prefident, let no man controvert.

111. ' The

111. ' The affembly of ten under a chief,
' *either the king himfelf, or a judge appointed by him,*
' muft confift of three, each of them peculiarly
' converfant with one of the three *Védas*; of a
' fourth, fkilled in the *Nyáya*, and a fifth in the *Mi-*
' *mánfà* philofophy; of a fixth, who has particularly
' ftudied the *Nirukta*; a feventh, who has applied
' himfelf moft affiduoufly to the *Dhermafáftra*;
' and of three *univerfal fcholars*, who are in the
' three firft orders.

112 ' One, who has chiefly ftudied the *Rig-*
' *véda*, a fecond who principally knows the *Ya-*
' *jufh*, and a third beft acquainted with the *Saman*,
' are the affembly of three under a head, who may
' remove all doubts, both in law and cafuiftry.

113. 'Even the decifion of one prieft, *if more can-*
' *not be affembled,* who perfectly knows the princi-
' ples of the *Védas*, muft be confidered as law of
' the higheft authority; not the opinion of myri-
' ads, who have no facred knowledge.

114. ' Many thoufands of *Bráhmens* cannot
' form a legal affembly for the decifion of contefts,
' if they have not performed the duties of a regu-
' lar ftudentfhip, are unacquainted with fcriptural
' texts, and fubfift only by *the name of* their facer-
' dotal clafs.

115. ' The fin of that man, to whom dunces,
' pervaded by the quality of darknefs, propound
' the law, of which they are themfelves ignorant,
' fhall pafs, increafed a hundred-fold, to the wretches
' who propound it.

116. ' This comprehenfive fyftem of duties,
' the chief caufe of ultimate felicity, has been de-
' clared to you; and the *Bráhmen*, who never de-
' parts from it, fhall attain a fuperiour ftate above.

117. ' Thus did the all-wife MENU, who pof-
I
' feffes

' feffes extenfive dominion, and blazes with hea-
' venly fplendour, difclofe to me, from his bene-
' volence to mankind, this tranfcendent fyftem of
' law, which muft be kept 'devoutly concealed
' *from perfons unfit to receive it.*

118. ' LET every *Bráhmen* with fixed attention
' confider all nature, both vifible and invifible, as
' exifting in the divine fpirit; for, when he con-
' templates the boundlefs univerfe exifting in the
' divine fpirit, he cannot give his heart to iniquity :

119. ' The divine fpirit alone is the whole af-
' femblage of gods ; all worlds are feated in the
' divine fpirit; and the divine fpirit, no doubt,
' produces, *by a chain of caufes and effects confiftent*
' *with free-will,* the connected feries of acts per-
' formed by imbodied fouls.

120. ' We may contemplate the fubtil ether in
' the cavities of his body ; the air in his mufcular
' motion and fenfitive nerves; the fupreme *folar*
' *and igneous* light, in his digeftive heat and his
' vifual organs ; in his corporeal fluids, water ; in
' the terrene parts of his fabric, earth;

121. ' In his heart, the moon; in his auditory
' nerves, the guardians of eight regions; in his pro-
' greffive motion, VISHNU; in his mufcular force,
' HARA ; in his organs of fpeech, AGNI ; in excre-
' tion, MITRA; in procreation, BRAHMA':

122. ' But he muft confider the fupreme om-
' niprefent intelligence as the fovereign lord of
' them all, *by whofe energy alone they exift* ; a fpirit,
' *by no means the object of any fenfe,* which can only
' be conceived by a mind *wholly abftracted from*
' *matter, and as it were* flumbering ; but which,
' *for the purpofe of affifting his meditation,* he may
' imagine more fubtil than the fineft conceivable
' effence, and more bright than the pureft gold.

123. ' Him fome adore as tranfcendently pre-
' fent

' sent in elementary fire; others, in MENU, lord of
' creatures, *or an immediate agent in the creation* ;
' some, as more diftinctly prefent in INDRA, *regent*
' *of the clouds and the atmosphere*; others, in pure
' air; others, as the moft High Eternal Spirit.

124. ' It is He, who, pervading all beings in
' five elemental forms, caufes them, by the gra-
' dations of birth, growth, and diffolution, to re-
' volve in this world *until they deferve beatitude*,
' like the wheels of a car.

125. ' Thus the man, who perceives in his
'. own foul the fupreme foul prefent in all creatures,
' acquires equanimity toward them all, and fhall
' be abfolved at laft in the higheft effence, even
' that of the Almighty himfelf.'

126. HERE ended the facred inftructor; and
every twice born man, who, attentively reading
this *Mánava Sáftra*, promulgated by BHRÍGU,
fhall become habitually virtuous, will attain the
beatitude which he feeks.

GENERAL NOTE.

THE learned *Hindus* are unanimously of opinion, that many laws enacted by MENU, their oldest reputed legiflator, were confined to the three firft ages of the world, and have no force in the prefent age, in which a few of them are certainly obfolete; and they ground their opinion on the following texts, which are collected in a work entitled, *Madana ratna pradípa.*

I. CRATU: In the *Cali* age a fon muft not be begotten *on a widow* by the brother *of the deceafed buftand*; nor muft a damfel, *once* given away *in marriage*, be given a *fecond time*; nor muft a bull be offered in a facrifice; nor muft a water-pot be carried *by a ftudent in theology.*

II. VRĬHASPATI: 1. Appointments *of kinfmen to beget children on widows, or married women, when the hufbands are deceafed or impotent,* are mentioned by the fage MENU, but forbidden by himfelf, with a view to the order of the four ages; no fuch act can be legally done in this age by any others *than the hufband.*

2. In the firft and fecond ages men were endued with true piety and found knowledge; fo *they were* in the third age; but in the fourth, a diminution of their *moral and intellectual* powers was ordained *by their Creator:*

3. Thus

3. Thus were fons of many different forts made by ancient fages; but fuch cannot now be adopted by men deftitute of thofe eminent powers.

III. PARA'SARA: 1. A man, *who has held intercourfe with a deadly finner*, muft abandon his country in the firft age; he muft leave his town in the fecond; his family in the third age; but in the fourth he needs only defert the offender.

2. In the firft age, he is degraded by mere converfation with a degraded man; in the fecond, by touching him; in the third, by receiving food from him; but in the fourth, the finner alone bears his guilt.

IV. NA'RADA: The procreation of a fon by a brother *of the deceafed*, the flaughter of cattle in the entertainment of a gueft, the repaft on flefh meat at funeral obfequies, and the order of a hermit, *are forbidden, or obfolete, in the fourth age.*

V. *A'ditya purána:* 1. What was a duty in the firft age, muft not, *in all cafes*, be done in a fourth; fince, in the *Cali yuga*, both men and women are addicted to fin:

2. Such are a ftudentfhip continued for a very long time, and the neceffity of carrying a waterpot, marriage with a paternal kinfwoman, or with a near maternal relation, and the facrifice of a bull,

3. Or of a man, or of a horfe: and all fpirituous liquor muft, in the *Cali* age, be avoided by twice born men; fo muft a fecond gift of a married young woman, *whofe hufband has died before confummation*, and the larger portion of an eldeft brother, and procreation on a brother's widow or wife.

VI. *Smriti:* 1. The appointment of a man to beget a fon on the widow of his brother; the gift of a young married woman to another bridegroom, *if her hufband fhould die* while fhe remains a virgin;

2. The

2. The marriage of twice-born men with damsels not of the same clafs ; the flaughter, in a religious war, of *Bráhmens*, who are affailants with intent to kill ;

3. Any intercourfe with a twice born man, who has paffed the fea in a fhip, even though he have performed an expiation ; performances of facrifices for all forts of men ; and *the neceffity of* carrying a water-pot ;

4. Walking on a pilgrimage till the pilgrim die ; and the flaughter of a bull at a facrifice ; the acceptance of fpirituous liquors, even at the ceremony called *Sautrámani* ;

5. Receiving what has been licked off, at an oblation to fire, from the pot of clarified butter ; entrance into the third order, or that of a hermit, though ordained *for the firft ages* ;

6. The diminution of crimes in proportion to the religious acts and facred knowledge *of the offenders* ; the rule of expiation for a *Bráhmen* extending to death ;

7. The fin of holding any intercourfe with finners ; the fecret expiation of any great crimes, except theft ; the flaughter of cattle in honour of eminent guefts, or of anceftors ;

8. The filiation of any but a fon legally begotten, or given in adoption *by his parents*; the defertion of a lawful wife for any offence lefs than actual adultery :

9. Thefe *parts of ancient law* were abrogated by wife legiflators, as the cafes arofe at the beginning of the *Cali* age, with an intent of fecuring mankind from evil.

ON the preceding texts it muft be remarked, that none of them, except that of VRÍHASPATI, are cited by CULLU'CA, who never feems to have confidered any other laws of MENU as reftrained

to

to the three firft ages; that of the *Smṛiti*, or facred code, is quoted without the name of the legiſlator; and that the prohibition, in any age, of *ſelf-defence*, even againſt *Bráhmens*, is repugnant to a text of SUMANTU, to the precept and example of CRISHNA himſelf, according to the *Mabábbárat*, and even to a fentence in the *Véda*, by which every man is commanded *to defend his own life from all* violent aggreſſors.

THE END.

www.ingramcontent.com/pod-product-compliance
Lightning Source LLC
Chambersburg PA
CBHW030254100426
42812CB00002B/428